KING'S MISTRESS, QUEEN'S SERVANT

Tracy Borman studied and taught history at the University of Hull and was awarded a PhD in 1997. She went on to a successful career in heritage and has worked for a range of historic properties and national heritage organisations, including the Heritage Lottery Fund, the National Archives and English Heritage. She is currently Chief Executive of the Heritage Education Trust and also works part-time for Historic Royal Palaces. She is a regular contributor to history magazines, including articles in BBC History magazine on the history of beauty and 18th century 'It' Girls. Her second book, *Elizabeth's Women: The Hidden Story of the Virgin Queen*, was published by Jonathan Cape in 2009.

ALSO BY TRACY BORMAN

Elizabeth's Women: The Hidden Story of the
Virgin Queen

TRACY BORMAN

King's Mistress, Queen's Servant

The Life and Times of Henrietta Howard

Tracy Borman

VINTAGE BOOKS
London

Published by Vintage 2010

2 4 6 8 10 9 7 5 3 1

Copyright © Tracy Borman 2007

Tracy Borman has asserted her right under the Copyright, Designs
and Patents Act 1988 to be identified as the author of this work

First published in Great Britain in 2007 by Jonathan Cape
First published in paperback in 2008 by Pimlico

Vintage
Random House, 20 Vauxhall Bridge Road,
London SW1V 2SA

www.vintage-books.co.uk

Addresses for companies within The Random House Group Limited
can be found at: www.randomhouse.co.uk/offices.htm

The Random House Group Limited Reg. No. 954009

A CIP catalogue record for this book
is available from the British Library

ISBN 9780099549178

The Random House Group Limited supports The Forest
Stewardship Council (FSC), the leading international forest
certification organisation. All our titles that are printed on
Greenpeace approved FSC certified paper carry the FSC logo.
Our paper procurement policy can be found at:
www.rbooks.co.uk/environment

Printed and bound in Great Britain by
CPI Cox & Wyman, Reading, RG1 8EX

To Alison, with love and thanks

Acknowledgements

My research has taken me to a wide range of archives, libraries and historic sites, and I have been fortunate to encounter many helpful and supportive people along the way. As well as the staff in the manuscripts room of the British Library and the Norfolk Record Office, I would also like to thank Karen Horn, formerly of the English Heritage Library, whose assiduous hunting down of books from across the country saved me many long hours and contributed enormously to my understanding of the period. Of the various historic sites that I have visited, Marble Hill has featured most prominently; I owe an enormous debt of gratitude to the English Heritage staff there, in particular Jacqui Degnan, Pauline France and Rheme Handhal, for all their help and enthusiasm. Additionally, I would like to thank Cathy Power for sharing her expertise and for organising a display of artefacts at Marble Hill to coincide with publication. Also Wendy Davidson and Lisa Hampton for arranging events and promotion, and my manager, Mark Pemberton. Thanks are due to the staff of Blickling Hall in Norfolk, and to those at Historic Royal Palaces, notably Susanne Groom, Joanna Marschner and David Souden for sharing their expertise on Henrietta's apartments and her companions at court.

The Marble Hill Society has, from the very beginning, been incredibly supportive and enthusiastic about the this book. In particular, I am very grateful to Mary Wackerbarth for so generously sharing her wealth of knowledge and research with me. It is thanks to Mary that the date of Henrietta's birth, for many years uncertain, was at last discovered. I am also indebted to the Chairman, John Anderson, for so actively garnering support from among the Society's members, and to Keith Hathaway and Janet Clarke for promoting it through guided tours and events.

I wish to thank my publishers, in particular Will Sulkin for having faith in the book and Ellah Allfrey for her insightful and sensitive editorship, and Hannah Ross for her excellent work on publicity. I am also extremely grateful to my agent, Julian Alexander, for his guidance, encouragement and impeccable sense of timing.

I have been very fortunate in having the unstinting support of my family and friends throughout. My biggest thanks go to Alison Weir, without whose generosity and encouragement this book would have remained an idea to be followed up at some undefined point in the future. I would like to thank my parents for their unfailing kindness, patience and support, my sister Jayne and her family, my friends Maura and Howard for being the first to read the manuscript through in its entirety, for coming up with the title, and for promoting the book so energetically. I am also greatly indebted to my dear friend Honor Gay for her boundless enthusiasm and interest in the subject and for her belief in me as an author, to Julian Humphrys for his inspirational finds in second-hand bookshops, to Doreen Cullen for her kindness, wisdom and patience, and to Tony Giardina and all the staff of Il Chicco in New Malden, whose incomparable cappuccinos have sustained me through many a difficult chapter.

Thanks are also due to all of the other kind and generous people who have given their support to this book in various ways, including Sam Hearn and the John Hampden Society, the endlessly creative Richard Knight and Mission 21, my website designer, Ian Robinson, Lucinda and Stuart Eggleton, Philippa Treavett, Richard Foreman, Kathleen Carroll and Len Clark.

Finally to Pete, for his love and support, and for making Twickenham as special to me as it was to Henrietta.

Contents

List of Illustrations

Section 1

1. Henrietta Howard, Countess of Suffolk (Thomas Gibson, Blickling Hall, The Lothian Collection ©NTPL/John Hammond); 2. Blickling Hall (author); 3. The 'Duel Stone' Cawston, Norfolk (author); 4. Sir Henry Hobart (attributed to William Wissing, Blickling Hall, The Lothian Collection ©NTPL/John Hammond); 5. Henry Howard, 10th Earl of Suffolk (Thomas Gibson, Magdalene College © Cambridge University); 6. Sophia Dorothea with her two children (Jacques Vaillant); 7. George I in his coronation robes, 1714 (Sir Godfrey Kneller, National Portrait Gallery, London); 8. George II and Madame von Wallmoden, 1738 (© The British Museum); 9. George II, c. 1727 (Charles Jervas, National Portrait Gallery, London); 10. Caroline Wilhelmina of Brandenburgh-Ausbach, c. 1727 (Charles Jervas, National Portrait Gallery, London); 11. *The Music Party* (Phillipe Mercier, National Portrait Gallery, London); 12. Henrietta Howard, Countess of Suffolk (Charles Jervas, National Portrait Gallery, London); 13. George II (Thomas Howard, National Portrait Gallery, London); 14. John, Lord Hervey of Ickworth (Jean Baptiste van Loo, National Portrait Gallery, London); 15. Sir Robert Walpole (Jean Baptiste van Loo, National Portrait Gallery, London); 16. Mary Bellenden, 1798 (engraving by James Heath after unkown artist, National Portrait Gallery, London); 17 Mary Lepel, Lady Hervey of Ickworth, 1798 (James Heath, National Portrait Gallery, London); 18. *Figures on the Bank of the Long Water*, Hampton Court Palace (Bernard Lens ©Yale Center for British Art, Paul Mellon Collection, USA/The Bridgeman Art Library)

Section 2

19. Caroline Wilhelmina (engraving by John Faber after Joseph High-more, National Portrait Gallery, London); 20. Henrietta Howard, Countess of Suffolk, with dog (John Faber, National Portrait Gallery, London); 21. George II (Thomas Worlidge, National Portrait Gallery, London); 22. *A Tea Party at Lord Harrington's House*, 1730 (Charles Philips, © Yale Center for British Art, Paul Mellon Collection, USA/The Bridgeman Art Library); 23. Alexander Pope with his dog Bounce, 1718, (Jonathan Riachardson, courtesy of Viscount Cobham, Hagley Hall, Stourbridge); 24. John Gay (George Perfect Harding after William Aikman, National Portrait Gallery, London); 25. Jonathan Swift, 1718 (Charles Jervas, National Portrait Gallery, London); 26. Jonathan Swift and Friends (Eliza Sharpe, National Portrait Gallery, London); 27. Henrietta appointed Mistress of the Robes (courtesy of the Norfolk Record Office); 28. Henrietta's divorce papers (courtesy of the Norfolk Record Office); 29. Plans for Marble Hill (courtesy of Norfolk Record Office); 30. Lady Suffolk's bedchamber at Marble Hill (English Heritage Photo Library © English Heritage); 31. Engraving of Marble Hill House from the river, 1749 (Augustin Heckell, courtesy of the London Borough of Richmond upon Thames Local Studies Collection); 32. & 33. Henrietta Howard and Charles Berkeley at the time of their marriage (Charles Phillips, from the private collection of Lord Braybrooke, on display at Audley End House, Essex); 34. John Hobart, 2nd Earl of Buckinghamshire, 1784 (Thomas Gibson, Blickling Hall, The Lothian Collection ©NTPL/John Hammond); 35. Henrietta Hotham (George Romney, English Heritage Photo Library © English Heritage); 36. Horatio (Horace) Walpole, 4th Earl of Orford (John Giles Eccardt © National Portrait Gallery); 37. A lock of Lady Suffolk's hair (by kind permission of the Trustees of Lambeth Palace Library); 38. Marble Hill House (English Heritage Photo Library © English Heritage)

Every effort has been made to trace and contact copyright holders. The publishers will be pleased to correct any mistakes or omissions in future editions.

Prologue

———————⟨◦⟩———————

HIDDEN AWAY AMONG THE archives of Lambeth Palace, the ancient residence of the Archbishops of Canterbury, is a collection of letters from the eighteenth century. The volume itself is relatively nondescript, but inside the front cover is a lock of hair. This is dark brown, almost chestnut in colour, and the years have not faded its lustre. It has apparently no connection with the letters contained within; the only clue to its provenance is given in the inscription beneath, which reads: 'Lady Suffolks hair'.

Henrietta Howard, later Countess of Suffolk, was the mistress of King George II. Described variously as 'the Swiss' (because of her apparent neutrality), the 'Cloe' of Pope's poem who was 'so very reasonable, so unmov'd', and by Swift as a consummate courtier who packed away her 'private virtues . . . like cloaths in a chest', she remains as much an enigma today as she was for her contemporaries. The impression of passivity and mildness that she conveyed belied a complex and fascinating character.

Henrietta was in fact far more than the mistress of a king. She was a dedicated patron of the arts; a lively and talented intellectual in her own right; a victim of violence and adultery; and a passionate advocate for the rights of women before the dawn of feminism. Her wit and intelligence shone through in a society that still viewed any evidence of 'learning' in women as unseemly. Her attacks on the injustice of marriage found expression in the letters she left behind, but more importantly in the actions that shocked her contemporaries and echoed the views that only started to gain ground with the 'Bluestocking' movement a generation later. Henrietta was a woman of reason in an Age of Reason. The mark that she left on the society and culture of early Georgian England was to resonate well beyond the confines of the court, and is still in evidence today.

Traces of Henrietta's remarkable life can be found in a host of different places: from the archives at Lambeth to her exquisite Thames-side villa, and from the verses and works of art that she inspired to – above all – the lively, witty and often scandalous letters of her voluminous correspondence. The latter lay neglected among the Hobart family papers until the nineteenth century, when they were discovered by a Victorian antiquary and passed to the British Library as being of sufficient interest for the nation to enjoy. It is these letters, more than any of the other historical sources, that provided the inspiration for my book. They give a fascinating insight into the glittering world of Georgian high society – its poets, playwrights, intellectuals and princes. They capture a forgotten age; an age of cultural enlightenment, high society, immorality and excess, and the gradual demise of monarchical – and male – predominance. They tell the story of a nation through the lens of a remarkable woman.

When all of these traces of Henrietta's past – the letters, memoirs, poetry and buildings – are pieced together, they reveal a life that was captivating as much for the dramatic events that it contained as for the character of the woman who lived it.

Chapter 1

'A Backwater in Time'

———◦———

THE ROAD THAT RUNS from Norwich to Holt intersects a bleak and featureless tract of the north Norfolk countryside. Fields stretch out on either side, interrupted by the occasional cluster of houses or woodland. When the road reaches the scattered village of Cawston, it passes a small enclosure on the east side, set back from the verge and obscured from view by the overgrown copse beside it. In the middle of this enclosure, bounded by railings, is a large stone urn mounted upon an imposing square pedestal. Years of exposure to the elements have taken their toll, but amidst the rust and moss that cover the decaying structure, it is just possible to make out the letters 'HH' chiselled into the crumbling façade.

Sir Henry Hobart of Blickling Hall was one of the most truculent squires in Norfolk. Active military service had provided a useful outlet for his aggression during his younger days, but now, aged almost forty, he expended most of his energy in politics and was a fierce proponent of the Whig party. From the start, this had brought him into conflict with a number of his fellow noblemen, and he now had a reputation as a troublemaker. 'I wish Sir Henry, instead of prosecuting his neighbours, would think of paying his debts,' complained Humphrey Prideaux, Dean of Norwich, adding: 'It may be his turn, sometime or other, to bear as much as he now acts.' His words were to prove prophetic.

In 1698, a county election brought about the downfall of many individual Whig members – Sir Henry included. His defeat was decisive and humiliating: he only achieved a miserable third place in the voting. Mortified by the result and the accompanying loss of status, and angry at the wasted expenditure that it had entailed, Hobart retired to Blickling to lick his wounds. Introspection and remorse were not qualities that he had in abundance, however, and he soon began casting about for someone to blame. He did not have to wait long to find the perfect scapegoat.

A report reached Hobart's ears that Oliver Le Neve of Great Witchingham, his neighbour and Tory rival, had been spreading rumours that he had committed an act of cowardice at the Battle of the Boyne, and that this had led to his election defeat. Given that the Boyne had been fought some nine years earlier, the report was probably scurrilous and put about by a mischief-maker. But, as one commentator observed, 'Sir Henry would not be satisfied without fighting', and he therefore seized upon the unlikely rumour as sufficient grounds. All of the fury and resentment that he had been harbouring since the election defeat now found full expression, and he immediately challenged Le Neve to a duel.[1]

Le Neve had no desire to quarrel with his formidable neighbour. He was by no means an aggressive man, and challenges and duels did not enter into his scheme of existence at all. Convivial and sociable, he had a wide circle of friends and devoted a large amount of his time to reading, gardening and hunting. Having been left a widower in 1696, he had recently married his second wife, Jane, and was looking forward to a life of uneventful domesticity at Great Witchingham. The arrival of Hobart's challenge shattered this tranquil prospect.

The strict rules of conduct governing late seventeenth-century society allowed Le Neve little choice but to accept the challenge. Hobart would brook no delay. He assigned the very next day for the duel and named the place as Cawston Heath, which was within easy reach of both men's estates. In contrast to his opponent, he relished the prospect of what looked set to be an easy contest. He was an exquisite swordsman; Le Neve was an amateur – and a left-handed one at that. Hobart also had the advantage of height and presented a tall and formidable figure against his opponent's much smaller and slighter frame. The outcome seemed all but assured.

Sir Henry was already at Cawston when Le Neve arrived at dawn the following day. The heath was a bleak expanse of grassland, flanked on either side by copses and hedgerows. The sultry August weather, which had threatened to break for some days past, must have added to the sense of foreboding as the pair faced each other. There is no record of either man having brought along a second, and the only known witness to the ensuing fight was a local serving girl who had hidden in some nearby bushes.

Within minutes, the duel began. Hobart drew first blood, wounding his opponent in the arm. In the confused mêlée that followed, Le Neve – whether by skill or chance – ran his sword deep into Sir Henry's belly. As his opponent fell to the ground, Le Neve swiftly mounted his horse and galloped off to Yarmouth, the nearest port, from where he intended to make his escape to the Continent.[2]

Whether the girl who had witnessed the duel raised the alarm, or Hobart had been accompanied by a second is not known, but he was shortly afterwards carried home to Blickling. His arrival caused great consternation amongst the household, and he was immediately conveyed to the principal bedroom of the house. By now he was bleeding profusely and in excruciating pain. It was said that his agonised screams could be heard throughout the grounds.[3] A surgeon was hastily summoned to the house, but his endeavours were in vain and Sir Henry died the following day.

Hobart's death caused a sensation across Norfolk and beyond. One of the first to record it was Narcissus Luttrell, who wrote in his diary on 25 August: 'Letters yesterday from Norfolk brought advice, that Sir Henry Hobart was killed in a duel by justice Le'neve: they fought on Saturday, and Sir Henry being run into the belly, dyed next day; Captain Le'neve was also wounded in the arm.' Within a few days, the news had reached as far as Bath, from where a local notable, Roger Townshend, wrote to his brother: 'Ye news of Sir Harry's having lost ye Election & yt of his death were equally surprising to me.'[4]

The almost gleeful way in which Sir Henry's peers exchanged reports of his death threw the genuine grief of his wife and eight young children into sharp relief. Among the latter was Henrietta, the middle daughter, who, aged nine, was the image of her late father. This tragic episode provided a foretaste of the drama and upheaval that lay ahead in what was to be a truly remarkable life. Henrietta's fate lay well beyond the safe confines of Blickling and would take her right to the heart of the royal court.

Henrietta Hobart was born on 11 May 1689, and baptised nine days later at St Martin-in-the-Fields, London. It was common for noble ladies from remote country estates to travel to London for their 'lying in' because of the superior medical care that was readily available in the capital – although even that was primitive by modern-day standards. As soon as her mother was well enough to travel, she was taken back to the family estate at Blickling.

Blickling had been in the hands of the Hobarts since 1616, when the first Sir Henry Hobart, with customary shrewdness, had acquired it at a knock-down price from the impoverished incumbents.[5] The Hobarts had made their name and fortune in law during Tudor times, and Sir Henry had risen to the esteemed position of Lord Chief Justice of the Common Pleas. He was acknowledged by his peers as a 'leading light' of that profession and 'renowned for his Learning'.[6]

Sir Henry had been keen to perpetuate his achievements and enhance the Hobarts' standing by investing in a country estate. He had had his eye on Blickling for some time. It was ideally situated, being some twenty miles north of the county's principal city, Norwich, and the same distance again from the picturesque coastline beyond. The surrounding countryside was characterised by wooded valleys, gently undulating fields and pastures.

But for all that, the house itself – a decaying, inconvenient medieval structure – hardly befitted a man of his stature, and many puzzled that he had gone to so much trouble to acquire it when he could have easily afforded to build a sumptuous new estate in the latest Jacobean style. But Blickling was associated with some of the most prominent figures in England's history. Harold Godwinson, Earl of the East Saxons and later King of England, owned it in the eleventh century, and it was then seized by William the Conqueror after his victory at Hastings. It was also the birthplace of Henry VIII's disgraced queen, Anne Boleyn, whose family owned it for eighty years.

Blickling Hall's distinguished past, and in particular its association with Anne Boleyn, was well known at the time, and would undoubtedly have been one of the main attractions for Sir Henry. He could not have imagined that two centuries later, the fate of one of his own descendants would also be dictated by a king's desire.

Having acquired the estate, Sir Henry immediately set about extending and updating it. He enlisted the services of one of the most celebrated architects of the day, Robert Lyminge, who had built the sumptuous Hatfield House for Robert Cecil. Sir Henry hoped to establish a dynasty at Blickling, and his ambitions were reflected in the new building. He ordered initials to be carved prominently in the stonework: H for himself and D for his wife, Dorothy. His son John and daughter-in-law Philippa were represented in the same way. Keen to preserve the links with the estate's illustrious past, Sir Henry also decided to incorporate some of the existing medieval and Tudor fabric into his new Jacobean mansion.

The remodelling of Blickling took more than a decade, but the result was a triumph. Lyminge had created an exquisite Jacobean mansion for his patron, the envy of the nobility for miles around. Contemporary visitors would have been impressed by the first sight of the building: the warm colour of its brickwork, the glittering of its many leaded windows, its festive turrets with their gilded vanes, the extravagant gables and the outstretched arms of the wings, flanked with dark walls of yew. Its appearance was to remain unchanged for centuries. In the 1930s, *Country Life* magazine enthused: 'The suddenness and completeness with which the scene bursts upon the eye strikes a simultaneous chord rather than a scale of impressions: a backwater in time ... a vanished line of Norfolk grandees, the generous vitality of Shakespeare's England, the childhood of Anne Boleyn, and, muted by the imprisoned mist of time, faint memories of famous knights, the pomp of bishops' courts, and the last of the Saxon kings passing through the water-meadows that gave his manor its name.'[7] Modern-day visitors to the house are treated to much the same view as Sir Henry would have enjoyed almost four hundred years earlier.

After Sir Henry's death, the estate passed to his son, John, who established Blickling as the principal family seat for the next twenty years. He was succeeded by his youngest daughter, Philippa, whose marriage to her first cousin, John, son of Sir Miles Hobart of Intwood, ensured that Blickling stayed in the Hobart family. It was during this time that the estate received its first royal visitor in almost two hundred years. In an attempt to secure the loyalty of this former Parliamentarian stronghold, Charles II went on progress to Norfolk in 1671.

To the royal court in London, Norfolk seemed a remote and self-contained province, situated far from the heart of national affairs. Its topography made it even more unwelcoming, bounded as it was by sea on the north and east, by the Wash and fenlands on the west, and by wild and lonely heathlands on the south-west. From the coastal regions of this vast county, it was easier to reach Holland than to negotiate the great forests, fens and heathlands on a journey inland to other parts of England.

This wild and isolated corner of the kingdom had a long history of rebellion and independence. Over the centuries, it had endured repeated invasions from Romans, Vikings and Normans. Many of these and subsequent invaders settled in the lands which they had come to ravage and loot. The sparse population of natives and settlers developed a character that was distinct from the rest of England and marked by a strong independence of spirit. The people have been described as 'reserved suspicious of "foreigners", by which they mean people from other English counties'.[8] This reserve and suspicion in turn bred political and religious dissent, which found its fullest expression during the Civil War, when the county rallied to the Parliamentarian cause against the King.

Norwich was, admittedly, the third city in the kingdom, but it had received scant attention from Tudor and Stuart monarchs. Charles II's visit was therefore the cause of great excitement. One of the few houses of sufficient stature for the King to visit was Blickling, and Charles made his way there with the Queen, Catherine of Braganza, the Duke of York and various other court notables as part of his progress. The visit represented something of a reconciliation. Charles was fully aware that Sir John Hobart had been one of Cromwell's most active supporters, both in the House of Commons and in county affairs. But in the spirit of appeasement that had served him so well, the King was gracious and charming to his Norfolk host. He even knighted Sir John's eldest son, Henry (Henrietta's father), who was then just thirteen years old. It was recorded that the royal party was 'most noblie and plentifully treated' in the Great Dining Room, but the apparent conviviality did not penetrate far beneath the surface. Sir John's political stance remained unchanged, and the King was later heard to comment on the 'hollow hospitality' he had received at Blickling.

Sir John Hobart returned to Parliament the following year, and after another decade of mutually exhausting political conflict, he died in 1683. And so Blickling passed to Sir Henry Hobart. It was by now an onerous legacy, for the estate was desperately in debt and already reduced to a quarter of the acreage it had possessed in 1625. He therefore set out to find a wife with a dowry large enough to ease his financial burdens. He evidently did not have to search for long, because the following year he married Elizabeth, co-heir to the famous judge, Sir

Joseph Maynard.[9] At the time of their marriage in 1684, Sir Henry was twenty-five years old, and his bride was seventeen. Elizabeth Maynard brought with her a £10,000 dowry, which afforded Blickling at least a temporary respite from its financial problems.

But Sir Henry soon plunged the estate into further debt. He had inherited his father's passion for politics and, like him, proceeded to enter into a series of cripplingly expensive election campaigns. The fact that he had been knighted by Charles II in no way reconciled Sir Henry to royal policy, and, like his father, he became an outspoken member of the Whig party. Within a few years of inheriting the estate, Sir Henry had almost brought it to its knees. He had little choice but to sell off considerable portions of it in order to keep his creditors at bay.

Untroubled by the knowledge that her father's profligacy was storing up problems for her future, Henrietta's childhood, and that of her siblings, was a happy one. Although Sir Henry's costly obsession with politics had burdened the Blickling estate with debts, there had still been money enough to provide the family with a good diet. The items listed in a bill paid to 'Goodwife Agness Parnell' included 'fresh herin', 'anchovises', capers, plums and coffee (something of a rarity outside London in the late seventeenth century).

Sir Henry also ensured that his children received an education befitting their noble status: like his great-grandfather and namesake, he had a strong sense of dynastic ambition. Provision was made for his son John to receive a private education when he came of age. His daughters, meanwhile, were well versed in the social skills required of young noblewomen. The household accounts include a receipt for thirty shillings paid to a dancing-master in March 1693 'for twice coming to Blickling to teach the young Ladyes to Daunce'.[10]

In the late seventeenth century, daughters were commonly given instruction in what was considered useful for their future way of life, in particular those accomplishments that were most likely to secure a wealthy husband. Most well-bred young ladies could play a musical instrument and were taught to dance, write, and in some cases speak modern languages such as French and Italian. Mary Dewes, a contemporary of Henrietta, reflected: 'In our childhood, writing, dancing and music is what is most attended to.'[11] The more challenging intellectual studies, meanwhile, were reserved for their male counterparts.

This was considered the natural order of things. Published two years before Henrietta's birth, the 'Treatise on the Education of

Daughters' warned: 'we should be on our guard not to make them [women] ridiculously learned. Women, in general, possess a weaker but more inquisitive mind than men; hence it follows that their pursuits should be of a quiet and sober turn. They are not formed to govern the state, to make war, or to enter into the church; so that they may well dispense with any profound knowledge relating to politics, military tactics, philosophy, and theology ... women are by nature weaker than men.'[12]

At the same time, however, there was the beginning of a subtle shift in the attitudes of many women in society. During the Civil War, with their husbands away for long periods fighting for Crown or Parliament, women had increasingly taken centre stage in the running of great houses and estates. With greater responsibilities had come a growing sense of independence. This had been augmented by the substantial loss of life among the male combatants, which meant that for many women, their new-found independence had been permanent.

Mary Astell, often hailed as the first English feminist, argued that if women were subservient to men, then it was due to inequality of education rather than to nature. She declared: 'I think Women as capable of Learning as Men are', and lamented that: 'Custom and Education have dwindled us into very Trifles! such meer Insignificants!'[13] Such ideas had become increasingly widespread by the dawn of the eighteenth century. Lady Mary Wortley Montagu, a contemporary and later acquaintance of Henrietta, regretted that women's education was so limited, and confessed to her daughter: 'The ultimate aim of your education was to make you a good wife.' She scorned the prevailing attitude, whereby 'the same studies which raise the character of a Man should hurt that of a Woman', so that she should 'conceal whatever learning she attains, with as much solicitude as she would hide crookedness or lameness'.[14]

The cry was even taken up by some leading men of letters in the early eighteenth century. Henry Fielding criticised 'the morose Schoolmen who wou'd confine Knowledge to the Male Part of the Species'. Jonathan Swift (who later became a close friend of Henrietta) satirised the state of affairs in his most famous work, Gulliver's Travels, in which Gulliver's master proclaims that it is monstrous of mankind 'to give the females a different kind of education from the males, except in some articles of domestic management'.[15]

It was not until the end of the eighteenth century that standards in women's education underwent a marked improvement. A century earlier, when Henrietta was growing up at Blickling, they were still woefully inadequate. But despite the limitations of her education, Sir Henry's third daughter had a keen intellect and thirst for knowledge, and the views that she was to express in adulthood suggest that she may well have absorbed some of the early feminist beliefs that were being propounded at this time. She certainly had a precocious talent for writing, which was later to find expression in her correspondence with some of the brightest stars of the Georgian literary world. But for now she enjoyed the traditional upbringing of a nobleman's daughter in the privileged confines of Blickling, surrounded by her many siblings.

The Hobart family's life seemed to be largely dictated by the forceful personality of Sir Henry. His quick temper and dictatorial manner were well known throughout the county and had won him respect and enemies in equal measure. They also ultimately led to his death. The only two portraits that Sir Henry commissioned were both of himself alone, and none of his wife or any of his eight children is known to have been painted during his lifetime. It may of course be that these were subsequently sold or lost, but it would be consistent with Sir Henry's character that he should dominate the portraiture at Blickling as much as he did his family's daily life there.

If the rumours put about by Hobart's adversaries were true, then this same self-interest extended to the family's finances. He was said to have deprived his wife of her rightful income and subjected her to a life of comparative hardship in order to fund his own extravagant lifestyle. Archbishop Prideaux told a fellow churchman: 'Here is a lady of one of ye best families in ye countrey who hath all her fortune in his hands, and he hath not payd her any interest these severall years, whereby she is put to great hardships for her subsistence.'[16]

Yet the grief that his death caused at Blickling suggests a genuine love and tenderness between Sir Henry and his wife and children. That Henrietta would cherish a fondness for Blickling for the rest of her life provides a testament to the happiness of her early family life there. The tenacity with which her mother pursued Sir Henry's murderer, who was eventually brought to justice in 1700, proves the sincerity of her love. So too the sums that were lavished on his funeral, despite the family's straitened circumstances. The household accounts include an order for a coffin lined with six yards of white baize, and the craftsmen spent two full days cutting out the inscription. Nine escutcheons were painted for the funeral and nine gold rings were bought for the bearer and minister, along with gloves of Cordova leather, fine black cloth, crape, silk hatbands, black silk hose, cotton stockings and a mourning sword.[17] Lady Hobart also ordered a monument to be erected on the spot where her husband fell.[18] It would mark the last duel ever fought in Norfolk.

With Sir Henry's mortal remains interred in the family vault at Blickling church, his wife had to shoulder the considerable burden of managing a large family and a debt-ridden estate alone. The eldest of her seven girls were the twins Mary and Anne, aged thirteen, and the youngest, Catherine, was just two months old. The only son and heir, John, was four years old and therefore far too young to take on the inheritance that would one day be his.

The list of Sir Henry's creditors had been steadily growing throughout the 1690s, and a number of the individual sums that he owed were substantial. The year before his death, one of his creditors had ridden in person to Blickling to serve a bill of £8,000 on the baronet. Hobart's old adversary, Prideaux, had predicted with barely disguised glee that this would 'reach a great part of his estate'.[19] Although many of Hobart's debts were associated with his expensive political campaigns, there were still more generated by the day-to-day running of Blickling Hall. The elegant new Jacobean house built by Sir John Hobart earlier in the century was now in need of repair, and the family accounts are riddled with bills for emergency works. Ongoing maintenance, such as thatching, added further to the Hobart family's debts, as did window taxes (whereby owners had to pay a set amount per window, making it cripplingly expensive for a property the size of Blickling) and estate staff. While the estate itself generated a reasonable amount of income from tenants and livestock, this was not enough to cover the mounting debts. Neither had Sir Henry left his wife and children sufficient financial provision in his will: all of it was tied up with the management of his lands and estates.[20]

Less than a year after her husband's death, Lady Hobart was forced to borrow money from local businessmen in order to make ends meet.[21] It was also rumoured that she planned to escape financial ruin by marrying again, and, within a year of the funeral, several rich men were named as prospective husbands. If Lady Hobart had such plans, they came to nothing. With no dowry, a notoriously encumbered estate, and a large number of dependents, she did not present an alluring prospect to the eligible noblemen of Norfolk, regardless of what her physical attractions might have been.[22]

Faced with mounting debts and a beleaguered estate, Lady Hobart had no choice but to seek help through her family connections. Her grandfather, Sir John Maynard, had been a famous judge and Member of Parliament, and had retained office as councillor to various governments during the turbulent periods of the Civil War, Commonwealth, Restoration and Glorious Revolution of 1688. He had married, as his fourth wife, Mary Charleton of Apley Castle. After his death, she had made another good match, to Henry Howard, 5th Earl of Suffolk. This made her one of the richest relations that Lady Hobart had, and although their family connection was somewhat tenuous, she wrote to ask for her assistance. To her delight, the Countess of Suffolk invited her granddaughter by marriage to spend the summer of 1699 at Gunnersbury House, which she had inherited from her first husband. Lady Hobart gratefully accepted, and she and her children duly made their way there.

Sir John Maynard had purchased Gunnersbury at the height of his fame. There had been an estate there since the Middle Ages. Alice Perrers, the mistress of Edward III, had lived there for a time, and it had subsequently passed to various other distinguished owners. In 1658, Sir John Maynard commissioned John Webb, a pupil of Inigo Jones, one of the most celebrated architects of the seventeenth century, to build a magnificent new house in the style of a Palladian villa. It was completed five years later and was one of the finest houses for miles around. It stood on a raised terrace in the surrounding parkland and commanded a much-admired view towards the Thames and beyond to Kew and Richmond. 'From the portico in the back front of the house, you have an exceeding fine prospect of the county of Surrey, the River Thames, and all the meadows on the borders for some miles, as also a good prospect of London, in clear weather,' enthused the writer Daniel Defoe.[23] At first-floor level was an elegant Corinthian portico, which looked out over a formal forecourt. The interior was no less impressive, with its grand imperial staircase, richly ornate saloon, and lavish furniture and tapestries throughout.[24]

Elizabeth Hobart and her eight young children lived in some considerable comfort at Gunnersbury and enjoyed the company offered by the Countess and her elderly husband. They were to make several more visits over the coming years, which in itself was a considerable feat given that it was almost 150 miles from Blickling. In an age when travel by road was still agonisingly slow, not to mention uncomfortable and dangerous, the journey would have taken at least a week.

Living at Gunnersbury gave Lady Hobart some much-needed respite from the onerous duties of running the Blickling estate. But it was not long before tragedy again blighted her family. In August 1701, during one of the family's sojourns at Gunnersbury, she was taken ill with what proved to be the final symptoms of consumption. Her condition worsened rapidly and she died on 22 August, three years to the day since her husband's death.[25]

The seven young Hobart girls and their brother were now orphaned. As the only son, John had inherited Blickling on his father's death, but being then just four years old, the estates were given over to trustees, who would administer them until he came of age fourteen years later. Protracted minorities such as these were always unsettling for estates, and this one was made worse by the financial burdens under which the family was struggling. Their prospects were now far from favourable.

Shortly after the death of their mother, the Hobart children moved back to Blickling. Although they returned to Gunnersbury the following summer, the trouble and expense of doing so meant that for the most part they stayed in Norfolk.[26] The link with the Suffolks was maintained by the terms of Sir John Maynard's will, which obliged the Countess (who was the trustee) to draw down the twice-yearly allowances for the Hobart children.[27] But the Earl and Countess of Suffolk remained rather distant figures in the lives of the children, and it was the two eldest, the twins Mary and Anne (now aged sixteen), who took charge of their upbringing.

The downward turn of fortune that had begun with the death of their father in 1698 dealt the young family another blow when, in the spring of 1702, Anne was taken ill and died a few days later. Their happy and carefree early childhood had been replaced by the constant fear of death and ill fortune. These fears were to be realised again and again, for during the following three years, three more of the siblings were borne to the churchyard at Blickling.[28]

By 1705, Henrietta, aged sixteen, was the eldest of the surviving Hobart children, and assumed responsibility for their care. They did have two uncles, John and Thomas, brothers of the late Sir Henry, but both were practising law in London and there is no record that they provided any assistance. Members of the household at Blickling would no doubt have supported the children as much as possible, but the main burden would still have fallen on Henrietta as the oldest surviving representative of the family. Her brother John and sisters Dorothy and Catherine were all under twelve years old. The latter fell dangerously ill the following year, and the abundance of apothecary bills among the family papers suggests that the threat of further tragedy continued to hang over Blickling. With her mother and elder sisters dead, and the estate virtually bankrupted by her late father, Henrietta's future looked bleak indeed.

Having taken on responsibility for the care of her siblings, she decided to appeal to the Suffolks for more active assistance. It was a step that she would soon live to regret.

Chapter 2

'Man's Tyrannick Power'

---◇---

HENRY HOWARD, 5TH EARL of Suffolk, was an old man of seventy-seven when his wife's young kinswoman Henrietta sought his assistance. He had held a few minor appointments during his life, including Commissary General of the Musters in Charles II's reign. A staunch Royalist, he had fought at the Battle of Roundway Down in 1643, but otherwise his military career had been of little note and he preferred the more leisurely pursuits that life in the country could offer. He was described as 'A Gentleman who was never yet in business, loves cocking, horse matches, and other country sports.'[1]

The Earl and his second wife Mary divided their time between Gunnersbury House and Audley End, the spectacular Jacobean mansion near Saffron Walden where he had spent his childhood. His impoverished elder brother James had been obliged to sell it to the Crown for use as a royal palace, but Charles II had soon tired of it, and succeeding monarchs had paid it little attention. In 1701, Sir Christopher Wren had urged King William III to rid himself of this unnecessary burden, and the house had duly been returned to the Howard family, which was now under the direction of the 5th Earl.

Henry Howard had had three sons by his first wife, Mary Stewart, the daughter and heiress of Andrew Stewart, 3rd Baron Castle Stewart, an Irish peer. It was said that the infusion of Irish blood into the Howard strain accounted for certain unpredictable elements in their offspring. The Castle Stewarts had a history of reckless behaviour, the 1st Baron having ruined himself through expensive living.

The youngest of the Howard sons, Charles, born in 1675, had pursued a military career, as was traditional for the younger sons of

noble families. At the age of twenty, he was awarded a captaincy in
Lord Echlin's Regiment of Dragoons (mounted infantry), and given
command of a troop. This was not as great an honour as it might
appear. Dragoons were third in rank behind the Household Cavalry
and Regiments of Horse, and attracted a much lower rate of pay.
Commissions were therefore less expensive, and this is possibly why
Charles ended up here rather than in one of the more prestigious regiments, for he had already frittered away most of his modest allowance.
Nevertheless, he retained the post for the following nine years. During
this time he served mainly in Ireland, but also saw action in the War
of the Spanish Succession, when he served as aide-de-camp to the
Duke of Ormonde in the Cadiz expedition of 1702. Later that year,
he was recommended for further promotion by the Earl of Nottingham.
In 1704, he was appointed a captain in Lord Cutts's Dragoons.
Nicknamed 'Salamander' on account of his courage in the hottest parts
of the battlefield, Lord Cutts had fought alongside the Duke of
Marlborough at Blenheim a few months earlier.

Charles may have led an exemplary military career, but this was in
sharp contrast to his private life. Free from the shackles of family
responsibilities (as the youngest of three sons, he was not expected to
inherit his father's title and estates) he indulged in a life of excess and
became addicted to drinking, gambling and whoring. A contemporary
observer described him as 'wrong-headed, ill-tempered, obstinate,
drunken, extravagant, brutal'.[2] The fact that he could conceal the darker
facets of his character beneath a veneer of charm and respectability
made him all the more dangerous.

Charles took a period of leave from his military service during 1705
and returned home to stay with his parents at Gunnersbury. He arrived
to find a guest at the house. Henrietta Hobart had been invited to live
at Gunnersbury on a more-or-less permanent basis. At sixteen years
of age, she was already an attractive young woman: her fine chestnut-
brown hair, large clear eyes and pale complexion gave her an appearance that was at once striking and untainted. She was also bright and
quick-witted, and had inherited the keen intellect of her learned forebears. But her mental and physical qualities were of less interest to
Charles than her potential fortune. As the eldest surviving daughter of
Sir Henry Hobart, she was entitled to a significant dowry when she
married, on which occasion she would also receive an inheritance from
her late great-grandfather, Sir John Maynard.

At thirty, Charles was fourteen years Henrietta's senior. What drew her to him is something of a mystery. In his published sketches of the principal characters at the Georgian court, Lord Chesterfield, Henrietta's friend in later life, shrewdly observed: 'How she came to love him, or how he came to love anybody, is unaccountable, unless from a certain fatality which often makes hasty marriages, soon attended by long repentance and aversion.'³ Perhaps she was taken in by his charming and easy manners. Perhaps his military bearing evoked memories of her cherished father. Or perhaps she saw this as the only means to ease the burden on her siblings, who were now apparently living under the sole care of the household staff at Blickling, for the terms of her father's will had ensured that her generous dowry would be protected even though the rest of his estate was in financial difficulties. What was more, she would also receive a regular – if modest – income paid every half-year after her marriage. Whether captivated or calculating, she very quickly decided to marry him.

For his part, Charles could appreciate the advantages of giving up his protracted bachelorhood for the sake of his young kinswoman. The Earl and Countess of Suffolk approved of and encouraged the romance. Henrietta presented a highly appropriate match for their troublesome youngest son. The aristocracy preferred to keep to its fairly close circle, and Henrietta was from one of the oldest and most respected noble families in East Anglia. Within a very short space of time, the pair were betrothed.

Henrietta may have been enraptured by her fiancé, but her uncle, John Hobart, was considerably less so. Charles Howard's reputation had apparently reached as far as his chambers in Lincoln's Inn Fields. Although he had had little to do with Henrietta and her siblings since their father's death, he now provided a valuable service by insisting upon drawing up a marriage settlement that would prevent Charles from getting his hands on a large part of her fortune. He made himself an executor of this settlement, along with the family's solicitor, Dr James Welwood. As one might expect from a family that had such a distinguished record in law, the settlement constituted an impenetrable barrier to Henrietta's future husband. It stipulated that £4,000 of her £6,000 dowry would be invested by her executors, and that the interest would provide her with 'clothes and other expenses of her person with which the said Charles Howard her intended husband is not to meddle or have any power or disposeing thereof'.⁴ Even if

Henrietta were to die before her husband, Charles would still be unable to access this money, for the arrangement provided that it would pass to her children. The foresight of Henrietta's family in insisting upon this arrangement was to prove all too justified.

On 2 March 1706, Henrietta Hobart married Charles Howard at the church of St Benet Paul's Wharf, in the city of London. St Benet's had been built by Wren in the style of a Dutch country church. Its dark red brick façade was offset by white marble swags and corner-stones, together with a decorative lead spire. The royal arms of King Charles II were mounted over the entrance, and the interior would have been illuminated by the bright spring sunshine flooding in through the vast windows on either side of the nave. The calibre of the building was further enhanced by a tomb within the chancel, which contained the mortal remains of Inigo Jones.[5]

The location of the church, opposite the College of Arms, made it a popular wedding venue for those in military service, and this could have been why Charles and Henrietta chose to marry here, rather than at either of their family's estates, as was more customary. The groom may have worn his military uniform, which consisted of a stiff-necked jacket with yellow cuffs, white breeches, black leather boots and a tricorn hat. But most gentlemen who served in the army wore their civilian clothes for formal occasions, with the addition of a sash across the chest to denote their military association.

Meanwhile, it was common for eighteenth-century brides to wear one of their 'best' or evening dresses, which were often white but could have been any colour, for there was no standard attire for weddings at this time.[6] A passing reference to some 'weding cloaths' in Henrietta's papers indicates that she at least had a new dress for the occasion. Her betrothed had been obliged to contribute £300 to her apparel, but this would prove to be one of the last sums he ever laid out on her behalf. Indeed, it seems to have exhausted his resources, because three months later he sold his commission in the Regiment of Dragoons for £700. His financial circumstances were now 'the reverse of opulent', as one contemporary observed.[7]

The Howards moved to London soon after their marriage, although the surviving records do not reveal in which part of the capital they were living – or in what degree of comfort. It might be supposed that the latter was not considerable, however, for they had barely enough money to live on. Now that Charles had sold his commission, their only source of income was the interest from Henrietta's personal fortune, which her executors had intended to ensure her comfort alone. Rather than providing for her clothes and other personal expenses, it was soon frittered away by Charles on drink and gambling.

The Howards' married life could not have got off to a worse start. In the face of financial hardship, the initial attraction that had brought them together quickly faded. Within weeks of their wedding, Charles's true character had been revealed all too clearly. His carelessness with money might have been forgiven, but his temper and violence could not, and Henrietta soon felt the full force of it. Her infatuation turned to hatred, and she bitterly regretted tying herself to such a loathsome character. Society viewed marriage as a binding and everlasting commitment, however, and no matter how miserable or badly treated a woman was, she was expected to stand by her husband. There was therefore nothing that Henrietta could do about it. As Lord Chesterfield later observed: 'Thus they loved, thus they married, and thus they hated each other for the rest of their lives.'[8]

There was another tie that bound Mrs Howard to her new husband. She had fallen pregnant almost immediately after the marriage, and on New Year's Day 1707 she gave birth to a son, whom she named after her father Henry. What should have been a joyful occasion merely served to put an increasing strain on the couple's relationship, not to mention their already limited resources.

Even as Henrietta was entering the final stages of pregnancy, Charles was scheming to get his hands on her fortune. Shortly before his son's birth, he brought a lawsuit in the court of Chancery against Henrietta's brother John, who he claimed had cheated her out of her full inheritance. According to his suit, he and his wife were entitled to the £4,000 that her executors had tied up in investments. John Hobart's lawyers, meanwhile, pointed out that according to the terms of the marriage settlement, Henrietta was entitled only to the interest on that sum. Among the Hobart family papers are several boxes of correspondence relating to the case. It was to drag on for the next six years, and by the time it was concluded in 1712, most of the money had dwindled away.

The interesting – and potentially lucrative – diversion that Henrietta had presented during their courtship was now tedious to Charles, and the added burden of a new baby to provide for made him crave the freedoms that he had enjoyed to the full as a bachelor. He therefore sent his young wife and infant son to live in the country while he remained in London. The 'mean lodgings' that he hired for them in Berkshire, and that Henrietta still recalled vividly in an accusatory letter written to him some years later, formed a sharp contrast to the comfort that she had enjoyed in her early years at Blickling and Gunnersbury.[9] There was barely enough food to live on, and if she ever wished or needed to travel anywhere, she was obliged to hire a coach from Reading, like any commoner. Even the more straitened circumstances in which she had lived after her father's death were as luxury compared to her onerous new life.

Charles, meanwhile, was busy squandering their limited funds on a life of excess in London. Henrietta rarely saw or heard from him during her first year in Berkshire, and he only deigned to make one or two visits. She grew increasingly miserable with her solitary existence, and felt keenly the shame of living in such mean circumstances with her new son. In 1709, therefore, after two years alone, she resolved to go to London and seek out her husband. What she found there was shocking, for Charles had soon fallen back into his old ways. Any residue of tender feeling that she had felt towards him was now destroyed for ever.

Nevertheless, the prospect of returning to her miserable life in the country was scarcely more appealing to Henrietta than that of staying with her errant husband. At least the latter offered some hope, however misguided, that she would be able to reform his debauched habits. This proved to be a hopeless cause, however, and within a year he had run up huge debts from his addiction to the capital's gambling tables and brothels. Henrietta now suffered the humiliation of having their goods seized and being ejected from their lodgings in both London and Berkshire.

Homeless and in debt, they had no choice but to call upon Charles's wealthy family for assistance. His father had died in 1709, and his eldest brother Henry had succeeded as 6th Earl of Suffolk. Henry had little time for the feckless Charles, but judged it the lesser of two evils to have him close at hand, where his wayward behaviour could be checked, than to risk his bringing further disgrace on the Suffolk family name in London. He therefore allowed the couple and their young son to come and live at Audley End. That he did so reluctantly and with ill grace is demonstrated by the fact that he insisted on treating them as boarders and charged them a rent of £20 per year.

Charles found this situation equally repugnant, and it was not long before he strayed from the family home and resumed his life of immorality in London, leaving Henrietta alone with her brother-in-law and his wife. In fact, during the year and a half that the Howards boarded at Audley End, Charles spent only a fraction of his time there. When Henrietta came to make up the accounts with Lady Suffolk, she found that there was only five months' rent due from her husband because he had been absent for the rest of the time. But Charles proved incapable of honouring even this meagre sum. His patience tested too far, the Earl of Suffolk promptly expelled the couple from his house.

Determined not to suffer the humiliation of yet another separation from her husband, this time Henrietta insisted that they find lodgings together. Charles reluctantly agreed, but only on condition that they move to London, where his favoured haunts would be within easy reach.

At the beginning of the eighteenth century, London was a city shaped by the substantial rebuilding that had taken place after the Great Fire in 1666. This had focused initially on what is now the West End. A mass of houses had been built in the streets around Covent Garden, St James's Palace and Lincoln's Inn. Elegant squares had been created in Soho and Gray's Inn Fields, and avenues tightly packed with new houses had sprung up around them. Along the Strand, old palaces had been replaced by small streets and courtyards filled with lodgings. The city that had emerged by the end of the seventeenth century was marked by regular red-bricked streets and white stone churches, with the crowning glory of St Paul's Cathedral, newly rebuilt by Sir Christopher Wren. It was no longer two cities (Westminster and the rest of London) as it had been a century earlier, but 'one huge dragon of a town spread along the arc of the Thames'.[10]

Henrietta and Charles made their way back to London towards the end of 1711. The quality of lodgings that they could afford was hardly commensurate with what was expected of a noble couple, but having now alienated both of their families, they had little choice. They moved to St Martin's Street in Covent Garden, which was at this time an unfashionable and rather shabby part of the city. The gabled houses that lined the street had been built fifty or so years earlier and were now somewhat faded and in need of repair. The couple's lodging was secured for a rent of 35 shillings per week, which although more expensive than their house in Berkshire, was relatively cheap for London and would not have bought them any great luxury. They were able to afford only one servant, and even that was apparently on a part-time basis. The regular payments from Henrietta's dowry would have been enough for them to live on fairly modestly, but Charles was not one given to moderation. Within just seven months, he had spent all of their funds and they were again forced to seek shelter elsewhere.

Their family ties broken, the Howards turned to friends for assistance. Henry O'Brien, Earl of Thomond, was distantly related to them by marriage. A staunch Hanoverian and former Privy Councillor, he had gone on to a successful military career as colonel of a Regiment of Dragoons. After the death of his father, his mother had married Charles's brother Henry, 6th Earl of Suffolk, and lived with him at Audley End. Lord Thomond's estate, Shortgrove, was at nearby Saffron Walden, and he agreed that Charles and Henrietta could stay with him there for the summer of 1712. While he might have genuinely taken pity on the couple, it is more likely that he invited them as a deliberate slight to his stepfather. He did not charge them a rent, and they were only obliged to lay out a few guineas for the servants.

It was common for the nobility to stay at each other's country houses during the summer months, when stench and disease made the capital less attractive. The Howards might have succeeded in presenting it as such were it not for the fact that Charles left his wife alone there for all but two weeks of their sojourn while he returned once more to London.

The humiliation that Henrietta suffered was acute. Her husband had been with her for only a fraction of their six-and-a-half-year marriage, and during that time she had endured a seemingly endless cycle of cruelty, indignity and hardship. Her respectable life as a gentleman's daughter had been transformed into one of misery and humiliation as the wife of a notorious drunk and philanderer. The shame of her situation compelled her to live increasingly apart from society, 'concealing myself and my Misery from ye world', and quietly eking out the meagre funds that her husband's excesses left her with in order to preserve a semblance of respectability. But with Charles showing no inclination to be discreet in his pursuits, this was an ever more impossible plight.

Charles's neglect betrayed what was by now a complete lack of affection towards his young wife – a fact of which she was all too painfully aware. Among Henrietta's correspondence is a letter that she wrote to her husband some twenty years later. This letter, which runs to several pages, makes up for the absence of surviving correspondence from the early years of the Howards' marriage. Even though it was written two decades after the events it describes, its accuracy is proven by various other sources, notably the legal papers within the Hobart family archives and eye-witness accounts given at the time of their divorce.

'During ye space of 6 years and a haf yt you pretended to live with me, you were absent above half of ye time,' she complained. 'Your absence plainly show'd ye greatest indifference.' This was hardly the married life that Henrietta had imagined during her childhood at Blickling. But loneliness, shame and neglect were as nothing to what she was about to endure. In the same letter she reflected: 'I must confess them periods of splendour and happiness comparatively with the dreadful Scenes that followed which I tremble even to repeat, and which humanity wou'd force ye most barbarous to commiserate.'[11] At least while Charles was so often absent, Henrietta was shielded from the effects of his temper. Living with him on a daily basis would prove a far worse fate.

The couple were forced to take up lodgings together in London when they had exhausted Lord Thomond's hospitality. Although they had lived rent-free that summer, Charles had continued to fritter away their resources, and they were now able to afford only the meanest of dwellings in Beak Street, an unsavoury part of the capital. What was worse, Charles had by now accumulated such substantial debts that they were obliged to assume a false name in order to escape his creditors. So it was that a 'Mr and Mrs Smith' and their young son moved into Mr Penhallow's lodgings towards the end of 1712.

Living under the same roof as his wife and child did nothing to check Charles's habits; if anything, it made them worse. To drinking and gambling were added 'other pleasures which a wife is entitled to call crimes', for Charles continued to prefer the company of whores to that of his young spouse. Such was his indifference towards Henrietta that he did not attempt to conceal the fact from her.

While Charles enjoyed a life of excess and increased the burden of their debts, Henrietta and their six-year-old son Henry were forced to endure penury and degradation. 'I there Suffer'd all that Poverty and ye whole train of miseries that attend it can suggest to any ones imagination, nor was this all, I was unpitied by him who had brought me into these calamities, I was dispised and abused by him tho' he often knew me under the pressure and Smart of hunger ... he has known me rise and go to bed without meat, when he could have come home in surfeits to me who was actually starving.' Her drawn and wasted appearance attracted the pity of a neighbour, Mrs Anne Cell, who often invited her to take dinner or supper at her house. Henrietta accepted gratefully, but Mrs Cell guessed that she would not have done so 'had she not been in ye utmost want'.[12] Her clothes also betrayed the impoverished situation into which she had sunk. They were by now so worn and threadbare that her landlady, Mrs Hall, offered to mend them for her in exchange for Henrietta looking after her young child for a few hours.

In the shame and humiliation that such circumstances wrought upon her, Henrietta must have been glad of the need to disguise her true identity with a false name. Her only solace was her son, upon whom she lavished as much care and attention as her circumstances would allow. Neighbours observed that the pair were inseparable, and that Henrietta was constantly looking out for Henry's welfare – giving him the best offerings from their meagre fare, repairing his clothes while her own were threadbare, and keeping him amused during the long and lonely days in their shabby lodgings.[13]

When Charles was at home, he treated his wife little better than a servant. She cooked, cleaned and carried out any other task that her husband demanded. Mrs Hall described how she once saw Henrietta struggling to carry a grate 'with a Red Hot fire in it' from one room to another and back again on the same night, while her slothful husband looked on.[14] The couple were evidently no longer able to afford enough coal to heat more than one room at a time.

The harder Henrietta worked, the more disdain she incurred from her husband. According to Mrs Cell, she behaved in 'ye most Engaging & obedient manner that was possible' towards him, but he never showed any tenderness or compassion towards her.[15] The couple's debts continued to mount and Charles was obliged to keep a low profile at home. Frustrated at being deprived of his treasured vices, he sought solace in tormenting his young wife. Frustration turned increasingly to violence, and Henrietta now bore the full brunt of her husband's temper.

Although Charles's frequent absences had caused misery and humiliation for his wife, she soon came to realise that they were far preferable to the times when he was with her. In a testament that she later wrote about her marriage, she recalled that 'such frequent separations screened me in some measure from the effects of your temper which I afterwards severely felt'.[16] With the prospect of violence ever present, Henrietta lived in a state of permanent terror. Her landlady noticed that she seemed to always be 'under a Constant Awe, & Apprehension, scarce daring even to speake to him'. She often saw her in tears, which she believed was 'owing to his ill usage of her'.[17]

Trapped in a loveless and violent marriage, forced to endure poverty and deprivation, and unable to call on friends or family for help, Henrietta's plight was now desperate. But she refused to follow the path to certain ruin that her husband was driving them along. In the depths of her misery, she hatched a plan to restore their fortunes. The means of salvation was a far cry indeed from the insalubrious lodgings of London's Beak Street.

The Electoral court at Hanover, in Germany, had for some time been a source of great interest and speculation for politicians and courtiers in England, for it was from here that the successor to Queen Anne looked set to hail. The House of Hanover's claim to the British throne had arisen from a period of turbulence and dynastic uncertainty in Britain towards the end of the seventeenth century. In the 'Glorious Revolution' of 1688, the Catholic King James II had lost his kingdom to his nephew and son-in-law, the Protestant William of Orange. William, who ruled from 1689 until 1702, and his wife and co-ruler Mary II (James's elder daughter) had no direct heirs. Their successor, James's younger daughter, Anne, had had many children from her marriage to Prince George of Denmark, but none had reached adulthood. William, Duke of Gloucester, the last to survive, had died in 1700. This had made the issue of the succession, which had been pushed to the fore when James II had been driven from the throne, even more acute. In order to exclude the Jacobite claimants and a variety of other Catholic individuals with better claims than the Hanoverians, Parliament had passed an Act of Settlement in 1701 which had provided for the succession of the Electoral House of Hanover.

The Hanoverians' claim to the British throne derived from King James I's daughter Elizabeth, who in 1613 had married Frederick V, Elector Palatine. In 1658 their youngest daughter, Sophia, had married Ernest Augustus of the staunchly Protestant house of Brunswick-Luneburg, in north Germany. The marriage had been an outstanding success in dynastic terms, bringing forth six sons and a daughter, all of whom had survived into adulthood. Widowed in 1698, Sophia was now the heiress-presumptive to the British throne.

Political events in Germany must have seemed very distant to the Howards. Indeed, in their impoverished state, even the court in London was well beyond their reach. But they nevertheless inspired Henrietta's plan for advancement, for she seized upon the idea that they could go to Hanover in an attempt to secure themselves positions in the future royal court. Given that she and her husband were out of society, and therefore not party to the latest news from court, it is extraordinary that she should conceive such a plan on her own. Her correspondence contains no clue as to what provided the inspiration.

It was certainly a bold move. Throughout history, royal families have been petitioned for favour by high-born ladies and gentlemen, and the Hanoverians were no exception. But Henrietta had little apart from her aristocratic connections to recommend her, and these were in a country with which the Hanoverians were not yet familiar: it is doubtful that Electress Sophia would have known of either the Hobarts of Blickling or the Howards of Audley End. Neither would Henrietta be able to impress the German courtiers with fine clothes or extravagant hospitality: the voyage alone would take up most of any funds that she managed to raise. The plan therefore rested upon Sophia having enough of an eye to the future to fill her court with English nobility, regardless of the paucity of their means.

Henrietta risked everything to bring her plan to fruition. Heavily in debt and with no more funds to call on, she decided to sell what little furniture and goods they had left, 'Beds & Bedding not Excepted'.[18] The shame of doing so was great, and Henrietta disguised herself with a hood and cape as she made her way to the nearby merchant's, where she sold every last piece. This raised enough money to pay for the voyage to Hanover. The road to salvation was now tantalisingly close. But for all her careful planning, she had not accounted for one crucial detail: the need to keep the money safe from her husband's grasping reach.

Henrietta had told Charles about the Hanover scheme and had persuaded him of the need to sell their goods in order to fund it. But while she had enthused about everything that was to be gained from a connection with the Electoral family, all Charles had seen was the prospect of some ready money. As soon as she returned with it, he stole and squandered the lot.

Henrietta was devastated. She seemed destined to live a life of abject poverty, no matter how hard she tried to claw her way out of it. Her plan had not only failed, it had left her worse off than she had been before. With no resources, in either money or goods, the Howards were now unable to meet their weekly rent payments. Although their landlady, Mrs Hall, had been sympathetic towards Henrietta's plight, she could not afford to let the couple live in her house for nothing, and they were once more obliged to seek new lodgings.

Still going by the name of Smith to protect Charles from his creditors, the couple lived in a succession of cheap lodgings. The first of these was in Red Lion Street, Holborn, which was further east than Beak Street, in an even less desirable neighbourhood. Charles's creditors soon caught up with him and, fearing arrest, he left Henrietta on her own as he sought alternative shelter. Her husband's absences were no longer a thing to be feared, however; they brought her a welcome respite from his cruelty.

Left to her own devices, Henrietta's thoughts again turned to Hanover, and she began to save what little money she could from the modest half-yearly allowance provided by her inheritance. Charles was, unfortunately, integral to her plans. Their chances of success would be far greater if they were presented to the Hanoverian court as a respectable noble couple; the strict codes that governed high society would not have tolerated a noblewoman making the journey without her husband. Neither could they escape the country and travel under false names, since it was their family name that was the key to their success. But if Charles were to come out of hiding, he would almost certainly be arrested at the behest of his creditors. Henrietta took the bold step of going in person to entreat them to give him more time to pay his debts. The names of these creditors are not provided in Henrietta's papers. We only know that she went to see them because of the long letter she wrote to her husband many years later, in which she recalled this and other episodes from her miserable early married life. That she succeeded in winning a temporary reprieve is as much a testament to her determination to improve her situation as it is to her skill in negotiation.[19]

Having eased the burden of their debts, albeit temporarily, it was with renewed vigour that Henrietta now set about raising what money she could for the voyage. She gave up the rooms that she and her young son had shared in Red Lion Street and moved into Charles's squalid lodgings.[20] These consisted of one 'very bad Room', and the rent was one tenth of what their first London lodgings had cost almost three years before. Charles was evidently content to live in squalor if it meant he could spend what little money he had on drinking and whoring. Henrietta found him fully engaged in both pursuits when she and Henry arrived towards the end of 1713. By now she was all but immune to his depravities. As long as she could drag him away from them long enough to save the family from utter ruin, she would be content.

Living in a 'wretched manner' and with no furniture left to sell, Henrietta cast about for other means to raise the money for Hanover. Some years before, she had been obliged to pawn the few items of jewellery she owned, and she now sold them all for good. But this still did not give the Howards sufficient funds for the voyage. Increasingly desperate, Henrietta contemplated selling her own hair and visited several wig-makers. Even this sacrifice was not enough, however, for the highest price she was offered was a mere eighteen guineas, which was significantly less than she had hoped for. Rather than being humbled by the fact that his wife was prepared to take such a step, Charles sneered that she should have accepted the money because it was more than her hair was worth.[21]

Eventually, after more than a year of carefully putting by what she could from her inheritance, Henrietta had accumulated enough money to fund their trip to Hanover. While she was delighted at being at last able to carry out her plan, the prospect of Hanover also brought with it some anguish, because it meant being separated from her young son. Whether she could not afford to take him with them, or whether she judged the voyage too hard for a seven-year-old boy is not certain. Neither is it clear to whom she entrusted his care, although the strongest possibility is that he was taken in by his paternal uncle at Audley End. Whatever the case, Henry had become her only joy and comfort during the years of misery and hardship she had suffered, and the prospect of leaving him behind must have been painful.

Thus, with only her wayward husband for company, and no great prospect of success, Henrietta set sail for Hanover.

Chapter 3

Hanover

◁○▷

T HE ELECTORATE OF HANOVER lay between the Elbe and Weser
rivers, the North Sea and the Harz mountains, in what is today
north-west Germany. Lacking both strong natural defences and
manmade fortifications, this loosely united patchwork of territories was
seen as easy prey for invaders, and therefore relied heavily upon the
protection of the Holy Roman Empire, of which it formed part. The
lack of unity within the Empire, however, made it an unreliable source
of security, and Hanover's vulnerable geographical position was further
weakened by the lack of an army large enough to see off any would-
be attacker. The Electorate therefore needed to find a powerful international ally, and thanks to the Act of Settlement of 1701, there was
an ideal candidate: Britain, a country whose population and military
forces dwarfed those of Hanover, now became her chief hope.

When Queen Anne named the Hanoverians as her successors, it
had a dramatic effect upon the prestige and importance of the Electorate.
This in turn had a marked impact upon its architecture and culture.
Hanover had changed little since medieval times. At the turn of the
seventeenth century, when the nearby court began to rise in status, the
appearance of the old city of Hanover was transformed. Handsome
new public buildings and houses sprang up on every side, and the outskirts
of the town, beyond the walls, also began to expand. It became the
resort of wealthy nobles, eager to enhance their position at court, and
new entertainments were introduced for their amusement.

For all of Hanover's improvements, it remained rather modest
in scale and did not really compare with the magnificent new towns
and cities that were springing up across Europe at this time. A

contemporary English traveller, Lady Mary Wortley Montagu, described it as 'neither large nor handsome', and the only thing that she found worthy of note was the opera house, which she declared was one of the best she had seen and even eclipsed that of Vienna.[1] Lady Mary's acerbic accounts form one of the best sources for Hanover and its court during this period. Although sometimes exaggerated for effect, they provide a shrewd – often unforgiving – reflection of the characters and customs within.

If Hanover was – at least in Lady Mary's eyes – an unimpressive provincial town, it did have one important asset, and that was its proximity to the Electoral court, which for most of the year resided at the palace of Herrenhausen, some two miles away. Herrenhausen was built in 1665 by John Frederick, Duke of Hanover, and substantially remodelled by the last Elector, Ernest Augustus, in the late seventeenth century. The palace was wide and low, consisting of just two storeys. The main building sprawled across three sides of a great courtyard, with terraces on the right and left over the ground floor, and a magnificent double stone staircase forming its centrepiece. It was flanked by several smaller houses occupied by officials of the court, and a vast range of stables that could accommodate up to six hundred horses. It also boasted a splendid orangery, decorated with frescoes that depicted scenes from the Trojan War, which housed a vast array of exotic fruits.

The most celebrated feature of Herrenhausen, however, was its magnificent gardens. These were modelled on Versailles and were designed to inspire awe. The palace was approached by an imposing double avenue of limes, which gave way to 120 acres of terraces, fountains and statues of mythological beings, fenced about with high, maze-like hedges of clipped hornbeam. Enclosing the whole was an enormous moat, 86 feet wide, on which ornamental gondolas would float during the summer months. Even the most critical of visitors could not fail to be impressed. Lady Mary admitted that the grounds were 'very fine' and was surprised by 'the vast number of orange trees, much larger than I have ever seen in England, though this climate is certainly colder'.[2]

The palace and gardens of Herrenhausen were built to enhance the status of the Electorate, as well as to give pleasure to the occupants and visitors. Under the rule of the late Elector and his lively spouse, Sophia, the court soon gained a reputation for being the gayest in Germany, and its splendour was out of proportion with the importance of their modest dominions. This was to change with the death of Ernest Augustus and the accession of his son, George Louis, to the Electorate in 1698.

Of medium height and build, with the typical Germanic features of fine hair and light blue eyes, George bore no trace of his Stuart ancestry. While his father had been every bit the genial and charming prince, George was by contrast a dour man, unrefined in taste, uncouth in speech, and excessively fond of order and routine. Naturally shy and uncommunicative, he was suspicious and aloof in his dealings with others. But he was honest and straightforward and loathed the intrigue and double-dealing that was so often a feature of court life. He also had great personal courage and had distinguished himself on a number of military campaigns. While acknowledging these virtues, contemporary observers were less than kind in their assessment of George's character. The Earl of Chesterfield described him as 'an honest, dull, German gentleman', while Lady Mary Wortley Montagu called him 'an honest blockhead . . . more properly dull than lazy'.[3]

George Louis was as penurious as his father had been extravagant, and cut back on all unnecessary expenditure. The resulting impact on court life was bemoaned by contemporaries. The waspish Duchess of Orléans wrote: 'It is not to be wondered at that the gaiety that used to be at Hanover has departed; the elector is so cold that he turns everything into ice – his father and uncle were not like him.'[4] The Duchess was, admittedly, biased, for she had long harboured a dislike for most of the Hanoverian family. If the court was not quite so dull as she claimed, however, it was still less refined than it had been in the days of the old Elector.

The great German philosopher Leibniz, who was a favourite at court, described one of the revelries held there in imitation of a sumptuous Roman banquet. The Elector and all the ladies and gentlemen of the court were dressed in Roman costume, and there were singers, dancers, drummers, huntsmen blowing horns, slaves, and all manner of raucous entertainments. Unfortunately, things got rather out of hand when a quarrel arose between one of the noble couples present. Fuelled by rage (and no doubt an excess of wine), the lord threw a goblet at his lady's head, and there ensued a monumental battle, much to the amusement of the onlookers, who assumed it was part of the entertainment. This incident was typical of the Hanoverian court, both in Germany and later in England, where great state occasions so often descended into farce.

The coarseness of the Hanoverian court in the early eighteenth century extended to the Elector's personal life. Since the age of sixteen, when he had made his sister's governess pregnant, George Louis had held the view that women were essential for the normal entertainment of a full-blooded man, and scorned the idea that sentiment should enter into it. Marriage, meanwhile, was simply a biological and political necessity. Love certainly seemed to have had little to do with his choice of a wife. At the age of twenty-two, he had married his first cousin, Sophia Dorothea, heiress of the Duke of Celle, who was then just sixteen years old.

It was not a happy union. Sophia Dorothea's immature and flighty nature clashed with George Louis's sternness, and his frequent absences on military campaigns doomed their marriage to failure within a few short years. Both found solace in various lovers, but one of Sophia Dorothea's choices was to prove her downfall. The charismatic and glamorous Count von Königsmarck could not have been more different from her dull and boorish husband, and Sophia Dorothea was captivated. The two became lovers, but the affair did not remain a secret for long, and when Königsmarck suddenly and mysteriously disappeared, it was rumoured that George Louis had had him murdered. George promptly divorced his wife and imprisoned her at Ahlden Castle, while he assumed custody of their two children.

Henceforth George Louis preferred the company of mistresses, and there was no talk of his taking another wife. He favoured one mistress above all others: Melusine von der Schulenburg, who in 1690 was appointed lady-in-waiting to his mother, Electress Sophia. Within a year she had become his lover, and in 1692 she gave birth to their first daughter. Madame Schulenburg lived with George Louis to all intents and purposes as his wife, and when he succeeded to the Electorate in 1698, her position became even more influential.

Contemporaries were bemused by the Elector's choice of mistress, for she was hardly the most attractive lady to grace the Hanoverian court. Her tall and emaciated frame earned her the nickname of 'the Maypole', and a bout of smallpox in her youth had left her pockmarked and virtually bald. Her attempts to remedy these defects with thick make-up and an unsightly red wig only made things worse, and her overall appearance was compounded by an appalling dress sense. Perhaps the lady's real attraction for George Louis, though, lay in the similarity of their characters. In a letter written to a friend back in England, Lady

Mary Wortley Montagu snidely observed that Madame Schulenburg was 'so much of his own temper, that I do not wonder at the engagement between them. She was duller than himself, and consequently did not find out that he was so.'⁵ She was also very faithful to him – a quality that he valued highly in lovers and ministers alike.

The same fidelity did not extend to George Louis himself, for he took a number of other mistresses. The most prominent (in more ways than one) was Madame Kielmansegg, whose mother, the Countess Platen, had been the long-standing mistress of George's father. Madame Kielmansegg was as different to Schulenburg as it was possible to be – except for the fact that she was equally unattractive. A lively and vivacious woman, she was flamboyant in everything she did. In contrast to Schulenburg's avaricious nature, she was exceedingly extravagant in her personal tastes, and rumour had it that her morals were as loose as her purse strings. George Louis' son, who hated her, once declared that she had slept with every man in Hanover – an allegation she countered by producing a certificate of moral character signed by her husband. This might have proved a more convincing defence had she not deserted him for another man some years earlier.

Kielmansegg's appearance presented a sharp contrast to that of her rival mistress. Her enormous bulk earned her the nickname of 'the Elephant', and her permanently flushed complexion and ostentatious black wig did her no favours. One of the best, and most amusing, contemporary descriptions of her was provided by Horace Walpole, who had met her when he was a child and had been terrified by her overbearing girth. He described her as being 'as corpulent and ample as the Duchess [Schulenburg] was long & emaciated. Two fierce black eyes, large & rolling beneath two lofty arched eyebrows, two acres of cheeks spread with crimson, an ocean of neck that overflow'd & was not distinguished from the lower part of her body, and no part restrained by stays – no wonder that a child dreaded such an Ogress.'⁶

The Elector's unusual taste in women did little to enhance his reputation. The Earl of Chesterfield described Schulenburg and Kielmansegg as 'two considerable samples of his bad taste and good stomach', and claimed that they 'made all those ladies who aspired to his favour, and who were near the statutable size, strain and swell themselves, like frogs in the fable, to rival the bulk and dignity of the ox'.⁷

The prominence of George Louis' mistresses was one of the most notable features of the Hanoverian court in the early eighteenth century.

Another was the role of his mother, the Electress Sophia, whose forceful personality wielded a great deal of influence over the court's social and political life. Fiercely intelligent, she read and corresponded widely and was fluent in five languages. She possessed a naturally cheerful and lively disposition, and enjoyed excellent health – due in no small part to her passion for outdoor exercise. Even in old age, she would spend two or three hours every day pacing up and down the gardens of Herrenhausen, tiring out many a young courtier who kept her company.

Electress Sophia was immensely proud of her British ancestry. Although she had never set foot in England, she took a keen interest in her future subjects and was said to be more English than German in her tastes and habits. Unlike the rest of the Hanoverian family, she spoke the language perfectly and kept herself well acquainted with events there. She even instructed her immediate circle to call her 'Princess of Wales', though in reality she had no claim to that title.

Relations between Electress Sophia and her son were notoriously hostile. Sophia found George Louis' lack of refinement irksome, and lamented the decline of court life that she had witnessed since he had inherited the Electorate. She found some solace, however, in her grandson, the Electoral Prince George Augustus, and his wife Caroline, whose bright and engaging presence offered a much-needed boost to life at Herrenhausen.

The only son of George Louis by Sophia Dorothea, George Augustus was born at Herrenhausen on 10 November 1683. Although he would have detested the comparison, he bore a strong resemblance to his father, being short and stout, with a quick, springy step that was described by less generous observers as 'strutting'. Together with his bulbous eyes and a complexion that was often given to flushing, this gave him an appearance that bordered on the comical. To George Augustus, his father was a cold and distant figure who took little interest in his upbringing, preferring to leave this to Sophia Dorothea, who doted on him. George Augustus adored her in return, and was therefore devastated when, at the age of eleven, he was snatched from her arms and placed under his father's guardianship following his parents' divorce.

Sophia Dorothea was desperate to see her children, but the letters she wrote to her estranged husband begging him to grant her wish went unanswered. George Augustus was occasionally allowed to visit his maternal grandparents, who fuelled his antagonism towards his father. He never gave up hope of seeing his beloved mother again, and it was said that he once escaped the confines of Herrenhausen and got as far as Ahlden, where he swam across the moat and almost succeeded in gaining entry to the castle before he was apprehended.

George Augustus grew to loathe the father who had so cruelly separated him from his mother. His feelings were reciprocated in full. Indeed, there was something of a tradition of hatred between fathers and sons in the Hanoverian line. Rather than showing any sympathy towards George Augustus for the sudden loss of his mother, the Elector mocked and bullied him for weakness, and was fond of making half-veiled threats to disinherit him. This in turn fostered a strong sense of insecurity in the young prince.

Bullying aside, George Louis took little interest in the upbringing of his son, and it was his mother, Electress Sophia, who took over. As she had no great love for her own son, it may be supposed that her grandson's hatred for him grew even stronger under her tutelage. The Electress made no secret of the fact that George Augustus was her favourite grandchild, and she indulged rather than checked his wayward behaviour. As a result, he grew up spoilt and with a lofty sense of his own importance.

Ironically, while George Augustus loathed his father intensely, he developed a personality that was remarkably similar in many respects. He was boorish, unrefined, obstinate and avaricious. Having received the traditional training of a German prince, he also shared his father's passion for military affairs. He never developed any real talent in this respect, but like his father he was brave in the line of fire. He was to distinguish himself in 1708 at the Battle of Oudenarde, where he had his horse shot from under him. The greatest military leader of the age, the Duke of Marlborough, praised his conduct, and the poet Congreve wrote a ballad in honour of 'young Hanover brave'.

For all his courage on the battlefield, the Electoral Prince was prone to petulant outbursts and his temper could flare up at the slightest provocation. One contemporary said of him that he 'looked on all the men and women he saw as creatures he might kick or kiss for his diversion'.[8] Another wrote that he 'had rather an unfeeling than a bad heart; but I never observed any settled malevolence in him, though his sudden passions, which were frequent, made him say things which, in cooler moments, he would not have executed'.[9]

The strong sense of insecurity that his father had engendered in him at an early age plagued George Augustus throughout his life. He found refuge in an obsession with facts and figures, and developed a slavish, almost manic attention to detail which found expression in his fascination for genealogy. He knew the complicated family trees of all the princes of Europe and could recite them with absolute accuracy. His knowledge of military regiments, orders and uniforms was equally precise and could never be faulted. Subjects such as these formed the basis of his conversation, and his companions at court were treated to many long hours of it. He did not so much win arguments as bore his opponents into submission. One courtier lamented his 'insisting upon people's conversation who were to entertain him being always new, and his own being always the same thing over and over again'.[10]

George Augustus's obsession with detail also materialised in a love of order and routine. His days moved with clockwork regularity, and his eye was exceptionally quick to spot anything that was at odds with the established order, especially when it concerned the ceremonials at court. He hated the unexpected, and even the most minor disruption would make him fly into a rage. Meals were regular and to the moment, as was every other aspect of his daily routine. 'Little things, as he often told me himself, affected him more than great ones,' the Earl of Chesterfield observed. The Prince's eldest daughter, Anne, later concurred with this. 'When great points go as he would not have them, he frets and is bad to himself,' she told a friend at court, 'but when he is in his worst humours, and the devil to everybody that comes near him, it is always because one of his pages has powdered his periwig ill, or a housemaid set a chair where it does not use to stand, or something of that kind.'[11]

Such an acute obsession with order, coupled with an extraordinary ability to retain the most detailed facts and figures, may simply have been traits inherited from his Guelph ancestors. While he had much in common with his father, however, George Augustus's personality was more extreme in many respects, and it is possible that there was a medical reason for this. In fact, he displayed some of the main traits of Asperger's syndrome.[12]

George's love of routine extended to his sexual relations, which he conducted in as well regulated a manner as he would an inspection of infantry. There was certainly no absence of passion, though, and he shared the same animal appetites as his father. He was highly energetic, eager for satisfaction, and not over-delicate as to how it was gratified. Having been raised predominantly by women, he felt safe in their company and preferred it to that of men. But he rarely developed any great affection for them and, like his father, believed that their primary function was to meet his physical needs.

However, the Electoral Prince was not as coarse and unfeeling as this portrait suggests. His confidence may have been difficult to gain, but once won, his loyalty was sincere and enduring. Furthermore, as well as military training, he had also acquired more refined princely accomplishments. His education included the classics, and he was given a good grounding in modern languages. He could speak French and Italian, and his knowledge of English was sound, even if he retained a marked German accent. But this was where his academic achievements ended. Like his father, he was contemptuous of intellectuals and men of letters, famously declaring: 'I hate boets and bainters both.' He often told courtiers that when he was a young boy he had despised reading and learning as other children did, not merely upon account of the confinement they entailed, but because he viewed them as 'something mean and below him'.[13] It is extraordinary, then, that he should have chosen for his bride one of the most accomplished and intellectual princesses in Europe.

Wilhelmina Caroline, Princess of Brandenburg-Ansbach, was born in the palace of Ansbach, a small town in south Germany, on 1 March 1683. She was the elder of the two children of Johann Friedrich, Margrave of Brandenburg-Ansbach, and his second wife, Eleanore Erdmuthe Louisa. Like that of George Augustus, Caroline's childhood was dominated by women. Her father died when she was just three years old, and she was raised by her mother until she, too, died ten years later. Caroline was subsequently taken into the care of her guardians, the Elector of Brandenburg and his wife, Sophia Charlotte, who became Queen of Prussia in 1701. It was she who exerted the greatest influence over her young charge. Electress Sophia Charlotte presided over a liberal, cultivated court, where intellectual discussion was actively encouraged, and Caroline was introduced to some of the greatest intellectuals and artists of the day, including Voltaire and Handel. Her favourite was the celebrated German philosopher and mathematician Gottfried Wilhelm Leibniz, with whom she developed a close friendship. They spent long hours together discussing philosophical, historical and religious questions. With regard to the latter, Caroline was a staunch Protestant and even turned down the prospect of what would have been a prestigious marriage to Archduke Charles, the future Holy Roman Emperor, on the basis that it would have meant converting to Catholicism.

Politics was also a passion for Caroline, and early on she developed a lust for power that was to stay with her for life. In certain respects she had the makings of a consummate politician. She was shrewd, wily, lavish in her compliments and often sparing with the truth. According to Lady Mary Wortley Montagu, she had a 'low cunning, which gave her an inclination to cheat all the people she conversed with', but at the same time she lacked 'understanding enough that falsehood in conversation, like red on the face, should be used very seldom and very sparingly'.[14]

Like her future husband, Caroline could speak French, and she later employed an Englishwoman to read to her, although she herself admitted that she found some difficulty in speaking the language. Perhaps because of the absence of any formal education when she was a child, her spelling was idiosyncratic and her handwriting poor. The Electoral Prince once observed that she 'wrote like a cat'.[15] On the whole, Caroline's intellectual abilities and tastes could perhaps be described as wide, but not very deep. They might have been completely absent for all George Augustus cared. What interested him were the reports of her physical charms.

Caroline was comely in a soft, flaxen, Aryan way. Contemporary portraits of her as a young woman show her with fair, fine and abundant hair, and blue eyes that matched those of her future husband. Her skin had an attractive rosy hue and was remarkably soft. She was quite small in stature, but robust rather than delicate. Her greatest asset (and the one that attracted most admiration from her male suitors) was her ample bosom, which she displayed to maximum advantage. She was well aware of her charms, and her poise and coquetry served to enhance her overall attractiveness.

The courtship of the Electoral Prince George Augustus and Caroline of Ansbach reads like a work of romantic fiction. The story goes that George rode out to the palace of Triesdorf, where Caroline was staying for the summer. He disguised himself as a young nobleman travelling for pleasure and assumed a false name to complete the ruse. Acting incognito would allow him to find out if he could love the Princess, and if she could love him, without bringing the considerable factor of his true status to bear. It was also expedient because of the hatred that Caroline's guardian, the King of Prussia, harboured for George's father. George was said to have fallen in love with the Princess at first sight. Her fair hair and large breasts were exactly to the taste of this lustful young prince. An envoy in Hanover reported that as soon as he met her, 'he would not think of anybody else'.[16]

Caroline was more calculating in her assessment of the Prince. Although she went along with the pretence of his being an ordinary young nobleman, she knew full well that he was really the heir to the Electorate of Hanover, and potentially to a much greater prize – the throne of Great Britain. She was also shrewd enough to realise that for all his bluff and bluster, here was a man who could be manipulated and subjected to her will. From the very start, she seemed to know instinctively how to play him. She appealed to his vanity and insecurity by professing a most ardent devotion to him, as well as a fervent desire to fulfil his every whim. His irascibility and petulance she met with soothing patience and apparent submissiveness, and for much of the time she was pursuing her own ambitions by appearing to comply with his. George may have been blind to her manipulative nature, but contemporary observers were not. One of these noted: 'Her first thought on marriage was to secure herself the sole and whole direction of her spouse; and to that purpose counterfeited the most extravagant fondness for his person; yet, at the same time, so devoted to his pleasures (which she often told him were the rule of all her thoughts and actions).'[17]

Caroline was not completely devoid of affection for her young suitor, however. Of an energetic and vigorous constitution, she shared his earthy nature, and the couple were thoroughly to enjoy their marriage bed. Nevertheless, it was the Prince's powerful status that attracted her most, and she readily accepted his offer of marriage. Their betrothal was formally announced in July 1705, and they were married at the beginning of September in the chapel of Herrenhausen. Eager though he was to claim Caroline for his wife, George was bored by the tediously long ceremony and dozed off during the sermon, much to the amusement of the congregation. The Duchess of Orléans rather crudely observed: 'What good news for the bride that he should be well rested.'[18]

The Princess manipulated her new husband from the start. She suggested that his family had shown him a lack of respect by presenting his bride with inadequate gifts. At the very least, she said, they ought to have given her all of his mother's jewels. It did not take much to inflame George's hatred of his father, and he now also turned on his grandmother, the Electress, 'which ended in such a coldness towards all his family as left him entirely under the government of his wife'.[19] In driving a wedge between him and his family, Caroline had succeeded in strengthening her own hold over him. This episode set the tone for what was to be an enduring, if subtle, subjugation of George to his wife's will, and before long he came to rely on her utterly.

Their marriage soon brought forth the expected heirs. The Electoral Princess gave birth to a son, Frederick, on 1 February 1707. Three further children followed in quick succession: Anne (1709), Amelia (1711) and Caroline (1713), and there were more to come. This strengthening of the Hanoverian dynasty could not have been more timely. Early in 1714, rumours reached Herrenhausen that the English Queen was fading fast.

Soon Hanover was thronging with well-born English adventurers, all anxious to pay homage to their future sovereign. The Electress was by now an old woman of eighty-four, so many hedged their bets by also seeking favour with her son, the Elector George Louis. Both of the main political parties in England, the Whigs and the Tories, sent emissaries, ostensibly to pay their respects, but in reality to gain the upper hand with the Hanoverians. At that time, the court of Hanover was apparently 'as much divided into Whig and Tory as the court of England'.[20]

All English visitors of any standing were received and entertained like invited guests. The Electress relished the prospect of taking the throne of her ancestors, and welcomed her future subjects with enthusiasm. Among them were Henrietta and Charles Howard. They arrived in Hanover early in 1714, after travelling 'in the meanest and most fatiguing manner', as Henrietta later recorded.[21] Their meagre funds had allowed them none of the comforts usually enjoyed by well-bred travellers. They took what lodgings they could afford in the town and prepared to make their court to the Electoral family at Herrenhausen. They had been out of polite society since their marriage, and there is no evidence that they had any acquaintances in Hanover to effect an introduction. Everything now rested upon their ability to render themselves agreeable to the Electoral family and thus pave the way for appointments in the future royal household. If they failed, they would have no choice but to return to England and face certain ruin. The modest allowance from Henrietta's dowry would not be enough to satisfy the growing list of creditors.

This was a daunting enough prospect in itself, but was made even more so by Charles. Rather than helping his wife to carry out her plan, he chose instead to torment her. More irritable than usual due to the long and arduous journey, he took his temper out on her with violence. 'When I came to Hanover and hoped to enjoy some respit from my troubles, I found ye uneasiness of yr Temper, render'd me void of almost a moments rest.' He also resumed his old habits, apparently set on establishing the same reputation in Hanover that had besmirched him in London. To Henrietta's utter dismay, he succeeded, and before long his activities were 'so visible as to be remark'd by all our acquaintances'.[22] She had to act quickly before the name of Howard was rendered unacceptable at the palace of Herrenhausen.

Henrietta went at once to apply for an introduction to the Electress. When this was granted, she summoned all her resolve and endeavoured to make herself as engaging as possible to the 'heiress of Great Britain'. Sophia was delighted with this new arrival at court. That Henrietta was English and of noble status certainly helped pave the way to her favour. But it was her pleasant, amiable manner and cultivated intellect that set her apart from the many other English adventurers who crowded the state rooms at the palace. In comparing her character to a book, a contemporary observed that it was 'a compleat treatise on subjects moral, instructive, and entertaining, perfectly well digested and connected, the stile is admirable, the reasoning clear & strong'.[23] Mrs Howard was certainly far superior in intellect and conversation to the Hanoverian ladies at court, and before long she had become a welcome guest in Sophia's apartments.

Henrietta's success in impressing the Electress proved that she had the makings of an excellent courtier. She had used just the right amount of artfulness and flattery to secure Sophia's good opinion, and had successfully concealed her real motives in doing so. She later confessed to a friend that she had found the Electress's conversation 'extremely light and without any gravity'. But her flattery had not been entirely false. She seemed to genuinely like the Electress, and enjoyed the opportunity to spend time with such a lively and sociable woman. She was also impressed by Sophia's skill in languages, and recounted how she had seen her 'keep up a conversation with four or five persons of different languages who spoke only their own, at the same time, & when she wanted to speak to them all together, she spoke Latin'.[24]

Henrietta soon became all but a lady-in-waiting to the Electress, and as such entered fully into the various diversions of court life at Herrenhausen. Whenever possible, Sophia entertained her English visitors personally. She frequently gave dinner parties at the palace, and these occasions were certainly more lively when she was present than when the English visitors were treated to the company of the Elector alone. Lord Johnstone, who was among the guests, described the entertainments to his friend the Earl of Oxford: 'The gaiety and diversion of the court consist entirely in a regular promenade that is made every evening in the orangery and garden of Heerenhuysen and lasts for 2 or 3 hours, in which the old Electress, who is near 84, performs a miracle, fatiguing all the company with walking after her without in the least incommoding herself.'[25]

Another English visitor was the poet and playwright John Gay, who was at that time struggling to make a name for himself in England. At twenty-eight, Gay was one of a group of like-minded young authors and wits in London who had recently formed the Scriblerus Club. The other members included Alexander Pope, Jonathan Swift and John Arbuthnot, Queen Anne's physician. The club had political as well as literary interests, and its members were staunch supporters of Lord Bolingbroke, the Tory peer who was wrestling for power with the Earl of Oxford. Gay dedicated *The Shepherd's Week* to him; this was published in April 1714 and was undoubtedly one of his best works so far. Shortly afterwards he was appointed secretary to the Earl of Clarendon, a Tory envoy hoping to win support for his party in Hanover, and the pair arrived there in June 1714.

Gay soon became a regular fixture at the Electoral palace, and wrote to a friend back in England: 'I go every night to court at Herenhausen, the Place & Gardens more than answer'd my expectations.' He immediately won favour with the Princess, who was charmed by his liveliness and wit, and in particular by the poems that he wrote for her. He confided to his friend: 'the Princess hath now ask'd me for my Poem, and I am obliged to make Presents to 3 or 4 Ladys besides'. One of these ladies was Henrietta, who was delighted with her new companion at court, and the pair established a firm and lasting friendship. Gay's enthusiasm for the Hanoverian court was less enduring, however, and within a few weeks of his arrival he was complaining: 'We have not much variety of Diversions, what we did yesterday & to day we shall do to morrow, which is, go to court and walk in the Gardens at Heernhausen.'[26]

As Henrietta's circle of acquaintance grew, her position at court became increasingly prominent. Electress Sophia delighted in having her nearby at the nightly dinners and receptions, and loved to exchange gossip about the assembled guests. One evening, at a court ball, Henrietta was standing behind the Electress's chair when, pointing to Madame Schulenburg, who was within earshot, Sophia cried: 'Look at that Mawkin, and think of her as being my son's passion!'[27] Henrietta was mortified by the Electress's lack of discretion, until she remembered that the object of her derision could not speak English.

Electress Sophia was not the only one who was charmed by the young English noblewoman, for Henrietta also succeeded in winning the favour of the Electoral Princess. In her, Caroline found a much-needed outlet for her intellectual interests. She had soon learned to suppress these in front of her husband, who could not abide intellectual discussion, so she was overjoyed at being able to converse freely with Mrs Howard. When the latter expressed an admiration (possibly diplomatic rather than real) for the teachings of Leibniz, Caroline was enraptured, and promptly appointed her one of her 'dames du palais'. Henrietta's joy was complete when, shortly afterwards, Electress Sophia promised that she would make her a Woman of the Bedchamber should she live to be Queen of England. There was, moreover, an understanding that if she died before succeeding to the English throne, her grandson's wife, Caroline, would honour this promise.

But Henrietta could not yet feel secure. There was still a chance that political events in England might take a different turn and deprive the Hanoverians of their inheritance. The Jacobite faction was growing in strength, and the prospect that it offered of placing a British rather than a German-born king on the throne was an enticing one. As late as December 1713, Princess Caroline had written to her friend Leibniz: 'You do well to send me your good wishes for the throne of England, which are sorely needed just now, for in spite of all the favourable rumours you mention, affairs there seem to be going from bad to worse.'[28]

Moreover, it was not enough for Henrietta alone to secure an appointment: to be sure of success her errant husband would also have to find favour. Henrietta did everything she could to help by recommending him to the Electress and Caroline, earnestly hoping that they had not already learned of his unsavoury reputation. But it was the male members of the Hanoverian family who Charles would have to impress, because it was in their households that he would need to find employment. This was made even more difficult by the fact that, unlike his mother, the Elector had no love of the English and disapproved of their presence at his court. Against all the odds, Charles succeeded in winning him over. Perhaps his vulgarity appealed to George Louis, who had no time for the niceties of polite conversation and court etiquette. Or perhaps his wife's efforts had reaped some reward. Whatever the case, Charles was able to secure the promise of an appointment in the royal household as soon as the Hanoverians took up residence in England.

Their task accomplished, the Howards became a regular feature of the court. As Henrietta's intimacy with Caroline grew, so did her acquaintance with the Princess's husband, George Augustus. The Electoral Prince approved of his wife's companion. She displayed all the qualities that he admired in a woman: modesty, discretion and – above all – obedience. As Lady Mary Wortley Montagu shrewdly observed: '[he] judged of the merit of all people by their ready submission to his orders'.[29] The Prince was also drawn to Henrietta's physical charms. Now aged twenty-five, she had blossomed into an attractive woman. The fashionably pale skin that others had to attain with cosmetics was hers by nature. Her fine features were perfectly framed by her long hair, which fell in soft curls down her back, and her figure (although less ample than Caroline's) was slim and elegant. But it was her presence, just as much as her appearance, that made her alluring. Softly spoken, she chose her words carefully and was exceptionally discreet. Her eyes seemed to betray a secret pleasure or amusement, and the fact that she rarely revealed her private thoughts and feelings gave her an enigmatic quality.

Henrietta's main charm for the Prince, however, was the patient interest she showed in his tedious conversation. He would spend hours regaling her with minute descriptions of the military campaigns in which he had fought, or reciting the intricacies of European royal genealogy. A woman of keen intellect like Henrietta could not have found any genuine pleasure in such monotonous subjects, but she was shrewd enough to flatter the Prince's vanity by appearing fascinated. Caroline was apparently content to allow their acquaintance to develop, no doubt glad to be relieved of the tedium of her husband's company for an hour or so each day. The Electress was equally approving, and was said to have remarked: 'It will improve his English.'[30]

There was some speculation among the courtiers who observed Mrs Howard's friendship with the Prince as to whether it went beyond the platonic. George was a highly sexed young man and had already taken several mistresses since his marriage. Speculation aside, however, there is little else to suggest that Henrietta and George had begun a physical affair at this stage. It is unlikely that a woman who had hith-erto proved a model of such decency and propriety as to border on the prudish would so easily have surrendered her virtue. This would in any case have risked, rather than enhanced, her new-found favour at the Hanoverian court. A prince could more easily cast aside a mistress whom he had tired of than a respectable and suppliant companion whose friendship both he and his wife valued highly. Henrietta was already too skilled a courtier to jeopardise the prize that she had so nearly won by entering on such a reckless course.

Reports of Queen Anne's deteriorating condition were now arriving at Herrenhausen on an almost daily basis. But the health of her successor-in-waiting was also beginning to fail. The Electress feared that her cher-ished ambition to be Queen of England would be snatched from her by death, and confided to Leibniz: 'She [Queen Anne] will have to hurry up with her dying if I am to be Queen.'[31] The eyes of the world were now on the two aged matriarchs, and speculation was rife as to which of them would die first. Despite her advanced years, Sophia seemed the more likely to outlive her rival. She had enjoyed excellent health, and her mind was as sound as ever. As she herself had once commented, 'creaking wagons go far'. However, it was whilst displaying this excellent constitution and taking one of her accustomed brisk walks in the grounds of the palace, on 19 June 1714, that Sophia suddenly collapsed, having suffered what appeared to be a massive stroke. Caroline rushed to her side, but the Electress died in her arms a few moments later.

The Electress's death again threw the Hanoverians and their English dependants into uncertainty. According to the 1701 Act of Settlement, the Elector would now succeed as heir to the English throne, but this rested on Queen Anne's approval, and she had a well-known distaste for her distant German relatives. She also had little choice, for none of her children had survived into adulthood, and it would have been inconceivable to revoke her Protestant dynasty in favour of the Jacobites. If Anne had to accept a Hanoverian succession, however, she stead-fastly resisted suggestions that the Electoral family should visit her in England, saying that it would be akin to seeing her coffin before she was dead. She had taken a violent dislike to George Louis when he had come to pay his court to her many years before with the intention of strengthening their alliance through marriage, and had swiftly nipped any such proposals in the bud. Yet with the prospect of a Jacobite succession being no more appealing to her than that of a boorish Hanoverian, she eventually agreed formally to name the Elector as her heir.

Electress Sophia had missed out on being Queen of England by the narrowest of margins, for just a few short weeks after her death, Queen Anne herself lay dying. As her life hung in the balance, antici-pation at Hanover reached fever pitch, and almost hourly updates of the Queen's condition were dispatched from the English court. On 31 July, the Earl of Oxford reported: 'This day, about 10 o'clock, it was apprehended her Majesty was just expiring, but by the strength of her nature, she recovered out of that fit. There is so little hope of her recovery that an express is this day sent to the court of Hanover to desire his Electoral Highness immediately to come to England. It is thought by the physicians that she cannot live many days.'[32] The physi-cians were right. Less than twenty-four hours later, the Queen was dead. Henrietta's fate was now irrevocably tied to Britain's new Hanoverian royal family.

Chapter 4

St James's

————◁◇▷————

WHEN THE MESSENGER ARRIVED at Herrenhausen with news of Queen Anne's death, the Elector was asleep in bed. It being a dispatch of such importance, permission was granted to wake him. On hearing that he was now King of England, George merely grunted, turned over and went back to sleep. His snores were soon heard reverberating along the corridors of the palace.

The reaction in England was equally muted. The expectation of a Jacobite uprising came to nothing, and the succession of the Hanoverian king was remarkably peaceful: 'not a mouse stirred against him in England, in Ireland or in Scotland'. Two days after Queen Anne's death, heralds proclaimed George I king before the gates of St James's Palace, Charing Cross, Temple Bar, Cheapside and the Royal Exchange.[1]

George I was in no hurry to take up his new crown. His interests did not extend far beyond the borders of his beloved Hanover, and he had always disliked the English with their liberal and upstart ways. 'His views and affections were singly confined to the narrow compass of his Electorate,' sneered Lord Chesterfield. 'England was too big for him.'[2] Certainly in terms of size alone, George I's new kingdom dwarfed his native lands. In 1714, Britain's population stood at around 5.5 million, while Hanover's was less than one tenth of that.

But there were more fundamental differences. In Hanover, the Elector reigned supreme over a population grown accustomed to obedience and discipline. All expenditure over £13 had to receive his personal sanction, and the army was regarded as his private property. England, meanwhile, was the most fractious, constitution-ridden country in Europe, and the power of the monarch was significantly limited. He was unable to levy new taxes, abolish privileges or make new laws without Parliament's consent. Neither could he order the imprisonment or execution of any subject, or confiscate their lands or property. The last monarch to undermine these liberties had been executed.

It was therefore with good reason that the Duchess of Orléans feared that George I's succession to the British throne would lead to catastrophe. 'I wish our Elector could have another kingdom, and our King of England his own, for I confess that I don't trust the English one iota, and fear that our Elector, who is now King, will meet with disaster. If his rule in England were as absolute as our King's here [in France], I have no doubt that right and justice would reign, but there are altogether too many examples of the unfair way in which the English treat their kings.'[3]

George I lingered in Hanover for a full six weeks before reluctantly assembling his entourage and beginning the journey to England. Even then, progress was slow. The stately retinue, which included the Prince, Mesdames Schulenburg and Kielmansegg, the King's two Turkish Grooms of the Chamber, and seventy-five other German courtiers and servants, was stopped time and again to receive the congratulations of mayors and burghers in the cities through which it passed. When it reached Holland, the final stopping-place before the voyage across the Channel, a series of receptions and addresses occasioned yet more delay. When the royal yacht at last embarked, it was tossed about on rough seas and then detained off Gravesend by thick fog for several hours. The very elements surrounding his new kingdom seemed as inhospitable as the people within to George, who heartily wished himself back in Hanover.

Finally, on the evening of 18 September 1714, the royal yacht emerged through the fog that had now drifted inland along the Thames, and landed at Greenwich. It was greeted by the firing of cannons, the ringing of bells and the flying of flags. The citizens of London, who had been instructed to 'put themselves out of Mourning' for Queen Anne in preparation for his arrival, thronged along the riverside to catch a first glimpse of their new King.[4] Among them was a great number of privy councillors, lords spiritual and temporal, and place-hunters of every variety, all elbowing and jostling their way into the royal presence. The object of their veneration was, however, in an ill humour, his patience tested by the tiresome journey. He dismissed them all with scant ceremony and hastened to bed.

Not to be deterred, vast crowds again gathered at Greenwich the following day, a Sunday. They stood and cheered for hours to attract the royal attention and were eventually rewarded with an appearance by the King and his son at the windows of the palace. *The Weekly Journal* reported: 'His Majesty and the Prince were graciously pleased to expose themselves some time at the windows of their palace to satisfy the impatient curiosity of the King's loving subjects.' They would get a more fulsome reward the next day, which had been appointed for the King's public entry into London and was declared a general holiday. This time, George was unable to dispense with the ceremonials for which he had had so little patience at Greenwich, and he was forced to endure the full pomp and pageantry of a royal procession through the capital.

The day had dawned clear and fine, and as the royal party set out from Greenwich Park at two o'clock that afternoon, the sun was shining brightly. The procession, in which a strict order of precedence was followed, presented an impressive sight to the assembled crowds. First came the untitled aristocracy, the lowliest of the ranks, but as only those who could afford a coach drawn by six horses were permitted to take part, many were absent. They were followed by knights bachelors, baronets, the Lord Chief Justice and other senior officers of the law, the privy councillors, bishops, and, finally, the highest-ranking officials in the land: the Lord Chamberlain, the Lord President of the Council, the Lord High Treasurer and the Lord Chancellor.

The climax of this magnificent procession was the carriage bearing the King, which was more splendid than all the rest. Fashioned out of glass, fringed with gold and emblazoned with the royal arms, it was drawn by eight horses with postilions. Amidst all this unparalleled splendour, George I presented something of an anticlimax. Although he occasionally leaned forward and, with his hand on his heart, bowed to the cheering crowds, his face was fixed in a grim expression that betrayed his utter distaste for the elaborate ceremonials. His already sour temper was irritated further by the Prince, who, sitting beside him, was all smiles and conviviality.

Behind the royal carriage came a series of coaches bearing the various Hanoverian courtiers, officials and servants that George had brought with him to England. The assembled crowds were astonished by the sight of the King's two Turkish grooms, Mahomet and Mustapha, whom he had acquired on one of his military campaigns. But they were as nothing compared to the two extraordinary creatures that had the privilege of being the King's mistresses. Since the very earliest times, kings of England had chosen some of the most beautiful women in the kingdom as their intimate companions. In recent memory, Charles II's court had been graced by a host of glamorous ladies of pleasure whose beauty was immortalised by poets and portrait-painters. The citizens of London who lined the route of the royal procession were therefore ill prepared for the vision of their new King's rather unusual taste in women. As the carriage passed by bearing the corpulent mass of Madame Kielmansegg, who was squeezed up against the emaciated frame of Madame Schulenburg, a gasp of dismay reverberated among the crowds, shortly followed by peals of laughter and a chorus of raucous jibes.

The firing of cannon signalled the arrival of the procession into the City of London, and the King and his entourage looked across the river to the imposing fortress of the Tower. The Lord Mayor greeted them in Southwark, where the coaches came to a rather prolonged halt as the royal party was treated to a series of formal addresses. Transcribed in full in the following day's newspapers, these ran into several pages and would have tested the patience of even the most accommodating of princes. But the Hanoverian King was not noted for this virtue and, worse still, could barely understand a word of English. The many fine words extolling his 'most illustrious merit' therefore served merely to aggravate his already frayed nerves, and were greeted with nothing more than an occasional grunt, signalling impatience rather than approval.

When at last the speeches were over, the cumbersome entourage crossed the Thames at London Bridge and made its way to Wren's great masterpiece, St Paul's Cathedral, where four thousand children chanted 'God save the King!' Throughout the sprawling city, the processional route was lined with troops and crowds, and flowers were thrown from the windows and flag-draped balconies above. The pealing of church bells competed with the shouts and cheers from the assembled masses, which grew ever louder as they consumed the wine and ale that flowed from specially constructed fountains.

It was eight o'clock in the evening – some six hours after it had left Greenwich – before the procession arrived at its final destination of St James's Palace. The festivities outside continued long into the night, however, with bonfires lighting up the streets and squares, while people feasted on roasted meats washed down by numerous barrels of beer. As the gates of St James's closed on the royal retinue, the new

King heaved a sigh of relief, glad to be free at last from all the tedious pomp and ceremony. But the palace in which he now found refuge did little to soothe his ill temper.

St James's Palace had been built by Henry VIII in the 1530s on the site of a former leper hospital, and although subsequent monarchs had made some improvements, it was plain and old-fashioned, with its red-brick Tudor façade and maze of small rooms within. It was neither impressive to visitors nor comfortable for the royal family. In his 'Critical Review of the Public Buildings . . . in and about London and Westminster', James Ralph wrote: 'so far from having one single beauty to recommend it, that 'tis at once the contempt of foreign nations and the disgrace of our own'. Corroborating this, Charles de Saussure, a contemporary Swiss traveller, declared that it 'does not give you the impression from outside of being the residence of a great king'. Even Englishmen thought it somewhat lacking in stature. In his *Tour Thro' . . . Great Britain*, Daniel Defoe observed: 'The King's Palace, tho' the Receptacle of all the Pomp and Glory of Great Britain, is really mean, in Comparison with the rich Furniture within, I mean the living Furniture.'[6]

St James's had become the principal royal residence after 1698, when fire had destroyed Whitehall Palace, but it had only ever been intended as a temporary base until the latter was rebuilt. As this had still not happened by the time George I arrived in England, he had no choice but to set up court here. St James's plain and decaying Tudor exterior suffered by comparison with the stately magnificence of Herrenhausen, and George took an instant dislike to it. He thought little better of the adjoining park, even though it was one of the most attractive in London. Lined with imposing avenues along which notables could drive in their splendid carriages, St James's Park had been opened up to pedestrians by Charles II. Even on the most inclement of days, it was filled with people of all kinds, from 'welldressed Gentlewomen' to 'staymakers, sempstresses and butchers' daughters', who presented a colourful scene as they promenaded up and down its tree-lined paths and lakes.[7] Its beauty was lost on the new King, however, who thought it would make a better turnip field and proposed closing it to the public so that it could be ploughed up for that purpose. When he asked his Secretary of State, Lord Townshend, how much it would cost, the latter wryly replied, 'Only three crowns, Sir.'[8]

Barely had George I set foot in St James's Palace than he was yearning to be back at Herrenhausen. The buildings, the parks, the customs, and above all the people of his new dominions were all distasteful to him, and he found little to please him. Aware that the affairs of court and government could not be put off, he resolved to make them as palatable as possible by surrounding himself with German advisers and staff. Chief among them were three ministers who became known as the 'Hanoverian Junta': Bothmer, Bernstorff and Robethon. The first of these had been George's agent in London during the reign of Queen Anne, and his knowledge of English affairs was unrivalled among the German contingent. Bernstorff had enjoyed a long and distinguished political career in Hanover, rising to the position of Prime Minister. As the officer responsible for Sophia Dorothea's strict imprisonment, he had the full trust and admiration of the King, which gave him a great deal of influence. Robethon, meanwhile, was a former private secretary to William of Orange and was employed by George before he became King to carry confidential correspondence from informants in England.

All three men were greedy, grasping and corrupt, making full use of their influence with the King to amass large fortunes in bribes from place-hunters at court. The Hanoverian ladies were little better. Mademoiselle Schutz, a niece of Baron Bernstorff, alienated the English peeresses at court by making a habit of borrowing their jewels and forgetting to return them. Before long she had accumulated a considerable collection of treasures, which she took with her when she returned to Hanover. The King's two mistresses lost no time in exploiting their positions to bring them financial reward, and both were brazen in their greed for gold. When the Duke of Somerset resigned as Master of the Horse, Madame Schulenburg cheekily proposed that the post be left vacant so that the revenues could be given to her. Much to the disgust of the English courtiers, George assented to her request, and the profits – amounting to some £7,500 a year – fell into his mistress's eager hands.

Tensions soon arose between the Hanoverians and the English at court, and criticism of the King's entourage began to appear in pamphlets and newspapers. One decried them all as 'pimps, whelps and reptiles', and the unpopularity of these 'hungry Hanoverians' began to spread among the people. The simmering resentment at court soon spilled out into open sniping between the opposing factions. A lady-in-waiting recorded how, one evening, the Countess of Buckenburg launched a verbal attack on English ladies, saying that they always presented themselves 'pitifully and sneakingly' and that they 'had their heads down, and look always in a fright'. German ladies, on the other hand, she said, 'hold up their heads and hold out their breasts, and make themselves look as great and as stately as they can'. Lady Deloraine promptly retorted: 'We show our quality by our birth and titles, Madam, and not by sticking out our bosoms.'[9]

Within weeks of arriving in England, George I and his entourage had succeeded in antagonising large swathes of the court and the population at large. They had little choice but to accept him as their King, however, and preparations were made for his coronation. His daughter-in-law, Caroline (now Princess of Wales), was sent for from Hanover. She arrived with two of her children, Princesses Anne and Amelia, in mid-October. The youngest child, Caroline, was left behind on account of illness, and the eldest, Prince Frederick, also remained in Hanover by command of the King. The Princess of Wales was welcomed by her husband when she landed at Margate, and together they made the journey back to London in state. Their arrival was greeted by demonstrations of joy, with cannons fired from the Tower and St James's Park, and bonfires lit across the city. The people hoped that, in the absence of a queen, the Princess would bring some much-needed sparkle to a court that had already become staid and dull.

The first impressions were promising. Caroline seemed to strike a chord with the citizens of London. One newspaper enthused: 'The whole conversation of the town turns upon the charms, sweetness and good manner of this excellent princess, whose generous treatment of everybody, who has had the honour to approach her, is such that none have come from her without being obliged by some particular expression of her favour.'[10] Caroline was as forthcoming and affable as the King was withdrawn and sullen, and she threw herself into the ceremonies and diversions of court life with vigour. The evening after her arrival in England, she attended a drawing room at St James's and delighted the guests by playing cards and chatting amiably to them for several hours. During the days that followed she went on promenades in the parks, attended receptions and assemblies, and welcomed company into her apartments at the palace. So bewildering was her array of social engagements that she complained of having scarcely enough time to prepare for the coronation.

This event took place on 20 October 1714, a week after Caroline's arrival. As it was the inauguration of a new line of kings, the English people were determined to put aside their growing resentment of George I and celebrate the occasion with unprecedented splendour. Just as on the day of the King's entry into London, huge crowds lined the streets along which the coronation procession would pass, and Westminster Abbey was crowded with nobles, peers, ministers, officials and ambitious men and women seeking places at court, each anxious to find favour with George I. Even the Jacobites turned out to greet him, although their smiles were somewhat forced. One member of the congregation described them as 'looking as cheerful as they could, but very peevish with Everybody that spoke to them'.[11] They had prayed for rain, but the day was clear and bright, and the warm October sunshine gave an extra brilliance to the magnificent costumes and decorations.

The King was dressed in robes of crimson velvet, lined with ermine and bordered with gold lace. He wore the collar of St George, and on his head the cap of estate adorned with a circle of gold encrusted with diamonds. Despite the magnificence of his attire, however, he did not present a very majestic figure, and the sourness of his countenance suggested that he was no more eager to take up his crown than he had been when he had first arrived in his new kingdom.

Once inside Westminster Abbey, the traditional coronation ceremonies were observed. Owing to the King's ignorance of English, these had to be explained to him by the high officials standing nearby. As they could speak neither German nor French, however, they had to resort to Latin as the only common language between them. George's foreignness was even more obvious when it came to the part of the service at which he was required to repeat the anti-Catholic declaration. He did so with such a strong German accent as to render it completely unintelligible, and he could have been renouncing something entirely different for all the loyal Protestants standing by knew.

Such mishaps aside, the ceremony proceeded along the accustomed lines, and at two o'clock in the afternoon, having received the coronation ring, orb and sceptre, the crown of Great Britain was lowered on to the head of the first Hanoverian king. The beating of drums and the sounding of trumpets inside the Abbey gave the signal for cannons to be fired across the city, which in turn prompted celebrations among the citizens of London and the population at large, lasting long into the night.

Amidst the festivities, however, were signs of discord. Jacobite riots broke out in Bristol, Norwich and Birmingham, and in London shouts of 'Damn King George!' were heard amidst the more traditional salutes to the new sovereign. The discord went to the very heart of the ceremonials. During the coronation banquet in Westminster Hall, the King's champion rode into the hall and, as tradition dictated, laid down a challenge to any person who did not acknowledge George as King of England. To the astonishment of the assembled guests, a woman promptly threw down her glove and cried out that His Majesty King James III was the only lawful owner of the crown and that the Elector of Hanover was a mere usurper. She was hastily ushered from the hall and the festivities resumed, apparently unabated. But the incident had betrayed a growing resentment of the foreign king.

With the coronation over, the King and Prince and Princess of Wales set about the business of appointing the members of their households. Noblemen and women jostled with low-born adventurers in the state rooms of St James's Palace, all hoping that the efforts they had already made to secure a place would pay off. Among them were Mr and Mrs Howard, who had arrived from Hanover shortly before the coronation. Henrietta knew that this was her only chance to avoid falling back into the misery and deprivation of their former life in London. Although her scheme to win favour at Herrenhausen had proved a resounding success, the promises made to her there already seemed a distant memory, and there was no guarantee that they would be honoured now that the Hanoverians had come into their inheritance. What was more, with no queen consort, places in the household of the Princess of Wales were highly sought after, and competition was fierce.

Mrs Howard hastened to pay her respects to the Princess at the earliest opportunity, and was relieved when she was welcomed into her apartments at St James's. She was joined by many other ladies of high-born status, each hoping to outdo the other in the hunt for the most prestigious places. Lady Mary Cowper, who was to be appointed a Lady of the Bedchamber, noted in her diary that she had made her way to court early one morning soon after the coronation in order to wait upon the Princess, but had found the Duchess of St Albans 'upon the same errand', along with the Duchess of Bolton, Charlotte Clayton and Mrs Howard.[12]

Caroline had already made two appointments to her household before arriving in England. Elizabeth, Countess of Dorset, and Louisa, Countess of Berkeley, were both awarded positions as Lady of the Bedchamber. Five more were subsequently appointed to this role: the Duchesses of St Albans, Bolton, Montagu and Shrewsbury, and Lady Cowper. The post that Henrietta had been promised was that of Woman of the Bedchamber. Five days after appearing at St James's, and several agonising months after first being promised the post, she finally got her reward. Along with Mary Selwyn, Mrs Pollexfen and Charlotte Clayton, she was appointed a Woman of the Bedchamber to the Princess of Wales on 26 October 1714.[13]

Henrietta's achievement should not be underestimated. In the fiercely competitive world of the court, social 'quality' was not enough to secure an appointment, and there were many more people fulfilling this criterion than there were places available. Lady Irby, for example, who, like the Howards, had fallen on hard times, appealed for a place in the Princess's household on the grounds that this was the only way that she could be made 'easy in her fortune'. Like so many others, she failed in her quest.[14] Having a relation or patron at court was a key advantage, and most of those who sought positions without it (of whom Henrietta and her husband were numbered) were disappointed. Money was another useful tactic, and many place-seekers offered bribes to those close to the royal family in return for their putting in a good word. Again, this had not been an option for the Howards, who were still heavily in debt and could secure no further credit.

But the overriding criterion for success was the ability to spend a great deal of time and effort at court. 'Tenacity of purpose and determination to succeed were as important as the much-derided courtierly attributes – the ability to fawn and flatter,' observed one contemporary.[15] Lady Mary Wortley Montagu, whose husband was among those seeking a place at George I's court, urged him not to be modest and self-effacing, but to push others out of the way and continue asking until he got what he wanted: 'I don't say it is impossible for an impudent man not to rise in the world; but a moderate merit, with a large share of impudence is more probable to be advanced, than the greatest qualifications without it.'[16]

Henrietta was of a naturally modest and reserved manner, and it must have taken a substantial effort for her to push herself forward sufficiently. The years of misery inflicted on her by her husband were

no doubt a powerfully motivating factor, and the resilience that they
had given her enabled her to practise that other necessary quality of
tenacity. Her position secured, she turned her attentions to her errant
husband, hoping that he would manage to stay out of trouble long
enough for the promise made to him in Hanover to be honoured. It
seems that he did so, for shortly afterwards he became Groom of the
Bedchamber to the new King.

Although they were now in separate households, the Howards were
given apartments together at St James's Palace. They were among only
a small number of household servants who enjoyed this honour. The
palace was too small to accommodate all those who had a right to lodgings, and the majority went instead to Somerset House on the Strand,
the great mews houses at Charing Cross, or were scattered about in
Whitehall. Having apartments at St James's was not necessarily indicative of great favour, however: these tended to be reserved for the
Bedchamber staff, whose duties required them to have quick and easy
access to their master or mistress.

Most staff lodgings at the palace consisted of several rooms, and
some were even large enough to house the officer's own family and
servants. That said, accommodation for the household staff at St James's
was considerably less luxurious than that enjoyed by the royal family
in the state rooms above, and it left much to be desired in the way of
comfort and hygiene. Damp was rife throughout the apartments, and
the only ventilation came from the persistent draughts caused by broken
windows still awaiting repair. Washing facilities were almost non-
existent, while chamber pots were frequently used by both sexes
'amongst a cloud of witnesses'.[17]

Nevertheless, the Howards' new apartments were undoubtedly
preferable to the squalid lodgings in which they had been living before
their sojourn in Hanover. They also had the significant advantage of
being rent-free. In addition, the couple now received a regular wage:
£500 per year for Charles and £300 for Henrietta.[18] This was supplemented by an allowance for food when the court was in the 'country'
– usually Hampton court or Windsor – for the summer. Above all,
their court appointments gave them that most valuable asset, for which
Henrietta had been striving ever since her wedding day: security.

Chapter 5

In Waiting

———◇———

DURING THE REIGN OF England's new king, George I, the structure of both the male and female royal households changed little from what it had been under his predecessors. Since the reign of James I, there had been four main departments: the Lord Chamberlain's department, the household below stairs under the Lord Steward, the stables under the Master of the Horse, and the Bedchamber under the direction of the Groom of the Stole. With the exception of the first of these, which was the largest and had several different offshoots, each had a clearly defined purpose. The stables department looked after the King or Queen's horses and carriages, and its leading officers became personal royal servants when the sovereign was out of doors. The household below stairs was a vast supply department that acquired, prepared and distributed food, drink, fuels and other necessaries throughout the court. The Bedchamber staff, among whom Henrietta and Charles were numbered, were the personal servants of the monarch in his or her private apartments. As such they were among the most sought-after positions because they had the greatest access to the sovereign.

The royal household had, however, decreased considerably in size due to rising costs. Under Charles I, it had comprised 1,450 staff; a hundred years later, George I employed 950. The majority of these were located within the Lord Chamberlain's department, which employed an average of 660 staff, while the Bedchamber was the smallest department with just thirty. However, there were many more men and women working at court than those who were listed as official servants. All of the greater and many of the minor household officers employed servants of their own, some of whom did their master's work. Often, therefore, an appointment in the household could bring a regular income and access to the sovereign without any arduous duties. Taking the official servants and their own staff together, well over a thousand men and women were connected with the royal household in some way. This was a vast number, particularly when compared to the households of the nobility, the greatest of whom had only fifty servants, and most of whom had fewer than thirty.

In addition to the household structure that was already established for George I when he arrived at St James's, he also brought seventy-five of his own servants from Hanover. His two Turkish Grooms of the Bedchamber served the majority of his personal needs, and a number of bedroom pages did the rest. Furthermore, the new King had such a strong aversion to formal etiquette that the traditional duties performed by the bedchamber staff, such as the elaborate dressing ceremonies, were no longer required. Their activities were therefore limited to introducing men into the King's rooms and accompanying him when he went out of his apartments. During the early years of his reign, George lived as private a life as possible. Even on the rare occasions that he dined in public, his bedchamber staff were not required to serve him on bended knee, as court etiquette usually dictated. As a result, these posts became little more than sinecures.

The King chose not to appoint a Groom of the Stole until 1719. For the first five years of his reign, therefore, the Gentlemen of the Bedchamber were the most senior officials in that department. These posts were the preserve of the nobility, and most were held in conjunction with positions in government. Below them were the Grooms of the Bedchamber, of whom Charles Howard was one. Seven out of the eight Grooms had a military background, as was traditional for this position. The Grooms were the middle rank of servants in the Bedchamber and should have been kept busy with a range of tasks connected with the King's person, including helping him to wash and dress. But although they were almost always in attendance, this was more for public show than for practicality, thanks to George I's reliance on his German servants. The absence of any onerous duties no doubt suited the slothful Charles Howard perfectly.[1]

His wife had a rather less easy time of it. In contrast to the King, both Caroline and her husband embraced every element of the traditional court ceremonies. This entailed a busy life for all those who attended them. The structure of their households mirrored that of the King, although the staff were paid significantly less. The Princess's Bedchamber was presided over by the Duchess of St Albans as Groom of the Stole.[2] Below her were the Ladies of the Bedchamber, who were all peeresses and undertook the most honourable and ceremonial duties of that department. They oversaw the work of the lower-ranking bedchamber staff and acted as companions to the Princess. They also waited on her during formal dinners, receptions and other state occasions. Not being a peeress, Henrietta was barred from this rank of servant, and was instead among the Women of the Bedchamber, who made up the middle tier of staff. Below them were the sempstresses, laundresses and other more menial servants.

As Woman of the Bedchamber, Henrietta was one of only a small number of servants who had close and regular contact with the Princess. She and the seven other women who held this post took it in turns to be 'in waiting' – that is, on duty in the palace. During her periods of waiting, Henrietta was in more or less constant attendance on her mistress. Her day began early, as she was required to rise before the Princess and be ready to come into her bedchamber as soon as she awoke. Her first task was then to pour out the water in which the Princess washed, or on the days when she bathed, to fill the bath with the hot water that the Page of the Backstairs brought up in great ornamental ewers. The washing or bathing over, Caroline's private chaplain was summoned and she would hear morning prayers, usually within the bedchamber itself. This was an important part of the Princess's daily ritual. She was devoutly religious and, though raised as a Lutheran, became an enthusiastic follower of the Anglican faith once in England.

After prayers came the ceremony of dressing the Princess in her day clothes – or 'shifting', as it was known. This was the most strictly ordered of all the bedchamber rituals. Each attendant looked after a specific item of clothing, which varied according to their rank. The Women of the Bedchamber, assisted by the laundresses and sempstresses, were responsible for the Princess's underwear. Her outer garments, which were more valuable and elaborate, were commissioned and cared for by the Ladies of the Bedchamber, under the watchful eye of the Groom of the Stole. After the attendants had ensured that the correct garments were ready, the Woman of the Bedchamber would set them out in order and then hand each item in turn to the Lady of the Bedchamber, who would assist the Princess in putting them on.

This painstaking procedure would continue from the linen undergarments to the skirts and outerwear, right down to accessories such as gloves and fans. The final touches would then be put in place, namely dressing her hair and fastening on her jewellery. This would be performed by the Woman of the Bedchamber under the supervision of the Lady, who would discuss with her mistress which jewels she wished to wear that day.

The ceremony of dressing over, the Princess would venture out into the court, attend formal occasions, make visits or go to chapel, depending on the day of the week. Whatever she was doing, her bedchamber ladies and women were in waiting all the time, in case they were required to run errands for her or attend to her appearance. In the early evening, Caroline would return to her private apartments, where she would spend her time reading, talking or playing cards with her ladies. If there were any formal entertainments later in the evening, such as a drawing room or assembly, both the Ladies and Women of the Bedchamber would accompany their mistress. Finally, the Princess would retire and the rituals of the morning would be performed in reverse, with the ladies and women undressing their mistress and preparing her for bed. Often it could be as late as two o'clock in the morning before they were able to retire themselves.

Henrietta's work as a Woman of the Bedchamber was not hard as such, and was certainly less physically demanding than her years of serving her husband, but it was constant and often unpredictable, depending as it did upon the whim of the Princess. The hours were also very long, and she would have had precious little time to herself. Even when she was not actively attending to the Princess, she would have been surrounded by the other Women and Ladies of the Bedchamber who were in waiting. Although friendships did develop between them, these were overshadowed by the fierce rivalry that dominated Caroline's household, as each member of it vied for favour. There was more or less constant bickering, and heated arguments could flare up over the most trivial of matters. Lady Cowper, whose diary is rich in gossip and scandal from the court, described one such occasion: 'This day was passed in Disputes amongst us Servants about the Princess's kissing my Lady Mayoress, and quoting of Precedents.'[3] Henrietta tended to keep out of these petty disputes, anxious to avoid anything that might jeopardise her newly won position. Her neutrality and discretion won the admiration and respect of the other ladies, and while they might quarrel among themselves, they rarely quarrelled with her.

There was one exception. Charlotte Clayton, another Woman of the Bedchamber, was a favourite of the Princess, but sensed that in Mrs Howard she had a rival. She knew that Henrietta's association with Caroline went back further than her own, to the court in Hanover, and she was suspicious of the way in which Henrietta held herself aloof from the bickerings of the household. Part of Mrs Clayton's insecurity no doubt sprang from her own rather obscure background. Her husband was a lowly clerk of the Treasury, and she had only risen to the position in the Princess's household thanks to her acquaintance with the Duchess of Marlborough. She had won Caroline's admiration by affecting to share her views on religion, and had steadily increased her influence over her mistress.

Mrs Clayton was a woman of considerable cunning, and used her advantageous position to win titles and riches for both herself and her family. She once received a pair of diamond earrings as a bribe for securing a prestigious post at court for the Earl of Pomfret. Decked out in these jewels, she went to visit the Duchess of Marlborough, who was entertaining Lady Mary Wortley Montagu. As soon as Mrs Clayton had left them, the Duchess exclaimed: 'What an impudent creature, to come hither with a bribe in her ear!', to which Lady Mary replied: 'Madam, how should people know where wine is sold, unless a bush is hung out?'[4]

Henrietta struggled to hide her dislike for Mrs Clayton, and as her own influence in the Princess's household grew, the rivalry between them intensified. Their animosity did not escape the sharp eye of John, Lord Hervey, who claimed that at its root lay not just rivalry, but a profound difference in character. 'Mrs Clayton and Mrs Howard hated one another very civilly and very heartily, but not in equal constraint,' he wrote, 'for whilst Mrs Clayton was every moment like Mount Etna, ready to burst when she did not flame, Mrs Howard was as much mistress of her passions as of her limbs, and could as easily prevent the one from showing she had a mind to strike, as she could the other from giving the blow. Her passions, if I may be allowed the comparison, were like well-mannered horses, at once both hot and tractable.'[5]

Her influence with the Princess may have been inferior to Mrs Clayton's, but in terms of popularity among the ladies at court, Mrs Howard far outstripped her rival. As well as the Ladies and Women of the Bedchamber, she also befriended the Maids of Honour – the unmarried ladies who were the Princess's main companions at court. These well-born young ladies were amongst the liveliest and most vivacious at St James's – if not in the whole of England. Most were still in their teens, and their beauty and giddiness lent a much-needed brightness to life at court. Principal among them was Mary Bellenden, daughter of John, 2nd Lord Bellenden. Her voluptuous beauty and high spirits made her the darling of the court. Horace Walpole talked of the 'universal admiration' for her, adding, 'Her face and person were charming, lively she was even to etouderie,[6] and so agreeable that she was never afterwards mentioned by her contemporaries but as the most perfect creature they had ever seen.'[7]

Mary Bellenden's closest rival at court was Mary ('Molly') Lepel, who combined beauty and charm with a lively wit and intellect. Her more poised style and ability to please won her the admiration of some of the greatest intellectuals of the day, including Voltaire, who wrote a poem in her honour. Lord Chesterfield said of her: 'She has been bred all her life at Courts, of which she has acquired all the easy good breeding and politeness without the frivolousness. She has all the reading that a woman should have, and more than any woman need have.'[8]

Among Miss Lepel's many admirers was the waspish courtier Lord Hervey. Hervey was handsome in a delicate sort of way, and his slender, mincing figure bordered on the effeminate. He had a voracious sexual appetite that was satisfied by both men and women, and he was described as being as much a fop as a rake. Alexander Pope excoriated his immorality and christened him 'Lord Fanny', who 'now trips a lady, and now struts a lord'. Hervey's acerbic wit and love of gossip found full expression in his memoirs, which recorded – and often exaggerated – the daily round of events and scandal at the Georgian court. Despite his sexual ambivalence, Hervey married Molly Lepel – apparently for love, for she had no fortune – and she bore him eight children.

The eldest among the Maids of Honour was Mary Meadows, who did her best to keep her unruly companions in order. She had quite a task, especially with Sophia Howe. This young lady owed her position at court to the fact that she was the great-granddaughter of Prince Rupert, brother of old Electress Sophia. Miss Howe was exceedingly gay and flighty, and her irrepressible humour frequently bordered on the coarse. On one occasion, she had a fit of giggles during a service in the royal chapel at St James's, earning her a severe reprimand from the Duchess of St Albans, who told her she could not have done a worse thing. 'I beg your Grace's pardon,' Miss Howe tartly replied. 'I can do a great many worse things.'[9]

Sophia Howe was not the only Maid of Honour to fail in her religious devotions. The Chapel Royal soon became a magnet for all the beaux at court, and a great deal of ogling and giggling went on, especially during Bishop Burnet's long sermons. The situation became so intolerable that he complained to the Princess, who eventually agreed to his suggestion that the Maids of Honour's pew should be built up so high as to shield them from their admirers. This sparked one such admirer to lament:

> And now Britain's nymphs in a Protestant reign
> Are boxed up at prayers like the Virgins of Spain.[10]

The liveliness of Princess Caroline's household, and that of the Prince of Wales, formed a sharp contrast to the general tenor of life during the early years of George I's reign. The new King was fifty-four when he ascended the throne, by which age his habits and principles of thought were firmly entrenched. He was not inclined to change either for the sake of his new court, and instead continued the routines that he had established as Elector. These had been simple in Hanover and remained so in England. He wanted very few of the innumerable rights and courtesies to which he was entitled. He was a shy and reserved man, and the notion of traditional royal ceremonies such as the levée, during which the King invited members of the court into his bedchamber to observe his dressing, were abhorrent to him. He would have none of them.

George I hated fashionable society and shunned it whenever possible. He rose early but did not emerge from his bedchamber until noon, when he went into the adjoining closet to receive his ministers and other visitors. These audiences generally lasted until three o'clock in the afternoon, when the King again retired to his bedchamber. He ignored the Stuart tradition of dining in public, choosing instead to take his meals in private, waited on by his faithful Turkish servants. Late in the afternoon, he would venture out to take a walk alone in the gardens of St James's. On Sundays he was forced to spend more time in public because of the requirement to attend chapel. But even then, few courtiers would catch more than the briefest glimpse of him as he hurried back to his private apartments after the service, and he rarely spoke to any of the dense throng lining the corridors.

The King spent most of his leisure hours in the apartments of his two favourite mistresses, Mesdames Schulenburg and Kielmansegg. These were situated as far apart in the palace as possible, with George's apartments in between, because the two women hated each other. One of the more innocent pleasures that he enjoyed with Madame Schulenburg was to sit and watch her cut figures out of paper, an occupation that would hold him in thrall for several hours.

But George was not a total recluse. In the evenings, he sometimes slipped out of St James's and went to the theatre or opera with a small party of intimate friends. He shied away from the royal box, however, preferring to watch the performances incognito. Since he knew little English, he favoured ballets and pantomimes. His companions were almost always women, and despite his reserve, he enjoyed flirting with them. His dalliances occasionally attracted unwanted attention, however. One evening, in a moment of impetuosity, he kissed the hand of the Dowager Duchess of Ancaster, who was sitting next to him. In her surprise, she rose and made a low curtsey, which unfortunately drew the attention of the ladies nearby, who 'clapped their fans to their faces, and tittered'. It was reported that 'The whole house was astonished', and that the King's display of gallantry was 'pretty near to a declaration of love'.[11]

Very occasionally, George would join the Princess's evening parties for half an hour, but he always resisted her invitation to take part in the card tables. This was not due to any aversion to gambling: George loved to play cards, but he preferred to do so with a select group of friends in private houses.

The new King's reluctance to show himself in public did nothing for his popularity. His English subjects grew increasingly disdainful of him, and of his mistresses, whom they thought resembled more the ugly sisters of pantomime than the beauteous creatures they were accustomed to in the royal court. One day Madame Kielmansegg was taking a ride in a carriage when she was accosted by a jeering mob. Leaning out of the window, she called: 'Goot people, why you abuse us? We come for all your goots!' To which a voice from the crowd shouted back, 'Yes, damn ye, and for all our chattels too!'[12]

A rather more serious indication of a lack of public support for the new regime came less than a year after George I's accession. His preference for German habits and customs over English ones also extended to his views on foreign policy. He persuaded Parliament to release funds for the military campaigns in which he was engaged on Hanover's behalf. He also implemented a foreign policy that was almost entirely dictated by his desire to augment Hanover's status, even though it sacrificed British interests – and coffers. This sparked widespread resentment among both his ministers and his subjects.

The Jacobites, who had been steadily gaining support on both sides of the border, seized the chance to further their own cause at the expense of the King's, and started to gather their forces. They planned three risings: 'James III and VIII', who was in exile on the Continent, was to land in the south-west of England and lead a march to London. At the same time, Jacobite forces in the Borders and Scottish Highlands were to be mobilised. This was the people's chance to rid themselves of 'German George' and restore the rightful Stuart king to the throne. James's health was drunk in public and at private dinners by passing the wine glass over the water bottle to signify 'the King over the water'. There was a flurry of pamphlets and ballads denouncing the Hanoverian regime and urging people to rise up in support of their rightful king. Meanwhile, George I doggedly persisted with his pro-Hanover policy, flying in the face of public opinion, and either refusing to believe in the threat to his crown or caring little for it.

In the event, the Jacobite risings came to nothing. Poor leadership and indecision, coupled with effective government intelligence, nipped the south-west rebellion in the bud. On the Borders, the Jacobite forces advanced as far as Cumbria and captured Preston, but were then outnumbered and obliged to surrender. The rising in Scotland was initially successful, and both Perth and Aberdeen were captured. But again lack of leadership prevented them from pushing home the advantage. If the Jacobite risings had failed to achieve their objective, however, they had provided a very clear demonstration of the anti-Hanoverian feeling across the country at this time. Thenceforth, George would ignore public opinion at his peril.

With the popularity of the King at an all-time low, the Prince and Princess were quick to seize the advantage. They made themselves as affable and visible as George was dour and reserved. While he stubbornly pursued his German habits and interests, they loudly expressed their love for all things English. The Prince proclaimed: 'I have not von drop of blood in my veins dat is not English.' This may have been a little more convincing if it had not been expressed with such a strong accent, and had it not been well known that he in fact had even more German blood in his veins than his father. He went further still by announcing at a reception one evening that he thought the English were 'the best, handsomest, the best-shaped, best-natured and lovingest people in the world, and that if anybody would make their court to him, it must be by telling him that he was like an Englishman'. This delighted the English courtiers but horrified their German counter-parts, who 'could not contain themselves, but fell into the violentist, silliest, ill-mannered invective against the English that was ever heard'. They had further cause for complaint when Caroline took up her husband's theme and declared that she would 'as soon live on a dunghill as return to Hanover'.[13]

How sincere these expressions were is uncertain, but the fact that the Prince and Princess voiced them and made an effort to understand and speak English (admittedly not very competently) gave them a huge advantage over the King. What really swung the tide of popular opinion in their favour, though, was not their words but their actions. Spying the gap that George I had created by refusing to enter into court cere-monials and other formal occasions, they threw themselves headlong into the full round of engagements offered by fashionable society, deter-mined to add some much-needed glamour and vitality to the Hanoverian court. As Lord Hervey observed: 'the pageantry and splendour, the badges and trappings of royalty, were as pleasing to the son as they were irksome to the father'.

The Princess gave a series of balls and masquerades at Somerset House and St James's Palace, to which all of London's most elegant noblemen and women flocked. She also held formal drawing rooms two or three evenings a week, where guests were treated to lively conver-sation, music and cards. The latter became all the rage, and before long the whole court was gripped by gambling fever. Lady Cowper recounted that on one occasion 'There was such a court I never saw in my life. My mistress and the Duchess of Montagu went halves at hazard and won six hundred pounds. Mr Archer came in great form to offer me a place at the table, but I laughed and said he did not know me if he thought I was capable of venturing two hundred guineas at play, for none sat down to the table with less.'[14] High play was accompanied by deep drinking, and things occasionally got out of hand. At a drawing room one evening, a gentleman present, who had evidently taken great advantage of the royal hospitality, fell out with another guest, and in the fray 'pulled him by the nose'. He was promptly thrown out for being 'drunk and saucy'.[15]

The Prince and Princess did not confine their entertainment to the court, but made sure that they were seen in all of London's most fashionable retreats. The capital was at that time a city built for entertainment: assembly halls, pleasure gardens, coffee houses and gambling rooms were springing up everywhere, and the great aristocratic mansions were being transformed to suit the new social tastes of the privileged classes. There was greater vibrancy in the arts, and a host of new theatres were opening up in London's West End. The royal couple were very fond of operas and plays, and were often to be seen in full state at the Haymarket or Drury Lane, enjoying everything from Shakespeare to the latest farce. Caroline even caused a scandal at court by going to see a risqué new comedy called *The Wanton Wife* – much to the horror of the Duchess of Roxburgh, who claimed that it was 'such a one as nobody could see with a good reputation'.[16]

On the evenings when there was no formal court occasion or play to divert them, the Prince and Princess would dine at the houses of great noblemen and women. Frequent mention is made in the newspapers and diaries of the time of a dinner at the Duchess of Shrewsbury's, a supper at my Lady Bristol's, or a ball at the Duchess of Somerset's. The couple always made sure that they were at their most affable and charming on such occasions, conscious that with the nobility rested one of the surest routes to good opinion among the population at large.

Their social pursuits did not stop during daylight hours. In the early months of the reign, they walked in St James's Park every day, accompanied by a fashionable crowd and those seeking to be so. Later on, the Princess discovered the gardens at Kensington Palace, which she greatly admired, and they soon became a popular destination for London's socialites. Entrance was by ticket only, so the general public could only watch from behind the gates, eager for a glimpse of the glamorous young royals.

In the fashionable world, dinner was taken in the middle of the day, and, unlike the King, Caroline and George upheld the Stuart tradition of dining in public. Ordinary people would flock to watch the spectacle of the royal couple and their guests eating, and would endure many hours of being squeezed and jostled in the galleries that lined the dining room. This became such a popular pastime that a ticketing system had to be introduced.

Like everything else at court, mealtimes were governed by rigid codes of etiquette and ceremony, which were then mirrored in fashionable households across England. Guests would walk into the dining room in strict order of rank, ladies first. The mistress (in this case the Princess) would sit at one end of the table, surrounded by the most important female guests. The other would be occupied by her husband and all of the gentlemen present. This division of the sexes often led to overexuberance among the male diners, whose boisterous habits of drinking loud healths and reciting lewd ballads went unchecked by the ladies seated a safe distance away.

Some attempts to curb these excesses were made later on in the century by John Trusler, who published *The Honours of the Table*, a series of rules for behaviour during meals. This advised that it was vulgar to eat too quickly or too slowly, as it showed that one was either too hungry or did not like the food. Guests should also avoid smelling the meat whilst it was on the fork because it implied that they suspected it was tainted. Trusler warned of a number of other faux pas. 'It is exceedingly rude to scratch any part of your body, to spit, or blow your nose ... to lean your elbows on the plate, to sit too far from it, to pick your teeth before the dishes are removed.' And woe betide anyone who had the call of nature during meals. If it was too urgent to be ignored, then they must steal from the table unobserved and return without making any mention of where they had been. Jonathan Swift poked fun at such rigid strictures in his satirical handbook, *Directions to Servants*, which recommended practices that would have made Trusler faint away in horror: from combing one's hair over the cooking, to eating half the meat before it went to table, and keeping quiet about any lumps of soot that accidentally fell into the soup.

The obsession with order and ceremony at the royal table was matched by the lavishness of the fare that was served. Enormous quantities of food were consumed by the assembled guests, and the predominance of meat astonished foreign visitors. 'I always heard that they [the English] were great flesh-eaters, and I found it true,' wrote one. 'Among the middling sort of people they had 10 or 12 sorts of common meats which infallibly takes their turns at their tables.'[17] The first course to be served almost always consisted of various types of meat, some of which was accompanied by sauces. Stewed or potted venison, pork sausages, 'jugged' pigeons, pheasant with prune sauce – all made their way to the tables at court. Vegetables such as turnips, carrots and parsnips were served occasionally, but many people believed them to be bad for the health and steered well clear. Dessert was the final course to arrive. Strawberry fritters, whipped syllabubs, jellies and sweetmeats were favourites with the sweet-toothed Georgians. A healthier option of fresh fruit was also included, and the privileged classes were treated to exotic varieties such as pineapples, peaches and grapes, which were grown in the hothouses that had started to spring up across the country. This sumptuous feast would have been washed down with wine, followed by coffee or hot chocolate, and all three beverages would have been generously sweetened with sugar.

It is hardly surprising that after the last dishes had been cleared, the Prince and Princess would retire to their apartments for a post-prandial nap. But they were soon back on the social round. For Caroline, this involved making calls. Ladies of quality passed most of their afternoons going from house to house drinking tea, which was a luxury commodity in those days. Etiquette demanded that if a caller came while the lady of the house was out and left a card, that visit must be returned the following day. This meant that members of fashionable society were constantly flitting around London in sedan chairs and carriages, catching up with their obligations and making calls of their own choosing.

Gentlemen, meanwhile, idled away many hours in the new coffee houses that were opening up across the capital, such as White's Chocolate House in St James's Street or Lloyd's of Lombard Street. Here they would read newspapers or debate political matters whilst enjoying their coffee or hot chocolate. One foreign traveller to London was astonished by the number of these establishments, and by the variety of pursuits that went on within them. 'Some coffee houses are a resort for learned scholars and wits; others are the resort of dandies or of politicians, or again of professional newsmongers; and many others are temples of Venus.'[18]

Such was the social whirl into which Caroline and George threw themselves. They were swept up by, but at the same time dictated, the fashionable life of London. At a public dinner one day, they were delighted to see the 'country folks' wearing straw hats, and when the

Princess noticed that one girl had come without hers, she sent her home to get it. This prompted several of the gentry present, who were eager to win favour with the royal couple, to don straw hats the following day.

The Prince and Princess certainly seemed to have the knack of courting ordinary people and high society alike, and they were loved for it. Their charm offensive worked so well that just a few months into the reign, the foreign traveller and diarist Sir Dudley Ryder noted: 'I find all backward in speaking to the king, but ready enough to speak to the prince.'[19]

Knowing that his son was more popular with the English than he was himself irritated George I intensely and fuelled the growing discord between the two. But rather than focusing upon improving his own public profile, he handed the Prince and Princess a further advantage by announcing that he was leaving for a visit to Hanover. He had been itching to do so ever since he had inherited the British crown: he missed the order and familiarity of the court at Herrenhausen, and in particular the obedience of his people there, who were a good deal less trouble-some than his fractious English subjects. His timing could not have been worse. Sympathy for the Jacobites remained strong, and people were still smarting from the heavy expenses to which he had subjected them in pursuance of Hanoverian interests. It was in vain that his ministers pressed these points upon him, and the King left London in June 1716. Those who watched him go said that he was the most animated they had seen him since his arrival in England.

Much to the Prince's resentment, the King did not trust him enough to make him regent during his absence. Instead, he revived a title that had not been in use since the Black Prince's time in the fourteenth century – that of 'Guardian of the Realm and Lieutenant'. This carried less authority than the position of regent, and George further restricted his son's powers by insisting that the Duke of Argyll, the Prince's trusted friend and adviser, should be dismissed. The Prince was livid and his wife was 'all in a flame', but in the end they relented, and the King, having won his point, set out for Hanover.[20]

Chapter 6

The Swiss Cantons

◄◦►

NO SOONER HAD THE royal yacht set sail than George and Caroline were acting the part of King and Queen in all but name. Their court was even livelier than before. They kept open house and lived from morning to night in a perpetual round of gaiety. A little over a week after the King's departure, they left the cramped confines of St James's and repaired to Hampton Court, Henry VIII's magnificent pleasure palace by the Thames. Their very journey was a spectacle to behold as they made a progress up the river in state barges hung with crimson and gold, and headed by a band playing music.

The Prince and Princess passed the whole of that summer at Hampton Court, and everything they did was on a grand scale. As a public relations exercise, it was faultless: by demonstrating what a brilliant court they could hold, they simultaneously drew attention to the sharp contrast with George I's staidness and reserve. They gathered around them the glitterati of Georgian society: all of its wittiest, most beautiful, wealthiest, cleverest and most talented members were there. Ordinary people, too, flocked to Hampton Court, eager to witness the most extravagant royal entertainments since the decadent days of Charles II.

They were not disappointed. The Prince and Princess appeared in public several times a day. It was one of the finest summers for years, and in the mornings they would take the air on the river in richly decorated golden barges, hung with curtains of crimson silk and wreathed with flowers. One of the visitors noted with some astonishment that 'all sorts of people have free admission to see them even of the lowest sort and rank', shrewdly adding: 'They gain very much upon the people by that means.'[1]

In the afternoons, the Prince and Princess would walk in the elegant palace gardens for two or three hours, followed by the Maids of Honour and their beaux. The Prince would then play a game of bowls with the gentlemen of the court, while his wife and her ladies sat in the nearby pavilion and chatted, played cards and drank tea until dusk.

The eager crowds were sometimes treated to another glimpse of the royal party in the evening, when they chose to take supper in public. After this, there would be the traditional court pastimes of music, dancing or cards. More often than not, though, they each had private suppers and parties in their apartments, attended by a few select friends. It was often late into the night before everyone finally retired. This pattern was repeated day after day and night after night. It was a bewildering round of entertainments that would have exhausted even the most energetic of courtiers, but the fact that Caroline was at this time heavily pregnant with her fifth child made her stamina all the more impressive.

The gaiety and diversions of court life during that summer at Hampton Court extended to the ladies and gentlemen of the royal household. Chief among them was Henrietta. During her two years in the Princess's service, she had developed social graces commensurate with the most seasoned courtier. Her lively wit and keen intellect were feted throughout the court, and her discretion, mildness and good nature won her many friends among the Maids of Honour and other members of the court. 'She has as much Good nature as if she had never seen any Ill nature, and had been bred among Lambs and Turtle-doves, instead of Princes and Court-ladies,' Pope once said of her, and this view was shared by many others.

On the evenings when her mistress chose to dine privately, Henrietta held supper parties in her own apartments at Hampton Court. These were likely to have been on the eastern range of the new palace built by Wren, overlooking the magnificent 'Fountain Court'. If so, they were directly above those occupied by the Princess and were linked to her State Bedchamber by means of a small staircase. This meant that Henrietta could swiftly respond to any summons from her mistress that might arrive while she was off duty. The Maids of Honour nick-named these chambers 'the Swiss Cantons', and Mrs Howard 'the Swiss', on account of the neutral position she occupied between conflicting interests at court.

Discretion was a rare quality among members of the Georgian

court, with its daily round of scandals, and Henrietta's companions
were grateful for it. Flirtations (or 'frizelations', as Henrietta called
them) were a common feature of the evening parties in the Swiss
Cantons. These were lively gatherings, attracting some of the wittiest
and most vivacious members of the court. Among them was Philip
Dormer Stanhope, later Earl of Chesterfield. An exuberant young man
of twenty-two, he had a somewhat unprepossessing appearance. Lord
Hervey described him as being 'as disagreeable as it was possible for
a human figure to be without being deformed ... He was very short,
disproportioned, thick, and clumsily made; had a broad, rough-featured,
ugly face, with black teeth, and a head big enough for a polyphemus.'
But Stanhope's intellect and humour more than made up for his physical deformities. His amusing letters and anthologies were celebrated
throughout the court. Dr Johnson described him as a 'lord among wits',
and even Lord Hervey admitted that he had 'more conversable entertaining table-wit than any man of his time', adding: 'he affected following
many women of the first beauty and the most in fashion'.[2]

Among these was Henrietta. She and Stanhope had first met a year
earlier, when he had been appointed a Gentleman of the Bedchamber
to the Prince of Wales. She delighted in his company, which enlivened
the monotony of her duties at court, and he was similarly enchanted
by her gentle wit and intelligent conversation. The two soon became
close friends, and the bond between them was strengthened by their
shared experiences in the household of the Prince and Princess.

Undoubtedly the greatest of the wits and poets to frequent
Henrietta's apartments that summer, though, was Alexander Pope. Like
Chesterfield, Pope's physical stature made him somewhat disadvan-
taged. He was just four feet six inches in height and had a humped
back. His physique was further hampered by a fragile constitution, and
he was dogged by ill health throughout his life. Chesterfield referred
to his 'poor, crazy, deformed body' as a 'mere Pandora's Box, containing
all the physical ills that ever afflicted humanity'. His face bore noble
and intelligent features, however, and the famous eighteenth-century
artist Sir Joshua Reynolds found it a fascinating subject: 'He had a large
and very fine eye, and a long handsome nose; his mouth had those
peculiar marks which are always found in the mouths of crooked
persons; and the muscles which ran across the cheek were so strongly
marked that they seemed like small cords.'[3]

But Pope's physical defects were eclipsed by the brilliance of his poetry, and by the time Mrs Howard made his acquaintance, he had already become one of the leading lights of the literary world in Georgian England. In 1709 he had published the *Pastorals* to great acclaim, followed by *An Essay on Criticism* and the mock epic *Rape of the Lock* three years later. His most famous work, though, was his translation of Homer's *Iliad*, published around 1714, which had achieved such widespread popularity that even George I and his son were among the subscribers. Pope's literary talent was matched by his skill in conversation, which was littered with irreverent observations and flattery, and he soon became a firm favourite with the Princess's ladies.

As well as poets, wits and Maids of Honour, Henrietta's supper parties also included the most illustrious member of the Hampton Court set: the Prince of Wales himself. Attracted more by the charms of the Maids of Honour than by the diverting conversation, George became a frequent visitor to Mrs Howard's apartments. He found the hostess's modesty and discretion appealing, and was flattered by her patient interest in his tediously long accounts of the military campaigns in which he had fought. The attention he paid to her led some to speculate that they were already lovers.[4] Pope hinted at it in a poem written to the Maids of Honour at around this time:

> But should you catch the Prudish itch,
> And each become a coward,
> Bring sometimes with you Lady R– [Rich]
> And sometimes Mistress H–d [Howard]
> For Virgins, to keep chaste, must go
> Abroad with such as are not so.

It is not clear whether Pope was implying that Mrs Howard and Mrs Rich were not virgins or that they were not chaste. The fact that Lady Rich was well known for her marital infidelity does lead one to suspect that it was the latter. While it was entirely acceptable for a prince of the royal blood to bed ladies at court, it was less so if they were married. In Henrietta's case, this was complicated by the fact that her husband worked in the King's service, and Charles Howard's notoriously volatile nature made it all the more necessary for her to keep such rumours from him. It is therefore unlikely that she would have enjoyed the humour in Pope's verse. Besides, there is little to suggest that her relationship with the Prince had gone beyond harmless flirtation at this stage.

The summer of 1716 at Hampton court passed in a round of receptions, parties, recitals and other diversions. All the gaiety and flirtation
that had been suppressed in the dowdy rooms of St James's now burst
into life. In a letter to Henrietta written a dozen or so years later, Molly
Lepel wistfully recalled 'a thousand agreeable things' from that time. 'I
really believe a frizelation wou'd be a surer means of restoring my spirits
than the exercise and hartshorn I now make use of,' she wrote. 'I don't
suppose that name still subsists, but pray let me know if the thing it
self does, and if ye meet in the same cheerfull manner to supp as
formerly; are ballads or epigrams the consequence of these meetings?
is good sence in the morning and wit in the evening the subject or
rather the foundation of the conversation?'[5]

Beneath the frivolity that summer was an undercurrent of political
scheming. Hampton Court became a magnet for dissenters from the
existing regime, including malcontent Whigs, supporters of the Tory
opposition, and even some suspected Jacobites. The Duke of Argyll
was among the Tory contingent, despite having been dismissed from
his offices at George I's explicit instruction. Meanwhile, the King's
faithful servant Bothmer was playing spy and sending frequent reports
back to his master in Hanover.

The two principal ministers in government, Lord Townshend and
Sir Robert Walpole, decided that swift action was required to prevent
the royal couple from falling completely under the spell of the
Opposition. Walpole went to see for himself what was happening at
Hampton Court, and was dismayed to find that Argyll was frequently
granted private audiences with the Prince and Princess. He wrote
anxiously to Townshend: 'You can entirely conjecture what must be
the consequence of these appearances ... They have such an effect
already, as draws the tories from all parts of the neighbourhood, gives
such a disgust to the Whigs as before michaelmas I may venture to
prophecy, the company here will be two of the king's enemies.'[6]

Townshend went at once to join his fellow minister at the palace.
It is proof of the influence that Henrietta now had – or was perceived
to have – that he paid his court first to her in the hope that by these
means he would 'insinuate himself mightily in the favour of the Prince'.
In so doing, he had underestimated that of Princess Caroline, who was
affronted by his neglect. A word from her woman of the Bedchamber,
Lady Cowper, urging him 'how wrong his usage of the Princess was,
and how much it was for his interest to get her on their side', made

him quickly change tactics.[7] Before long, Townshend had succeeded in winning favour with the royal couple, and a political crisis for the Whigs was averted – for the time being at least.

As summer drew to a close, the royal party bade farewell to Hampton Court and made their way back to St James's Palace. A few days after their arrival, the Princess went into labour. All the gaiety and harmony that had existed that summer quickly evaporated, and tensions again arose between the Hanoverian and English courtiers. A German midwife had been assigned to oversee the birth, but she claimed that the English ladies of the household had threatened to have her hanged if the baby died. With Caroline becoming increasingly agitated as her pains came in ever stronger waves, the midwife stood by, refusing to touch her unless she and the Prince agreed to defend her against such threats. Upon hearing of this, George flew into such a rage that he vowed to throw the perpetrators out of the window. Lord Townshend eventually managed to restore order by taking hold of the midwife, shaking her and making 'kind faces' in order to bring her to her senses. This furore can hardly have been soothing for the Princess, who was suffering a traumatic labour, and after several days she was delivered of a dead prince.

Further trouble was to come, for as Caroline lay recovering in her bedchamber, the King was making his way back from Hanover. He arrived in London at the beginning of December in a foul temper, fuelled by a tiresome journey and fierce resentment at having to take leave of his beloved homeland. There he had been feted and honoured as a ruler should be, in stark contrast to the treatment he had received from his upstart English subjects. Ministers, diplomats, princes and courtiers had all come to pay their respects to him, and there had been assemblies and receptions every night in celebration of his longed-for return. Free from the onerous customs of the English court, the King had been a changed man. 'His Majesty dines and sups constantly in public,' one visitor to Hanover reported. 'The court is very numerous, and its affability and goodness make it one of the most agreeable places in the world.' His two years in England seemed little more than an unpleasant dream. Lord Peterborough, who was among the guests at Herrenhausen, noted that the King was so happy that he believed he had 'forgotten the accident which happened to him and his family on the 1st August 1714'.[8]

But all good things come to an end, and it was with the bitterest regret that George reluctantly departed from Hanover in order to resume his royal duties in England. The frequent reports he had received about his son's increasing popularity prompted him to do so, and also exacerbated his already sour temper upon his arrival at St James's. The simmering resentment that had long existed between the King and the Prince of Wales was now on the verge of breaking out into open hostility. Any pretence at civility was abandoned, and they barely acknowledged each other in public.

The political malcontents at court were quick to seize upon this opportunity to further their ambitions, and worked hard to widen the gulf between father and son. Within a few months of the King's return, the carefree summer at Hampton Court seemed a distant memory, and the court was now beset with tension and suspicion. The King was desperate to escape these troubles by returning to Hanover, but his ministers warned him of the danger of doing so in view of the Prince's growing influence and popularity. At length they persuaded him to stay in England and launch a summer of such lavish entertainment at Hampton Court that it would eclipse his son's of the previous year and thereby bolster his own public image. George duly made his way there in July 1717, accompanied by the Prince and Princess.

The King was far from being a lively and genial host, but he cast aside his natural reserve and entered into a full round of social engagements. He progressed to chapel every Sunday in full state, watched by the crowds of people who had travelled back to the palace once more. So many were there, in fact, that one contemporary lamented that London was 'now very empty since the Royal Family went to Hampton Court, where the public manner in which the King lives, makes it the rendezvous not only of the Ministers and great men but of the people of all ranks and conditions'.[9]

Despite his hatred of the custom, George I dined in public every Thursday, and held balls, dancing and other elaborate entertainments almost every day. As a deliberate snub, he excluded his son from these occasions, but he seemed to have a genuine affection for his daughter-in-law and invited her along to many of them. Caroline's physical charms were certainly not lost on him, and he was openly flirtatious, sometimes overstepping the bounds of decency with his lewd remarks. When she rebuffed his advances, he effected frustration and called her 'cette diablesse Madame la Princesse', but kept up his attentions to her all the same. This reduced the Prince to paroxysms of rage, and it was clear to everyone at court that a breach of monumental proportions was brewing.

George I had made a valiant attempt to create a vibrant court life at the palace that summer, and for a while it seemed that he would succeed in outshining the Prince's efforts. But he could not sustain it for long, and by the end of the royal party's sojourn, he had fallen back into his accustomed ways, shunning society for the company of his mistresses. With characteristic scorn, Lady Mary Wortley Montagu observed: 'Our gallantry and gaiety have been great sufferers by the rupture of the two courts here: scarce any ball, assembly, basset-table, or any place where 2 or 3 are gathered together. No lone house in Wales, with a rookery, is more contemplative than Hampton Court: I walked there the other day by the moon, and met no creature of any quality but the king, who was giving audience all alone to the birds under the garden wall.'[10]

In October 1717, the Prince and Princess returned to St James's Palace, where the Princess, heavily pregnant once more, began her lying-in. She gave birth to a boy, George William, on 2 November, and as this was the first prince of Hanoverian blood to be born on British soil, it was a cause for great celebration. Ministers, officials, courtiers and household staff, including Henrietta, crowded into the Princess's bedchamber to offer their congratulations. Even the King, who was still at Hampton Court, expressed his satisfaction and sent his compliments to their Royal Highnesses. But far from leading to a reconciliation between them, the new Hanoverian prince was to be the unwitting cause of an open rupture.

Upon his return to St James's, George I enquired into the ceremonies that were traditionally observed at the baptism of royal princes in England. He was informed that the custom was for the King to act as godfather and choose another from the principal lords at court. His gaze alighted upon the Duke of Newcastle, a mean-spirited and obnoxious nobleman whose eccentricities rendered him a laughing stock in polite society. Both the Prince and Princess despised him, but this only increased his suitability in the King's eyes, and George duly nominated him as the second godfather. The Prince was incensed at this deliberate provocation and immediately demanded that his father retract the offer. But the King was immovable, and ordered preparations to continue as before.

The christening took place in the Princess of Wales's bedchamber at St James's, and according to custom, she remained in bed while the invited guests assembled around her. The tension between George I and his son was palpable, and the guests watched anxiously as the latter visibly struggled to suppress his rage. Henrietta was present, and later described the extraordinary scene that followed to Horace Walpole, who recorded it in his *Reminiscences*: 'No sooner had the Bishop closed the ceremony, than the Prince crossing the feet of the bed in a rage, stepped up to the Duke of Newcastle, and holding up his hand and fore-finger in a menacing attitude, said, "You are a rascal, but I shall find you."' Unfortunately, thanks to the Prince's strong German accent and his own very nervous temperament, Newcastle thought he had said 'I'll fight you.' Appalled and confused, he rushed to consult his colleagues at court, and on their advice he went to the King and told him that he had been challenged. George did not wait to ask the Prince for his version of events, but instead took the remarkable step of placing him under house arrest. Henrietta recounted her astonishment when, going to the Princess's apartments as usual the following morning, she was stopped in her tracks by Yeomen of the Guard who 'pointed their halberds at my breast, & told me I must not pass'.[11]

The court had never known such drama, and the whole of London was agog with excitement. George had already earned a reputation for brutality among the English, who had heard the rumours about the murder of Count von Königsmarck and were now truly shocked that a king should arrest his own son. George called a cabinet, and was rumoured to have told his ministers that if he had been in Hanover he would have known precisely what to do with the Prince, but being in England he was forced to conform to the laws. The cabinet suggested negotiation, and emissaries were duly dispatched to Prince George, who was evidently somewhat unnerved by the incident and wrote letters full of respect for his father. They received no reply.

The Prince and Princess remained under arrest at St James's for four days, and Henrietta continued to be refused access to her mistress. The cabinet grew increasingly anxious. Aware of the Habeas Corpus Act, by which no one could be detained without just cause, they tentatively suggested to the King that the Prince's continued arrest might be regarded as a breach of the law. He grudgingly agreed to release his son, but rather than seeking a reconciliation, he promptly expelled the royal couple from court. In an act of spite, he also insisted that their children remain at St James's.

The division in the royal household had dramatic repercussions for Henrietta. She and her husband could no longer continue living together at St James's and serving their respective masters: a choice would have to be made between marital loyalty and official duty. This choice would have been far more difficult if the Howards had enjoyed any happiness together during their time at the palace. But Charles's ill treatment of his wife had resumed almost immediately after they had taken up residence there.

His temper was fuelled by incessant drinking, and he found fault in everything she did. Her clothes were not fine enough, her acquaintances were irksome, her hours of service to the Princess interfered with the time at which he liked to take his meals. When Henrietta sought to remedy whatever caused him displeasure, this merely served to anger him more. In a long and impassioned letter that she wrote to her husband a decade later, she recalled every detail of those miserable days: 'when under the dread of your resentment I got leave to dine or sup at the hours you liked I then too gave offence & you used to upbraid me with derision yt I was no longer in favour nor my attendance any longer necessary'. As time wore on, Charles's behaviour grew ever more deplorable, and Henrietta came to live in fear for her life: 'Your language to me was ye Grossest and most abusing,' she complained, 'you have call'd me names and have threatened to kick me and to brake my neck. I have often laid abed with you when I have been under apprehensions of your doing me a mischief and sometimes I have got out of bed for fear you shou'd.'[12]

Miserable though Henrietta's life with Charles had been, it was no easy step to forsake her marriage vows in order to continue in the Princess's service. Despite the lax morality that existed in the early Georgian court, the laws governing marriage were strict, and a woman was expected to tolerate all manner of ill treatment from her husband rather than risk the shame of separation. Violence, drunkenness and adultery were all too common in marriages, but they constituted insufficient grounds for action. Some women, such as Mary Astell (often hailed as the first English feminist), did speak out against this injustice: 'To be yok'd for Life to a disagreeable Person and Temper . . . to be denied ones most innocent desires, for no other cause but the Will and Pleasure of an absolute Lord and Master, whose Follies a Woman with all her Prudence cannot hide, and whose Commands she cannot but despise at the same time she obeys them; is a misery none can have a just idea of, but those who have felt it.'[13] But such opinions were rarely voiced in the early eighteenth century, and the vast majority of women felt compelled by society and the law to maintain their silence even if faced with the most extreme provocation.

Desperate to escape her miserable marriage, but equally afraid of destroying her reputation at a time when rumours were already circulating about her friendship with the Prince, Henrietta agonised over what to do. Not trusting any of her friends at court enough to confide in them, she committed her feelings to paper. Charles, she said, had ruled her 'with Tyranny; with Cruelty, my life in Danger', and she reasoned: 'Self preservation is ye first law of nature, are married women then ye only part of human nature yt must not follow it?' She went on to express views that were astonishingly radical for the time, arguing that women had 'superiour sense, superiour fortitude and reason' to men, and therefore questioning 'how dangerous is Power in womens hands? Do I know so many miserable wives from mans Tyranick power.' Henrietta knew, though, that reason and justice alone were not enough to protect her reputation if she were to leave her husband, and she ended her soliloquy with a note of despair: 'his honour is now mine: had I none before I married? Can I devide them? how loose his, and keep my own?'[14]

When the Prince and Princess had made the necessary preparations to leave court and Henrietta's decision could no longer be delayed, she attempted to discuss the matter with her husband in the hope of reaching a compromise. But Charles scorned the very idea that his wife should continue in the Princess's service, and a furious row ensued. In a show of defiance, Henrietta at once left their apartments without pausing to gather her belongings, and went with all haste to join her mistress.

Consumed with rage, Charles sent a message to her saying that he no longer considered her his wife and ordering the removal of her possessions from their apartments. Henrietta calmly complied with his wishes and sent a servant to carry out the task. Although she apologised for the 'impertinent' things she had said in the heat of the moment, she made it clear that her decision to leave was final. The thought of returning to her husband, whose punishment of her disobedience was bound to be severe, was now completely abhorrent to her. It was in vain that she reasoned with him to 'give me leave with the greatest submission, to desire you will reflect, upon all our former way of living, and those unhappy circumstances we have been in; and judge if the prospect of returning to that must not be very Terrible to me'.[15]

Furious at his wife's continued defiance, and egged on by the King, who was determined to make life difficult for his son and daughter-in-law, Charles wrote again to demand that she return to him, threatening to resort to the law if she refused. 'The unparalell'd treatment of your behaviour to me, has twice endanger'd my ruine; and since I find you persevere in your defiance to my recalling you home again, send this to acquaint you, what I am determin'd to do; I have consulted (I beleive) as good opinions for your comeing to me, as I know you have lately done to support the Contrary, and depend upon it I will put them in execution; therefore tis left to your Choice, forceing me to those measures, or avoiding them by Compliance; if you have any sense of Virtue left, or reflexion of reason, you shall find better treatment from me, then I am sure you must in your self be convinced you can deserve; but if this meets any farther denyal, I will immediately take such methods, as the Law prescribes in Your Case.'[16]

At the mention of legal action, Henrietta shrewdly changed tack and affected astonishment that Charles was demanding her return when he had 'expressly abandon'd me and dismiss'd me from living any more with you'. She added, with perhaps more conviction than she felt: 'I have but too good reason to fear worse treatment than I believe the law of England allowes, and in such cases I have always heard a wife is protected.'[17] Her refusal to give in to Charles's bullying won her the support of the Princess, in whose service she remained, free at last from her husband's tyranny.

But freedom had come at a price. Just as the King had retained the Prince and Princess's children at court, so Charles insisted that their young son Henry must stay with him. Worse still, he forbade Henrietta from visiting him, despite all her entreaties, and resolved to raise the boy to despise her. He could not have exacted a crueller revenge upon his wife's first act of defiance.

Chapter 7

'These fools may ne'er agree'

---<o>---

THE QUARREL IN THE royal household spawned a rush of ballads, pamphlets, reports and gossip. News of it had quickly spread throughout the court, and it was now the most popular topic of conversation in taverns and coffee houses across London. The people were at turns astonished and amused by this extraordinary occurrence, and it did little to enhance the popularity or prestige of the House of Hanover. One contemporary verse ran:

> God grant the land may profit reap
> From all this silly pother,
> And send these fools may ne'er agree
> Till they are at Hanover.

The Jacobites seized upon the controversy as yet another example of the Hanoverians' unsuitability for rule, and stirred up ill feeling across the country. The King's ministers urged him to make peace with the Prince of Wales, but he would have none of it. The division between father and son had been widening for many years, and would not be easily healed.

Following their expulsion from court, the Prince and his wife sought temporary shelter in the home of his Chamberlain, Lord Grantham, on Albermarle Street, Piccadilly. It was humiliating for the royal couple to be thus forced to turn to a servant, and quite where they would go after that was still uncertain. Together with their household staff and Maids of Honour, many of whom were weeping, they made a sorry procession on that cold November night. A confidential report contained within the papers of Henry Bentinck, 1st Duke of Portland, described how the Princess, who was still recovering from the birth of her son, in 'the utmost grief and disorder' swooned several times. The Prince was equally distraught, and cried nonstop for two hours.[1]

Caroline remained in a fragile condition, miserable at being separated from her children, the three young princesses Anne, Amelia and Caroline, and the newborn prince, George William, who had literally been taken from her arms. She was also anxious about what the future now held for her and her husband, and urged the Prince to write another conciliatory letter to his father, apologising for any offence that he had caused by this 'misunderstanding'. George grudgingly consented, but the ensuing dispatch had no effect: his father declared that he had had enough of the couple's insincerity to make him vomit. He did relent a little, though, and sent word to the Princess that if she was prepared to leave her husband then she would be welcome to live with her children at St James's. Caroline replied indignantly that her children were 'not as a grain of sand compared to him', and that she would stay with him at all costs. The sacrifice of leaving their children was, however, keenly felt by both the Prince and Princess. A few days after their expulsion, they returned in secret to St James's and snatched a few moments with them. The King was furious when he found out and sent a severe reprimand to his son, warning him that in future he must apply for permission to visit – and that even then it was unlikely to be granted.[2]

Much as he might have wished to, George was unable to remove his son from the line of succession or deprive him of the £100,000 allowance that he received from the civil list. He therefore sought ways to humiliate him. The Prince and Princess were denied their guard of honour and other marks of distinction, and foreign ambassadors and envoys were advised that if they visited the couple, they would not be received at St James's. The same went for all peers and peeresses, privy councillors and their wives, and other officials at court. Orders were also sent to all those who were employed in the service of both the King and the Prince that they must choose between them, and ladies whose husbands were in the King's household were likewise to quit the Princess's.[3] Henrietta had already made her choice, but those who had served in the royal household for many years were thrown into a great quandary. Among them was the Duchess of St Albans, who was forced to relinquish the most prestigious post in Caroline's household so that her husband could continue in service to the King.

Henrietta Howard (c. 1720).
Painted at the height of her power at court, this portrait shows
Henrietta dressed for a masquerade ball and holding a velvet mask.

Blickling Hall (the east front),
Henrietta's childhood home
in Norfolk.

The 'Duel Stone' originally
marked the spot on Cawston
Heath where Henrietta's father,
Sir Henry Hobart, was fatally
wounded in a duel. It was
subsequently moved a short
distance to its current location
on the Norwich to Holt road.

Sir Henry Hobart,
4th Baronet.
The portrait hangs
above the Grand
Staircase in Sir
Henry's ancestral
home, Blickling Hall,
Norfolk.

Henry Howard,
Henrietta's son by
her first husband,
Charles Howard.
The portrait hangs
at Henry's former
college, Magdalene,
Cambridge.

Sophia Dorothea of Celle, estranged wife of George I, with their two children, George (later George II) and Sophia Dorothea.

Engraving of George II and Madame von Walmoden, the mistress who replaced Henrietta. It was published in 1738, by which time the King and his mistress had become subjects of public ridicule.

George I in his coronation robes, 1714.

King George II and Queen Caroline Wilhelmina, c. 1727, the year of the coronation.

'The Music Party', 1733. This painting shows the twenty-six-year-old Prince Frederick with his three younger sisters; from left to right, Anne, the Princess Royal, Caroline and Amelia. The house in the background is Kew Palace.

Henrietta Howard, 1724.
This portrait, painted when
Henrietta was aged thirty-five,
was commissioned by her friend
Alexander Pope. It was later
given to Horace Walpole, who
displayed it at Strawberry Hill.

King George II,
aged sixty-one (1744).

(*Left*) Lord Hervey (c.1740–41). The waspish courtier is best known for his scandalous memoirs of the reign of George II. (*Right*) Robert Walpole, 1st Earl of Orford and Britain's first Prime Minister (1740).

(*Left*) Mary Campbell (née Bellenden), Maid of Honour to Princess (later Queen) Caroline and one of Henrietta's closest companions at court. (*Right*) Mary (Lepel), Lady Hervey of Ickworth. Known as Molly by her fellow ladies in waiting, she served in the Queen's household for some years before marrying Lord Hervey and retiring to his country estate at Ickworth, where she bore him eight children.

Engraving of courtiers enjoying Hampton Court Gardens (1733).

Worst of all, though, was George I's insistence that the royal grand-
children must remain at St James's. His stubbornness on this matter
was to have fatal consequences. Deprived of his mother's milk, the
newborn prince's fragile health began to falter. The King's ministers
urged him to relent, aware of the damage that would be done to his
public profile if the child died. He eventually agreed that the Princess
might attend her son, but found the thought of her presence at St
James's so repugnant that he sent the infant to Kensington. The little
prince's condition deteriorated rapidly in the damp confines of this
palace, and he died the following day. He was buried in Henry VII's
chapel in Westminster Abbey – and with him, it seemed, any hope of
a reconciliation.

Public sympathy was now firmly with the Prince and Princess of
Wales. Grieving for their son, they had the additional burden of knowing
that they would have to find a new residence. It was neither convenient nor appropriate for them to stay in the house of a servant for
long, and although Lord Grantham had done everything possible to
make them comfortable, their circumstances were 'much straitened'
from what they had been at St James's. So cramped was their accommodation, in fact, that they were obliged to sleep in the same room –
a highly unusual circumstance for a couple of royal blood. This meant
that the Princess's ladies would have to see the Prince in a state of
undress in order to attend their mistress. Horace Walpole recounts that
one evening, when both George and Caroline were ill with chickenpox,
Henrietta sat in between their beds and read them to sleep. Such discom-
forts apart, Lord Grantham's house was also unsuitable for receiving
officials and distinguished guests, and before long their court began to
dwindle. 'Many waited on them at their first going to Lord Grantham's,'
it was reported, 'but few since.'[4]

The Prince therefore started to look for a suitable alternative, and
soon afterwards took Savile House, a handsome – if rather small –
mansion in Leicester Fields (now Leicester Square), and ordered the
removal of his effects from St James's. The size of the house meant
that it, too, represented only a temporary base. Fortunately, however,
the building adjoining it, Leicester House, was also vacant, and the
Prince was able to secure it for the sum of £6,000. He and the Princess
duly moved there on 25 March 1718, accompanied by their households.

The distinguished history of Leicester House made it a fitting residence for the royal couple. It had been built by James I's famous

ambassador, Lord Leicester, in the early seventeenth century. In 1662 it had had its first royal tenant, in the form of George II's great-grand-mother, Elizabeth, Queen of Bohemia, and then played host to Peter the Great on his visit to England. It was a spacious two-storey house, fronted by a large courtyard and situated on the north side of Leicester Fields. Inside, it boasted a fine staircase and a series of handsome reception rooms, ideal for entertaining the couple's guests.

Before long, Leicester House had become a magnet for members of London's most fashionable society. At all hours of the day and night, the courtyard was crowded with coaches and sedan chairs, lords and ladies in sumptuous costumes and powdered wigs, and all manner of servants, footmen, bearers and stablemen. Disaffected Whigs and Tories also flocked there, eager to further their political ambitions by showing allegiance to the Prince. 'The most promising of the young Lords and Gentlemen of that party [the Whigs], & the prettiest & liveliest of the young Ladies formed the new court of the Prince and Princess of Wales,' recounted Horace Walpole.[5]

The Prince and Princess entertained even more lavishly than during their regency at Hampton Court. As well as drawing rooms every morning, there were receptions, balls and assemblies three times a week. On the rare occasions that no formal entertainments were held, the couple showed themselves at the theatre, opera or other public place, always surrounded by a magnificent suite of lords and ladies. London's social scene was more vibrant than it had been since the accession of the Hanoverians. 'As for the gay part of town, you would find it much more flourishing than you left it,' Lord Chesterfield told a friend. 'Balls, assemblies and masquerades have taken the place of dull, formal visiting-days.'[6]

In cultivating such a brilliant court, the Prince and Princess were effectively throwing down a gauntlet to the King in the battle for public opinion. He was quick to respond. With a substantial effort, he forced himself to abandon his natural reserve and threw open the doors of St James's for drawing rooms, balls and assemblies several times a week. Anxious to attract a good attendance, he extended the invitation to anyone who was well enough dressed to be admitted by the footmen guarding the doors, and also opened up the road through St James's Park to 'all coaches without distinction'.[7] When he moved to Hampton Court for the summer, he ordered that the festivities must eclipse those of the previous year. He held assemblies every evening, balls twice a week, and even endured the ordeal of dining in public every day.

But for all of George I's efforts, his court did not even come close to rivalling that of his son. One regular at St James's noted with some despondency: '[I] went to court but there were so few people the King did not come out so I went home.' Even Lady Mary Wortley Montagu, a stalwart supporter of the King, complained about the monotony of his entertainments, which she said comprised 'a perpetual round of hearing the same scandal, and seeing the same follies acted over and over'.[8]

Eventually the King tired of the pretence, and in May 1719 he set off once more for Hanover, leaving the few English noblemen and women who had not already deserted his court to make their way to Leicester House. The Prince was triumphant, and he and his wife launched themselves into the task of entertaining London society with even more vigour than before. During the summer months they repaired with their court to Richmond Lodge, which the Prince had acquired at around the same time as their London residence.

Rebuilt ten years earlier, the Lodge was an elegant country retreat set in the beautiful landscape of the Old Deer Park in Richmond, to the south of the present-day Royal Botanic Gardens. Bordered on one side by the River Thames and situated amidst some of the best hunting ground in England, the Lodge's main attraction was undoubtedly its location, particularly as it was also only eight miles from London. It had previously been owned by King William III, who had lavishly furnished the interior with damask curtains, velvet beds and rich mahogany panelling, much of which still remained. But the house had only ever been intended as a hunting lodge, and despite the enlarge-ments carried out by its subsequent owner, James Butler, 2nd Duke of Ormonde, it was still rather small for a royal residence. Accommodation for members of the household was therefore in short supply, and most were paid 'lodging money' for whatever shelter they could find. A terrace of four houses was later built on Richmond Green for Caroline's Maids of Honour, but in the meantime they were obliged to take their chances with the rest. As a Woman of the Bedchamber, Henrietta fared rather better, for it was essential that she had ready access to her mistress, so she was one of the lucky few who took up residence with the royal couple in the Lodge itself.

No sooner had the Prince and Princess of Wales moved to their

new summer retreat than Richmond became one of the most fashionable places to live outside London. 'This town and the country adjacent encrease daily in buildings,' Daniel Defoe observed in his *Tour
Thro'* . . . *Great Britain*, 'many noble houses for the accommodation of
such, being lately rais'd and more in prospect.'⁹ The spa waters of
Richmond were suddenly discovered to have miraculous healing qualities, and a pump room was swiftly built to serve the crowds of well-
bred ladies and gentlemen who now flocked there, along with an
assembly room, ornamental gardens and a lavish new theatre on the
Green.

For the royal party, the chief pleasure during the day was hunting,
a pastime to which the Prince was greatly addicted. The Princess usually
watched from the safety of her chaise, but her ladies did not escape
so lightly and were fully expected to take part. Henrietta wrote to her
friend John Gay: 'We hunt with great noice, and violence, and have
every day a very tolerable chance to have a neck broke.'¹⁰ The evenings
were passed with supper parties, cards or music, with the occasional
visit to the theatre, and the gaiety that prevailed was reminiscent of
that first summer at Hampton Court.

For the ladies and gentlemen of the royal households, this was truly
the best of times, and for none more so than Henrietta. She threw
herself with almost reckless abandon into the wide range of diversions
that were on offer, and was reported to have lost £100 at the card
tables during the first few weeks of her stay. On the evenings when
there was no formal entertainment, the brightest stars of the court all
flocked to the intimate supper parties she held in her rooms, and these
soon became legendary. 'The apartment of the bedchamber woman in
waiting became the fashionable evening rendezvous of the most distinguished Wits & Beauties,' recounted her friend Horace Walpole.¹¹

Some of the acquaintances she had made at Hampton Court two
years before now became her close confidants. Principal among them
was Alexander Pope, who was soon a regular visitor to both Leicester
House and Richmond Lodge. Henrietta possessed all the qualities that
Pope most admired in a woman. She had a lively wit and intellect, and
was always eager to hear his latest poetry and prose. Pope was also
drawn to women who had endured hardship, and he was aware of what
Henrietta had suffered at the hands of her husband since they had last
met. The combination of her quiet strength and vulnerability invoked
his compassion and admiration in equal measure.

Of all her friends, Pope was the most genuine. As a Roman Catholic, he was barred from public office and therefore did not seek advancement at court through her influence; rather, he frequented it because he enjoyed being at the heart of fashionable society. He had also set himself firmly against the royal family by sneering at them in his poems and satires. If anything, this served to increase his appeal for Henrietta, who secretly shared much of his disdain.

Pope's affection for her soon found expression in verse. 'I know a reasonable woman, Handsome and witty, yet a friend,' he wrote in his poem 'On a Certain Lady at Court'. 'Not warp'd by passion, awed by rumour, Nor grave through pride, or gay through folly; An equal mixture of good humour And sensible soft melancholy.' The last line proves that, unlike many of Henrietta's other acquaintances at court, Pope was not fooled by her cheerful disposition. He knew that it disguised a deeper unhappiness, caused by the cruel treatment that she had received from her husband and by the separation from her son. He referred to it again in a letter to a friend, in which he said that there was 'an air of sadness about her which grieves me', and went on to declare how much he admired the way she put her own unhappiness to one side for the sake of her companions: 'I have a sort of Quarrel to Mrs H[oward] for not loving Herself so well as she does her Friends: For those she makes happy, but not Herself.'[12]

For her part, Henrietta delighted in Pope's company. Trusting few at court, she found a welcome release in being able to confide in him. The same was true for Pope, who described her to another of the ladies at court as 'the most trusty of Friends'.[13] Henrietta was also greatly diverted by her friend's witty conversation and irreverent verse. One of his most amusing poems was written as if from his beloved dog, Bounce, to Henrietta's lapdog, Fop:

> We Country Dogs love nobler Sport,
> And scorn the Pranks of Dogs at court.
> Fye, naughty *Fop*! where e'er you come
> To fart and piss about the Room,
> To Lay your Head in every Lap,
> And, when they think not of you – snap!

On his visits to Mrs Howard's apartments, Pope was often accompanied by Charles Mordaunt, 3rd Earl of Peterborough and Monmouth.

The Earl's military, political and diplomatic careers had won him many honours, but he had always refused to bow to convention. He had joined the navy at the age of twenty, but had disagreed with the strategies followed in the war against Spain, so had promptly built his own ship – a forty-six-gun privateer that he named *Loyal Mordaunt*. This almost caused a diplomatic incident, because the Spanish feared that he would use it to attack their fleet and complained to Charles II, who ordered Peterborough to remain on dry land. The Earl had actively opposed Charles's successor, James II, and had been instrumental in paving the way for William of Orange to seize the crown in 1688. But his notoriously volatile behaviour made the new queen suspicious. 'Lord Monmouth is mad,' she confided in private, 'and his wife who is madder, governs him.' This wife was Carey Fraizer, whom Peterborough had been obliged to marry hastily and in secret after getting her pregnant.

The Earl had returned to favour at court after the accession of Queen Anne, and had been appointed Commander-in-Chief of her fleet in the war against Spain. He had subsequently been employed in various diplomatic missions on the Continent. But his unpredictable behaviour had made the British government nervous, and he had been recalled in 1714. 'It was impossible that a man with so much Wit as he shew'd, cou'd be fit to command an Army, or do any other Business,' observed Pope. The new Hanoverian King evidently shared his opinion, for Peterborough was instructed not to appear at court.

Following the split in the royal family, however, he became a regular guest at Leicester House. Now aged sixty, this 'rusty hero and roué' was still one of the liveliest gallants at court. His high spirits were matched by fast living, and he was as fond of drinking and gambling as of flattery and flirtation. On one occasion, he had driven his horses so hard that his coach had overturned, injuring him seriously enough to make him 'spit blood'. His friends had been so concerned for him that they had daily expected to hear news of his death, and were astonished when he made a rapid recovery. 'He outrode it, or outdrank it, or something, and is come home lustier than ever,' marvelled one of them. Peterborough's extraordinary energy and restlessness still led him on many overseas ventures, and he seemed to be forever flitting between the Hague and Vienna, Madrid and Copenhagen, or similarly far-flung places. Swift once said of him that he must know 'every prince in Europe's face', and that he 'Flies like a squib from place to place, And travels not, but runs a race.'[14]

Peterborough was an instant hit at court. His witty conversation and irrepressible flirtatiousness delighted the Princess's ladies. Horace Walpole described him as 'one of those men of careless wit and negligent grace who scatter a thousand bon-mots and idle verses'. None of the ladies received more attention from him than Mrs Howard. A self-confessed 'superanuated gallant', he was some thirty-one years her senior, but displayed the energy of a teenager as he laid siege to her affections with flattery, verse and letters. The latter ran to dozens of pages and were filled with wildly romantic sentiments. 'Your eyes were not more fatall to me the first Time I saw them, then my own have been false to my heart ever since,' he wrote, 'if I have not told you a thousand times yt I dye for you, this I might speak with truth to the Lady who has seized my soul.'

Apparently consumed by love, the Earl claimed that he trembled every time he came near the object of his affections: 'the first moments I approach her I can hardly speak; and I feel myself the greatest fool in nature nere the woeman in the world who has the most witt'.[15] He continued this theme in his 'Song' to her:

> When she comes in my way — the motion, the pain,
> The leapings, the achings, return all again . . .
> O wonderful creature! A woman of reason!
> Never grave out of pride, never gay out of season;
> When so easy to guess who this angel should be,
> Would one think Mrs Howard ne'er dreamt it was she?

The 'cruell mistresse' of Peterborough's heart countered his protestations with good-humoured scorn. His 'Song' she dismissed as 'the ridiculous cant of love', and the insincerity of his apparent devotion was exposed by her frank good sense. 'That you might mistake love in others I grant you, but I wonder how you could mistake it in yourself,' she chided. 'Consider, my lord, you have but one heart, and then consider whether you have a right to dispose of it, is there not a lady at Paris who is convinced that nobody has it but herself? Did you not bequeath it to another lady at Turin? At Venice you disposed of it to six or seven, and you again parted with it at Naples and in Sicily. I believe, my Lord,' she concluded, 'that one who disposes of his heart in so profuse a manner is like a juggler, who seems to fling away a piece of money but still has it in his own keeping.'[16]

Despite Mrs Howard's firm dismissal of Peterborough's romantic declarations, there was inevitable speculation at court that their acquaintance had deepened into intimacy. There is very little evidence to support this, however. Indeed, if there was ever so much as a suggestion of indecency in the Earl's intentions, he was met with a severe reprimand from Henrietta, and she lost all of the good humour with which she countered his more harmless flirtations. 'Can so much goodnesse be angry to such a degree as not to forgive a fault [that] can never be repeated?' pleaded Peterborough on one such occasion. 'Should the person who has robb'd me of my sences, be mercilessly severe to a mistaken expression?'[17]

In fact, for all his apparent devotion to Mrs Howard, Peterborough's real affection lay in an entirely different quarter. Around the time that he had first started to frequent Leicester House, he had met and fallen in love with Anastasia Robinson, a singer at the King's Theatre. His love for her was genuine and enduring, and he married her some years later. It was therefore fortunate that Henrietta never took his romantic declarations seriously.

The poet John Gay was another rival for Mrs Howard's attentions at court. A sociable and convivial man, he had an insatiable curiosity and lust for life, and was adored by his many friends. Gay's ballads and verse may have been of a more playful nature than Pope's, but he still enjoyed some notable successes, including *The Shepherd's Week*, *The Wife of Bath*, and his most famous work, *The Beggar's Opera*. The *Fables* that he had written for the royal children made him a welcome guest at court. Ever since his first encounter with the Hanoverians during his visit to Herrenhausen in 1714, he had been angling for an official post in the royal household. This was probably one of his motivations in cultivating Henrietta's acquaintance, as she was now rising to prominence at court, but he soon came to like her for herself, and their friendship was to continue long after it became obvious that she would be unable to help him.

Like Pope and Peterborough, Gay became a frequent visitor to Leicester House and Richmond Lodge, and when his travels took him away from court, he and Mrs Howard maintained a humorous and affectionate correspondence. In September 1719, he went to the Continent for a few weeks, and wrote to her from there: 'I have been looking every where since I came into France to find out some object that might take you from my thoughts, that my journey might seem less tedious, but since nothing could do it in England, I can much less expect it [in] France.'[18]

The poet and the courtier sharpened their wits on each other, and each helped to develop the other's literary talents. As a friend to some of the greatest writers of the age, Henrietta amassed a correspondence that reads like a who's who of Georgian England. Five large volumes of the letters that she received from the likes of Pope, Swift and Gay are among the manuscripts preserved within the British Library. These also contain the many drafts of letters that Henrietta sent in reply. They are scattered with crossings-out and half-finished sentences as she strove continually to improve her already engaging prose, and behind the hurried scrawl that races across the page, one can almost sense her frustration as she tried to attain the perfect phrase or retort. 'You will find that a woman's pen is not so ready as her tongue,' she once told Peterborough, 'for most women speak before they think, and I find it necessary to think before I write.'

The Earl was in fact one of her most challenging correspondents, for she was keen to dampen his elaborate professions of love with suitably acerbic replies. For this, she called upon her friend John Gay for assistance, and in return provided him with inspiration for his plays. 'I have some thoughts of giving you a few loose Hints for a satyr,' she wrote to him one summer at Richmond, 'and if you manage it right (and not indulge that foolish good nature of yours) I dont question but I shall see you in good employment before Christmas.'[19]

Although Gay was four years older than Henrietta, he had a helpless, almost childlike quality that appealed to her maternal instincts, and he came to rely on her sensible advice and patient affection. In contrast to many of his rather more feckless friends, who indulged and even encouraged his waywardness, Henrietta was a steadying influence on him. When he professed to be in love with an unsuitable young woman, she told him: 'I can no more aprove of your having a passion for that, then I did of your turning Parson.' She was constantly urging temperance and moderation when Gay's appetite for fine food and strong wine got the better of him. She even concerned herself with the suitability of his clothes, chiding him for going about 'so thinly Clad' in the middle of November.[20]

For all Gay's waywardness, he did occasionally offer Henrietta some sound advice of his own. He had been a frequenter of courts long enough to know how fickle, unstable and even dangerous they could be, and he counselled his friend on the qualities that were required to survive in such an arena. 'I have long wish'd to be able to put in practice that valuable worldly qualification of being insincere,' he wrote. 'Another observation I have made upon Courtiers, is, that if you have any friendship with any particular one you must be entirely govern'd by his friendships and resentments not your own . . . as men of Dignity believe one thing one day, and another the next, so you must daily change your faith and opinion. Therefore the method to please these wonderfull and mighty men, is never to declare in the morning what you believe 'till your friend has declar'd what he believes, for one mistake this way is utter destruction.' Gay made use of the word 'friendship' several times in this letter, but qualified it by saying: 'I know that I speak improperly for it has never been allow'd a court term.'[21] He would have done well to follow his own advice, but he was too bent on the pursuit of pleasure to give sufficient attention to his advancement at court. As a consequence, he was never to gain the privileged position there that he had hankered after for so long.

Mrs Howard's literary set at court was completed by Lord Chesterfield. Their friendship had flourished since the first summer at Hampton Court, and the fact that they both served in the royal household gave them a common bond, as well as ample opportunity to see each other. Their lively conversations were supplemented by a host of witty letters. Like Pope, Chesterfield lavished attention on Henrietta's dogs (even though he was wary of them), as well as on the lady herself. He wrote to her newborn puppy Marquise, expressing his pleasure on its 'happy delivery', and adding mischievously: 'I begg of you not to be at all concerned at any insinuations that may be thrown out, that your issue does not bear that resemblance to the Father, which it ought.' He also accused Henrietta of treating her dogs like children, which was probably only half in jest, for he knew well that she missed her son desperately.[22]

In between entertaining her friends and undertaking the many duties to which she was bound by the Princess, Henrietta had barely a moment to herself during the years at Leicester House and Richmond Lodge. 'I was and am in such a continual hurry,' she told Gay, 'that I don't know what I writ to Mr Pope yesterday, or what I write to you now.'[23] Pope himself was astonished by the frantic pace at which she and her fellow ladies at court were obliged to live. His description of their bewildering schedule provides an amusing insight into life in the

Georgian court. 'Mrs Bellenden & Mrs Lepell took me into protection
. . . & gave me a Dinner, with something I liked better, an opportunity
of Conversation with Mrs Howard. We all agreed that the life of a
Maid of Honour was of all things the most miserable; & wished that
every Woman who envyd it had a Specimen of it. To eat Westphalia
Ham in a morning, ride over Hedges & ditches on borrowed Hacks,
come home in the heat of the day with a Feavor, & what is worse a
100 times, a red Mark in the forehead with a Beaver hatt; all this may
qualify them to make excellent Wives for Fox-hunters, & bear abundance of ruddy-complexion'd Children. As soon as they can wipe off
the Sweat of the day, they must simper an hour, & catch cold, in the
Princess's apartments; from thence To Dinner, with what appetite they
may – And after that, til midnight, walk, work, or think, which they
please?'[24]

The frenetic pace of court life, with all its attendant pleasures and
entertainments, was a world away from Henrietta's former life with
Charles Howard. But she seemed to adapt to it admirably, and less than
a year after the Prince and Princess had moved to Leicester House, she
had become one of its brightest stars. That she had done so in a court
renowned for its fickleness and volatility makes her achievement all the
more impressive. 'Persons who have been us'd to Courts cannot be
greatly surpris'd at any sudden change of favor, or at seeing those who
lean'd against the Throne yesterday, beneath the Footstool to day,'
remarked one contemporary. 'Every thing rolls on here in the usual
manner, the same contriving, undermining and caballing at the back-
stairs, the great ones hurrying back and forward, and the little ones
crynging after,' observed another.

Those who ran the gauntlet of its intrigues, plots, backbiting and
factions had to be prepared to live their lives in the open, for there
were very few secrets at court. 'Whatever you say or do at court, you
may depend upon it, will be known,' Chesterfield counselled his son,
'the business of most of those who crowd levees and antechambers
being to repeat all that they see or hear, according as they are inclined
to the persons concerned, or according to the wishes of those to whom
they hope to make their court. Great caution is therefore necessary.'[25]

Principal among the qualities required to survive at court was the art
of dissimulation. 'Nothing in courts is exactly as it appears to be,' Lord
Chesterfield warned his son. 'Those who now smile upon and embrace,
would affront and stab each other if manners did not interpose.' Henrietta

had quickly come to terms with this and had tempered her behaviour accordingly. In private, however, she confessed that she found such insincerity profoundly distasteful. 'We seldome see a man the more favour'd or esteemed for his plain-dealing,' she lamented. 'The long disuse of it in courts has put it on the same footing with ill manners and ill breeding.' To her credit, rather than openly expressing opinions that she did not believe, for the most part she simply maintained a neutral silence. With her natural reserve and discretion, this was perhaps easier for her than it would have been for many others.[26]

It was by thus distancing herself from the intrigues of court that Henrietta achieved success. The modesty and discretion that she had displayed in her early days at court increasingly set her apart from the scores of giddy, gossiping, fickle ladies and gentlemen who frequented Leicester House. Some courtiers resented her for it, but most were full of respect. The commendations of her good character are numerous. Her cousin, Margaret Bradshaw, proudly declared that 'all ye court are fond of her, she being allways redy to do a good turn & selldom speaks ill of any one'. Her friends said the same. 'I believe and as far as I am capable of judging know her to be a wise discret honest & sincere courtier who will promise no farther than she can perform and will always perform what she does promise,' wrote one. Pope, who never stinted in his praise, told a friend who was about to meet her: 'What you'll most wonder at is, she is considerable at court, yet no Party-woman, and lives in court, yet wou'd be easy and make you easy.' In another letter, he claimed that Mrs Howard could 'teach two Countryfolks sincerity'. Even Swift, who later wrote a damning portrait of her, admitted: 'Mr Pope hath always been an advocate for your sincerity, and even I in the character I gave you of your self, allowed you as much of that Virtue as could be expected in a Lady, a Courtier and a Favorite.'[27]

While some expressed frustration that Mrs Howard was 'as close as a stopped bottle', her discretion won the trust and admiration of her fellow ladies at court. Mary Bellenden, a flirtatious and wayward Maid of Honour who had much to conceal, was certainly glad of it, and told her: 'I intirely confide in you upon all occasions, & believe you as I doe ye Gospel.' Henrietta no doubt owed much of her discretion to the years of having to endure her husband's drunkenness, violence and womanising while presenting a respectable demeanour to the outside world. Some courtiers mistook this for a want of feeling,

but Pope knew the truth and once told her: 'You, that I know feel even
to Delicacy, upon several triffling occasions.' Another close friend,
Horace Walpole, later commented: 'her patience and good breeding
makes her for ever sink and conceal what she feels'. Even Lord Hervey,
who disliked her, recognised that her apparent passivity hid a multi-
tude of sorrows, and remarked: 'few people who felt so sensibly could
have suffered so patiently'.[28]

Mrs Howard's calm, dispassionate manner may have had an additional cause. She frequently complained of pains in her head, and some
time in her late twenties or early thirties, she began to lose her hearing.
The two conditions could have been related, although it is just as likely
that the headaches were due to emotional rather than neurological causes.
The constant fear that her husband would make fresh trouble, together
with the pressures of her service to the Princess, must have made her
life at court stressful at times. Her deafness would not have helped the
situation, as it would have forced her to concentrate hard in order to
understand any of the conversations going on around her.

In 1727, when she was aged thirty-eight, she told Swift, who suffered
from the same affliction, that she had 'a bad head, and deaf ears', and
that these were 'two misfortunes I have labour'd under several Years'.
Six years earlier, Mary Bellenden (by then Mrs Campbell) blamed
Henrietta's failure to relay a message on either 'your memory or your
ears'.[29] Pope affectionately referred to his friend's disability in 'On a
Certain Lady at Court':

> 'Has she no faults, then (Envy says), sir?'
> Yes, she has one, I must aver:
> When all the world conspires to praise her,
> The woman's deaf, and does not hear.

To be hard of hearing in a world that fed on gossip, intrigue and
scandal was clearly a great disadvantage, and Henrietta resorted to the
most extreme measures to try to cure it. One surgeon even persuaded
her to have her jaw bored, which in the days before anaesthetic must
have been an agonising procedure. She took a long time to recover,
and later admitted: 'that pain of the opperation was almost insuportable
and the Consequence was many weeks of missery and I am not yet
free from pain'. This was enough to destroy her faith in the medical
profession, and when, two years later, another surgeon offered to test

his theory on her that since the ear was of no use in hearing, it should be removed, she politely declined.[30]

The extent to which Mrs Howard's deafness lay behind her apparent neutrality and discretion cannot be known for certain. Whatever was the case, these qualities now won her an admirer who was to change the course of her life for ever.

Chapter 8

'J'aurai des maîtresses'

———◦———

THE PRINCE OF WALES'S attentions to Henrietta had been increasing steadily since the summer at Hampton Court in 1716, and by the time the royal party moved to Leicester House the following year, ambitious courtiers and politicians were beginning to seek preferment through her intervention. While the friendship between them was becoming closer, it had not yet become a physical liaison. Indeed, the Prince's attentions were at that time focused upon another.

Mary Bellenden, who was lauded as one of the greatest beauties at court, had become the object of royal desire soon after the move to Leicester House. Lord Hervey claimed that she was 'incontestably the most agreeable, the most insinuating and the most likeable woman of her time, made up of every ingredient likely to engage or attach a lover'.[1] Like Henrietta, Miss Bellenden had attracted many of the poets and wits who hung about court, including Gay, who described her as 'smiling Mary, soft and fair as down'.[2] But their admiration was rather shallower than the esteem they held for Henrietta, for Mary had little of the wit and learning of her fellow court lady. This was no barrier to the affections of the Prince, with his aversion to intellectuals and abhorrence for learning in women. He therefore used every strategy he knew to get her into bed. Miss Bellenden felt no reciprocal passion, however, and rejected his clumsy advances. She later confided to Henrietta that her tactics had been to 'cross her armes' at him whenever he approached.[3]

But the Prince was not to be so easily deterred. Mary was notoriously short of money and often complained to friends of her penniless state. 'O gad I am so sick of bills for my part, I believe I shall never be able to hear 'em mention'd without casting up my accounts,' she told Henrietta. 'I have paid one this morning as Long as my arme, & as broad as my bum.'⁴ Knowing of the lady's impoverishment, George resolved to impress her with his wealth. One evening at court, he sat by her and, with a great flourish, took out his purse and began laboriously counting out his money. Miss Bellenden was singularly unimpressed. 'The Prince's gallantry was by no means delicate; & his avarice disgusted her,' wrote Horace Walpole, who later heard the whole tale from Henrietta. Mistaking her aversion for coyness, George repeated the performance a second time, at which the lady lost all patience and cried out: 'Sir, I cannot bear it! If you count your money any more, I will go out of the room.' As Walpole wryly observed: 'The chink of gold did not tempt her more than the person of his Royal Highness.'⁵

Mary Bellenden's decided rejection of the Prince's advances may seem surprising given the prestige that could be gained from a liaison with him. But she was in fact already deeply in love with another. Colonel John Campbell was one of the Prince's Grooms of the Bedchamber, and Mary had been instantly attracted to him. The Prince suspected that her affections lay elsewhere and tried to cajole her into revealing the identity of her lover by promising that he would do what he could for the couple, provided that she agreed not to marry without his sanction. Mary assented to the latter part of the bargain but would not tell him who her lover was. Then, fearing that he would discover it anyway and break up their liaison, she promptly did exactly what she had promised not to and married Colonel Campbell in secret. The Prince never forgave her, and whenever she appeared at court after that, 'tho trembling at what she knew she was to undergo', he always stepped up to her and 'whispered some very harsh reproach in her ear'.⁶

According to Hervey, Henrietta spied the opportunity created by Miss Bellenden's rejection of the Prince and stepped in to take her place in his affections. 'By this conduct she left Mrs Howard, who had more steadiness and more perseverance, to try what she could make of a game which the other had found so tedious and unprofitable that she had no pleasure in playing it and saw little to be won by minding it.'⁷ It seems unlikely, however that Henrietta set out to excite the Prince's passion in such a calculated fashion. Although living apart from her husband, she still took her marriage vows seriously, and her decision to leave him had only been made after the fiercest of battles with her conscience. She had been anxious to protect her reputation and avoid any further scandal, and had succeeded in winning respect throughout the court as a modest and virtuous woman.

It is doubtful that the Prince presented a more appealing prospect to her than he had to Mary Bellenden. His physical charms were rather limited. Always on the short and stout side, his figure had not bene-fited from the lavish dining that he had enjoyed during his years at court. Neither had his countenance been improved by the frequent bouts of rage that consumed him, which would inevitably cause his face to turn a deep red and his already bulbous eyes to bulge even more. Whenever his temper was severely provoked, he would make a ridiculous spectacle of himself by stamping and kicking his wig around the room: hardly the Prince Charming of romantic legend.

But for all that, the Prince of Wales was of course irresistible in one important respect: he offered the chance of prestige and influence at court. This was a seductive prospect for Henrietta, whose memo-ries of poverty and deprivation were still fresh in her mind. As her friend Horace Walpole shrewdly observed: 'nor do I suppose that love had any share in the sacrifice she made of her virtue. She had felt poverty, and was far from disliking power.'[8] She therefore began to encourage the Prince's increasingly obvious advances.

Love did not seem to feature very highly in the Prince's actions either. While he flirted with the ladies at court, he was passionately in love with his wife, and even after thirteen years of marriage still preferred her bed to any other. He would hasten there every evening after dinner, and whenever business took him away from court, he would whisk Caroline off to the royal bedchamber as soon as he returned, much to the ribaldry and amusement of the courtiers standing by. No other woman was even fit to 'buckle her shoe', he once said, and this was borne out by all of his actions.

Nevertheless, George, like his father, thought it essential to enhance his royal status (not to mention his male dignity) by cultivating an image as a man of gallantry. From the very earliest times, kings had taken mistresses, whether for status, companionship or physical gratification. Far from being hidden away, these mistresses often came to enjoy posi-tions of influence at court. They had close and easy access to the King, and were often confidantes and advisers as well as lovers. As such, they represented one of the surest means for statesmen, officials and ambi-tious place-hunters to gain favour with the sovereign. If a mistress fell pregnant, it was not uncommon for their bastard offspring to be given high-ranking positions or prestigious estates. One of the most lustful British kings of recent times had been Charles II, whose court was filled with the most beautiful women in Europe. Some of his former mistresses still frequented the early Georgian court, as did those of his successors. For example, the Duchess of Portsmouth bumped into Lady Dorchester, mistress of James II, and Lady Orkney, mistress of William III at a drawing room one evening. 'Who would have thought that we three whores should have met here!' the latter is said to have exclaimed.[9]

With such an impressive track record set by his royal forebears, Prince George was not about to let the side down. Furthermore, he was anxious to demonstrate by taking a mistress that he was not ruled by his wife. Horace Walpole derided him for being 'more attracted by a silly idea he had entertained of gallantry being becoming, than by a love of variety; & he added the more egregious folly of fancying that his Inconstancy proved he was not governed'. A mistress was there-fore as important a part of his household as a valet, coachman or Groom of the Stole. As Lord Hervey observed, the Prince seemed to 'look upon a mistress rather as a necessary appurtenance to his grandeur as a prince than an addition to his pleasures as a man'.[10]

Necessary she may have been, but it was equally imperative that a mistress should do nothing to disturb the rigid orders and ceremonials of the Prince's daily life. Henrietta was ideal in this respect. She was patient and compliant, and George rightly supposed that she would give him little trouble. Her discretion was an added bonus and would prevent any unnecessary tittle-tattle about his prowess as a lover.

The affair between Mrs Howard and the Prince of Wales was there-fore born less of passion than of convenience. George was expected to take a mistress, so he chose one who would cause as little disrup-tion to the order of his life as possible. Henrietta, meanwhile, was prepared to fulfil the role in expectation that it would augment her position at court and secure her future prosperity.

There are no surviving love letters or other contemporary accounts that suggest a tender or prolonged courtship. The affair probably began during the Prince and Princess's stay at Richmond, from June to September 1718. The atmosphere among the royal household was always more relaxed and convivial during these annual retreats, and the formal public occasions tended to be replaced by more intimate supper parties or evening strolls around the gardens and parkland surrounding the Lodge. The potential for discreet romantic liaisons was therefore greater than amidst the public formalities of Leicester House and St James's.

Princess Caroline was somewhat indisposed that summer, as she was expecting her seventh child and the pregnancy was proving a troublesome one.[11] Whether this prompted George to seek diversion elsewhere, or whether the long, sultry days during which he was surrounded by the alluring ladies of his wife's household sharpened his sexual appetite, is not certain. Whichever was the case, he now became fixated with 'pretty Mrs Howard', the modest and attractive lady whom he had first met four years earlier in Hanover.

The first indication that their relationship had developed from the platonic to the physical was an observation by a contemporary at court that the Prince had started to spend every evening (some 'three or four hours') in her apartments. At first they were joined by Miss Bellenden and some of the Princess's other ladies, but after a time his visits became 'uninterrupted tête-à-têtes' with Mrs Howard. In his diary of court events, Lord Egmont noted with some astonishment that George would 'spend hours alone with her when none else was admitted'. Their affair was conducted with the clockwork regularity so typical of the Prince. Onlookers at court noted that he would enter Henrietta's apartments at precisely seven o'clock every evening 'with such dull punctuality, that he frequently walked about his chamber for ten minutes with his watch in his hand, if the stated minute was not arrived'.[12]

Exactly how the Prince and Mrs Howard passed the three or four hours every evening alone together was a source of much speculation among the courtiers and politicians who hung about in the public rooms beyond. The rather clinical way in which he conducted the liaison, always with one eye on the clock, led some to doubt that he 'entered into any commerce with her, that he might not innocently have had with his daughter'.[13] The punctuality of the Prince's visits should not necessarily be taken as evidence of a lack of passion, however, for he was obsessed with routine and measured his movements by the clock. Just as he visited Henrietta at the same time every evening, so he always retired to his wife's bed for two hours after dinner, which was always taken at the same hour, and even the slightest deviation from his accustomed habits would send him into a fury.

Moreover, the Prince lacked the subtlety to conduct an affair purely for show and, in contrast to his new mistress, was not given to concealing his true emotions. 'The fire of his temper appeared in every look and gesture,' wrote Lady Mary Wortley Montagu, 'which, being under the direction of a small understanding, was every day throwing him upon some indiscretion.'[14] He was also of a very lascivious nature and sought women's company for physical rather than intellectual stimulation. Lord Chesterfield wrote of the 'animal spirits' which governed his actions, and Horace Walpole observed that 'unfortunately his Majesty's passions were too indelicate to have been confined to platonic love for a Woman'. He dismissed as 'a ridiculous pretence' the notion that theirs was a 'meer friendship', and pointed out that George was 'the last man in the world to have taste for talking sentiments, and that with a woman who was deaf!'[15]

The early Georgian court was, besides, hardly a temple of morality. Sex, scandal, flirtation, infidelity, intrigues and elopements were as much a part of daily life as the formal levees, dinners, drawing rooms and other ceremonials. Masquerade balls, which were a regular occurrence at Leicester House, became a cover for wanton behaviour. They presented infinite possibilities for amorous encounters, as masks and costumes released guests from the strict decorum that usually governed social occasions. Sultans were seen making love to nuns, and not all of the nuns were female. John James Heidegger, who as Master of the Revels presided over these gatherings, was denounced by a Middlesex jury as the source of all vice and immorality. In an effort to placate such prudish opinion, masquerades were subsequently renamed *ridottos*, but nothing else about them changed.

The ladies of the Princess's household were esteemed more for their beauty and vivacity than for their virtue. Prudery was viewed as a singularly unattractive quality in women. Pope wrote of it in a verse dedicated to the Maids of Honour at court:

> What is prudery?
> 'Tis a beldam
> Seen with wit and beauty seldom.
> 'Tis a virgin hard of feature,
> Old and void of all good nature

Most of these ladies were maids in name only and had precious little honour. Sophia Howe's wild spirits caused many lively scenes at Leicester House, and she also wreaked havoc during her visits to the country.

She wrote to Henrietta on one such sojourn: 'You will think I supose that I have had no flirtation since I am here but you will be mistaken,' and went on to boast of her various conquests.[16] Soon after her return to court, Miss Howe fell for the charms of a young gallant, Anthony Lowther, and eloped with him. But Lowther proved unworthy of the lady's affections, treating her cruelly and refusing to marry her. She was therefore forced to return to her mother's house, her reputation in tatters, and died – it is said of a broken heart – a few years later.

Sophia was far from being the only girl of uncertain virtue at court. Miss Mary Chamber, another friend of Henrietta, was devoted to the pursuit of pleasure and regaled her with lurid tales of her adventures. 'All sorts of Diversions are in great plenty here,' she once wrote from Tunbridge Wells, 'but I think Ravishing is the most prevailing entertainment.' She also recounted a trial that was the talk of the town, in which a man had been accused of forcing himself upon a woman. The case had been thrown out when the judge had asked the 'victim' to name the time and place that the accident had occurred, and she had answered 'that was impossible for her to tell because it lasted for a quarter of a year together'. Margaret Bradshaw, meanwhile, who was a relative of Mrs Howard, boasted to her that she fully expected to find favour with the King when she visited court, 'for my Bubbys are mightily grown since you saw me'. She added: 'I veryly beleve if he were once in my Parlour, & I in good humour he'd never go home again, for I have very wining ways with me when I think fitt to show my parts which I wont do to every body.'[17]

In such an environment, the likelihood of a platonic liaison between a highly sexed prince and an attractive Woman of the Bedchamber was slim indeed. Lord Hervey may have tried to downplay the affair out of loyalty to Princess Caroline, but Henrietta was far from being mistress in name only. Her closest friends knew the truth, although, as Horace Walpole observed, they pretended not to. 'From the propriety & decency of her behaviour [she] was always treated as if her virtue had never been question'd, her friends even affecting to suppose that her connection [with the Prince] had been confined to pure friendship.'[18] Henrietta's irreverent cousin, Margaret Bradshaw, showed no such discretion and teased her about the loss of her virtue: 'A Courtier is a detestable thing & I am glad none of my famely are so, for lett people come of Ever such honest parents, they are soon corruptyed. Mrs Howard's father was a sure naile [but] his Daughter proves a rotten Pegg.'[19]

There may have been another, more compelling, piece of evidence that the affair between the Prince of Wales and Henrietta Howard was of a sexual nature. Within her correspondence are two letters which contain the merest hint of a pregnancy. In August 1718, Carr, Lord Hervey, whose younger brother John kept him informed of events at court, wrote to Henrietta at Richmond: 'the most pleasing account I can have from Richmond will be that of your being in good health, & not wanting to be told you are grown bulky'. This may of course have been a light-hearted warning that she should avoid ruining her famously slim figure by overindulging in the rich foods that were on offer at court, and on its own it is certainly not enough to indicate that she was thought to be with child. But then a few months later, in May 1719, Mrs Howard received a letter from the daughter of James Welwood, her trusted Hobart family solicitor whom she had known since childhood. The postscript of the letter, apparently written in haste, reads: 'I wont say a word of the cradle.'[20]

There are no further references to this, and in fact Henrietta's correspondence becomes very patchy between the autumn of 1718 and the summer of 1719. This in itself may be significant, but it cannot be taken as reliable proof that she had borne her royal lover a child during that time. What is more convincing in this respect is that George was rumoured to have awarded Henrietta an annual pension of £2,000 from around the time that their affair began. This was a considerable sum (equivalent to more than £250,000 today), particularly for a man not renowned for his generosity. There is no trace of it in the official records, although the Treasury Papers for the year 1718 indicate that the Prince granted her an additional allowance of £100 per year, and several similar amounts are recorded in the years that follow. These papers also show that her apartments were made more comfortable by the addition of such luxuries as crimson silk-lined curtains and mahogany furniture.[21] Again, taken on their own, these gifts and grants of money indicate nothing more than that Mrs Howard was a favourite of the Prince, and are not substantial enough proof that they were intended to help support a child.

There is also the question of whether Henrietta, however discreet she was, would have been able to hide a pregnancy from the prying eyes of court. The full-skirted dresses that were then in fashion would have helped to conceal the physical signs. Furthermore, although she was required to be in more or less constant attendance, she was often reported to be indisposed, and on one occasion she had to be excused from duty for several weeks. If she had given birth during this time, then the child could quite easily have been passed off as her brother's. John Hobart had married in 1717, and his wife Judith had produced a child almost every year after that. The births and baptisms of five of the seven children were recorded in the register of Blickling church. The two exceptions were Robert, who died in infancy, and Dorothy, who was one of only two Hobart children to survive into adulthood.

This latter child would later come to live with Henrietta at court, following the death of John Hobart's wife in 1727. Although she was fond of children in general, Henrietta showed a partiality towards Dorothy that would last a lifetime. In the only known surviving portrait of the girl, there are striking similarities with the facial features of George II. She has the same large, almost bulbous eyes, together with a long straight nose and high forehead. Her appearance is also similar to that of George II's daughters by Caroline, in particular Princess Amelia.

The fact that it is almost impossible to say for certain whether Henrietta bore her royal lover's child poses an interesting question in itself. Royal bastards were hardly shocking: indeed, it had long been common for kings and princes to openly acknowledge and provide for them. They were, after all, valuable proof of their virility. So why would Henrietta try to conceal a pregnancy? That she had a husband was not reason enough on its own. There are many examples of married royal mistresses throughout history, and besides, Henrietta was already estranged from Charles. Furthermore, as the Prince's official mistress, it was a little late to be overcome by an attack of morality. But then Charles Howard was a violent man, and it is possible that Henrietta dared not risk provoking him by allowing it to be common knowledge that she was having another man's child. She may also have feared that this would prejudice her son Henry against her, and would make it even less likely that she could win custody of him.

Another possibility is that she was so proud of her reputation as a 'Woman of Reason', the darling of the poets and playwrights of Georgian England, that she did not wish it to be overshadowed by the knowledge that she had borne a royal bastard. This may also explain the ambiguity of her relationship with George. She could have encouraged the notion that it was entirely platonic because she wanted to be known as something more than just a royal mistress. She had long cherished intellectual ambitions and was a fierce critic of women's subservience to men, so it is likely that her affair with the Prince – while necessary to her advancement – was also something of an embarrassment to her. The truth of this would be borne out by subsequent events.

The lack of documentary proof to support either theory is frustrating. It is possible that this was destroyed, whether by Henrietta, her family, or the prudish Victorian editor who assembled her correspondence for publication. Or it may be that Henrietta was so successful in hiding the truth from her contemporaries that no evidence ever existed. Given the preponderance of published memoirs and letters from the period, the latter seems more likely. One can hardly imagine Lord Hervey omitting such a piece of scandal from his memoirs if it was known about at court. Whatever the case, the tantalising suggestion of a secret pregnancy adds to the enigma of Henrietta's character, as well as of her relationship with the Prince of Wales.

If Henrietta had hoped to gain considerable influence over the Prince through her affair with him, she was to be disappointed. George despised the way that his father was ruled by his two mistresses, Mesdames Schulenburg and Kielmansegg, and was determined not to fall into the same trap. According to her adversary at court, Lord Hervey, Henrietta was deeply embarrassed to be in the position of having all the semblance of power with no capacity to execute it. 'Notwithstanding her making use of the proper tools, the stuff she had to work with was so stubborn and so inductile that her labour was in vain,' he observed, 'her situation was such as would have been insupportable to anyone whose pride was less supple, whose passions less governable, and whose sufferance less inexhaustible.'[22]

The Prince was, apparently, under the influence of only one woman, and that was his wife Caroline. She appeared to manage him so expertly that she was able to get her own way without ever seeming to, and soothed his violent fits of temper with apparent compliance and humility. She spent many hours with her husband each day, schooling herself into 'saying what she did not think, assenting to what she did not believe, and praising what she did not approve', in order to insinuate her opinions 'as jugglers do a cord, by changing it imperceptibly, and making him believe he held the same with that he first pitched upon'.[23]

Caroline's skill in manipulating the Prince was well known at court. The ideal wife in Pope's *Of the Characters of Women* was based upon her:

> She, who ne'er answers till a Husband cools,
> Or, if she rules him, never shows she rules;
> Charms by accepting, by submitting sways,
> Yet has the humour most, when she obeys.

Lady Mary Wortley Montagu, meanwhile, claimed that the Princess 'had that genius which qualified her for the government of a fool', and that her first thought on marriage had been 'to secure herself the sole and whole direction of her spouse; and to that purpose counterfeited the most extravagant fondness for his person'.[24]

Caroline realised that to win real power, she needed an accomplice in government. Sir Robert Walpole, the chief minister, was the ideal candidate. The two were described as being like 'leaves on the same twig'. Both were cunning, intelligent, coarse-fibred, full of appetite for life and, above all, had an insatiable lust for power. Their alliance was forged by the knowledge that each was indispensable to the other. Walpole knew that in Caroline lay the real route to influence over the Prince. It was said that he had discovered early on that whatever 'galantries' the Prince might indulge in, 'the person of his Princess was dearer to him than any charms in his Mistresses'. Furthermore, although Henrietta was George's declared favourite, the wily minister perceived 'that the power would be lodged with the wife, not with the Mistress'. He therefore disregarded the latter and abstained from joining the throng in her apartments, which won him the lasting respect and trust of the Princess. In paying his court to her, rather than Henrietta, it was said he 'had the right sow by the ear'.[25]

Walpole also appealed to Caroline's vanity by telling her that he could do nothing without her, and that she was 'the sole mover of this court; whenever your hand stops, everything must stand still, and whenever that spring is changed, the whole system and every inferior wheel must be changed too'. The Princess was equally aware of how indispensable Walpole was to her plans: the Prince would tolerate advice from a minister, but he would never do so from a woman.

They were joined in their alliance by Lord Hervey, who was a staunch supporter of Walpole and outspoken in his Whiggish beliefs. In truth, however, it was his wit rather than his politics that really drew Caroline to him. She was delighted by the irreverence of his humour, which did not scruple to make fun of her husband, and the two became so close that there were inevitably scurrilous rumours that they were having an affair. Hervey was as disdainful of George as he was admiring of the Princess, and in his memoirs he portrayed him as an impotent fool who was entirely ruled by his wife.

The Prince knew people sneered that Caroline governed him, and he hated it. He would do everything possible to prove them wrong, often to the point of humiliating her in front of the entire court, laughing at her ignorance over matters of state or flying into a rage if she dared to voice an opinion that was not his own. The Princess met all of this with 'the obsequiousness of the most patient slave to the most intemperate master'. She returned every insult with flattery and every contradiction with acquiescence, and 'with the implicit resignation of the most rigid Christian, whenever he smote one cheek turned the other'.[26]

Caroline's tolerance of her husband's behaviour extended to his romantic liaisons with her ladies at court. Far from being affronted by his blatant infidelity, she seemed actively to encourage it on the grounds that anything that brought him pleasure was also a source of joy to her. One courtier observed that she was 'so devoted to his pleasures (which she often told him were the rule of all her thoughts and actions), that whenever he thought proper to find them with other women, she even loved whoever was instrumental to his entertainment'. If the late-eighteenth-century historian William Coxe is to be believed, this was all an act. 'Never wife felt or lamented a husband's infidelities more than herself,' he claimed, arguing that Caroline's 'forced complacency' was only achieved through a 'violent effort'.[27] But it is unlikely that she was suffering any such inner turmoil. Her tolerance almost certainly sprang from a calculated strategy rather than the saintly forbearance that she was so keen to display to the world, for it helped her to manipulate the Prince – provided that the object of his extramarital attentions was sufficiently malleable.

The Princess had, in any case, been bred to accept infidelity as the natural course of royal marriages. The courts in which she had undergone her royal training had hardly been conspicuous for their morality.

Electress Sophia had for years not merely tolerated but welcomed the Countess of Platen as the mistress of her husband. Her daughter, who had married the King of Prussia, had followed the same policy towards his other women. By contrast, the actions of George I's ill-fated wife, Sophia Dorothea, had provided an example of what not to do. Objecting to his blatant infidelity by taking a lover of her own had earned her a lifetime's imprisonment at Ahlden.

If Caroline had been raised a pragmatist in her views of royal marriage, then she also had another reason to accept her husband's infidelity with a readiness bordering on the enthusiastic. Being obliged to spend '7 or 8 hours tête-à-tête' with him every day was quite a burden, given his choleric temper, tedious conversation and boorish manners. The Princess was therefore only too happy to be relieved of his company for a few hours. Moreover, she judged that the mild and compliant Mrs Howard would pose little threat to her own hold over the Prince. 'Tho' she was at that time very handsome, it gave her Majesty no jealousy or uneasiness,' remarked one courtier.[28]

But Caroline was not a woman who left things to fate. For all of Henrietta's apparent modesty, she was still spending three or four hours alone with Prince George every day, and she might well use some of her acclaimed intellect to try to influence his opinions. She was also a magnet for members of the Opposition in government, notably Lord Bolingbroke, the powerful Tory peer who had been dismissed from his position as Secretary of State upon George I's accession. Some of her literary circle, including Pope and Gay, were also of that party, and used her evening gatherings to discuss affairs of state, as well as to exchange ideas for their poetry and satires. In courting such associates, Henrietta made an enemy of Sir Robert Walpole, the leader of the Whig administration in government and arguably one of the most powerful men in the country. Slowly but surely, two enemy camps began to form at Leicester House: the Whig party led by the Princess and Walpole, and the Tory sympathisers who attached themselves to the Prince of Wales's mistress. Given Caroline's clever manipulation of her husband, the former party was clearly in the ascendancy, but as long as Henrietta remained his mistress, she would always be a focus for the Opposition.

Caroline therefore did everything she could to minimise the risk posed by her rival. She began by using the means that were directly under her control, namely Henrietta's position in her household. As Woman of the Bedchamber, Henrietta had an array of duties to occupy her time. It was far from being the sinecure that many of the higher-ranking positions constituted. Yet she had so far been treated kindly by Caroline, who seemed to value her as much for her companionship as for her usefulness in the household. All of this was to change when she became the Prince of Wales's mistress. The Princess was determined that henceforth she would carry out every duty to the letter. Addressing Henrietta with great condescension as 'my dear Howard', she began to inflict ever more menial tasks upon her.

During the ceremony of dressing, it was the job of the Woman of the Bedchamber to hold the basin while the Princess washed. From now on, Caroline insisted that Henrietta perform this task on bended knee. Henrietta tolerated this at first, but as her mistress heaped more and more indignities on her, she rebelled. In a rare outburst of temper, 'with her fierce little eyes, and cheeks as red as your coat', she told her mistress 'that positively she would not do it'. The Princess, who recounted the whole incident to Lord Hervey, answered calmly but firmly, as one would to a naughty child: 'Yes, my dear Howard, I am sure you will; indeed you will. Go, go! fie for shame! Go, my good Howard; we will talk of this another time.'[29]

Determined not to suffer this humiliation again, Henrietta made enquiries into the exact duties of her role, and called upon precedents to help her. She sought the advice of Abigail Masham, former Woman of the Bedchamber to Queen Anne. Unfortunately, Mrs Masham confirmed that the post-holder was indeed required to kneel when holding the wash-basin, so the Princess had been entirely justified in her request.[30] What appeared on the surface to be a trivial matter was in fact a major point of principle, and Henrietta knew that henceforth she would have no choice but to submit to the Princess's requests. Caroline was triumphant and could not resist the opportunity to gloat. 'About a week after, when upon maturer deliberation she had done everything about the basin that I would have her, I told her I knew we should be good friends again,' she confided to Hervey, 'but could not help adding, in a little more serious voice, that I owned of all my servants I had least expected, as I had least deserved it, such treatment from her.'[31]

Caroline proved adept at using Henrietta's position in her household to reinforce her own superiority. That Henrietta had been her Woman of the Bedchamber for some years before the affair began was a distinct advantage, because it meant that the precedent of obedience had already been firmly set. It had been a very different situation for Catherine of Braganza, wife of King Charles II. Upon her arrival in England, she had been dismayed to discover that her husband-to-be had appointed his then heavily pregnant mistress, Lady Castlemaine, as her Lady of the Bedchamber. Catherine had demanded that the appointment be revoked, but Charles had been adamant, insisting: 'I like her company and conversation, from which I will not be restrained, because I know there is and will be all innocence in it.' He had later repeated the exercise with another mistress, Louise de Keroualle, Duchess of Portsmouth. His wife had been unable to hide her distress at this further indignity. 'This day, the Queen being at dinner, the Duchesse of Portsmouth, as a lady of the bedchamber, came to wait on her,' observed a bystander at court, 'which putt the Queen into that disorder that tears came into her eyes, whilst the other laughed and turned [it] into jest.'[32]

Caroline's manipulation of her husband's mistress was further aided by her knowledge of the latter's vulnerability. She knew full well that Henrietta's husband had frittered away their modest fortune on drinking and gambling, and that without her position at court, she would face almost certain ruin. She also knew that Henrietta's abiding terror was that she would be forced to return to this violent and abusive man, who had subjected her to years of misery before her escape to Leicester House. Moreover, etiquette demanded that no direct reference to the affair could ever be made by two well-bred women, so in theory at least Henrietta's only role at court was in the Princess's household. It was in any case uncertain how long the affair would last. All of this gave the Princess a significant advantage over her rival, and she did not scruple to remind her of it whenever possible. After the incident with the wash-basin, Caroline told Henrietta that 'she knew I had held her up at a time when it was in my power, if I had pleased, any hour of the day, to let her drop thro' my fingers – thus–.'[33] Henceforth, she could torment her Woman of the Bedchamber to her heart's content.

In examining Prince George's relationships with Caroline and Henrietta, it seems that there was almost a role reversal between the wife and the mistress. The passion he felt for the former was obvious to everyone at court, and it had diminished little during the thirteen years of their marriage. When he took other women, he delighted in telling Caroline every detail of his conquest: from wooing to sexual technique. He even wrote to her about them, and one letter, describing the seduction of a young woman he met in Hanover, ran to a staggering forty pages. In return, Caroline displayed all the traits of a mistress, by using his passion to further her political ambitions, by putting aside her intellectual tastes to feign enthusiasm for his tedious conversation, and by meeting his fits of temper and rudeness with meek compliance. Above all, she took pleasure in humiliating the woman who was bound to him by duty and convention.

George's relationship with Henrietta, meanwhile, was apparently governed more by the clock than by passion, and his primary motivation in taking her as his mistress seemed to be a desire to conform with tradition. If Henrietta's enemies at court were to be believed, he got little pleasure from their connection and came to resent her as much as he would a tiresome wife. Lord Hervey, who was among them, claimed: 'She was forced to live in the constant subjection of a wife with all the reproach of a mistress and to flatter and manage a man whom she must see and feel had as little inclination to her person as regard to her advice.'[34]

But the Prince was not completely devoid of affection for Henrietta. In his account of events at court, the politician and diarist John Perceval, Earl of Egmont, speculated that it was Henrietta's 'good sense and agreeable carriage' that drew George to her.[35] She may not have had his wife's voluptuous figure, but she was still an attractive woman. When the affair began, she was twenty-nine years of age and was widely admired for her 'handsome' and 'pleasing' appearance. Her best feature was her long hair, which Lord Chesterfield described as 'remarkably fine'. Its natural colour was chestnut brown, but Henrietta tended to lighten it with dye. This may have been for the benefit of the Prince, whose weakness for blondes was well known at court.

Henrietta's fair hair is shown off to great effect in a portrait of her commissioned by Pope. Wearing an elegant low-fronted dress with pearls looped across the bodice, revealing the chemise, she presents an attractive and enigmatic figure. Her skin has a soft ivory hue which contrasts with the deep blue of her eyes, and her steady gaze transfixes the viewer. Her high forehead and long nose make her a striking rather than conventional beauty, but she has a pleasing, dignified appearance that commands interest and respect in equal measure. With one hand raised to her cheek in an apparently contemplative pose, she appears every bit the enlightened philosopher, yet the faint smile that plays about her lips suggests humour and warmth. In another portrait, she is shown in a more formal setting, dressed for a masquerade ball in clothes of the latest fashion.

Her slim waist is made narrower still by a stiff-boned corset, and her hair is neatly tucked under a hat, but her dark eyes show an intelligence and independence that no amount of court etiquette can suppress.

Henrietta's sense of style was one of her greatest attractions. Horace Walpole said that she was 'always well drest with taste & simplicity'. At one state occasion, she and her fellow Woman of the Bedchamber, Mrs Herbert, were described as being 'the two finest figures of all the procession'. She had worn a scarlet dress with a silver trimming and appeared 'so rich, so genteel, so perfectly well dressed' that she won the admiration of many onlookers.[36]

Henrietta's features mirrored her passive demeanour. William Warburton, a leading theologian at court, described her as 'singularly young looking; she is incapable of the keen feeling and passionate sorrow which might mark the brow with lines and fade the cheek. The only expression of her face is a sweet and gentle repose.' Lord Chesterfield echoed his observations, and referred to her countenance as 'an undecided one' which 'announced neither good nor ill nature, neither sense nor the want of it, neither vivacity nor dullness'.[37]

Mrs Howard had a number of admirers at court, including the members of her literary circle, all of whom sought to immortalise her attractions in poetry and prose. She was Pope's 'handsome' woman of 'A Certain Lady at Court', the 'angel … so fair' of Peterborough's 'Song', and a 'shadow like an angel with bright hair' to John Gay. William Byrd, a pious American traveller and frequent visitor to Leicester House, met 'pretty Mrs Howard' soon after her affair with the Prince began, and was instantly smitten. His diary is full of references to conversations they had engaged in, and on one occasion he enjoyed her company so much that after leaving court he felt compelled to take a woman into his coach and 'commit uncleanness', before returning home to say his prayers.[38]

While Henrietta was not a conventional beauty, she certainly had something in her appearance or character that drew men to her. The Prince had singled her out from a host of – arguably prettier – ladies in his wife's household. There is also some indication that, at least in the early days of their liaison, he felt some affection for her. A gossip at court noted that she once received a 'billet doux' from her royal master, and when the Princess summoned her to attend, she hastily stuffed this down her bosom. In curtseying before her mistress, however, unbeknown to her the note fell out. When Caroline found it she called

Henrietta back and thrust the offending note at her, coldly bidding her to take more care of her secrets in future.[39]

If Prince George harboured a little more affection for his mistress, however fleeting, than her enemies at court have claimed, then their assertion that she had no influence over him should also be qualified. Henrietta was certainly never a mistress of the calibre of Louise de Keroualle or Anne Boleyn in terms of political power or social prestige. No landmark events of state can be credited to her influence. Neither was she able to secure great riches through her position. George was notoriously mean, and although he had increased her annual allowance when she became his mistress, this paled into insignificance when compared to the bounty received by other royal favourites. William III had given Elizabeth Villiers all of King James II's private estates in Ireland, the income from which was valued at £26,000 per year. The Duchess of Portsmouth, meanwhile, had received in excess of £100,000 in gifts and bribes from Charles II and his ministers, not to mention the priceless jewels and other 'trinkets' that her royal master gave her. The Venetian ambassador was astonished by 'the quantity of gold which the King has given and which he lavishes daily upon his most favoured lady'.[40]

Henrietta may not have been in the same league as these women when it came to being rewarded for sacrificing her virtue, but she was at least able to win favour for a number of her friends and family. John Campbell, Duke of Argyll, who was among her close associates, rose considerably in power and prestige in the Prince's court at this time. He was appointed Lord Steward of the Household, and in 1719 was created Duke of Greenwich. His younger brother Archibald, Lord Ilay, also a friend of Mrs Howard, experienced a similar upturn in fortune. While she resisted most applications from those seeking a particular place at court or in government, she did secure some prestigious appointments for her brother, John Hobart. He was made a Knight of the Bath in 1725, Treasurer of the Chamber in 1727, and Baron Hobart of Blickling in 1728.

As well as furthering the cause of those close to her, Henrietta was occasionally able to thwart the designs of her enemies at court. She lent her support to Sir Spencer Compton, Speaker of the House of Commons, in his battle for supremacy over Walpole, and was so successful in persuading the Prince of his merits that he later raised him to one of the highest offices in the land. In so doing, she set herself in opposition to the Princess, who was Walpole's greatest ally at court. Lord Hervey, who was also in their camp, observed with barely concealed resentment that the mistress was able to work on the 'susceptible passions' of the Prince, and thus 'had just influence enough, by watching her opportunities, to distress those sometimes whom she wished ill'.[41]

However great Henrietta's influence over her royal lover, it was the *perception* of power, rather than the reality of it, that mattered. When she became the mistress of the heir to the throne, her position at court was immediately transformed. In the social and political hierarchy of the royal court, not just in England but across Europe, the position of mistress to the King or Prince was one of considerable prestige. In counselling his son on the best means to gain favour, Lord Chesterfield wrote: 'There is at all courts a chain which connects the Prince or Minister with the page of the back-stairs or the chambermaid. The King's wife or mistress has an influence over him; a lover has an influence over her; the chambermaid or valet-de-chambre has an influence over both; and so ad infinitum. You must, therefore, not break a link of that chain by which you climb up to the Prince.'[42]

The theory that the perception of power alone was enough to enhance Henrietta's position at court was borne out by events. No sooner had she become the Prince's mistress than a host of officials, ministers, disaffected politicians and ambitious place-seekers flocked to her apartments. 'These quotidian visits which His Majesty when Prince was known to bestow upon her, of so many hours in the four-and-twenty, and for so many years together, had made many superficial courtiers conclude that one who possessed so large a portion of his time must have some share of his heart,' wrote Lord Hervey. 'This way of reasoning induced many to make their court to her, and choose that channel to recommend themselves to the Prince.'[43]

Among the most notable were the Duke of Argyll, who was in opposition to Robert Walpole, and his brother Lord Ilay, along with the Duke of Dorset, chief officer of the King's household, and Sir Spencer Compton. It seemed inconceivable to such men that the Prince would 'give all his leisure hours to a pretty and agreeable woman who had no weight in his counsels and perhaps as small portion of his person'.[44]

Lord Chesterfield realised what Lord Hervey chose not to: however much these place-seekers and politicians exaggerated Mrs Howard's influence, it was the perception that she had the means to grant their request that augmented it. His account proves that she was well aware of this fact too, and used it to her advantage: 'Her lodgings grew more and more frequented by busy faces, both of men and women. Solicitations surrounded her, which she did not reject, knowing that the opinion of having power often procures power. Nor did she promise to support them, conscious that she had not the power to do it.'[45]

As the mistress of the Prince of Wales, Henrietta therefore had to perform a rather delicate balancing act. She had to maintain her influential position by listening patiently to the many supplicants for her favour without actually consenting to their requests, and she had to ensure the security of her own appointment in the Princess's household by serving both master and mistress. If she alienated either, her position at court would be untenable and she would have no choice but to return to her abusive husband. The stakes had never been higher.

However, there was also the added complication of having to ensure that the Prince never suspected she was using her position as mistress to gain influence over him. The necessity of this had already been proved by an incident concerning her friend Lord Chesterfield, who had sought Caroline's intervention in order to secure a 'trifling favour' from the Prince. The Princess had agreed to help him, but subsequently forgot about it. When, a few days later, she remembered her promise, she summoned the Earl and apologised for her oversight, assuring him that she would speak to her husband that very day. But Chesterfield replied that she should not trouble herself because Mrs Howard had already performed the task. Indignant at this slight, Caroline promptly told the Prince that he had been unwittingly manipulated by his mistress, knowing that he would be 'very unwilling to have it supposed that the favourite interfered'. George reacted just as she had hoped, flying into a rage and refusing to see Henrietta for several days. Chesterfield, meanwhile, was obliged to stay away from court until the Prince's anger had subsided.[46]

The difficult and volatile circumstances that had to be navigated in order to retain her position at court would have defeated a less careful and astute mistress. But Henrietta proved herself equal to the task. By 1720, two years after her affair with the Prince had begun, she was still referred to as 'a great favoret of Pluto's [the Prince], & consequently of our Queens [Princess]'.[47] Furthermore, even though she had failed to progress the vast majority of applications for the Prince's favour, she was still besieged by persons of influence – and those who aspired to be so.

Despite her success, Henrietta was growing increasingly restless at court. The skilful manipulation and deception that was required to maintain her position did not come naturally to one who preferred neutrality to faction and intellectual pursuits to political power games. She had also recently lost two of her closest companions at court. Molly Lepel had succumbed to the charms of Lord Hervey and had moved to his country estate in Suffolk after their marriage. Mary Bellenden had also left court to get married, and although both women corresponded frequently with Henrietta, it was a poor substitute for having them close at hand. Indeed, if anything their letters made her even more wistful, as they told of the domestic bliss and tranquillity of their new lives in the country.

Above all, though, Henrietta missed her son. Almost three years had passed since she had seen him, and despite enquiring after him on numerous occasions, she had been able to glean precious little news. Her cousin, Margaret Bradshaw, found out that he had spent some time at a school near Salisbury, and applied to the master there to see the young boy. She told Henrietta: 'I have sent ten times to Doctor Dunsters to inquire after your Child & could never be inform'd tell this minute yt he was gon from thence', and assured her that if she had managed to see him, she would have 'fill'd his bely sum times with frute & tea'.[48]

It must have been a torment for Henrietta to know that her husband was in all probability raising their son to despise his absent mother. Urged on by her friends, she even contemplated snatching him from his school. But she was painfully aware that her position at court remained tenuous and that she could offer none of the security that the boy needed. As mistress to the Prince of Wales, she also had to be careful not to risk what would inevitably be a very public scandal, given Charles Howard's temperament. She therefore clung to the hope that Henry would one day return to her of his own free will. She confided this to Mary Bellenden, now Mrs Campbell: 'nor will I have any sinister methods made use of, but leave all to his Natural Inclinations forbidding all arbitrary Proceeding'.[49]

The desire to see her son drove Henrietta to risk the Prince's wrath by trying to persuade him to make peace with his father. At least then she might be permitted to visit Henry at St James's, whereas since the royal feud, that palace had been strictly off limits for members of the Prince's court. For once, she and the Princess were of one accord. Caroline also missed her children, and although the King had allowed her to visit them at Kensington, he was clearly determined to exercise strict control over their upbringing. He even referred the matter to the King's Bench, proposing that he should be responsible for the children's education and that they should be 'entirely under his command'.[32]

The chances of the King and Prince making peace seemed remote. 'Any persons that are turned out of doors at St James's are sure to find entertainment at Leicester Fields, so that the happy reconciliation is as near as ever,' wrote the Earl of Oxford to his wife in May 1718. The King's resentment towards his son was not to be dispelled so easily. It had been growing in intensity ever since the quarrel at the christening, fuelled by reports that reached him of the brilliance and popularity of the Prince's court, which to George I was a clear demonstration of impenitent rebellion. It was rumoured that at one stage he even contemplated seizing his son and conveying him to South America, 'whence he should never be heard of more'.[51]

Eventually, worn down by the pleadings of his wife and mistress, and grudgingly accepting the logic of Walpole's arguments about the damage that the ongoing feud was doing to the Hanoverians' public image, the Prince reluctantly agreed to offer an olive branch. On St George's Day, 23 April 1720, he wrote a conciliatory letter to the King. Upon receipt of this, his father sent word that he would receive him at St James's. Mrs Wake, wife of the Archbishop of Canterbury, encountered the Prince on his way to the palace and was so shocked by his grim countenance that she stopped him and asked if he had heard some terrible news about one of his children. 'No,' he sourly replied, 'I am going to wait upon my Father.'[52]

The pair met in the King's closet at St James's. The Prince managed to put on a reasonable show of contrition, but as he knelt before his father and vowed that he hoped never again to invoke his displeasure, the words must have all but choked him. The King turned pale and was 'much dismayed' at the sight of his son's apparent humility. Onlookers noted that he 'could not speak to be heard but by broken sentences, and said several times, "Votre conduite, votre conduite"'. The Prince promptly turned on his heel and hastened back to Leicester House. The whole encounter had not lasted above five minutes.[53]

The reconciliation, however fragile, sparked great celebrations throughout both courts. All those who had been obliged to resign their places because their spouse was in the opposing camp now faced the prospect of a return to service. Lady Cowper recalled that the square in front of Leicester House was 'full of coaches' and 'the Rooms full of Company; everything was gay and laughing; nothing but kissing and wishing of joy; and, in short, so different a face of things, nobody could conceive that so much joy should be after so many resolutions never come to this'.[14]

Elizabeth Molesworth, an acquaintance of Henrietta, congratulated her upon the part she had played in all this. 'I suppose you have had no small share in the joy this happy reconciliation has occasioned,' she wrote. The rejoicing spread throughout the country, although most used it merely as an excuse for overindulgence. Mrs Molesworth admitted that her husband had 'celebrated the news in a manner that allarmed the country people', adding that he was 'att present a little Disordered with that nights work'.[15]

The reconciliation was 'so little cordial', however, that it made precious little difference to relations between the King and Prince.[16] The former would not hear of the royal couple returning to live at St James's – not that his son had any intention of doing so. When the pair met at formal court occasions, as they were now regularly obliged to do, the atmosphere between them chilled the temperature in the room by several degrees. At the first drawing room to be held after the ceasefire, the King and his son stayed at opposite ends of the room with their respective entourages, 'which made the whole thing look like two armies drawn up in battle Array', observed one courtier present. They exchanged angry glances all evening, each ready to pounce at the slightest provocation. The same courtier noted: 'one could not help thinking it was like a little Dog and a Cat – whenever the dog stirs a foot, the cat sets up her back, and is ready to fly at him'.[17]

Relations were no better a few weeks later. A court newsletter described an encounter between George and his son at another reception. The King 'spoke not one word to him, good, bad, or indifferent'. The Prince, meanwhile, deliberately slighted the Duke of Newcastle by standing in his way and refusing to speak to him.[18]

Celebrations among the royal household staff and government officials therefore proved short-lived. If anything, the atmosphere at court was even worse than it had been before the split, and many wished for a return to the days when the two households had been completely separate. Those who had tried to curry favour with both sides during the breach now found themselves out in the cold.

Neither did the reconciliation bring happier times for Henrietta. Charles continued to refuse her access to their son, on which point he had the King's backing. Furthermore, she found herself the mistress of an increasingly bad-tempered and petulant Prince. The restlessness that she had begun to feel a few months before now turned into a desperate yearning to be free from the shackles of court.

Chapter 9

'A house in Twittenham'

◄◦►

T HE SOCIAL PRESTIGE OF Leicester House and Richmond Lodge waned considerably after the reconciliation. The Prince and Princess of Wales wisely recognised that it would no longer be appropriate to entertain in such a lavish manner as to outshine the formal ceremonials at St James's. Besides, they were able to preside over the latter from June 1720 when the King set sail for Hanover once more. However, another, more unexpected, factor was about to hasten the decline not just of the couple's two main residences, but of London's social life generally.

The South Sea Company had been established by the Earl of Oxford in 1711 to trade with South America, but also as an alternative source of government funds to the Whig-dominated Bank of England and East India Company. Eight years later, there was a scheme to use it to take over part of the government debt. Even though the company had no trade, this immediately prompted wild speculation, and it seemed that the whole of London was scrambling to buy subscriptions.

Edward Harley wrote in astonishment to his brother, who had founded the scheme: 'The demon of stock-jobbing . . . fills all hearts, tongues, and thoughts, and nothing is so like Bedlam as the present humour which has seized all parties, Whigs, Tories, Jacobites, Papists . . . No one is satisfied with even exorbitant gains, but everyone thirsts for more, and all this founded upon the machine of paper credit supported only by imagination.' Many gambled their whole fortunes on what they regarded as a sure prospect. The King himself ventured a considerable sum, and Henrietta also wagered some of her modest funds. She was apparently shrewd in her investment, for her friend

Elizabeth Molesworth wrote to express 'the additional pleasure of hearing you have been successfull in the southsea'.¹ Fortunes were made overnight, and people who had previously been barred from high society were now welcomed into the most exclusive circles.

By August 1720, the price of stock had risen almost tenfold. The inevitable crash, when it came, wreaked widespread devastation. Thousands were rendered destitute overnight. Those who had enjoyed a brief glimpse of high society were thrown back into their accustomed orders, and many aristocratic families were ruined. 'There never was such an universal confusion and distraction as at this time,' wrote one observer, 'many are ruined by their boundless avarice.' Alexander Pope, who had wisely resisted advice to buy some stock a few weeks before, told a friend that the crash had come 'like a Thief in the night, exactly as it happens in the case of our death'. He had little sympathy for those whose greed had lost them everything. 'Methinks God has punish'd the avaritious as he often punishes sinners, in their own way, in the very sin itself,' he wrote. 'The thirst for gain was their crime, that thirst continued became their punishment and ruin.'²

Dismay and devastation were rapidly followed by anger and revolt. There was a general cry for the King, the Prince and the government to be made accountable. All the anti-German feeling that had been bubbling under the surface for so long now burst forth in a torrent of protests, propaganda and violence. The German ministers and mistresses were a target for the people's vitriol, and they were accused of having been bribed with large sums to recommend the project. It was even suggested that the entire royal family should resign and go back to Hanover.

Ministers urged the King to return to England at once, and he reluctantly agreed. Furious at having his visit so abruptly curtailed, he arrived back in early November. There followed a fierce debate in the House of Lords, during which Lord Stanhope, the chief minister, was accused of being the cause of all the trouble. He was so enraged by this that he fell into a fit and had to be carried home, where he died the next day. The Secretary of State, who was ill with smallpox, went the same way shortly afterwards, and his father, the Postmaster-General, chose to poison himself rather than face the accusations against him. The Hanoverian regime was deep in crisis.

Out of the debris rose Sir Robert Walpole. Unlike so many of his peers, he had shrewdly sold his South Sea stock at exactly the right moment and had amassed a considerable fortune as a result. This later enabled him to build a lavish new mansion near the Norfolk coast which eclipsed all the aristocratic houses for miles around. Walpole hailed from that county, being the son of a Whig MP, and had soon inherited his father's passion for politics. Regarded as a 'violent' Whig during his undergraduate days at Cambridge, he was first elected to Parliament in 1701, and had risen rapidly through the ranks to become Secretary at War. His fortunes, and those of his fellow Whigs, had declined during the years of Tory supremacy under Queen Anne, but he had been quick to seize the initiative when the Hanoverians had come to the throne.

Walpole's coarse manners and vulgar speech were notorious. In parliamentary debates, he was simple and direct, while in private his language was as earthy as any squire's. Swift said of him: 'he's loud in his laugh, and he's coarse in his jest', while Chesterfield described him as 'inelegant in his manners' and 'loose in his morals'.[3] He enjoyed to the full every pleasure that Georgian England had to offer. He drank deeply, hunted hard and kept at least one mistress. He also played up to his rustic origins by munching little red Norfolk apples to sustain him during long parliamentary debates. The English people loved his vulgarity and plain-speaking, and he in turn understood their hopes and fears, which proved to be one of the most powerful advantages he had over his enemies.

Walpole's directness also appealed to the Princess, who knew that he would always tell her the truth, and who shared his base humour. He cultivated her favour by making sure that he attended court regularly, which he rightly perceived was an essential prerequisite to furthering his career. Lady Mary Wortley Montagu recalled that he was fond of the maxim that 'whoever expected advancement should appear much in public. He used to say, whoever neglected the world would be neglected by it.'[4]

With Lord Stanhope dead and the government in crisis, Walpole spied his chance for glory. He ensured that when the ministry was reconstructed, the chief power would reside in his hands. He became, in effect, Prime Minister (Britain's first), a post that he was to retain for the next twenty years. George I admired him greatly, once telling Caroline that he believed he could 'convert even stones into gold', and placed a great deal of trust in him.[5] Partly as a result of this, and partly because Walpole had failed to fulfil the promises that he had made at the reconciliation, the Prince disliked him intensely. Disaffected Whigs and Tories therefore flocked in ever greater numbers to Leicester House.

Chief among these was Henry St John, Viscount Bolingbroke. A fierce opponent of Walpole, Bolingbroke had risen to high office in Queen Anne's reign, first as Secretary of War and later Secretary of State. He had spent several years in exile on the Continent after the Hanoverians came to power, but was now back at court, eager to stir up trouble for the Prime Minister. Bolingbroke was a somewhat volatile character, given to extremes of behaviour. 'His virtues and vices, his reason and his passions, did not blend themselves by a gradation of tints, but formed a shining and sudden contrast,' wrote Lord Chesterfield.[6] His quickness of temper and boldness of action contrasted with his lively wit, charm and intelligence. It was no doubt the latter characteristics that attracted Henrietta, and he became a regular guest at her evening parties.

Bolingbroke was joined by William Pulteney, Earl of Bath, another opponent of Walpole. He had risen to the position of Secretary at War when George I became king, but had resigned this office during the schism of 1717 and had since failed to return to greatness. United in their opposition to Walpole, he and Bolingbroke set up an influential political journal, *The Craftsman*, which attacked the corruption that it claimed festered in the seats of power. Like Bolingbroke, Pulteney had 'lively and shining parts' and a 'surprising quickness of wit'. He had a particular talent for amusing ballads and poetry, with which he would entertain Mrs Howard and her companions at court.

Completing the trio was Dr John Arbuthnot, former physician to Queen Anne. He had long moved in Tory circles, and his opposition to Walpole's regime had found expression in the biting political satires, journals and pamphlets that spilled from his pen. In the society of wits, politicians and courtiers who thronged into the coffee houses of London, he played a central role. But for all that, he was remarkably modest and unassuming, and to his friends he was both generous and loyal. 'If there were a dozen Arbuthnots in the world I would burn my Travels,' Swift once declared. Henrietta also valued his friendship highly. They had met some years before when she had first taken up her post in the Princess's household, and had soon become close friends. Arbuthnot had apartments near hers at St James's and would attend her whenever she was sick. She had therefore been delighted when he had followed the Prince of Wales to Leicester House after the split of 1717.

Henrietta's association with Walpole's enemies was to drive an even deeper wedge between her and the Princess. But at the same time it won her the respect of the Prince, who delighted in anything that might antagonise the King. With members of the Opposition finding a warm welcome at Leicester House, the division in the royal household was almost as marked as it had been before the reconciliation, and life for those who served in it once more became a tale of two courts.

For Henrietta, the trial of serving both the Prince and Princess was starting to take its toll. She began to complain of violent headaches and was sometimes too ill to carry out her duties in Caroline's household. She also missed her friends Mary Bellenden and Molly Lepel (now Mrs Campbell and Lady Hervey respectively), especially when the court repaired to Richmond for the summer. Without their company, the Lodge was a considerably less diverting place than it had been during the preceding years, and Henrietta's main source of entertainment was the letters she received from her absent friends. They too longed to be with her: 'I wich we were all in swiss cantons,' lamented Mrs Campbell.[7]

Henrietta confided her increasing dissatisfaction with life at court to Mrs Campbell, but urged her to destroy the letters in case they should be seized by her enemies. Her friend wrote at once to reassure her: 'You may be sure I'll never name you for an author upon several accounts, nor indeed talk of any thing you writ for tis what I detest.' Their mutual friend, Lady Lansdowne, was also admitted to her confidence. 'I hope Dear Mrs howard you & I shall Live to see better days,' she wrote, '& love & honour to flourish once more.'[8]

Henrietta's growing aversion to her life at court was not only caused by the lack of close friends nearby. After four years, the Prince's passion for her seemed to be cooling. Theirs had never been a great love match, but Henrietta was well aware of how fragile her position would be if he rejected her. The first signs of his restlessness can be traced to early in 1722, when her friends observed her to be 'much in the vapours'. Rumours soon reached Mrs Campbell. 'I was told before I Left London, that somebody that shall be nameless, was grown sour & crosse & not so good to you as usual,' she wrote to her friend. As somebody who had also been the subject of the Prince's affections, Mary was able to empathise with Henrietta's predicament, and lamented that his coldness 'betrays the want of that good understanding, that both you & I so often flatter'd ourselves about, but these times I fear is over'.[9]

If Henrietta had been growing restless even before this turn of events, she now longed to be free from court. Those of her friends who had already left and found happiness heartily wished that she could do so too. 'It would make one half mad, to think of mis spent time in us both,' reflected Mary Bellenden, 'but I ame happy, & I wou'd to god you were so. I wish . . . that your circumstances were such that you might Leave that Life of hurry, & be able to enjoy those that Love you, & be a little att rest.'

His sense of timing as impeccable as ever, Charles Howard chose this moment to begin tormenting his wife once more. His premise was the royal reconciliation, which he claimed gave Henrietta even less cause to continue living apart from him. During the five years since she had left St James's, he had continued to enjoy the sordid pleasures that had diverted him during their life together. In so doing, he had plunged himself still further into debt, and therefore renewed his attempts to secure a greater portion of Henrietta's fortune than their marriage settlement had allowed him. He wrote to taunt his wife with the news that he was again suing her beloved brother 'for that Sum [£4,000] I have undergone much vexation', adding: 'I desire to know if you will oppose it, and am truly sensible of the folly I committed, in makeing you so Independent of me.'[10]

Howard's letter had the desired effect, and Henrietta at once admitted: 'to find you have a resentment against my Brother adds to my uneasinesse'. However, she insisted that she no longer had any power over the matter of her £4,000 inheritance. Fearing that he would use their son to blackmail her, she begged him not to 'Endavour any thing that may hereafter prove a disadvantage to the child,' adding that when they had lived as man and wife, 'I and the child [were] put in the fears of starveing through the whole course of our lives'. Her reply only served to ignite Charles's wrath, and rumours of her renewed marital strife soon began to spread throughout the court. 'I want to know if mr howard is come to town, & if he is not plagueing you,' wrote her friend Mary Bellenden, who had heard the news. Henrietta did what she could to limit the damage, urging her husband to keep a cooler head and arrive at 'a better opinion of me then your present warmeth will admit of'. Given Charles's notoriously hot temper, this was a vain plea. For the next few months, he continued to slander his wife 'in ye most inveterate and publick manner too coarse to be repeated and too great to leave the world unamazed'.[11]

Assistance came from a rather unexpected quarter. The Prince, tiring of his mistress and impatient with her troublesome husband, offered her a way out of court. He presented her with a gift of stock worth £11,500[12], together with 'a sett of Guilt Plate', some diamond jewellery, a ruby cross, a gold watch, and all the furniture and furnishings of both her own and her servants' rooms at Leicester House and Richmond Lodge. He also threw in a shipload of mahogany – a rare and much-prized commodity – which had just arrived in London. For a man notorious for his miserliness, this was an extraordinarily generous gift. That he intended it to buy Henrietta's independence from her husband was clear in the wording of the settlement, which stipulated that the Prince's gift was something 'with which the said Charles Howard shall not have any thing to doe or intermedle'. Instead, she was to 'use or dispose of the same as she pleases . . . as if she was sole and unmarryed'. Anticipating that she would use the money to buy a house of her own away from court, George made sure that her husband would be unable to touch this either: 'the premisses soe to be purchased to and ffor the sole proper peculiar and seperate use and Benefitt of the said Henrietta Howard alone and not for the use or benefit of the said Charles Howard her husband'.[13]

The Prince was right in his prediction about what his mistress would spend the money on. She had for some time longed to escape court for a home of her own. The previous year, she had confided to her friend Mary Campbell that she was 'Jealous for Liberty and property'.[14] Without the Prince's gift, this had seemed a distant prospect. Now it was suddenly within her grasp. Overjoyed at her unexpected turn of fortune, Henrietta at once set about making plans to build a house where she could escape the misery of her life at court. The need to keep this a secret was paramount. Even though the terms of the settlement made it nigh-on impossible for her husband to get his hands on the property, he had proved more than capable of making a nuisance of himself on numerous occasions in the past, and would no doubt do so again if he found out that his wife was about to gain her independence. The Princess, too, was eager to retain Henrietta at court for fear that her husband would find a mistress who threatened her own hold over him.

Henrietta went in secret to seek the help of an acquaintance, Henry Herbert, 9th Earl of Pembroke. Known as 'the Architect Earl', he had grown up at Wilton, near Salisbury, which was believed to be the work of Inigo Jones, the first great British admirer of the Italian architect

Andrea Palladio. Lord Herbert was a patron of Colen Campbell, the leader of the English Palladian revival, and he engaged his protégé in working up some initial designs for Mrs Howard's villa. These were conveyed in secret to her apartments at Richmond Lodge that summer. She was delighted with this first glimpse of her future retreat, but resisted the temptation to share her excitement with even her closest friends. One day, when she was called to Greenwich unexpectedly, however, she inadvertently left the plans visible in her apartments. It was fortunate that the person who discovered them was a trusted friend.

John Gay had paid an impromptu visit to Richmond Lodge and, on finding the royal party absent, had repaired to Henrietta's rooms to wait for her. When she had not returned by the end of that day, he wrote to tell her that he had called, and expressed his curiosity about the plans he had seen. Greatly alarmed, Henrietta wrote to him at once: 'I beg you will never mention the Plan which you found in my Room. There's a necessity, yet, to keep that whole affair secret, tho (I think I may tell you) it's almost intirely finish'd to my satisfaction.' Gay assured her: 'When I hear you succeed in your wishes, I succeed in mine, so I will not say a word more of the house.'[15]

Either Gay failed to keep his word, or Mrs Howard's excitement triumphed over her usual discretion, because before long her project had become one of the worst-kept secrets at court. But if the Princess knew about it, she was, for now, content to indulge her 'good Howard' in her ambitious scheme. She was, in any case, absorbed with housing plans of her own, for the Duchess of Buckingham was making overtures to the royal couple that they should lease her house on the west side of St James's Park. A natural daughter of James II, the Duchess was proud of her Stuart ancestry and rather disdainful of the Hanoverian royal family. The Princess had expressed an interest in the house at a recent court reception, but rather than deal with her directly, the Duchess chose Henrietta as an intermediary. 'I have express'd my intentions about the house in a way that several perhaps would not,' she wrote to her, 'considering the little care and regularity that is taken in the prince's family.' The terms she offered were £3,000 per annum to rent the house, or £60,000 to buy it outright.[16] This was unacceptable to the royal couple, and the scheme was dropped. However, Buckingham House was to be purchased by the Crown some forty years later, and in the early nineteenth century it was remodelled by John Nash and became known as Buckingham Palace.

Henrietta's project, meanwhile, was progressing apace. Having approved the designs, she now sought an appropriate location for her new house. Early in 1724, she instructed her friend the Lord Ilay, who was a trustee of her settlement from the Prince, to purchase some land in an area known as Marble Hill, situated by the Thames at Twickenham.

By the early eighteenth century, the village of Twickenham, lying some ten miles south-west of London, had become one of the most desirable places to live for those wishing to escape the noise and smells of the capital. Just two hours by barge from London, and within easy reach of Hampton Court and Richmond Lodge, it became a magnet for members of fashionable society who sought rural tranquillity combined with ready access to the court. Lord Ilay himself had built a mansion there, the handsome Whitton Place, and he was surrounded by a host of other noble residents. The politician and government official James Johnston, a younger son of Lord Wariston, had modelled the elegant Orléans House on his country seat in Lombardy. The portrait painter Thomas Hudson lived nearby, as did Lord Strafford, the Dowager Countess of Ferrers and Lady Fanny Shirley. Lady Mary Wortley Montagu, who spent every summer there with her husband at the elegant Savile House, wrote to a friend in 1722: 'I am at Twickenham where there is at this time more company than in London.' So rapidly was the village expanding that later the same year, she told her friend that it had 'become so fashionable, and the neighbourhood so enlarged, that 'tis more like Tunbridge or Bath than a country retreat'.[17]

But perhaps the most important influence on Mrs Howard's choice of location was the proximity of her friend Alexander Pope. He had moved to the village in 1719 and had built a new villa on the proceeds from his translation of Homer's *Iliad*. Henrietta was captivated by his descriptions of the peace and tranquillity of the place compared to London. 'At Twickenham the World goes otherwise,' he wrote. 'We have as little politicks here within a few miles of court ... as at Southampton.'[18]

Delighted at the prospect of a new neighbour, Pope offered to help his friend with the design of her house and, in particular, its grounds. A keen gardener, he soon began to spend so much time at Marble Hill that he neglected his writing. 'My head is still more upon Mrs Howard and her works than upon my own,' he confessed to a friend in September

1724. He may well have drawn inspiration from the magnificent grounds of his friends the Digby family at Sherborne in Dorset, where he had stayed that summer. 'I have spent many hours here in studying for hers, & in drawing new plans for her,' he told his friend Martha Blount. His subsequent account of the parkland at Marble Hill showed that there was a direct correlation between the two. 'The Valley is laid level and divided into two regular groves of horse chestnuts, and a bowling green in the middle of about 180 foot. This is bounded behind with a canal [the Thames].' The elegant layout of Marble Hill's gardens was to remain unchanged for the next forty or so years. An account of 1760 described the 'fine green lawn, open to the river . . . adorned on each side, by a beautiful grove of chestnut trees'.[19]

Before long, Henrietta's other male acquaintances at court were falling over themselves to help. The Earl of Peterborough seemed even more eager than she was to see it completed. 'I was impatient to know the issue of the affaire, and what she intended for this autumn,' he wrote to Pope, 'for no time is to be Lost either if she intends to build out houses or prepare for planting.' He promised to call on Pope as soon as possible so that they could go together to Marble Hill.[20]

An amusing rivalry developed between the men involved in Mrs Howard's project, as each battled to outdo the others' efforts. 'Fair Lady, I dislike my Rivalls amongst the living, more then those amongst the dead,' wrote a peevish Lord Peterborough, 'must I yield to Lord Herbert, and Duke Ily, if I had built the castle of Blenheim, and filled the Land with Domes and Towers, I had deserved my fate for I hear I am to be Layed aside as an extravagant person fitt to build nothing but palaces . . . I can even wish well to the house, and garden under all these mortifications, may every Tree prosper planted by what ever hand, may you ever be pleased & happy, whatever happens to your unfortunate Gardiner, & architect degraded, & Turned of.'[21]

Allen Bathurst, 1st Earl of that name, was another rival for Peterborough to contend with. In common with an increasing number of Henrietta's friends, he was an ardent Tory, and, having lost the polit-ical prestige he had enjoyed under Queen Anne, he was now in constant opposition to Walpole's regime. Bathurst was renowned for his wit and counted some of the greatest literary figures of the day among his friends, including Congreve, Prior and Swift. He was also a close friend of Pope, who had recently introduced him to Mrs Howard. She was instantly captivated by his humour, and in particular his willingness to poke fun at the court. 'I am convinced I shall make but an awkward Courtier,' he told her in one letter, claiming that the last time he had been presented at Richmond, 'the folks I met there ... looked upon me as a wild Beast whose teeth and Claws had been lately pulled out'.[22]

Their friendship became close enough to cause a scandal at court. 'I, who smell a rat at a considerable distance, do believe in private that Mrs Howard and his lordship have a friendship that borders upon "the tender",' wrote Lady Mary Wortley Montagu to her sister. Dismissing everything that Henrietta had pleaded to the contrary, she continued: 'as there is never smoke without some fire, there is very rarely fire without some smoke. These smothered flames, tho' admirably covered with whole heaps of politics laid over them, were at length seen, felt, heard, and understood.'[23]

Before long, news of the suspected affair had reached the Prince. According to Lady Mary, he told his mistress that if she 'shewed under other colours', he would withhold her salary. If her account is to be believed, Bathurst was subsequently ordered to stay away from Richmond, and the matter was never spoken of again. There is little other evidence to support this, however, and the Earl was in fact welcomed back to court on many subsequent occasions.

Tender or not, Henrietta's friendship with Bathurst proved useful in the design of her new house. Like Pope, he was a keen gardener and had a magnificent park of his own near Cirencester. He was eager to assist in the layout of the grounds at Marble Hill, and told Pope that he planned to wait on their mutual friend there as soon as possible. He later sent some lime trees to be planted in her gardens.[24]

While Henrietta was grateful for her friends' help with her new villa and its grounds, she was not about to leave such an important project to well-meaning amateurs, and instead enlisted the services of some of the greatest architects and gardeners of the day. For the grounds she engaged Charles Bridgeman, landscape gardener to the King himself. Bridgeman was already much in demand and Pope had recently seen his work for Viscount Cobham at the celebrated gardens of Stowe. He visited Marble Hill with Henrietta and Pope in the summer of 1724, but there followed a delay of some weeks before he gave his opinion. He wrote to the latter in September explaining that he had been very busy, but assuring him that he had 'begun on the plan, and have not left from that time to this so long as I could see, nor shall [I] leave it till 'tis finished which I hope will be about tomorrow noon'.[25]

The laying out of the grounds at Marble Hill was to continue for some years. In the meantime, Henrietta commissioned Roger Morris, a little-known but talented architect, to build 'the naked carcass of a house'. He was paid £200 on account and started work straight away. Henrietta was far from being a passive observer of all this activity. Her interests extended well beyond the 'tea and scandal' with which the poet Congreve identified her sex.[26] She was passionately interested in, and had a sound knowledge of, the architectural styles that were prevalent in England at that time. As the 'Honourable Mrs Howard' she was included in the list of subscribers to the third volume of Colen Campbell's *Vitruvius Britannicus* in 1725. This included the designs for Marble Hill, although secrecy was still observed, for it was referred to simply as 'A house in Twittenham'. Henrietta also subscribed to both volumes of William Kent's *The Designs of Inigo Jones* in 1727.

Mrs Howard's friends and family were well aware of her passion for architecture, and often sought her advice on the design of their own homes. Lord Chesterfield wrote to her from his ambassadorial residence in the Hague in 1728 complaining that, having commissioned a spacious new apartment, he was 'at present over head and ears, in mortar'. Fearing that he might have judged the dimensions incorrectly, he pledged to 'submit to you and Lord Herbert; who I hope will both be so good as to give me your sentiments upon it'. Many years later, Henrietta's nephew John appealed to her during his modernisation work at Blickling, which he claimed his wife and sister were ruining with ill-advised schemes of their own. 'Your authority is necessary to silence them,' he insisted.[27]

The influence that Henrietta had on her own house can be clearly traced. Its harmonic architectural proportions owed much to the Palladian style that she so loved. As such, it was at the very forefront of fashionable taste, for this style was only just beginning to take hold in England. Its origins lay in the 'Grand Tour' of Europe, which had become an essential component of a gentleman's education. The Tour followed an established route which took in some of the greatest classical sites on the Continent, such as Rome and Pompeii. This in turn sparked an interest in the designs of the sixteenth century architect Andrea Palladio, whose villas were based on the strict numerical ratios and geometrical symmetry of his Greek and Roman forebears. The overall effect was one of elegant simplicity, and the Georgians loved it.

The period gave rise to some of the greatest Palladian creations of English architectural history: from the remodelling of Stowe and Woburn Abbey to the building of Prior Park in Somerset and Nostell Priory in Yorkshire. Marble Hill was on a much smaller scale, but was still regarded as one of the finest Palladian villas in England. 'I long to see what I'm told is the prettiest thing of the size that can be seen,' wrote Henrietta's friend Lady Hervey.[28] It was also one of the earliest, for it was not until after 1730 that the movement really started to take hold.

But Marble Hill was more than just a purely academic exercise; a slavish homage to the designs of Palladio. Not for Mrs Howard the rigid symmetry of Lord Burlington's house at nearby Chiswick, which was devoid of such luxuries as bedrooms and kitchens, and was variously described by contemporaries as 'rather curious than convenient' and 'too small to live in, but too large to hang on a watch chain'.[29] For all its elegance, both inside and out, Marble Hill was a house designed for a lady to live in and receive company, and Henrietta ensured that it was practical as well as aesthetically pleasing.

The house had two main entrances, for guests would arrive either by the road to the north or the river to the south. Most would have chosen the latter, as this was by far the most comfortable way to travel and avoided the dust, discomfort and danger of the bumpy roads, which were also riddled with highwaymen. Pope had fallen foul of them while Marble Hill was being built. On his way home one evening, his coach had been overturned when it crossed a broken bridge. He had been thrown into the river and had been 'up to the knots of his periwig in water' before the coachman had broken the windows and dragged him out. Pope's hand had been so badly cut that it was feared he would lose the use of his little finger '& the next to it'.[30] A surgeon had been hastily summoned from London, and had confirmed that the hand would be permanently crippled.

The scene of sylvan calm that is presented to modern-day visitors as they gaze across the Thames towards the graceful house beyond is rather different to how it would have looked in the early eighteenth century. The river would have been bustling with traffic: from elegant courtiers flitting between St James's or Hampton Court and their country retreats, to barges laden with goods pulled by dray horses plodding along the path. A contemporary engraving depicts the view that would have unfolded before them as the river wound westwards away from

Richmond. A sweeping wide avenue of chestnut trees led the eye up the gently sloping bank towards the elegant villa – described as being 'as white as snow' – that sat in the centre of the view. It was, and remains, a perfect composition, an image of beauty, taste and simplicity. 'Among all the Villas of this neighbourhood, Lady Suffolk's, which we sail past, on the left, a little below Twickenham, makes the best appearance from the river,' claimed a guide written for Georgian river tourists. 'It stands in a woody recess, with a fine lawn descending to the water, & adorned with wood well-disposed.'[31]

After strolling through the avenue, guests would arrive in the elegant entrance hall. With its precise symmetrical proportions, including four carefully positioned columns, this imitated the central court of a Roman house. Pope told Henrietta that it was 'the most delightful room in the world except where you are'.[32] An intimate breakfast parlour had been built downstairs, overlooking the river, while a grand staircase, fashioned from the mahogany that the Prince had given her, allowed visitors to parade in style up to the stately Great Room. Favoured guests might ascend the inner stone staircase to retire in one of the three fine bedrooms on the third storey, or to view portraits in the long gallery that ran alongside. Eight garrets were squeezed under the eaves for the servants, who used the same concealed stairs to reach the service wing. On the outside of the house, meanwhile, Henrietta ordered that balconies be added to the south front so that she could admire the fine prospect towards the Thames, Ham House and Richmond Hill.

The clarity of Henrietta's vision for the house suggests that she had filled many long hours at court planning every aspect of it in her mind, even though the need for secrecy had prevented her from committing these thoughts to paper. She made the most of the times when the court was at nearby Richmond to inspect the work in progress, and was so immersed in this task that she was no longer able to maintain a regular correspondence with her absent friends. 'How does my good howard doe, me thinks I Long to [hear] from you,' wrote Mary Campbell in August 1724. 'I suppose you are up to the ears in bricks & mortar, & talk of freez & cornish Like any Little woman.' She added that she was about to pay a visit to Colonel Fane's new Palladian-style house at Mereworth in Kent, 'where I intend to improve my self in the terms of art, in order to keep pace with you'.[33]

While she was heavily involved in the design, Henrietta's duties at court allowed her only the occasional visit to Marble Hill. This was a source of great frustration, for the house was rapidly becoming her sole source of comfort. Instead she had to make do with the news that her friends sent back to her from there. Work certainly seemed to be progressing apace, for within just a few short months, Pope was able to report: 'Marblehill waits only for its roof – the rest is finished.'[34] He must have been referring to the 'carcass' only, for there was still a great deal to do on the rest of the house. Nevertheless, the speed at which Morris and his men were working was impressive.

Frustrated by her confinement at court and impatient with her now onerous duties for both the Prince and Princess, Mrs Howard received some welcome relief in the form of a new visitor to Leicester House. Jonathan Swift was Dean of St Patrick's Cathedral in Dublin, but was better known for his literary genius than his spiritual endeavours. A close friend of Pope, Gay and Arbuthnot, he had risen to prominence during the reign of Queen Anne, when he had put his considerable literary talents to good use on behalf of the Tories, and before long he had become their leading propagandist. Despite winning favour with the Queen, he had been unable to secure a position at court, and on her death he had returned to his native Dublin, where he soon afterwards took up his post at St Patrick's.

Swift was not neglected by his friends back in England, who struck up a regular correspondence with him and continually begged him to return. As an incentive, Pope offered to introduce him to his friend Mrs Howard, whom he was confident Swift would admire as much as he did. 'I can also help you to a Lady who is as deaf, tho' not so old as your self,' he told him. 'You'll be pleas'd with one another, I'll engage, tho' you don't hear one another: you'll converse like spirits by intuition.'[35] Pope was right. When Swift finally gave in to his entreaties and paid a visit to England in the spring of 1726, he quickly forged a close friendship with Mrs Howard. It was fortunate that they conversed by word rather than intuition, for their good-humoured sparring kept their friends entertained during many a long evening at Leicester House. Their lively exchanges continued by letter after Swift had left England, and read like a duel of wits.

Swift's most famous work, *Gulliver's Travels*, was published – anonymously – shortly after his departure. This satirical tale was based upon certain characters within the Georgian court, including the royal family themselves. Henrietta read it with delight, and her next letter to Swift was loaded with references to it. Copying the style of the inhabitants of Lilliput, she wrote diagonally down one side of the paper and up the other. She also wove in various characters and scenes within the book, such as the 'Brobdignag Dwarf' and the 'Academy of Lagado', and signed the letter 'Sieve Yahoo' – the name that Gulliver gives to ladies at court. Swift pretended to be bemused by the missive, claiming that it was 'the most unaccountable one I ever saw in my life', and that he had been unable to 'comprehend three words of it together'. 'The perverseness of your lines astonished me,' he continued, and said that he had puzzled over its meaning for four full days before a bookseller had sent him a copy of *Gulliver's Travels*. He added that he had rather resented being 'forced to read a book of seven hundred pages in order to understand a letter of fifty lines'.[36]

For all their literary sparring, it seemed that Swift and Mrs Howard had a great deal of affection for each other. She gave him a ring as a token of her esteem, which he wore constantly to remind him of his new friend, and in return he presented her with a gift of luxurious Irish plaid 'made in Imitation of the Indian wherein our Workmen here are grown so expert'. Henrietta was so delighted with this that she proudly showed it off to the Princess, who immediately seized it for her own use.[37]

Like Henrietta's other male friends, Swift involved himself in the development of her new house. He was rather less serious in the task than Pope and Peterborough, however, and his chief preoccupation seemed to be with the wine cellar. He styled himself 'chief butler and Keeper of the Ice House', and told Henrietta: 'I hope you will get your house and wine ready, to which Mr Gay and I are to have free access when you are safe at Court.'[38] Swift did make a more practical contribution to the house by helping his new friend with the furnishings. He supplied more of the Irish plaid cloth, and this was used for bed hangings and curtains in the bedroom that subsequently become known as the 'Plaid Room'.

Much as she yearned to join her friends at Marble Hill, Henrietta was delighted by their obvious enjoyment of her new house, which was detailed in the many accounts that they sent her. Their lively party was broken up in August, when Swift returned to Ireland. His departure was greatly lamented. ''Tis a sensation like that of a limb lopp'd off,' Pope told him. 'One is trying every minute unawares to use it, and finds it is not.'[39] Henrietta was now among the circle of Swift's English friends who wrote to him regularly, and sometimes they composed joint missives for his entertainment. One of the most amusing was a recipe for 'Stewing Veal', which was laden with nonsensical puns. Its inspiration was the fact that Swift had complimented Pope's cook on the veal stew that she had served during a supper party at Twickenham. His friends used the recipe as a metaphor for the ingredients they thought should go into his sermons. It was written in Gay's hand, but there were contributions from Pope, Bolingbroke, Pulteney and Henrietta. They urged him to cut these up 'in a few pieces' in order to make them more palatable for the congregation.

Swift thanked them for it, but said he wished 'the measure of Ingredients may prove better than of the Verses', and added that he would like a recipe for 'a Chicken in a wooden Bowl from Mrs Howard, upon which you may likewise exercise your Poetry, for the Ladys here object against both'.[40] Not wishing to be outdone on the rhyming stakes, he ended with a short verse lamenting the recent misfortunes that had befallen his friends in England:

> Here four of you got mischances to plague you
> Friend Congreve a Feaver, Friend Howard an Ague
> Friend Pope overturned by driving too fast away
> And Robin at Sea had like to be cast away.

Swift may have numbered Henrietta among the friends whom he missed now that he was back in Dublin, but his interest in her was not entirely selfless. Tired of being so far away from the centre of political life, he hankered after a place at court. Despite assuring his new friend that he was 'no Courtier, nor have anything to ask', he clearly saw her as one of the best means to advancement.[41] He expressed his delight that the Princess had shown him such favour when he had been at Leicester House, although he claimed that he had not sought it: 'For I am not such a prostitute flatterer as Gulliver, whose chief study is to extenuate the vices and magnify the virtues of mankind.' He begged Mrs Howard to make sure that her favour would continue now that he was back in Ireland.

Henrietta served Swift well, not just with the Princess (who encouraged their correspondence), but with the court in general. 'My correspondents have informed me that your Ladyship has done me the honour to answer severall objections that ignorance, malice, and party have made to my Travells,' he wrote in November 1726, 'and bin so

charitable as to justifie the fidelity and veracity of the Author.' Grateful
for her assistance, he added: 'This zeal you have shown for Truth calls
for my particular thankes, and at the same time encourages me to beg
you would continue your goodness to me.' Realising the importance of
retaining Mrs Howard's favour, Swift showered her with witty and
amusing letters to fill her tedious hours at court. He even threw in a
bit of romance for good measure, going so far as to suggest marriage
– something that he could hardly promise, given his ecclesiastical duties.
Henrietta was well aware of his insincerity and gave short shrift to his
ridiculous proposal. 'I had rather you and I were dumb as well as deaf
for even then that shou'd happen,' she admonished him.[42] Suitably chastened, Swift resorted to less romantic means to win her favour in future.

Diverting though his letters were, Henrietta had more pressing
matters to attend to at court, for her husband Charles was once again
making trouble. He had been fighting a protracted and costly legal battle
with his brother, Edward, for the past few years. When the 7th Earl
of Suffolk died in 1722, he complicated the succession by settling Audley
End House and estate on Charles, who was the younger of his two
uncles, thereby passing over Edward, who succeeded to the earldom.
Edward contested the will, and the two brothers fought it out in the
courts, running up huge costs in the process. Eventually, in June 1725,
they entered into articles of agreement whereby Charles could retain
the house and estate on condition that he paid Edward £1,200 out of
the rents and profits. He was also to bear all the legal costs. Although
Charles agreed to this, he did not put the necessary arrangements in
place to levy the annual payments out of the estate, and two years later
his brother was still pressing for them.

Rather than sort out the estate, Charles preferred an option that
was both simpler and, for him, more entertaining: to torment his wife
until she agreed to give him the money. That Henrietta was using the
Prince's generous gift to build herself a house away from court was no
longer a secret. Charles knew how much she valued her independence,
and would therefore also have guessed how much the house meant to
her. He could not have been presented with a more perfect means of
blackmailing her.

'Mr Howard, having a mind to turn his reputed cuckoldom to the
best account, began to give his wife fresh trouble,' related Lord Hervey,
'and in order to make her pay for staying abroad pretended an inclination to have her return home.'[43] Enlisting the support of George I,

who was ever glad of an opportunity to annoy his son, Charles wrote
to Princess Caroline in the spring of 1727, telling her that he had 'again
receiv'd his positive directions, that she immediately retires from her
Employment under your Royal Highnesse'. He professed his 'unhap-
pinesse in this difficulty', claiming that he would not have dared put
forward such a request had it not been expressly commanded by the
King.[44] The Princess showed the letter to Mrs Howard, who immediately sent back a terse response to say he had indicated neither where
she should go nor in what manner he would provide for her if she left
her mistress's service.

But Charles was not to be bowed by his wife's defiance, and assured
her that 'all attempts you can use to the Contrary will be in vain'.[45]
Besides, he had a few more tactics up his sleeve. One of them was to
call upon the highest ecclesiastical power in the land to help fight his
case. William Wake, Archbishop of Canterbury, was not of a mind to
be drawn into an affair that had all the makings of a public scandal.
He also distrusted the man who had just related the tale of his wife's
disobedience. On the other hand, he strongly disapproved of marital
infidelity, particularly when it concerned the heir to the throne. He was
also aware that if Mr Howard chose to invoke the law, there was not
a court in the land that would support the wife against the husband,
regardless of who her lover was. He therefore wrote to the Princess
of Wales, urging that her husband's and the King's honour were at stake
because if Charles pursued his case through the law, it would 'make a
great noise'. Wake concluded that he hoped she would take 'some
method to prevent any such writ being brought to your House by
getting the Lady out of it'.[46]

The Princess did not particularly want to endure a public scandal,
but she was determined to keep Henrietta at court in order to maintain the delicate balance of power. She cleverly replied that if Mrs
Howard wished to return to her husband then she would willingly
release her – a thing that she knew full well was the last thing on earth
her Woman of the Bedchamber would ever do.

Henrietta used all her powers of reason in attempting to make
Charles drop his case. She reminded him that when she had left their
apartments at St James's following the royal quarrel, he had 'directly
dismissed' and 'absolutely discharged' her, saying that he never wanted
to see her again. 'What refuge more safe, more honourable or more
rational can a wife so abandoned by her Husband have recourse than

to Continue in the service of the Princesse of Wales,' she argued. Knowing full well that reason alone would not work with her husband, however, she sought the intervention of the Hobart family solicitor, Dr James Welwood, who went in person to try to persuade him. Unfortunately, this served only to provoke him further. Welwood told Mrs Howard that Charles had appeared 'highly incensed' and had fiercely denied the allegation that he had abandoned her. He therefore advised her to remain calm and sit it out until her husband tired of the whole affair.

He had reckoned without the tenacity of Mr Howard, who had his eyes on a much greater prize than his wife's return and was not about to give up so easily. Believing that if he caused enough embarrassment, either his wife or the Prince would pay him off, he resorted to increasingly dirty tactics, warning Henrietta that her continued disobedience threatened to ruin their son's reputation, and that the boy had been greatly upset by the whole sorry affair. 'How ungratefull and shocking A part he must share in life, to hear the reproaches of your Publick defiance to me, and what the World will interpret the occasion of it,' he surmised, concluding that she should give up her case at once if she cared at all for the 'small Posterity of A child you seem'd to love'. His words must have wounded Henrietta deeply, but she refused to allow him to use their son as a pawn in his evil game. 'You mention Sir a tender subject indeed, my Child,' she replied. 'I wish to God he was of a riper age to be Judge between us, I can not but flatter my self he would have more Duty and humanity than to desire to see his Mother exposed to misery and want.' She berated her husband for using the young boy in 'ye disputes yt have hapned between his father and mother' in order that he could pursue his 'precarious expectation of court favours', and begged him to speak no more of this 'preposterous reconciliation'.[47]

But Charles knew that he had hit upon one of the surest means of distressing his wife, and he continued to bait her on the subject. Scorning her 'feigned' tenderness towards her son, he told her that the boy would never choose her over his father. 'No artifice, or Temptation of Reward upon earth, will ever Prevaile with him to desert me, or disobey my Injunctions.' Henrietta replied that she 'hardly dare trust my weakness upon that subject', but insisted that although Henry's tender age made him 'susceptible of impression good or bad' she could not believe that he would 'persevere in forgetting he has a mother'.

What she then went on to say was a testament to the grief that she had suffered over her son – as well as the depth of her hatred for his father. 'I am not willing to sopose he will long neglect a parent who has not forfeited ye duty he owes her but if this of all other evils is yet reserved for me I must bear it with patience and submit to my fate,' she wrote. 'If I were now to dye he might say he had a mother to whom he had not paid the respect yt was due, so on the other side if he deserts me however lamentable the stroke is to me, I must and will think as in cases of mortality that I once had a Son.'[48]

This statement put paid to any further attempts by Charles to use their son against her. If she was prepared to give him up for good rather than submit to her husband's demands, then it was futile to pursue this line of argument any longer. Henrietta was playing a dangerous game. The ensuing years would prove that she had far from given up hope of reclaiming her son, but she knew it was vital to convey this impression now in order for Charles to spare him the shame of being involved in their increasingly public battle.

Furious that what he had assumed was a certain route to victory had backfired on him, Charles resorted to the only other means he could think of: violence. He managed to secure a warrant from the Lord Chief Justice which gave him the right to seize his wife 'wherever he found her'. 'This step so alarmed Mrs Howard,' observed Lord Hervey, 'who feared nothing so much as falling again into his hands', that she became a virtual prisoner at Leicester House.[49] She knew that she was safe from Charles as long as she remained there, for it was surely too extreme a measure – even for him – to attempt to take his wife by force out of the Prince of Wales's palace.

This confinement could not last for long, however. Summer was fast approaching, and with it the royal household's traditional removal to Richmond. This presented a very real danger for Henrietta. Etiquette would not allow a mere Woman of the Bedchamber to travel in the Princess's coach. She would therefore have to follow behind in a much less secure carriage, which it would have been all too easy for Charles to ambush. Neither could the royal party travel in secret: their annual pilgrimage to Richmond attracted thousands of spectators, and the magnificence of their stately procession did not exactly blend in with the surroundings. Henrietta therefore hatched a plan with her friends the Duke of Argyll and Lord Ilay to make her escape to Richmond in one of their coaches. They would leave early in the morning, some four hours before the royal coach. Once there, she would be lodged at Argyll's house in Petersham, rather than in the residence close to Richmond Lodge that she had recently shared with the Maids of Honour.

The plan worked brilliantly, and Mrs Howard was soon safely installed at the Duke of Argyll's house. The whole experience had terrified her, however, and even now she did not dare to set foot outside her safe house. 'I have not been abroad since I left London,' she wrote to Dr Welwood, apparently having been excused from her duties to Caroline, 'nor have I Courage yet to venture out.'[10] Her terror must have been great indeed, for not even the prospect of seeing her beloved Marble Hill again could incite her to leave Argyll's house. It was a miserable summer that she spent there, knowing that the manifestation of her independence was taking shape, brick by brick, just a few minutes away down river, and tormented by the thought that she might never be able to enjoy it. Her friends shared some of her frustration. 'Really it is the most mortifying thing in nature, that we can neither get into the court to live with you, nor you get into the country to live with us,' Pope wrote to her from nearby Twickenham, 'so we will take up with what we can get that belongs to you, and make ourselves as happy as we can, in your house.'[11]

Work at Marble Hill was progressing apace, and it was now so near completion that Henrietta had engaged a housekeeper and established a small farm in the grounds to supply the house with fresh milk, eggs and other dairy produce. While she was confined at Petersham, her friends were able to take full advantage of the daily improvements that were being made to her new home. Pope was a frequent visitor to the house, and tried to keep his friend's spirits up by supplying her with regular updates on its progress. 'We cannot omit taking this occasion to congratulate you upon the increase of your family,' he wrote, 'for your Cow is this morning very happily delivered of the better sort, I mean a female calf; she is like her mother as she can stare . . . We have given her the name of Caesar's wife, Calf-urnia; imagining, that as Romulus and Remus were suckled by a wolf, this Roman lady was suckled by a cow, from whence she took that name.' He went on to say that he and Gay had celebrated this momentous event with a 'cold dinner' at the house, which included wine, meat, fish and 'the lettice of a greak Island, called Cos'. He added: 'We have some thoughts of dining there to morrow, to celebrate the day after the birth-day, and on friday to celebrate the day after that, where we intend to entertain Dean Swift.'[51]

Pope's exuberance was premature. Shortly after he had dispatched this letter, events at court brought work on Mrs Howard's beloved house to a sudden halt.

Chapter 10

'Dunce the second reigns like Dunce the first'

———————◇———————

ON 13 NOVEMBER 1726, Sophia Dorothea, estranged wife of George I, died at Ahlden Castle, where she had been held captive for thirty-three years. The King celebrated the occasion by making a rare public visit to the theatre with his mistresses on the very day that he received the news. But for all his bravado, he was secretly troubled by a prophecy that had been told to him some time before, that he would follow his wife to the grave within a year.

The following summer, he announced that he was once again going to visit his beloved German dominions, and on 3 June he set off with his favourite mistress, Madame Schulenburg. Five days later, he had reached Delden, on the border with Germany, where he rested at the house of a local nobleman. In high spirits at the prospect of his imminent arrival at Herrenhausen, he ate an enormous supper, which included several watermelons. His host urged him to stay the night and give his stomach chance to digest the feast, but George was impatient to reach Osnabrück, the palace of his birth, and set off again at full speed in the early hours of the morning.

According to a contemporary account, just as the royal coach was about to depart, somebody threw into it an old letter from Sophia Dorothea lamenting her cruel fate and reminding her husband of the prophecy about his death.[1] Whether it was this or the surfeit of watermelons is not certain, but shortly afterwards the King was seized by an 'apoplectick fitt' of such violence that he fell to the floor of the coach. Greatly alarmed, his attendants brought the coach to an abrupt halt and prepared to carry him to a place of refuge. But George, by now furious in his impatience, urged the coachmen to speed on with the journey, crying: 'To Osnabrück, to Osnabrück!'

As the coach thundered along the treacherous roads, jolting the anxious passengers within, the King fell in and out of consciousness. His attendants looked on in panic, certain that he could not cling to life much longer. Finally, late into the following night, the castle of Osnabrück came into view, and upon arrival George I was borne at once to the bedchamber. No sooner had he been laid out on the bed than he was seized with a 'violent cholick of which he suffer'd very much for about 30 hours'.[2] His long struggle came to an end as the clock struck midnight on 11 June, and he breathed his last in the very room in which he had been born, sixty-seven years earlier. The prophecy thus fulfilled, Sophia Dorothea had won her revenge, albeit from beyond the grave.

Lord Townshend, who had accompanied the King on his journey to Hanover, dispatched a messenger with all speed to England. Four days later, the servants at Sir Robert Walpole's London residence on Arlington Street were disturbed by a frantic knocking at the door. They opened it to find a messenger, greatly agitated, telling them that he had an urgent dispatch for their master. On hearing that Sir Robert was not at home, the man set off for Richmond, where the Prince and Princess were enjoying their traditional summer retreat. He had got as far as the outskirts of Chelsea when he encountered the very object of his mission, who stopped him and asked what business caused him such haste. When the breathless messenger told him that he carried news of the King's death, Sir Robert made him hand over the dispatch so that he could take it in person to the Prince.

It was a sultry June day, and the Prince and Princess were taking their customary afternoon rest when their chief minister arrived, sweating and agitated. He at once applied to the Duchess of Dorset to be admitted to the royal presence, but was informed that they were sleeping and could not be disturbed. Sir Robert urged that his business would brook no delay, and the Duchess, with many misgivings, eventually agreed to wake them.

Furious at this interruption to his accustomed routine, the Prince immediately sent back word that he 'considered the minister very bad and impertinent at daring to come into his house and disturb him, and that he might go away again, for he would not see him'. Walpole continued pressing, however, which put his master into 'such a state of fury that he was on the point of rising to throw Sir Robert out of the room'.³ Eventually, the Princess managed to calm her husband by persuading him that Walpole would never dare to risk his wrath in such a manner unless the news was of the greatest importance.

Flustered and cursing, Prince George emerged from the royal bedchamber, half dressed and still muttering oaths against his chief minister. Walpole promptly lowered his great bulk down on one knee and kissed the Prince's hand, before imparting the news that his father was dead and he was therefore the new King of England.

Throughout history, heirs to the throne have been awestruck and humbled upon hearing that they have at last come into their inheritance. When Elizabeth I received the news that she was Queen of England, she sank to her knees in the gardens at Hatfield Palace and proclaimed in Latin: 'This is the Lord's doing: it is marvellous in our eyes.' If the chroniclers had been close at hand that hot June day in Richmond to capture George II's first words on hearing that he was now King, they might have been somewhat disappointed. There was no declaration of humility at God's greatness, nor was there a vow to serve his country with all his energy and passion. Instead, England's new King appeared first perplexed, then enraged, and at last spluttered: 'Dat is von big lie!' before prancing out of the room.

The rather bewildered Walpole was left struggling to haul himself back to his feet, having received scant reward for his eagerness to be the first to tell the royal couple these momentous tidings. Once he had recovered his senses, George told his minister to take his instructions from Sir Spencer Compton, speaker of the House of Commons and Treasurer of the Prince's household. As it was the chief minister's responsibility to make arrangements for the new government, the implication was that Walpole could consider himself dismissed from this office. His enemies were triumphant. William Pulteney was rumoured to have poisoned the Prince against his minister by blaming him for the humiliating terms of the reconciliation with the late King. Henrietta, a supporter of Compton, used her influence with the Prince to blacken Walpole's character still further. It was an easy task: George was minded to dislike any whom his late father had favoured. As he made his way back to London, filled with dismay at this sudden loss of power, Walpole could only hope that Caroline would use her accustomed wiles to persuade her husband of his folly.

George and Caroline now made hasty preparations to leave Richmond that afternoon. By the time they arrived at Leicester House, the courtyard was crowded with people, all anxious to pay homage to the new King and his consort. Lord Hervey, who had travelled with the royal party, described the scene. 'The square was thronged with multitudes of the meaner sort and resounded with huzzas and acclamations, whilst every room in the house was filled with people of the higher rank, crowding to kiss their hands and to make the earliest and warmest professions of zeal for their service.'[4]

For the ensuing four days, during which the royal couple were at their old residence, the crowds grew even greater, everyone present anxious to win favour and position. The contrast with the previous few years, when the house had been well and truly eclipsed by St James's, could not have been greater. 'Leicester House, that used to be a desert, was thronged from morning to night,' observed one courtier. It was with some amusement that Pope noted 'the strange spirit and life, with which men broken resume their hopes, their sollicitations, their ambitions', and urged a friend to join him in watching 'the fury and bustle of the Bees this hot season, without coming so near as to be stung by them'.[5]

Sir Spencer Compton basked in his newfound influence and popularity as eager politicians and courtiers beat a path to his door. He held receptions and supper parties that rivalled the new King's for splendour and elegance, and was gracious and charming to everyone he met. By contrast, Sir Robert Walpole, once so powerful at court, was treated like a social pariah. His ally, Lord Hervey, described how he walked through the public rooms at Leicester House 'as if they had still been empty', and observed: 'His presence, that used to make a crowd wherever he appeared, now emptied every corner he turned to, and the same people who were officiously a week ago clearing the way to flatter his prosperity, were now getting out of it to avoid sharing his disgrace.'[6] But Walpole was shrewd enough to know that the fickleness of a court that had been so quick to reject him could just as easily turn in his favour. Aware that his rival Compton, for all his charm, had not the ability to manage government effectively, he resolved to wait patiently for the tide to turn.

He did not have to wait for long. Compton's first official task was to draft the new King's speech for his Accession Council. It was a task to which he found himself unequal, and he begged Walpole to help him. Spying an opportunity to undermine his rival, Sir Robert readily agreed. Compton subsequently presented the finished speech to George as his own, but was dismayed when the King asked that part of it be revised. Knowing that he could not undertake this himself, he had to again summon Walpole to do it for him. His incompetence thus discovered, and the Queen having worked on her husband in the meantime, Compton's short-lived ascendancy in government was soon afterwards brought to an end. Walpole pushed home his advantage by offering to secure the King a vastly increased income from the Civil List. Appealing to George's greed was a sure way back to favour, but the minister now faced the considerable challenge of persuading Parliament to agree to the increase. Thanks to his oratory and manipulative skills, Walpole eventually succeeded, and the new sovereign was granted a staggering sum in excess of £900,000 per year. With Walpole thus restored to favour, the courtiers who had spurned him just a few days earlier now declared undying allegiance.

The collapse of Compton's brief ascendancy was the cause of some disappointment for the more loyal of his supporters, chief among whom were Henrietta and her friends Pulteney and Bolingbroke. According to Hervey, their own status at court declined as a result. 'His reputed mistress, Mrs Howard, and the speaker his reputed minister, were perceived to be nothing, and Mr Pulteney and Lord Bolingbroke ... less than nothing,' he wrote. 'It appeared very plain that His Majesty had no political regard for the first, no opinion of the capacity of the second, a dislike for the conduct of the third, and an abhorrence for the character of the last.'[7] This acerbic courtier was, however, very firmly in Caroline and Walpole's camp and was therefore apt to underplay the influence of their enemies at court.

In fact, George II's accession brought his mistress into much greater prominence than before and significantly enhanced her prestige. Although the extent of her influence was more ambiguous, this did little to dissuade the many who dismissed the Queen as a 'mere cypher', believing that 'the whole power and influence over the King was supposed to be lodged in the hands of Mrs Howard'. Her apartments were suddenly thronging with ambitious place-seekers, convinced that winning her favour was the surest means of securing advancement from the King. 'The busy and speculative politicians of the antechamber, who knew everything, but knew everything wrong, naturally concluded that a lady with whom the King passed so many hours every day must necessarily have some interest with him, and consequently applied to her,' observed her friend Lord Chesterfield.[8]

Applications came from every direction. Those who could not make it to court wrote to plead for Henrietta's favourable intervention. Lady Chetwynd expressed her profound regret at not being able to pay her respects to the Queen in person, especially as the posts that her husband had held during the late King's reign were now at risk. 'Unless their Majesty's by your kind intercession, shall shew us some mark of their Royall favour,' she wrote plaintively, 'we shall be obliged by necessity to find some other corner of the world to pass the remainder of our day's in.' Mrs Howard's distant kinsman, the Right Honourable Richard Hampden, complained of the persecution that he had suffered at Walpole's hands in the previous reign, which he claimed had left him heavily in debt. 'I humbly intreat to know if I am to expect wherewith to bye bread from this Royal Family,' he wrote, 'otherwise I must very soon take some service in some other family, to prevent my starving.' Another correspondent was the celebrated writer and poet Dr Edward Young, whose witty satires had kept Henrietta amused during many a long day at court, and who now sought something from her in return. 'If my case deserves some consideration, & you can serve me in it, I humbly hope, & believe you will,' he pleaded.

Others resorted to bribery in an attempt to win Mrs Howard's favour. This was a rather unwise policy, given the obvious contempt that she had shown for such base practices in the past – which was, admittedly, rare for a courtier. Some five years earlier, the Honourable Mrs Pitt, mother of the future Lord Chancellor, had offered her 1,000 guineas to secure her brother a post in the Prince of Wales's household. Her request had met with such a sharp rebuke that she had hastily written to beg forgiveness 'for ye freedom I have taken', adding that she had intended the money as a present rather than a bribe.

Henrietta gave similarly short shrift to any hint of financial reward made by her many petitioners upon George II's accession. One such offender was the Honourable Walter Molesworth, who wrote: 'I conceive that the late incident [George II's accession] has given you an increase of power, which may bear some proportion to the benevolence of your mind.' If she agreed to further his application for a Groom of the Bedchamber post, he promised 'whatever conditions or provisions you may annex to this favour'. His letter went unanswered, but its contents had so offended Henrietta that she made her displeasure known to

Molesworth's sister-in-law when she came to court. Chastened by the harsh words that he had heard second-hand, he wrote to beg forgiveness, assuring her that 'to shock your delicacy, as in common prudence it was not my business, could not consequently be my meaning'.⁹

Henrietta found all this attention overwhelming. It seemed that the sudden enhancement of her position at court had brought her anxiety rather than glory, for she feared that she would be unable to fulfil all – indeed, any – of the requests with which she was now besieged. The pressure sparked a recurrence of the severe headaches that she had begun to suffer during the previous few years. Her friend Martha Blount, to whom Pope had introduced her, wrote anxiously: 'I thought the kindest thing I could do was not to trouble you with any visits or letters, and I wish others had been as considerate of you, for the contrary (I hear) has had the effect I apprehend'd it would, of making you ill.'¹⁰

While Henrietta found the burden of her new prestige intolerable, her friends predicted that it would bring her great fortune and influence. Martha tried to lift her spirits by assuring her: 'I have rejoyced, and shall always, at every thing, that happens to your advantage.'¹¹ Others shared her optimism, if not her consideration. Jonathan Swift, who had hastened back to London upon hearing news of George II's accession, wrote to ask if Henrietta might approach the King to see whom he intended for the chancellorship of Dublin University. He assured his new friend that such was her current standing at court, that even the most tenuous association with her was sure to bring him favour. 'There are, madam, thousands in the world, who, if they saw your dog Fop use me kindly, would the next day in a letter tell me of the delight they heard I had in doing good; and, being assured that a word of mine to you would do anything, desire my interest to speak to you to speak to the Speaker [Sir Spencer Compton], to speak to Sir R. Walpole to speak to the King, etc.'¹² In the event, Henrietta was able to do little for him, and he returned to Ireland later that year, bitter in his disappointment.

As well as hoping for a position himself, Swift was also eager to see his friend John Gay in gainful employment. Gay had haunted the court for more than thirteen years, but while the royal family had delighted in his lively company, witty plays and irreverent satires, they had given him no material reward for his attendance. Now, though, with his friend Mrs Howard in such an influential position, there seemed a greater prospect of this than ever before. A post such as Lord of the Bedchamber to the King would have provided Gay with a regular

income and only the lightest of duties. Indeed, he could have afforded
to employ a servant to do most of these for him if he had wished.
Instead, however, he was offered one of the lowest-paid and least prestigious posts in the royal household: Gentleman Usher to Princess
Louisa, then a child of two years old. This was a studied insult on the
part of the Queen, who resented all the attention that her husband's
mistress was receiving and was determined to show the world where
the power really lay. She may also have been behind the King's refusal
to grant Swift his much-sought-after position.

Gay declined the post and withdrew from court. He told Pope and
Swift: 'now all my expectations are vanish'd; and I have no prospect,
but in depending wholly upon my self, and my own conduct', but added:
'As I am us'd to disappointments I can bear them, but as I can have
no more hopes, I can be no more disappointed, so that I am in a blessed
condition.'[13] Swift was rather less philosophical. In his disappointment
for himself and his friend, he railed against Henrietta for failing them
both. 'I always told you Mrs Howard was good for nothing but to be
a rank Courtier,' he wrote to Gay. 'I care not whether She ever writes
to me or no, She had Cheated us all, and may go hang her Self.'[14]

Gay, to his credit, begged Swift to treat their friend with more
justice and to realise that she had done everything in her power to help
them. But the Dean would have none of it. In vain, Henrietta's other
friends pleaded with him to see sense. Pope urged: 'that Lady means
to do good, and does no harm, which is a vast deal for a Courtier'.
His words met with a sharp rebuke from Swift, who declared: 'I take
Mr Pope and Mr Gay, who judge more favourably, to be a couple of
simpletons.'[15] Time did not lessen his resentment. In December 1731,
he told Gay: 'I have long hated her on your account, more because you
are So forgiving as not to hate her.'[16] As late as 1733, six years after the
event, he was still writing lengthy letters on the subject to his friends
back in England. One of these, Lady Betty Germain, was also a close
acquaintance of Henrietta, and the two were dining together when a
letter from Swift arrived. Upon scanning its contents, Lady Betty was
so shocked that she immediately hid it away in her pocket. She subsequently chastised him and reasoned: 'were it in people's power that live
in a Court with the appearance of favour to do all they desire for their
friends they might deserve their Anger & be blamed when it does not
happen right to their minds, but I believe never was the case with any
one'.[17]

Swift's cruelty towards Henrietta was not restricted to private correspondence. He also wrote a damning epistle and 'Character' of her,
which were later published. The first was addressed to Gay, and ran
thus:

How could you, Gay, disgrace the muse's train,
To serve a tasteless Court twelve years in vain!
Fain would I think our female friend [Henrietta] sincere,
'Till Bob [Sir Robert Walpole], the poet's foe, possess'd her ear.
Did female virtue e'er so high ascend,
To lose an inch of favour for a friend?
Say, had the Court no better place to choose
For thee, than make a dry-nurse of thy Muse?
How cheaply had thy liberty been sold,
To squire a royal girl of two years old:
In leading strings her infant steps to guide,
Or with her go-cart amble by her side!

The 'Character', meanwhile, was written before the Gentleman Usher
post had been offered to Gay, and was therefore prompted solely by
Swift's own disappointment. 'She abounds in good words and good
wishes, and will conduct a hundred scheams with those whom she
favours, in order to their advancement,' he wrote, 'although at the same
time she very well knows, that both are without the least probability
to succeed.' He concluded: 'her talents as a Courtier will spread, enlarge,
and multiply to such a degree, that her private virtues, for want of
room and time to operate, must be folded and layd up clean like cloaths
in a chest . . . it will be her prudence to take care that they may not be
tarnished or moth-eaten, for want of opening and airing and turning
at least once a year'.[18]

For a long time Henrietta remained patient and forgiving towards
Swift, despite his unjust treatment and false friendship. She continued
to press his cause with the Queen and to enquire after him through
their mutual friends. However, when after four years he was still making
bitter accusations and trying to incite her friends to desert her, she at
last retaliated. 'You seem to think that you have a Natural Right to
Abuse me because I am a Woman and a Courtier,' she wrote in
September 1731. 'I have taken it as a Woman and as a Courtier might,
with great resentment; and a determined resolution of Revenge.'

Referring to a recent controversy at court in which Swift had been
falsely accused of disloyalty to the Queen, she continued sardonically:
'Think of my Joy to hear you suspected of Folly, think of my Pleasure
when I enter'd the list for your justification. Indeed I was a little discon-
certed to find Mr Pope took the same side; for I wou'd have had the
Man of Wit, the Dignified Divine, the Irish Drapier have found no
friend but the Silly Woman, and the Courtier.' She concluded with one
last attempt at reconciliation. 'Am I to send back the Crown and Plad,
well pack'd up in my Character? Or am I to follow my own inclination, and continue very truely and very much your humble Servant.'[19]

But Swift could neither forgive nor forget what he saw as Mrs
Howard's callous disregard for her friends' advancement, and he went
to the grave hating her. This is in stark contrast to Gay, who soon got
over his disappointment and did not in any case blame her for it. He
was, indeed, to prove the most loyal of friends, and the two maintained
an affectionate correspondence for the rest of his days.

These were tense times for Henrietta. She knew that if she was retained
as both royal mistress and Woman of the Bedchamber after the
Coronation (which was traditionally the time when most people were
either reappointed or dismissed from their places), her position would
be a good deal more secure.

While Mrs Howard's future hung in the balance, work on her beloved
Marble Hill was called to an abrupt halt. Swift wrote a satirical 'dialogue'
between Marble Hill and Richmond Lodge, in which the former lamented:

My House was built but for a Show
My Lady's empty Pockets know:
And now she will not have a Shilling
To raise the Stairs, or build the Ceiling;
... No more the Dean [Swift], that grave Divine,
Shall keep the Key of my No-Wine;
My Ice-House rob, as heretofore,
And steal my Artichokes no more;
Poor Patty Blount no more be seen
Bedraggled in my Walks so green;
Plump Johnny Gay will now elope;
And here no more will dangle Pope.

Plans were already well underway for the Coronation, and the new King was determined that it should eclipse his late father's in every respect. He and Caroline ordered robes fashioned from purple velvet trimmed with ermine and wide gold braiding. The Queen Consort gathered together as many jewels as she could lay her hands on: not just her own, but those belonging to ladies of quality across London. Henrietta was closely involved in the preparations, along with the other Women of the Bedchamber, and as the Coronation drew closer, her hopes grew that she was now too indispensable to her mistress to be dismissed.

On the morning before the Coronation, the Queen's robes and jewels were carried to the Black Rod's Room at the House of Lords, which had been appointed for her dressing. All of her servants except the Women of the Bedchamber were dispatched there in the evening so that they could be ready to receive her. At last the day itself arrived. The eleventh of October 1727 dawned clear and bright, and extraordinarily warm for the time of year, which surely augured well for the new reign. Caroline rose early and, being in a state of 'undress', was conveyed in secret to the House of Lords. Mrs Howard, who followed in a hackney chair, noted that particular care was taken that 'it should not be suspected when her Majesty passed the Park'. Once there, she and the other Women of the Bedchamber busied themselves with dressing their mistress in her state robes. The Queen's magnificent gown was so weighed down with jewels that she later complained it had fatigued her greatly to walk about in it.[20]

The elaborate ceremony of the dressing over, Caroline was escorted to Westminster Hall to join her husband. The procession to the Abbey began at noon, and the crowds that had been gathering since dawn were overawed by the spectacle. 'No words (at least that I can command), can describe the magnificence my eyes beheld,' wrote Mrs Pendarves, who had managed to position herself by the doors of Westminster Hall.[21] The procession included everyone from the young women appointed to scatter sweet-smelling herbs and flowers at their majesties' feet, to kettle-drummers, choir boys, heralds, sheriffs, peers and peeresses, bishops, earls and dukes.

Beneath a glittering canopy made from gold cloth adorned with tiny gold and silver balls and bells walked the Queen in her jewel-encrusted gown, which 'threw out a surprising radiance', literally dazzling the spectators. Her train was borne by the three royal princesses, who were dressed in gowns of purple velvet and ermine, trimmed with silver. They were followed by four ladies of the Queen's household, including Mrs Howard and her fellow Woman of the Bedchamber Mary Herbert. Their gowns were so splendid that one onlooker claimed they were 'the two finest figures of all the procession'.[22] Henrietta was dressed in scarlet, which was perhaps intended to single her out as the King's official mistress, for it was not a colour that she usually chose to wear. Her gown was lined with richly embossed silver, and her long hair was worn loose about her shoulders.

At the end of the procession came the King himself. Drawing his rather squat frame up to its fullest possible height, he strutted out in the magnificent robes of state that had been made for the occasion. But for all his efforts, he could not escape the vague hint of ridiculousness that so often marked his public appearances. After the cool shelter of Westminster Hall, the unseasonably warm October sunshine came as something of a shock, and he soon became uncomfortably hot in the heavy velvet and thick ermine of his robes. He therefore retreated ever further under the canopy above him as the procession went on – so much so that the crowds complained they could not see him. To make matters worse, his crimson velvet cap, which was also lined with ermine, was too large for him and kept falling over his eyes. By the time the procession finally reached the Abbey, his notoriously short temper was on the verge of boiling over.[23]

Fortunately, the coronation ceremony itself passed without incident. After all the customary prayers, oaths and sermons, the King was presented with the royal orb and sceptre and, as he knelt before the Archbishop, the crown of state was lowered on to his head. 'A visible satisfaction was diffused over every countenance as soon as the coronet was clapped on the head,' observed Lady Mary Wortley Montagu, who was among the congregation. The shouts of the guests and the sounding of trumpets within the Abbey provided the signal for the great guns in St James's Park and the Tower of London to be fired. After the *Te Deum* had been sung, the Queen advanced for her coronation, flanked by Mrs Howard and three other women of her household. Together they removed her velvet cap and stood ready to pin the crown into place once it had been set there by the Archbishop of Canterbury. This done, the royal couple made their way to the nearby thrones and received Holy Communion.

It was almost three o'clock in the afternoon when the ceremonies ended and the procession was ready to return to the great hall of Westminster. Here a sumptuous banquet had been prepared for the King and Queen and their three hundred or so guests. The galleries up above were open to the public, and thousands had queued for hours to secure a place. Mrs Pendarves was among them, having been at the hall since half past four that morning. Despite making such an early start, she had found herself amongst 'so violent a crowd that for some minutes I lost my breath, (and my cloak I doubt for ever)', and claimed: 'I verily believe I should have been squeezed as flat as a pancake if providence had not sent Mr Edward Stanley to my relief.' After a great struggle, she eventually managed to secure a good vantage point 'without any damage than a few bruises in my arms and the loss of my cloak'.[24]

Mrs Pendarves, and the hundreds of others who crowded into the galleries, were richly rewarded for their endeavours. The hall had been lavishly decorated for the occasion. It was illuminated by more than 1,800 candles, their effect made even more dazzling by the gilded branches on which they were suspended. Thanks to the expert organisation of the Master of Ceremonies, Master Heidegger, within three minutes of the King arriving at the hall, all of these were lit and everyone in the room was filled with astonishment at this 'wonderful and unexpected illumination'.[25]

At the top of the room was a raised dais on which sat the newly crowned King, his Queen Consort, and their family. Beneath them were the nobility and other persons of quality, all dressed in rich and brightly coloured gowns and suits, who sat along tables arranged in neat rows stretching the length of the hall. As the aroma of the roasted meats, spiced game and other delectable dishes from the sumptuous feast floated up to the galleries above, many spectators, who had been on their feet for twelve hours or more, almost fainted away with hunger. Taking pity on them, some of the noble guests seated below filled their napkins with food and hoisted them up on ropes made from knotted garters.

When the feast and ceremonies were over, the royal family retired, followed by their attendants and guests, and were carried back to St James's 'very fatigued and weary'. As soon as all the guests had departed, the great doors of the hall were thrown open, and the huge crowds that had gathered outside were allowed to take possession of the remains of the banquet – including not just the food, but the table linen, plates, dishes, cutlery and anything else they could lay their hands on. Watching from the galleries above, Charles de Saussure described what followed. 'The pillage was most diverting; the people threw themselves with extraordinary avidity on everything the hall contained; blows were given and returned, and I cannot give you any idea of the noise and confusion that reigned. In less than half an hour everything had disappeared, even the boards of which the tables and seats had been made.'[26]

It was as if the celebrations and festivities, the cheers and emotion with which the people of England had greeted their new Hanoverian King had been but a dream.

Chapter 11

'The Indissolvable Knot'

———————◁○▷———————

THE CORONATION OVER, GEORGE II and his consort soon settled back into the routine of court life that they had established as Prince and Princess of Wales. The euphoria with which the people of London had greeted their new King and Queen soon disappeared, however, and in the cold light of day their appraisal of them was rather less favourable than it had been in the warm October sunshine outside Westminster Abbey. Ironically, for all the bitter hatred that he had felt towards his father, George was coming to resemble him more and more in both opinions and behaviour. 'Dunce the second reigns like Dunce the first,' sneered Pope in a poem published soon after the Coronation. The lofty professions of admiration for the English people and their country that he had aired so often as Prince were now shown to be false, and he began to demonstrate a bias towards Hanover that even his father would have been proud of.

As George's eyes were cast in the direction of his homeland, his English subjects began to resent the enormous allowance that had been bestowed on their avaricious King from the Civil List, and the heavy burden of taxation that had come with it. There were mutterings that all he cared about was 'money and Hanover', and their respect for him was further diminished by the fact that he seemed to be unwittingly dominated by his wife. Rumours of her manipulation had been circulating around the court for some time, and now spilled out into the coffee houses and taverns of London. The subject proved excellent fodder for the pamphleteers and poets. A particularly popular verse ran:

You may strut, dapper George, but 'twill all be in vain:
We know 'tis Queen Caroline, not you, that reign –
You govern no more than Don Philip of Spain.
Then if you would have us fall down and adore you,
Lock up your fat spouse, as your Dad did before you.

This was soon picked up by the staff at St James's, and before long the whole court was sniggering about it. When at last it reached the King's own ears, he was so furious that he stamped up and down, his face ablaze, and spluttered a series of oaths, half German, half English, making himself even more ridiculous than he appeared in the verse. He demanded that the traitorous author be brought before him. Information was surprisingly unforthcoming, however, and the culprit remained at large.

There was more of a grain of truth in the lines that had caused such hilarity. Caroline's ascendancy, cultivated by Walpole while she was Princess, was greatly strengthened now that she was Queen. 'The whole world began to find out that her will was the sole spring on which every movement in the Court turned,' observed Lord Hervey. 'Her power was unrivalled and unabounded.'[1] Meanwhile, *The Craftsman*, the most prominent opposition newspaper, likened Caroline's machinations to a game of chess, with Walpole as the knight: 'see him jump over the heads of the nobles . . . when he is guarded by the Queen, he makes dreadful havoc, and very often checkmates the King'.[2]

Caroline knew that the only way to govern her husband was to give every appearance of being utterly subservient to his will. 'Tho his affection and confidence in her were implicit, he lived in dread of being supposed to be governed by Her,' observed Horace Walpole. He went on to describe the 'silly parade' which she and his father, Sir Robert, would orchestrate in order to hide their collaboration from the King. Whenever the latter found them together in conversation, the Queen would immediately rise and curtsey, and meekly offer to leave the room so that the men could continue their business without the distraction of a silly woman. Sometimes George was content for her to retire, but more often than not he condescendingly bade her to stay. Either way, she invariably succeeded in persuading him of the wisdom of their chief minister's advice, but in such a way that he believed he had arrived at that opinion of his own accord.[3]

The King may have been duped by his wife's clever manipulation, but it was all too obvious to the rest of the court. 'She managed this deified image,' observed Lord Hervey with some admiration, 'as the heathen priests used to do the oracles of old, when, kneeling and prostrate before the altars of a pagan god, they received with the greatest devotion and reverence those directions in public which they had before instilled and regulated in private.' Her husband was so blissfully unaware that he was being hoodwinked by his wife and minister that he made himself increasingly ridiculous to those who knew better by boasting that he reigned supreme. On one occasion, he treated an assembly of courtiers to a proud speech about the superiority of his power compared with that of his predecessors. Charles I had been governed by his wife, he claimed, Charles II by his mistresses, James II by his priests and William III by his men. Worst of all, his father had been governed by 'anyone who could get at him'. At the end of this address, he turned to his smirking audience and, with a self-satisfied and triumphant air, demanded: 'And who do they say governs now?' They remained politely silent.[4]

Jealous of her power and alive to anything that threatened it, Caroline seemed bent on ensuring that her will held sway throughout the court. But the wily courtiers were not to be so easily fooled as the King, and Caroline lacked the subtlety to bring them all under her influence. They were careful enough to flatter her vanity, however, and make her think that they obeyed her. Thus she was played at her own game. 'The Queen's greatest error was too high an opinion of her own address and art,' observed Horace Walpole. 'She imagined that all who did not dare to contradict her, were imposed upon; & She had the additional weakness of thinking that she could play off many persons without being discovered.'[5]

Henrietta knew the Queen's tactics all too well. Wary of the enhancement of the mistress's prestige after George's accession, Caroline did everything she could to restrict her influence. Not content with preventing Mrs Howard's close friends from gaining their sought-after positions at court, she undermined those who already had places in the household and implied that her husband's mistress was unfaithful to him politically as well as sexually. Caroline was particularly vindictive towards Lord Chesterfield, one of her husband's Gentlemen of the Bedchamber, who she knew made fun of her in his poems and puns. Chesterfield was fond of gambling, and one night at court he won such a large sum of money that he asked Henrietta if she could keep it safe in her apartments. The door to these was visible to the Queen from her own rooms, courtesy of an 'obscure window ... that looked into a dark passage, lighted only by a single lamp at night'. Having witnessed Chesterfield's furtive entry into her Woman of the Bedchamber's apartments, Caroline went at once to tell the King that the pair were conducting an illicit affair. Enraged by such an underhand betrayal, George ensured that the Earl would henceforth receive no favour at court. Chesterfield was subsequently dispatched to the Hague, where he languished in virtual exile for five years as ambassador.

Caroline was aware that an increasing number of dissident Whigs and Tories were flocking to Mrs Howard's evening supper parties, among them the powerful Lord Bolingbroke and William Pulteney, and she was anxious to ensure that Henrietta did not succeed in winning favour for them with the King. The advantage that her Woman of the Bedchamber had secured in helping Compton to triumph over Walpole in the early days of George II's reign may have been short-lived, but it had served as a warning to Caroline, and she was anxious to avoid any such disruption to her plans in future. Lord Chesterfield recorded how she would therefore make the mistress feel her inferiority by preventing the King from visiting her room for three or four days at a time, 'representing it as the seat of a political faction'.[6]

Whether it was due to the Queen's tactics or George's own inclinations, Henrietta's relationship with him was visibly deteriorating within a few short weeks of the Coronation. He was impatient with her in public, and although he continued his evening visits with the same clockwork regularity as before, he seemed to derive little pleasure from them. Rumours of a rift began to spread beyond the court, and soon even her friends in the country heard of it. Henrietta tried to play them down by saying that the King's coldness towards her was due not to a decline of his affection but rather to his natural shortness of temper, which he displayed with many other people at court. But this only served to make her friends more suspicious that something was badly wrong between them. 'I very much applaud your discretion on retiring when-ever you beheld the clouds gather,' wrote Lady Hervey from Ickworth, 'but I own I suspect you of bragging when you tell me of avoiding the sunshine; to my certain knowledg that is a precaution that has long been unnecessary, so indeed my dear madam that sun had not darted one beam on you a great while, you may freeze in the dog days for all the warmth you'll find from our Sol.'[7]

Henrietta's company and conversation, which had previously been so diverting for the King, seemed to be an increasing source of irritation, and he began to find fault in everything she did. On one occasion, a year after the Coronation, she unwittingly said something to cause offence when they were walking together in the gardens at St James's. This met with such a furious rebuke from the King that she feared she had been dismissed altogether. 'I beg to know ... how soon it will be agreeable to you that I leave your famely,' she wrote to him afterwards, 'for with the utmost respect permitt me to say; that from your Majesty's behaviour to me, it is impossible not to think my removal from your presence must be most aggreable to your inclinations.' She was clearly still perplexed as to what had sparked his fury, and pleaded: 'as I am very sensible that I am under your displeasure, so I am intirely ignorant in what manner I have incurr'd it'. In desperation, she tried to win back his favour by stressing the longevity of their attachment and her unswerving loyalty to him throughout it. 'Were I allow'd to pursue the same way in thinking of your Majesty that I have for fourteen years past; I shou'd then think it impossible that such a tryfle cou'd wear out the remembrance of a fourteen year attachment with unwearied duty, and respect for you.'[8] She evidently succeeded on this occasion, and the King gave no indication that he wished to discontinue her as his mistress.

The courtiers who seized upon the King's increasing display of short temper with Henrietta as a complete loss of favour were either misguided or mischievous. The source of most of these rumours can be traced back to Lord Hervey, who despite being married to Henrietta's close friend Molly, was very firmly in the Queen's camp and therefore always quick to discredit her rival whenever he had the opportunity. George had retained Henrietta as his mistress for almost a decade, which was longer than any of his previous mistresses. What was more, he had continued to spend a great deal of time with her – between three and four hours every evening, as well as occasional meetings in the day – during most of which the couple had been alone together. It should not, therefore, be too surprising that once the novelty of the situation had worn off, and any initial burst of passion had cooled, the King was more inclined to display his natural short-temperedness with her. Indeed, the Queen, whom he undoubtedly loved very deeply, had been the subject of his wrath on numerous occasions, and he had often reduced her to tears in front of the whole court. The ebbs and flows of this choleric little man's humour should not, therefore, be taken as reliable proof of which way his affections lay.

Nevertheless, even a temporary loss of favour was unsettling for Henrietta, who still relied heavily on her position at court to save her from ruin. This was therefore the worst possible moment for her estranged husband to begin a fresh onslaught.

Charles Howard had been put out of his place upon the death of George I, and as a result was now more desperate for money than ever. His brother Edward was still pestering him for the £1,200 that he had agreed to pay him each year as part of their recent court settlement. Added to this were the spiralling debts that he was accruing from his expensive habits. As was his custom, rather than seeking to pay these off through honourable means, Howard chose to persecute his wife until she would agree to give him the money he needed.

Like so many others at court, Charles believed that now Henrietta was mistress to a king rather than a mere prince, she would be in a much better position to assist him. He therefore renewed his campaign against her with even greater vigour than before. This time, he had no patience for putting his demands in writing: his wife had proved that he was no match for her when it came to reasoned and protracted debate. Neither was he prepared to use the law or the Church to further his cause, as both had proved inadequate in the past. Instead, he opted for a far more peremptory (and familiar) course of action: violence.

Late one night, after the court had retired, he forced his way into the inner courtyard of St James's and shouted his demands so loudly that the whole palace was woken from their slumbers. Before the guards could seize him, he broke into the royal quarters and succeeded in reaching the apartments of the Queen herself. Startled by this sudden intrusion, she demanded to know what Howard's business was. Unabashed, he told her that he would have his wife leave her service and return to him at once. He added that if he was not permitted to do so that very night, then he would seize Henrietta from Her Majesty's coach the next time the royal family ventured out.

Caroline was not a woman to be cowed by such threats, and retorted that he might 'do it if he dare'. For all her bravado, however, she was clearly alarmed at being alone with such a notoriously volatile man as Howard, and later confessed to Lord Hervey: 'I was horribly afraid of him ... all the while I was thus playing the bully. What added to my fear upon this occasion ... was that I knew him to be so brutal, as well as a little mad, and seldom quite sober, so I did not think it impossible that he might throw me out of the window.' Anxious for her own safety, she edged closer to the door so that she might make her escape if he became violent. Feeling more secure, she told him very firmly that she would neither force his wife to go to him if she had no mind to it, nor keep her if she had. Charles retorted that he would apply instead to the King, which irked Caroline so much that she told him to save himself the trouble 'as I was sure the King would give him no answer but that it was none of his business to concern himself with my family'.⁹ At this point, the palace guards burst into the room and removed Howard by force.

Henrietta was mortified when she heard of the incident. Anxiety that it would exhaust what little patience the King had left with her combined with terror that her husband would strike again. The bitter irony of her situation was not lost on her. As Lord Hervey neatly put it: 'A husband ordered her home who did not desire to have her there, and a lover was to retain her who seemed already tired of keeping her.' It was an intolerable position to be in, and the part that she now had to act was 'equally extraordinary, difficult and disagreeable'.¹⁰

In desperation she abandoned her customary discretion and poured out all her fears and torment in a letter to her old friend Alexander Pope. He was so aghast upon receiving this that he wrote back to her by return of post, offering all the words of comfort and support that he could think of. 'I do not Only *Say* that I have a True Concern for you: Indeed I feel it, many times, very many, when I say it not. I wish to God any method were *soon* taken to put you out of this uneasy, discomforting situation.' Although it must have seemed an unlikely prospect to him, he urged his friend to take comfort from the thought that her husband's outrageous behaviour might turn their son against him, and thereby make him reflect that 'possibly his Mother may be yet worse used than himself'. But Pope knew Mrs Howard well enough to realise that all this must be having a devastating effect upon her. 'You, that I know feel even to Delicacy, upon several triffling occasions, must (I am sensible) do it to a deep degree, upon one so near & so tender to you.'¹¹

His fears were realised, for within a matter of days the sorry affair had taken its toll on his friend's health. She was struck down with such violent pains in the head that she was forced to take to her bed for several weeks. Even after she returned to her duties in the Queen's household, the headaches continued to plague her. 'I have been in the most exquisite [pain] for many days,' she wrote to Chesterfield in the Hague, 'which left so sensible a feeling for some weeks that I could attend to nothing else.' Frustrated by his inability to help her from such a distance, the Earl tried to lift her spirits with a series of witty letters on the subject of her illness. 'I can't help being very angry at your head for having given us both so much pain,' he wrote. 'I have known some Ladys heads very troublesome to others but at the same time very easy to themselves; yours is just the reverse.' Henrietta was still suffering the after-effects of her illness the following summer, and Dr Arbuthnot wrote to express his anxiety that she had not fully recovered.[12]

These were miserable times for Henrietta, worn down as she was by ill health and frustrated by the confinement that Charles's threats made necessary. The King's obvious impatience with her and the Queen's skilful manipulation of them both had turned her life at court into a relentless ordeal. Added to this was the knowledge that Marble Hill – the source of so much joy and hope just a few months before – now stood empty and unfinished. Even if she had had the money to complete it, she could not risk leaving the safety of the court and settling there, because she was bound to fall straight into her husband's hands.

Thwarted by the guards at St James's and by his wife's powerful protectors at court, Argyll and Ilay, from forcing his way into Henrietta's presence, Charles resorted to tormenting her with letters and messages. One evening, when she was with her friends Gay and Arbuthnot in her apartments at St James's, their light-hearted conversation was rudely interrupted by a messenger from her husband. He announced that he had come to secure Henrietta's agreement to pay Charles's brother the annual sum of £1,200, and that as he was due to dine with his master later that evening, he required her immediate response. At turns embarrassed and angered by this intrusion, she told him that she would not meddle in anything that related to the brothers' agreement about the Suffolk estate. The man pressed her further, however, saying that as well as the £1,200, her husband demanded that she settle the interest from her £4,000 inheritance on their son. Henrietta knew full well that doing so would be as good as handing it over to Charles himself, and absolutely refused. She added that she had 'starv'd with Mr H, & would not put herself in a circumstance to starve without him'. To this, the messenger responded that his master had 'not above four hundred a year'. Henrietta threw back that she had 'not many times, while with him, known where to get four hundred pence'.[13]

This incident threw the misery of Henrietta's situation into sharp relief. Not since the early days of her marriage had she felt so trapped. She confided to her lawyer and close friend, James Welwood, that she found it utterly impossible ever to live with her husband again, but equally so to resign her position at court, 'which service defends me from that poverty and want and that more insoportable misfortune of being illtreated'.[14] Feeling increasingly isolated at court, and being perpetually tormented by her husband, Mrs Howard began to consider taking the radical and, for the time, shocking step of suing for a legal separation.

In the early eighteenth century, marriage was very much considered to be for life. Except in the most extreme cases, once the wedding vows had been exchanged, there was no going back. Both the law and society forbade it. Contemporary tracts referred to marriage as an 'indissolvable Knot', and those women who dared to voice dissatisfaction with their lot were dismissed as vain and ungrateful. 'The Institution of Marriage is too sacred to admit a Liberty of objecting to it,' one nobleman warned his daughter. 'You are therefore to make the best of what is settled by Law and Custom, and not vainly imagine, that it will be changed for your sake.' The author of 'The Real Causes of Conjugal Infidelity and Unhappy Marriages', meanwhile, laid the blame of such troubles firmly at the door of 'the too great Liberty allowed our Women'.[15]

Only a very small number of women dared openly to criticise the unfairness of the situation. Mary Astell was one of the most vocal, and railed against a system in which 'Wives may be made Prisoners for Life at the Discretion of their Domestick Governors'. But such women were seen as blasphemous troublemakers; the product of too much learning and too little authority. Any man who sided with them was similarly shunned by society. One of these rare types was the author Daniel Defoe, who in 1724 published 'The Great Law of Subordination'. In this he claimed that 'the case of women in England is truly deplorable, and there is scarce a good husband now to twenty that merited that name in former times; nor was beating of wives ever so much the usage in England, as it is now'.[16]

Domestic violence was wholly disregarded by the law as being sufficient grounds for separation or divorce: indeed, most men hardly viewed
it as grounds for complaint. As late as 1753, the law still dictated: 'If
the wife be injured in her person or her property, she can bring no
action for redress without her husband's concurrence, and in his name,
as well as her own.'[17] Divorce was in fact such a rare and extreme
measure that it took an Act of Parliament to bring it about. From the
mid-seventeenth to the mid-nineteenth century, only four divorces were
obtained by women, and all involved extraordinary expense, trauma,
and – ultimately – disgrace. Even the less extreme legal actions were
similarly beset with difficulty. Annulments were so staggeringly unusual
that the very word would have been little understood in the context of
marriage. Another option was legal separation, but to gain this a female
petitioner had to go through the church courts and prove both adultery and life-threatening cruelty.

There was a third, slightly less problematic, alternative which was
to draw up a private deed of separation – in effect, an 'informal divorce'.
This latter option was by far the most common, though compared to
the number of women who chose to stay in their miserable marriages,
it was still very rare. Again there were powerful social prohibitions
against it, and the legal and financial risks were considerable. In most
cases, the wife would forfeit any income she might have from real estate,
as well as any future earnings or legacies, all her personal property, and
– worst of all – custody of any children. Indeed, the most vindictive
husbands could claim the right to total control over their children and
exclude their wives from even seeing them, let alone influencing their
upbringing. Charles Howard was already exercising this right to the full,
and there was absolutely no reason to expect that he would change his
behaviour if legal action was brought against him. The only way to
minimise the risks involved in these informal divorces was to secure
the best possible legal representation and draw up a very carefully
worded deed of separation.

Henrietta must have felt that in James Welwood she had the former
safeguard, and driven to desperation by her intolerable situation, she
instructed him to begin proceedings. Dispatching the letter in secret,
she urged him 'to have some body prepose to Mr H. to Enter into
articles', so that in future 'it may not be in the power of our Enemies
again to Torment us'. She added that as a meeting was both imprac-
tical and inadvisable under the circumstances, he must instead write to

her with his thoughts on 'this project of negotiating with Mr Howard for a separation'.[18] Perhaps not surprisingly, there is no trace of Welwood's response in the family papers, but he evidently agreed with his client's suggested course of action, for he subsequently began preparing the ground.

Welwood already had Mrs Howard's own testimony about her marriage, because earlier that year she had written a long and detailed account of it in a letter to her husband, and had wisely kept a copy for herself. It is clear from this that she was already considering legal proceedings at this time. 'You urge ye marriage Duty which I have perform'd and you have violated,' she argued. 'Ignorant as I am I must tell you yt there are circumstances which have at least suspended my Duty towards you who have made marriage an instrument of cruelty and have otherwise broken those laws you now vainly plead.' The letter ends with a reasoned, but rather inaccurate, claim that through his abusive behaviour he had forfeited any right to use the law against her. 'I am bound to preserve my life by a law superior to any claim of a husband, and I must tell you yt one who has broke other parts of his Matrimonial vow, has no right to possess himself of his wifes person.'[19]

Compelling though this account was, Welwood knew that on its own it was insufficient to prove Howard's infidelity and violence beyond doubt. For this, he would need to secure testimonies from independent witnesses, which was no easy task. The Howards had been living apart for over a decade, and during the early years of their marriage, Henrietta had been so humiliated by her husband's drunkenness and womanising that she had done her best to hide their situation from the world. Added to this was the fact that legal separation was so frowned upon that most people would have shied away from getting involved in any way. Thanks to sheer persistence, however, Welwood was eventually able to track down two credible witnesses who were willing to put such considerations aside.

Mrs Anne Hall and Mrs Anne Cell had been landlady and neighbour respectively to the Howards when they had lived in cheap lodgings in Soho. Their testimonies provided damning evidence against Charles. Both women told of his violence, cruelty and insobriety; that he would often reduce his wife to tears with his harsh words and even harsher actions, and that while he frittered away their money on his sordid habits, she would suffer 'as poor & as mean a manner as she could possibly be left to live in'. By contrast, Mrs Howard, they said, always behaved in 'ye most Obliging Courteous & Obedient manner', and never did anything to provoke or deserve her husband's ill treatment.[20]

Welwood could not have wished for more compelling testimonies than these. The two women had simultaneously upheld his client's character while damning that of her husband, and, crucially, their accounts tallied exactly with Henrietta's own. But he was not to enjoy the satisfaction of reading them, for no sooner had he dispatched his clerk to take their statements than he was struck down by a sudden illness and died. Henrietta was distraught. Not only was her legal separation now thrown into jeopardy, but she had lost a dear and trusted friend who had served her faithfully for many years.

In her grief, she cast about for allies at court. Thomas, 1st Baron Trevor, was Lord Privy Seal and a distinguished jurist. He was distantly related to Henrietta, for his grandfather, John Hampden, 'The Patriot', was her great-grandfather. At what stage Mrs Howard sought his intervention in her marital dispute is not clear, but he was certainly assiduous on her behalf. Without the formidable legal brain of James Welwood, she felt much less confident in pursuing her case through the law alone. She therefore resorted to the one thing that she knew her husband valued above all others: money. Having precious little of this herself, she urged Lord Trevor to seek her royal mistress's help in the matter. He duly secured an audience with the Queen and humbly requested that she pay Charles Howard the £1,200 in order to retain his wife in her service. His request was given short shrift. Caroline began by pleading poverty, saying that although she would do anything to 'keep so good a servant as Mrs Howard about me', she really could not afford such a sum. She later confessed to Lord Hervey that she had greatly resented this application, considering that it was 'a little too much not only to keep the King's guenipes . . . under my roof, but to pay them too'.[21]

The Queen's outright refusal to help, coupled with the fact that Henrietta had not applied to her in person, shows how hostile relations now were between the two women. Whether this prompted Henrietta to dispense with intermediaries and apply directly to her royal master is not certain. But against all the odds, the notoriously frugal King came to her rescue. On his orders, her annual allowance was increased by £1,200, thereby enabling her to pay her husband the exact sum that he demanded. An agreement was subsequently drawn up that provided Charles with an annuity during the lifetime of his brother, the 8th Earl of Suffolk. Thus, as Lord Hervey gleefully observed, 'this affair ended, the King paying the £1,200 a year for the possession of what he did not enjoy, and Mr Howard receiving them, for relinquishing what he would have been sorry to keep'.[22]

Bitter experience had taught Henrietta that money alone could not keep Charles at bay for long, however, and that he would soon fritter it away in the taverns and whorehouses of London. She therefore resumed the proceedings for a legal separation, confident in the knowledge that this time she had the means to make her husband agree to it. Her old friend the Duke of Argyll took up the case that Dr Welwood had so ably prepared, and instructed his lawyers to draft a deed of separation. They more than earned their fee, for the resulting document was so carefully worded and impenetrable that in signing it Charles Howard would have to relinquish all future claims to his wife and her money.

The deed opened with a declaration that 'henceforth during their joint Lives there shall be a Totall and Absolute Separation between them'. The pages that followed were filled with precise instructions and strictures that Mr Howard was to abide by in relation to his wife, notably that he must not 'by any means or on any pretence whatsoever claime seize Restrain or detain' her. Furthermore, he was to be as cut off from her purse as he was from her person, and every possible income, property or possession that Henrietta owned or might own in the future (apart from the £1,200 allowance) was to be kept well beyond his reach. Such resources were to be employed by Mrs Howard as she chose, and in return she was to forfeit any claim to her husband's fortune, such as it was. Above all, though, she was to be at liberty to 'Reside and Inhabit at her free will and pleasure in such place or places as she will see fitt in the same manner as if she was sole'.[23]

Thus drafted, the deed was passed to Charles's lawyers for their consideration. Their client objected to just one clause, but it was a significant one: that neither Henrietta nor her representatives could execute any further deeds or acts to consolidate the separation. Taken to their ultimate conclusion, these acts could have enabled the instigation of divorce proceedings, and this he was determined to thwart. Undoubtedly it was a desire to keep one final thread, however fine, in place so that his wife could never feel completely free of him, rather than any more sentimental feelings, that drove him to do so. Anxious to bring the matter to a swift conclusion, Henrietta agreed to his demand, and the words 'except his consenting or agreeing to a Divorce' were added to the clause, interlined between the original text.

The deed of separation was signed by Charles and Henrietta Howard on 29 February 1728, almost twenty-two years to the day since they had exchanged their wedding vows at St Benet's Church. Their miserable, destructive marriage was at last at an end.

Henrietta's relief was overwhelming. She could hardly believe that the heavy burden of fear under which she had laboured for so many years had finally been lifted. Her friends were overjoyed to witness the transformation in her. 'She is happier than I have ever seen her,' John Gay wrote to Swift a few days later, 'for she is free as to her conjugal affairs by articles of agreement.' Martha Blount concurred. 'Mrs Howard is well, and happier than ever you saw her,' she told Pope, 'for her whole affair with her husband is ended to her satisfaction.'[24]

Her joy was compounded the following year when work on her beloved Thames-side villa was finally completed. The King's additional allowance, coupled with the separation, had freed her from her husband's debts and given her a much greater measure of financial security. She was therefore able to instruct her architect, Roger Morris, to resume his work at Marble Hill. Substantial progress had been made by the end of 1728, and the 'Principall Story, two sweepe Wall and 4 Buildings in the Garden' had all been finished. Henrietta was now able to turn her attention to the interior furnishings, and was delighted when her friend Lord Chesterfield wrote to her from the Hague to say that he had spied 'an extream fine Chinese bed, window Curtains, Chairs, & c.' for sale at a very reasonable price. He assured her: 'If you should have a mind to it for Marble Hill, and can find any way of getting it over; I will with a great deal of pleasure obey your commands.' A few months later, the finishing touches to the exterior were made, and on 24 June 1729 Henrietta settled the final account of £763 for 'the finnishing all workes . . . and all Demands'.[25]

Mrs Howard's satisfaction at the completion of Marble Hill, a project that had taken more than six years and overcome many obstacles along the way, must have been great indeed. But it must also have been tempered by the frustration that she was not at liberty to enjoy her new retreat. The Queen showed no inclination to release her from service; indeed, she seemed to derive great satisfaction from the knowledge that her husband was tiring of his ageing mistress. If anything, this made her more determined than ever to ensure that she remained at the palace so that he would not be able to find a more alluring replacement.

Thus, even though the past year had given Henrietta much greater independence than ever before, she was still tied to a life that had ceased to bring her any joy. Moreover, she could no longer comfort herself with the knowledge that it was necessary for her survival: with Charles Howard being as good as out of the picture, she did not need her position at court to protect her.

The letters she wrote to her friends betray her growing restlessness and frustration, and the entertaining accounts of their own lives away from court made her even more wistful. 'I am glad you have past your time so agreeably,' she wrote to Gay during one of his jaunts to Bath, adding: 'I need not tell you how mine has been employ'd.' To Swift, she lamented: 'I have been a Slave 20 years without ever receiving a reason for any one thing I ever was oblig'd to do,' and concluded: 'I wou'd take your giddiness, your head-ake or any other complaint you have, to resemble you in one circumstance in life.'[26]

It was to be some considerable time before Mrs Howard was finally granted her wish.

Chapter 12

'Comforting the King's Enemies'

———◁◦▷———

IN 1729, WHEN HENRIETTA reached the age of forty, she should have been enjoying the fruits of her long struggle for independence. She had finally succeeded in ridding herself of her violent husband, who had been a thorn in her side for more than twenty years. She had also built a splendid home for herself away from court. But life at St James's had long since lost its appeal.

'No mill-horses ever went in a more constant, true or a more unchanging circle', complained Lord Hervey, 'so that by the assistance of an almanack for the day of the week and a watch for the hour of the day, you may inform yourself fully, without any other intelligence but your memory, of every transaction within the verge of the Court.'[1] George II's love of routine had set the tenor of life at his court ever since his residence at Leicester House, and while the round of receptions, balls and other formal occasions that he had established as Prince of Wales were diverting enough at first, after more than twelve years they were driving virtually everyone at court to distraction.

The days were filled with levees, walks or formal audiences, while the evenings were taken up with drawing rooms, balls, assemblies, or more low-key entertainments such as cards. While the public drawing rooms and assemblies afforded the opportunity of conversing with one's friends or making new acquaintances, the crowds that thronged into the palace often made these stiflingly hot and (eighteenth-century hygiene not being particularly advanced) malodorous affairs. 'There was dice, dancing, crowding, sweating and stinking in abundance as usual,' complained Lord Hervey after returning from one such gathering.

For the privileged few who were also required to attend the private

evenings, these occasions were purgatory. They could set their watches
by the time that the King sat down to quadrille or commerce, and
would look on in almost mournful silence as he continued to play for
the requisite number of hours, oblivious to the boredom of his guests
and attendants. The Duke of Grafton would routinely doze off after
an hour or so, remaining in that condition for the rest of the evening.
Lord Grantham, meanwhile, would try to stave off tedium by wandering
from room to room 'like some discontented ghost, that oft appears,
and is forbid to talk', and moved about 'as people stir a fire not with
any design in the placing, but in hopes to make it burn a little brighter'.[2]
At last the King would lay down his cards and stand up, giving the
signal that the assembled company was dismissed. Those who still had
enough energy and spirit would go to supper, but most would retire
to bed, greatly fatigued by another interminably long and dreary evening.

When the court moved from St James's to Hampton Court or
Kensington, the change of scene prompted no alteration to the accustomed routine. Henrietta now knew every royal residence intimately,
and any interest or appeal that they may once have held had long since
faded. She complained to friends about the tedium of her life.
Chesterfield, who was still enjoying a lively time of it in the Hague,
sympathised with his old friend back at court. 'I find by your account
that Kensington is not at present the seat of diversions,' he wrote. He
added that he hoped his letters would provide a welcome, albeit brief,
distraction for her, and urged her to fill her 'idle time' by writing back
to him.[3]

Mrs Howard did indeed rely more and more on letters to and from
her friends outside court to relieve the boredom of her life within it.
One of her most frequent correspondents was Lady Hervey. Following
the gentle pursuits of a country lady at her Ickworth estate, surrounded
by her children, she had the life for which Henrietta yearned. For her
part, though, Lady Hervey was restless and longed for the days when
they had been giddy young maids together at court. 'I pass my mornings at present as much like those at Hampton Court as I can,' she told
her friend, 'for I divide them between walking and the people of the
best sence of their time, but the difference is, my present companions
[books] are dead, and the others were quite alive.' Henrietta soon
dispelled such pleasant illusions of what she was missing out on at
court, and assured her that it was 'very different from the Place you
knew'. The 'frizelation, flurtation and dangleation' that had preoccu-

pied the young ladies in earlier times were no more, she said, and added: 'to tell you freely my opinion the people you now converse with are much more alive than any of your old acquaintance'. The wry humour of Henrietta's letter betrayed a deep longing to escape her life at court, and she ended by confiding '[I] do envy what I cannot posses.'[4]

Lady Hervey, Mary Bellenden, Sophia Howe and the other lively beauties who had graced the court during Mrs Howard's heyday had been supplanted by a new generation of young maids, even more giddy and wild than their predecessors. Chief among them was Anne Vane, who had been appointed a Maid of Honour in 1725. A clever young woman with a propensity for intrigue and deceit, Miss Vane's morals were dubious, to say the least. Horace Walpole described her as 'a maid-of-honour who was willing to cease to be so – at the first opportunity'.[5] At one stage, she was rumoured to be pregnant, having taken a rather hasty vacation to Bath on the grounds of ill health. She wrote to Henrietta from there, complaining of the 'aspersions I labour under, for I am inform'd that tis whisper'd about the court that I am with Child'. She claimed that this had done 'infinite hurt' to her health, but clung to the rather vain hope that it had not done the same to her reputation.[6]

Miss Vane was as indecent in her speech as in her actions. In her analogy of the ladies at court being like volumes in a library, Lady Hervey had described her as 'very diverting & may be read by people of the meanest as well as by those of the best understanding being writ in the Vulgar Tongue'.[7] She had good reason to be snide, for it was rumoured that her husband was one of a string of men at court who had fallen for Miss Vane's ample charms.

The lady's most famous lover, though, was Frederick ('Fritz'), Prince of Wales, who had finally been allowed to come over to England in 1728 after being detained in Hanover at his father's orders for fourteen years. He was smitten with Miss Vane from their first meeting and trailed after her like a lovesick puppy. When she at last succumbed to his advances (which in truth did not take long), she used all her feminine wiles and cunning to ensnare him even more than he had been at the beginning. Her hints about fine clothes and rich jewels were quickly taken, and she even persuaded Frederick to set her up in a home of her own. He duly purchased a house for her in London's fashionable Soho Square, where she lived in some style, receiving company and holding receptions as if she were the Prince's wife rather than his mistress. Anne rewarded her royal lover by giving him a son, whom he doted upon. It was rumoured, however, that Lord Hervey was the real father. Anxious not to lose the Prince's favour, Miss Vane publicly insisted that the child was his and, as if to prove the point, had him christened Cornwell fitzFrederick.

Mrs Howard had neither the energy nor the inclination to keep up with all the scandals created by Miss Vane and her fellow Maids of Honour. Their 'merry pranks' disturbed her sleep, as they scurried around the palace at night, giggling and committing all kinds of mischief. On one occasion they stole out into the gardens at Kensington and ran around flinging open and rattling people's windows until soon the whole palace was awake. Henrietta complained about this incident in a letter to Lady Hervey, who wrote back in sympathy: 'I think people who are of such very hot constitutions as to want to be refresh'd by night-walking, need not disturb others who are not altogether so warm as they are.'8

The daytime activities offered little respite for Henrietta. When the court was at Hampton or Windsor, the ladies were expected to join in the hunting, as they had in former years. This was a far greater challenge to the King's middle-aged mistress than it was to the giddy teenagers in his wife's household. Henrietta bore it stoically, but her increasingly fragile constitution soon rebelled, and the headaches that had plagued her in the past returned with a vengeance. 'As your Physician I warn you against such violent exercise,' scolded Lady Hervey. 'All extreams are I believe equally detrimental to the health of a human body, and especially to yours, whose strength like Sampson's lyes chiefly in your head.'9

Mrs Howard's growing loneliness at court was partly eased by the contact she had with John Hobart, 'the best of brothers'. Thanks to her, he had been appointed a Treasurer of the Chamber on George II's accession, and owned a house close to court on Pall Mall. Although the management of his estate at Blickling kept him away from London for long periods at a time, his daughter, Dorothy, often came to stay with Henrietta in her apartments at court. She delighted in these visits, for she had always doted on the child and a close bond had developed between them. Mrs Howard's friends referred to her as an 'indulgent mother', and to Dorothy as 'your child'. Whether their expressions were meant literally is uncertain.

Apart from John and Dorothy, Henrietta had no close family left.

The two sisters who had survived with Henrietta into adulthood, Dorothy and Catherine, were both now dead. The elder of them, Dorothy, had died unmarried at Bath in 1723. Catherine had married General Charles Churchill, a Groom of the Bedchamber, which suggests that she had been a visitor to her sister at court, but death had robbed the latter of her company in 1726.

The family member whose presence Henrietta missed most, however, was her son Henry. Almost thirteen years had passed since she had last seen him, and during that time she had been able to glean precious little news of him. Thanks to her friends outside court, she had learned that he had been sent to a private school in 1720 under the tutelage of Dr Samuel Dunster, a High Church parson who had a living in Paddington. He had subsequently followed the traditional education of a young nobleman by attending Cambridge, where he had been enrolled as a student at Magdalene College in 1725 at the age of eighteen.

Lord Peterborough had discovered that the boy had been sent to an academy in Paris after graduating from university. At Henrietta's entreaty, he had changed the plans he had had for his own son so that he could enrol him at the same place and thus secure regular reports of his welfare. Peterborough had also hoped that his son might speak favourably to the young man of his mother, and thereby undo some of the damage that Charles's evil influence had wreaked. The fact that there are no further references to him in Peterborough's correspondence suggests that the plan failed. Nor is there any evidence that Henry ever tried to contact his mother directly after he returned to England in 1728. He had not lost touch with his family altogether, though, for that same year he was elected the Member of Parliament for Bere Alston in Devon, which was part of the Maynard family estate. Henrietta's brother, John, had inherited it in 1720 and wielded a strong influence in the local elections, which suggests that he helped his nephew to secure the seat. Whether he thereby hoped to engineer a reconciliation between his sister and her son is not certain.

If Henry was grateful for the advantage he had gained from his mother's connections, he did not show it. His father had evidently done too good a job in raising him to hate her. This is borne out by references in letters from Henrietta's friends. Pope was aghast at 'the odd usage of Mr Howard to his son', but tried to reassure Henrietta that Henry would surely have inherited enough of her own good nature to resist his father's attempts to warp him. It soon became clear, though, that he had adopted his father's attitude towards her, as well as a fair portion of his nature. Indeed, he had evidently made this aversion so clear that she had been afraid to encounter him. When Lord Bathurst invited her to stay with him at Cirencester in the summer of 1734, she at first resisted on the grounds that she had heard her son was there, and asked Pope to find out if this were true. Bathurst wrote at once to reassure her: 'My castle is not molested by your fair son.'[10] Henrietta's fear of Henry must have been real indeed for her to have changed from longing to see him to doing all she could to avoid him.

The ever-increasing certainty that her son was lost to her for ever must have caused Henrietta great anguish during her long hours of solitude. Weighed down by this sadness, and weary of her life at court, she had a further reason to wish to be free of it. The waning of George II's affections towards her had until now only manifested itself in the occasional outburst of temper. Much as he loved the routine of their liaison, he was growing tired of his long-term mistress. Her body was losing its appeal, and her increasing deafness hampered the long conversations they had enjoyed in the past. After her legal separation from Charles Howard, however, the King's apathy turned to open aversion. On one occasion he charged into the Queen's room while Mrs Howard was arranging a piece of fabric around her mistress's décolletage, and snatched it from her, crying: 'Because you have an ugly neck yourself, you hide the Queen's!' According to Horace Walpole, this and similar incidents were repeated on numerous occasions.[11]

Other courtiers began to notice that the King's nightly visits to his mistress's chambers were becoming much shorter than they had been, and sometimes there was a total intermission. The tension between the pair soon spilled out from their private apartments into the open court. All those who saw them together at the commerce table or other evening entertainment observed that they were 'so ill together that, when he did not neglect her, the notice he took of her was still a stronger mark of his dislike than his taking none'. At Richmond Lodge, where the walls were thin enough for private conversations to be overheard, Lady Bristol, a Lady of the Bedchamber whose apartment adjoined Henrietta's, reported that she often heard the King speaking to his mistress in an 'angry and impatient tone'. One evening (her ear no doubt pressed close to the wall), she could discern Mrs Howard's subdued tones for a long time, as she tried to persuade him about some political matter. At length, Lady Bristol heard him exclaim: 'That is none of your business, madam; you have nothing to do with that.'[12]

Her husband's obvious irritation with his mistress was no doubt a source of satisfaction to Caroline, who had always been jealous of her rival. Yet she still refused to release Henrietta from service, for the danger that George might find a more attractive replacement was even greater now that she herself had started to lose her sexual appeal for him. Bearing ten children had taken its toll on her figure, and her fondness for chocolate had further increased its rotundity. In fact, she had grown so fat that she struggled to keep up with the King on their customary long walks in the gardens at Kensington, and by the time they returned, her ladies noticed that she was always red in the face and sweating profusely. She often had to plunge her gouty legs into icy-cold water before these excursions so that she was able to set out at all.

A more worrying complaint that had been festering for some years was also now causing her real discomfort. During the birth of her last child, Louisa, in 1724, she had developed an umbilical hernia. Knowing that the King could not tolerate any sign of physical infirmity or illness, she had taken great care to hide this complaint from him, and nobody knew of it but her German nurse and her most trusted Lady of the Bedchamber, Mrs Clayton, who had discovered it by accident. 'To prevent all suspicion her Majesty would frequently stand for some minutes in her shift talking to her Ladies,' recounted Horace Walpole, 'tho labouring with so dangerous a complaint.'[13]

In May 1729, tired and frustrated with his bloated wife and ageing mistress, George II sought refuge in the one place on earth he desired to be more than any other: Hanover. He had long cherished a desire to return to the country he had not seen since his father's accession some fifteen years earlier, and this had intensified after he himself had become King and abandoned any pretence of loving England. The people were now as irksome to him as they had been to his father, and he found fault in everything they did – from their manners and customs to the very fabric of their political constitution. He even insisted that his cooks learn how to prepare traditional German dishes, and became so fond of 'Rhenish soup' that it was hardly ever off the menu.[14] All this generated a great deal of bad feeling among his English subjects, who needed little excuse to revert to their accustomed xenophobia.

George cared little for their resentment, however, and began to establish a regular pattern of visits to his homeland. Whilst he enjoyed these immensely, his courtiers there were subjected to the same monotony of routine that their counterparts in London suffered on a daily basis. 'Our life is as uniform as that of a monastery,' complained one of his English retinue at Herrenhausen. 'Every morning at eleven and every evening at six we drive in the heat to Herrenhausen through an enormous linden avenue; and twice a day cover our coats and coaches with dust. In the King's society there is never the least change. At table, and at cards, he sees always the same faces, and at the end of the game retires into his chamber. Twice a week there is a French theatre; the other days there is a play in the gallery. In this way, were the King always to stop in Hanover, one could take a ten years' calendar of his proceedings, and settle beforehand what his time of business, meals, and pleasure would be.'[15]

When her royal master was away in Hanover, Henrietta was at least free from his bouts of temper and hostility towards her. But she was still left serving a spiteful and vindictive mistress, and the tedium of court life was only slightly alleviated by the King's absence. Frustration, melancholy and downright boredom soon took their toll on her health. In July 1730, she fell ill with a 'severe fitt of Collick'. The Queen refused to excuse her from her duties, however, and she complained to Gay: 'I am now in close waiting, my spirits very low, and my understanding very weak.'[16] She had barely recovered from this when in October she was struck down by a fever. This time Caroline was forced to relent, and Henrietta kept to her bed for several days 'in extreme pain'.[17] It took her some months to get over this, and it was only at the end of the year that her friend the Duchess of Queensberry was able – with some relief – to speak of her recovery. 'I am ... very very glad that you are better & think of life,' she wrote, 'for I know none who one could more wish to have live than yourself.'[18] Although Henrietta weathered this particular attack, she continued to be plagued by ill health throughout the years that followed.

But in 1731, her luck suddenly changed. Relief came from a wholly unexpected quarter. So many times in the past, her husband had tormented her when she was at her lowest ebb, but this time he was the cause (albeit inadvertently) of great joy. On 22 June, his brother

Edward died and he succeeded as 9th Earl of Suffolk. By the terms
of their separation, Henrietta was entitled to style herself Countess if
her husband inherited the family title and estate. What was more, the
late Earl had defied convention (or more precisely his brother, whom
he despised) by bequeathing all that remained of his fortune to his
long-suffering sister-in-law. Thanks to his protracted legal wranglings
with Charles, this had dwindled to some two or three thousand pounds,
but to Henrietta it was still a considerable sum.

Her new title, though, meant more to her than any amount of
money. She had at last won some recompense from the husband who
had subjected her to years of misery and hardship. As Countess of
Suffolk, she was unlikely ever again to return to that wretched state,
for with such a prestigious title came the potential for influence and
money. This had a profound effect upon her position at court. A
countess could not hold such a lowly position as Woman of the
Bedchamber. The Queen would therefore either have to release her
from service altogether, or promote her. If she chose the latter, the
options were limited. The rank immediately above Henrietta's former
one – that of Lady of the Bedchamber – was a possibility, but her new
status entitled her to aim even higher. Indeed, the most prestigious
position in the Queen's household was now open to her: that of Mistress
of the Robes.

Henrietta now faced the prospect of a substantial promotion if she
stayed at court, or the freedom and independence for which she had
so long fought if she was allowed to quit it. It was a prospect at once
delightful to the mistress and galling to the Queen, who for years had
derived petty satisfaction from subjecting her rival to menial tasks. For
her part, the new Countess of Suffolk no doubt preferred the option
of escaping court altogether and settling at her beloved Marble Hill,
but her mistress still had an eye to the delicate balance of power that
she had so long maintained at court, and was not about to let a mere
title disrupt it. She therefore gave Henrietta the choice of becoming a
Lady of the Bedchamber or Mistress of the Robes. The latter post was
then occupied by the Duchess of Dorset, but Caroline was still obliged
to offer it to Henrietta.

Henrietta of course chose the more prestigious position. It was
hardly a difficult decision, and she confessed to a friend that she 'did
not take one moment to consider of it'. She 'kissed hands' for the post
on 29 June, and the following day an official letter of appointment was

drawn up. Queen Caroline's 'Right Trusty and Welbeloved Cousin', the Countess of Suffolk, was henceforth the most senior member of her household.[19]

Henrietta's new position came with a salary of £400 a year and a substantially reduced set of duties. No longer would she be required to undertake such menial tasks as spending hours on bended knee holding a heavy ornamental wash basin while the royal person was cleansed by her ladies. In fact, she was no longer concerned with any of the Queen's more personal requirements, for her responsibilities were now confined to the rather more pleasant task of overseeing the royal wardrobe. Even then, the majority of the work was carried out by the Ladies of the Bedchamber, who commissioned new garments and ensured that everything was in place for the daily ceremony of dressing. Lady Suffolk might also be required to attend formal state events such as the reception of ambassadors, or the lavish dinners and assemblies that were periodically held at court to celebrate royal birthdays, the anniversary of the coronation, or other notable events. But these were hardly burdensome duties, and the post was a sinecure compared to that which she had formerly held. Gone were the days of having to be always on hand to answer the Queen's slightest whim. Indeed, regular attendance at court was not a requirement for the Mistress of the Robes.

'Every thing as yet promises more happiness for the latter part of my life then I have yet had a prospect off,' Henrietta wrote expansively to Gay. 'I shall now often visit Marble-Hill my time is become very much my own; and I shall see it without dread of being oblig'd to sell it to answer the engagements I had put myself under to avoid a greater evil.'[20] The 'engagements' that she referred to were the financial provisions that she had made for her husband as part of their legal separation. The £1,200 she had agreed to pay him each year had only been for as long as his brother lived, so it had now ceased. Free from this heavy financial burden, as well as from practically all her onerous duties at court, Henrietta had just cause for celebration.

Her friends rejoiced at her sudden change of fortune. 'Your Letter was not ill-bestow'd,' wrote Gay, 'for I found in it such an air of satisfaction that I have a pleasure every time I think of it.' He and the other members of her circle gently teased her by adopting a formal style to their correspondence and insisting upon calling her 'Your Ladyship'. Dr Arbuthnot led the charge. 'I have the honour to congratulate your ladyship on your late honour and preferment', he wrote, 'and the obliging manner that I hear the last was conferred.' Lady Hervey went one step further by calling her friend 'dear Swiss Countess'.[21] Henrietta pleaded with them to revert to their former way of addressing her, but she was nevertheless proud of her new title, and henceforth signed her letters 'H. Suffolk'.

Only Swift, who still harboured a bitter resentment against her, sounded a false note on the occasion. Although he had not written to her for years, he could not resist doing so now. 'I give you joy of your new title,' he sneered, before warning of 'the consequences it may have, or hath had, on your rising at court'. He went on to remind her that he had prophesied in his 'Character' that if she ever became a great lady, the impact upon her attitudes and behaviour would inevitably be a negative one.[22] But nothing could dampen Henrietta's spirits – not even the fresh trouble that was brewing with her husband.

Although he had inherited all the titles and estates that were due to him, Charles had been incensed by his late brother's deliberate slight in leaving his money to Henrietta. Fury combined with greed, as well as his customary readiness to torment his wife, and he immediately contested the will. 'I am persuaided it will be try'd to the utmost,' Henrietta told Gay, but added: 'poor Lord Suffolk took so much care in the will he made, that the best lawyers say's it must stand good'. Her friend's reply was sympathetic. 'I dont like Lawsuits,' he wrote. 'I wish you could have your right without 'em.' But he evidently perceived that she was not overly troubled by her husband's actions, for he concluded: 'As you descend from Lawyers, what might be my plague perhaps may be only your amusement.' Charles was so intent upon overthrowing the will, however, that he poured all his energies into the task, even disregarding the arrangement of his brother's funeral in the process. 'Mr Howard took possession of Body and goods,' his wife reported in early July, 'and was not prevail'd upon till yesterday, to resign the former for Burrial.'[23]

The new Earl of Suffolk would doggedly pursue his battle against the will for the next two years, even though the last thing he needed was to run up substantial legal costs. While he enjoyed undisputed possession of the Audley End estate, it was heavily burdened with debt. There was already a mortgage of £5,000 (with accumulated interest) on the house and lands, which dated back to the time of the 6th Earl. His successor, meanwhile, had run up debts amounting to more than £8,000. Charles was continually being pressed for payment of these, to say nothing of his own obligations (which were now considerable), and he was eventually forced to seek an act empowering him to raise money by sale or mortgage so that he could settle them. His inheritance had therefore brought him nothing but worry, vexation and trouble. His wife, by contrast, could enjoy all the benefits of her new title without being associated with any of the Earl's debts: her carefully worded deed of separation had made sure of that. Revenge had been a long time coming, but it was all the sweeter for it.

The promotion of George II's mistress to her new title and position attracted a great deal of interest in both the press and the court. It was reported in all the major newspapers, from *The Craftsman* to *The Gentleman's Magazine*. At court, meanwhile, the chief speculation was who would succeed Lady Suffolk as Woman of the Bedchamber. 'I hear no one but Mrs Claverin named for Mrs Howard's place,' wrote the Countess of Pembroke to Charlotte Clayton, who, as Henrietta's long-standing rival in the Queen's household, was galled by her promotion. The Countess tried to console her friend by adding that Henrietta's new position did not seem to have brought her much joy. 'She has come in the Queen's train to the drawing-room ... and has appeared with the most melancholy face that was possible.'[24]

Any anxiety Henrietta may have had that the Queen would disregard her new position and continue to inflict menial tasks upon her was dispelled on her very first day as Mistress of the Robes. She offered to dress her mistress's head as before, but Caroline insisted that protocol should be followed and therefore gave this task to a lower-ranking servant. Lady Suffolk was obliged to do nothing more taxing than present her jewels. The Queen remained as good as her word, and in return Henrietta was assiduous in carrying out her new duties. These were much better suited to her, for she had always had a natural sense of style and did her best to improve that of her mistress. Her correspondence shows that she went to great lengths to procure luxury fabrics and adornments for the royal wardrobe, even sending specific requests to any of her acquaintances who were travelling abroad. The Earl of Essex, a former Gentleman of the Bedchamber and now the

King's ambassador in Sardinia, was particularly helpful in this respect. At Henrietta's request, he purchased everything from fine Italian leather for the Queen's gloves to lavish gold fabric for her dresses.[25]

Lady Suffolk soon developed a reputation for being one of the most successful dressers the Queen had ever had. Just a few months after her appointment, the Duke of Dorset (whose wife had ceded the post to her) wrote of the celebrations in Dublin for the King's birthday, and claimed: 'I believe more rich clothes were never seen together, except at St James's, and some of them so well chosen, that one would have sworn a certain Countess of my acquaintance had given her assistance upon this occasion.' Two years later, she was entrusted with the considerable responsibility of ordering the clothes 'and other necessaries' for the Princess Royal's wedding.[26]

Henrietta derived a great deal more satisfaction from her new position than she had as Woman of the Bedchamber. But its real appeal lay in the opportunity it gave her to pursue a life away from court. She was quick to take full advantage of this. During the summer immediately following her appointment, she spent a great deal of time at Marble Hill, arranging the interiors, organising the household, receiving friends, holding supper parties, and – above all – simply relishing being in the home that she had spent so many long hours dreaming about. One of her most frequent visitors was Alexander Pope. The fact that their letters dried up at around this time suggests that they were able to converse in person far more than before. Lady Suffolk must have been overjoyed that she was now so often in the company of the man who had proved her most loyal and supportive friend during the past few years of strife.

As well as visiting Marble Hill, Henrietta also went on an excursion to Highclere in Hampshire, the estate of Robert Sawyer Herbert, with whom she had become acquainted when he was a Groom of the Bedchamber to George I. His estate was a convenient distance between Marble Hill and Amesbury, where the Duchess of Queensberry lived with Gay as a more or less permanent guest, and the two friends met there that summer. 'Those that have a real friendship cannot be satisfied with general relations,' Gay wrote when he heard of the trip. 'They want to enquire into the minute circumstances of life that they may be sure things are as happy as they appear to be.'[27]

Spending time with her friends that summer was a source of great joy for Henrietta, but it was also one of frustration. If she had longed to be free from court before, now that she had had more than the briefest glimpses of what her life could be like, she was desperate to escape for good. But Caroline was no more inclined to release her than she had been in the past. Even though George was spending more and more time in Hanover, where he was cultivating new romantic liaisons, she still saw Henrietta as instrumental to her hold over him. Knowing from bitter experience that it was futile to try to go against her mistress's wishes, Henrietta instead began to further isolate herself from the established regime, including Walpole's Whig ministry.

As early as 1729, she had set herself firmly in opposition to the Prime Minister by supporting her friend Gay in a fierce controversy prompted by one of his plays. *The Beggar's Opera* had been performed to great acclaim at the theatre in Lincoln's Inn Fields the previous year, and the royal family themselves had been among the many who had thronged to see it. The play had made fun of Walpole and contained characters who were clearly supposed to be his wife and mistress. The joke was lost on neither the audience nor the minister, and the latter was furious at being so humiliated. The King and Queen had greatly enjoyed the performance, however, so he could do little to prevent its circulation. Only when he heard that Gay was about to put a sequel, *Polly*, into rehearsal did he decide to act.

By all accounts, *Polly* was an even more blatant attack on Walpole because it represented him as a highwayman, robbing the good people of England. The minister heard of this and immediately ordered the Duke of Grafton, who as Lord Chamberlain presided over such matters, to ban the play 'rather than suffer himself to be produced for thirty nights together upon the stage'. If it could not be performed, however, it could still be printed, and Gay's friends advised him to publish it by subscription. At a stroke, the court was divided between those who supported the existing political regime and thus declined to subscribe, and those who demonstrated their opposition to it by adding their names to the list.

The Duchess of Queensberry placed herself very firmly in the latter camp by touting the play everywhere, including the court. She even invited the King himself to subscribe – an act of bare-faced audacity since his own Lord Chamberlain had banned its performance. In truth, George was rather amused by this, particularly as the Duchess was such a comely and vivacious addition to his assemblies. However, after relating to the Queen what had happened, he quickly changed his view, and the next day sent word to the Duchess that she was banned from court. Undeterred, the latter replied that she was 'surprised and well pleased that the King hath given her so agreeable a command as to stay from Court, where she never came for diversion'.[28]

With the Duchess of Queensberry in exile, Henrietta stepped in as Gay's chief advocate at court. She urged her royal masters to reconsider their ban on his play, arguing that it was stirring up resentment across the capital. She also attested to the author's excellent character and sincere loyalty to the Crown. 'Mrs Howard hath declared herself strongly both to the King and Queen as my advocate,' Gay wrote to Swift in March 1729. In defending her friend so vehemently, Henrietta placed herself in direct opposition not only to the sovereigns, but also to their most powerful minister in government, and therefore put her own position at court in jeopardy. John Arbuthnot wrote anxiously to Swift: 'he [Gay] has gott several turnd out of their places, the greatest ornament of the Court Banishd from it for his sake, another great Lady in danger of being chasé likewise'.[29]

The controversy eventually died down, but Gay had achieved notoriety as a result. As Arbuthnot wryly observed: 'The inoffensive John Gay is now become one of the obstructions to the peace of Europe, the terror of Members, the chief author of the Craftsmen, and all the seditious pamphlets which have been published against Government.'[30] This deterred many at court from having any contact with him, but Henrietta remained steadfast in her loyalty, making a point of seeing him often and maintaining a regular correspondence. She was equally supportive of the Duchess of Queensberry, who took Gay to live with her after the controversy, and the two became firm friends. Henrietta would often write letters to them both at Amesbury, and would receive joint replies in return. In an age when correspondence was frequently intercepted, particularly to and from the court, this was nothing less than an act of open defiance.

Mrs Howard's friendship with Gay deepened as time went on. His witty and irreverent letters kept her amused during her long hours at court, and she often expressed a longing to see him. The poet valued their friendship just as much, and even contemplated buying a house next to Marble Hill so that the pair could see each other often once Mrs Howard was finally able to leave court. But death was to rob them of their happy schemes.

Gay had always lived somewhat hedonistically, pursuing pleasure wherever it lay – from the spas of Bath, Tunbridge Wells or the Continent, to the pleasure gardens and country estates of his fashionable friends. He enjoyed his fill of rich food and fine wine along the way, and with a tendency towards laziness and an aversion towards any form of exercise, he grew exceedingly fat. Nevertheless, he always seemed in the rudest of health, so when he was struck down by a fever at the end of 1732, his friends were confident that he would soon recover. Their shock and devastation was profound indeed when, a few days later, the much-loved poet died. 'Would to God the man we had lost had not been so amiable or so good,' wrote Pope to Swift on hearing of his death, 'but that's a wish for our sakes, not for his. Sure, if innocence and integrity can deserve happiness, it must be his.' Swift did not open this letter for five days, having had 'an impulse foreboding some misfortune'. When he eventually managed to steel himself to read its contents, he was so distraught that for many months afterwards he could not even bear to hear Gay's name mentioned, for it brought on fresh waves of grief.

None mourned Gay's passing more than Henrietta. They had been close friends for almost twenty years and had shared the joy and sadness of each other's lives in equal measure. Gay had been the first to learn of his friend's plans for Marble Hill, and it was to him that she had written upon hearing that she had become a countess. Even when she had failed to secure him a position at court, he had remained loyal to her. Their affection was mutual and sincere.

In her grief, Henrietta turned to the Duchess of Queensberry, who felt the loss of her friend and lodger deeply. The two women had loved Gay as faithfully as he had loved them, and they were to miss his amiable presence for many years to come. 'I often want poor Mr Gay, & on this occasion extreamly,' wrote the Duchess to her friend in 1734. 'Nothing evaporates sooner than joy untold, or told, unless to one so intirely in your interest as he was, who bore at least an equal share in every satisfaction or dissatisfaction which attended us . . . tis a satisfaction to have once known so good a man. As you were as much his friend as I, tis needless to ask your pardon for dwelling so long on his subject.'[31]

The volume of Lady Suffolk's correspondence increased after Gay's death, as she tried to find solace among her remaining friends. The Earl of Chesterfield became a particularly frequent correspondent, and his lively accounts of the society and entertainments at the Hague provided a welcome diversion from life at court. His friendship had something else in common with Gay's, for the Earl was moving increasingly into opposition to Walpole's ministry. After years of pleading to be allowed home from an embassy that had long since lost any appeal, Chesterfield's wish was finally granted and he arrived back in England in early 1732. He was soon presented with an excellent opportunity to avenge himself on the minister who had ensured his virtual exile on the Continent.

Walpole was now at the height of his power. He bullied and cajoled the Cabinet into submission, he exercised almost complete ascendancy in Parliament, and he enjoyed the full confidence of both the King and Queen. He therefore had few qualms about introducing a scheme that under any other circumstances would have posed a serious risk to his position. Ever since the Glorious Revolution of 1688, the greatest burden of taxation had fallen upon land, but Walpole proposed to ease this by bringing the tobacco and wine duties under the law of excise. This would have effectively put a stop to the wholesale smuggling of these commodities, to which customs officials had hitherto turned a blind eye. George and Caroline, who knew that the Civil List depended to a significant extent upon the duties raised from tobacco and wine, gave their hearty approval to the proposal. Walpole was confident that it would breeze through Parliament without opposition, but this turned out to be a grave miscalculation.

Both within and outside Parliament, huge numbers of people rose up against the scheme, fearing that it was the start of a slippery slope that would end in every necessity of life being taxed. Walpole stoutly denied this, but suspicions had been aroused and there followed a rush of pamphlets and newspaper reports claiming that it was part of a much bigger plan. Meanwhile, a group of peers holding offices in the royal household gathered together and began plotting the overthrow of Walpole's measure. They included the Earl of Chesterfield and two other members of Mrs Howard's circle, the Duke of Argyll and William Pulteney. Thanks to their intervention, and to the huge tide of popular opposition, the minister was eventually defeated and his Excise Bill was thrown out by Parliament.

There were scenes of great rejoicing across the capital, and the

peers who had led the rebellion were triumphant. The Queen, meanwhile, was as devastated as her minister, and her husband was outraged.
He demanded to know the names of the upstart peers. Lord Hervey
was delighted to supply them, and as he read each one out in turn, the
King spluttered, 'Booby!', 'Blockhead!' and 'Whimsical fellow!', vowing
to exclude them from court for good. Walpole took rather more direct
action, and none felt it more keenly than Lord Chesterfield. Two days
after the Excise Bill had been dropped, he was climbing the great staircase at St James's Palace to attend the King as usual when he was halted
by a guard and presented with a summons demanding that he surrender
his office and absent himself from the court. Astonished at such an
abrupt dismissal after so long a service to the Crown, Chesterfield
insisted upon an audience with the King. Once admitted to the royal
presence, he proceeded to make a well-reasoned and dignified protest,
pointing to his eighteen years of good service and insisting: 'I declared
at all events against a measure that would so inevitably lessen the affections of Your Majesty's subjects to you . . . I thought of it as the whole
nation did.'[32] But George would have none of it, and Chesterfield was
obliged to retreat in disgrace to his father's estate in Yorkshire.

As she had with Gay, so Henrietta maintained her friendship with
the Earl as openly as before, and the two exchanged regular correspondence for the duration of his time in exile. She wrote to him as
soon as he had left court, and he was clearly grateful for this proof of
her loyalty. 'This is the case of your letter, which, though I should at
all times have valued as I ought, yett in this perticular Juncture, I must
look upon it, as a most uncommon and uncourtlike piece of friendship,' he replied, adding: 'It may, for ought I know have brought you
within the statute of Edward the Third,[33] as aiding, abetting and
comforting the King's Enemies, for I can depose that I am an enemy
of the King's, so that, by an induction not very much strain'd, for the
law, your generosity has drawn you into high treason.' Although he
wrote this somewhat light-heartedly, he was only half in jest, for he
knew how much his friend risked in allying herself with a disgraced
courtier and an avowed enemy of the most powerful politician in the
land. He also knew that written communication was as clear an indication of her allegiance as if she had invited him to tea in full view of
the court. 'As to the contents of your letter, did you reflect upon the
strict examinations it was to undergo before it reached me', he chided,
reminding her that it would have been subject to the 'penetration' of

Edward Carteret, the Post-Master General, as well as 'others of not inferior abilitys, and known Dabs, at finding out misterys'.[34]

In his exile, Chesterfield gathered about him a number of disaffected peers, including the Duke of Argyll, who had accompanied him to Yorkshire. Henrietta's friends Lords Bathurst and Cobham were also among the party. But the most formidable member of the group was undoubtedly Henry St John, Viscount Bolingbroke. Although he had been debarred from his seat in the House of Lords upon his return from exile on the Continent in 1725, Bolingbroke was a man of considerable cunning and intelligence, more so even than his despised rival Walpole. During the crisis over the Excise Bill, he had succeeded, through his political writings and his genius for intrigue, in doing more than any other man to stir up public feeling against the measure. With his exceptional powers of organisation, he had used the members of the Opposition as puppets in his game to defeat the Prime Minister. Lady Suffolk's private supper parties had provided the cover for many of their meetings, as they carefully planned the storm that would bring the mighty Walpole to his knees. Their eventual victory was only slightly marred by the minister's continuance in office, and Bolingbroke stepped up his campaign with even greater vigour than before.

He soon found an ally who was at once more powerful and more dangerous to Walpole than the King's mistress. Frederick, Prince of Wales, had been a thorn in his parents' side ever since arriving back in England five years before. He had grown up bitterly resenting them for leaving him behind in Hanover when his grandfather George I had become King. Any expectation that he would soon be sent to join them had turned into fierce disappointment when, year after year, he had been kept at Herrenhausen, apparently to satisfy their desire to retain a representative of the Hanoverian family there. Only when he had deliberately gone against George II's wishes by entering into negotiations for a politically unsuitable marriage had his parents grudgingly acceded that he was more trouble away from them than he would be with them.

Frederick landed in England in December 1728, aged twenty-one. His arrival was greeted with none of the ceremony that would be expected for a royal prince, and instead he was obliged to enter St James's Palace by the back stairs. This rather inauspicious beginning was a sign of things to come. Although Caroline made an effort to be amiable at first, George did little to hide his distaste for this troublesome young upstart. Before long, relations were as frosty between them

as they had been between George II and his late father. 'Whenever the
Prince was in a room with the King, it put one in mind of stories one
has heard of ghosts that appear to part of the company and are invisible to the rest,' observed Lord Hervey. 'Wherever the Prince stood,
though the King passed him ever so often or ever so near, it always
seemed as if the King thought the place the Prince filled a void space.'[35]
The Hanoverian tradition of loathing between fathers and sons was
thus rigorously upheld.

Frederick was as affable and cultured as his father was sour and
boorish. He also had a love of intrigue, and naturally became a focus
for all those who opposed the King or Walpole. The wits and writers,
in particular, found favour with him, for he had a genuine apprecia-
tion of the arts and a respect for talent. Chesterfield and Pulteney both
appealed to him, and he was greatly in awe of Bolingbroke, who became
his political mentor. Under his guidance, the Prince secretly stirred up
opposition to Walpole's excise scheme and played a key part in its overthrow.

Riding high on their success, Bolingbroke and his allies launched
another attack on Walpole in 1734. Their cause this time was the repeal
of the Septennial Act (whereby parliaments lasted for seven years) and
the revival of triennial sessions. Thanks to Bolingbroke's work behind
the scenes, Walpole was greeted by a hostile Commons when the House
convened to debate the issue. But he rose admirably to the challenge
and used the full force of his political skill and articulation to swing
opinion his way. Decrying his absent rival as an 'anti-minister', he
succeeded in defending the Act and was triumphant in the general election that followed. Bolingbroke was now ostracised at court and forced
to pursue his activities even more covertly.

The disgrace of Bolingbroke, Chesterfield and others among
Henrietta's circle not only set her further apart from the court, but also
demonstrated how far she had fallen from the King's favour. Her subtle
advocacy of such friends had, in the past, helped to protect their positions, even if it had not greatly enhanced them. As her own position
at court became less and less important to her, however, she had grown
more outspoken in defence of her political allies. That she was prompted
by a strong ideological commitment to Toryism is uncertain. She was
connected by birth and marriage to Whig families and had never openly
expressed views either way. It is just as likely that she supported men
such as Bolingbroke for the simple reason that she saw them as friends.

Perhaps she also realised that their political stance presented her with
an opportunity to break from the court. According to Hervey, she was
'for ever thwarting his [the King's] inclinations, reflecting on his conduct,
and contradicting his opinions', as well as criticising his ministers, in
particular Walpole.[36] The King met her entreaties with increasing impatience, and rather than furthering her friends' cause, she began to
hamper it.

Not all Lady Suffolk's acquaintances were so controversial, however,
and as the years went by she gradually widened her circle of friends
away from court. Principal among them was Lady Elizabeth ('Betty')
Germain, daughter of the 2nd Earl of Berkeley. Lady Betty had been
a lady-in-waiting to Queen Anne before marrying John Germain, a Dutch
soldier rumoured to be the illegitimate son of Prince William III of
Orange (and hence a half-brother of King William III) in 1706. Although
the couple had three children, none had survived beyond infancy and
Lady Betty was left alone when her husband died in 1718. A spirited
and intelligent woman, she had befriended Jonathan Swift as a child
when her father had taken his family to Ireland upon being appointed
a Lord Justice, and the two had remained close. Given Swift's hostility
towards Henrietta, it is doubtful that he was the cause of their introduction. More likely was either that they had met on one of Lady Betty's
visits to court, or that the Duchess of Dorset, at whose house in Knole
Lady Betty lived after she became a widow, had introduced them.
      The first reference to Lady Betty in Henrietta's correspondence was
in the summer of 1730, although the affection that clearly already existed
between them suggests that they had become acquainted earlier than
that. As well as having a love of wits and the arts in common, the pair
shared a passion for porcelain, and over the years would regularly buy
each other gifts for their collections. They spent time together at Windsor
in 1730 when the court adjourned there for the summer, and got on
so well that Henrietta was quite bereft when her friend left for Tunbridge
Wells. She wrote several times to Mary Chamber, Lady Betty's niece,
to enquire after her health. 'The repeated messages I receive from you
. . . occasions me much wonder,' Miss Chamber replied from Tunbridge
Wells. 'Surely my last letter to you so fully and so particularly related
the state of Lady Betty's health, that I imagined you could not have
required more information upon that subject.'[37]

The sincerity of their attachment was proved when, two years later, Lady Betty vigorously defended Henrietta against her old friend Swift's bitter attack. 'Im sorry to find our tastes so different in the same Person,' she wrote to him, 'and as every body has a Natural Partiality to their own opinion, so tis surprising to me to find La: Suffolk dwindle in yours who rises infinitely the more and the longer I know her.'[38]

Grateful though Henrietta was for this kind intervention, it was as nothing compared to what was arguably the greatest service that her new friend performed for her. Early on in their acquaintance, Lady Betty introduced her to her brother.

George Berkeley was some three or four years younger than Henrietta. He was the youngest son of the 2nd Earl of Berkeley, and had become acquainted with the court from an early age because his elder brother, James, had been a Lord of the Bedchamber to George I. He had been raised at the family estate in Gloucestershire with his sister before receiving the traditional education of a young gentleman, attending Westminster School in 1708 and entering Cambridge three years later, aged eighteen. He had enrolled at Trinity College, where his keen intellect and irreverent humour had made him an instant hit with the most lively young lords there. Among them was Lord Chesterfield, with whom George had soon become close friends. When he graduated two years later and went travelling abroad, Chesterfield greatly lamented his absence. 'Your departure, dear George, has been very unsuccessful to us,' he assured him, 'for as soon as you went away we immediately lost the name of the Witty Club, and I am afraid we shall soon dwindle into no club at all.'[39]

Berkeley had an aptitude for politics, and in 1720 he became MP for Dover, representing the town in the following two parliaments. He did so on the side of the Whigs, for he was at that time a supporter of Walpole. It may have been thanks to the latter's influence that he was appointed Master Keeper and Governor of St Katharine's Hospital in London on 28 May 1723, a post he was to hold for life. However, he was to change allegiance when he became acquainted with William Pulteney, a staunch member of the Opposition, during the last year of George I's reign. The pair shared a rather coarse sense of humour, and their letters were at times so indecent that large sections were edited out by the prudish nineteenth-century antiquary who later published them. Writing from the races at Newmarket in 1726, Pulteney described two horses that had particularly caught his eye, 'Prick Louse' and 'Sweet Maidenhead'. He went on to complain about the inclement weather, which he said had affected his joints, but turned this into a jest by adding: 'now I am cold I should find some soreness, or stiffness, about me, the last of which, I promise you, is no where but where it should be'.[40]

Berkeley matched his friend pun for pun, and on one occasion wrote a poem that was so vulgar it has until now remained buried in the archives of the British Library. His inspiration was the story of a woman in Godalming who in 1726 had caused a stir by claiming to have given birth to a family of rabbits. The poem begins:

> A woman long thought barren
> Bears Rabbits – gad! so plentifull
> You'd take her for a warren.

It then goes on to describe how a local landowner was brought in to examine the unfortunate woman:

> On tiptoe then this squire he stood
> But first he gave her money
> And reaching high as ere he could
> Said sure I feel a Coney
> Is it alive? St André cry'd
> It is, I feel it stir
> Is it full grown? the squire reply'd
> Yes sure, see here's the furr.[41]

Berkeley was rumoured to be as fond of Pulteney's wife as he was of the man himself. Indeed, it was said that he so persistently laid siege to her affections that he eventually incurred his friend's wrath and was 'mortally hated' by him henceforth. But the source of these rumours was unreliable, to say the least. It was Lord Hervey who put them about, and he was such a devout enemy of Lord Pulteney that the pair were later to fight a duel over an assumed slur in the press, even though this practice had been banned.

Although his friendship with Pulteney brought out a vulgar side to his character, George Berkeley's tastes and interests were on the whole as refined as any young gentleman's. He took great pleasure in the society of cultured wits and men of letters, and was a close friend of William Congreve, one of the greatest poets of the age. John Gay was also very fond of him, and he was among the pall-bearers at the latter's funeral in 1732. Alexander Pope was another of his acquaintances, and George paid regular visits to his house in Twickenham. His affable manners and good humour rendered him a pleasant and popular member of Georgian society, although his increasingly recalcitrant political views kept him away from the more favoured circles at court.

Berkeley's character was reflected in his appearance. He was not handsome by any means, but had a mild and pleasing countenance and eyes that sparkled with gentle humour. He did not enjoy the best of health, having suffered with gout from a relatively young age. He bore this complaint with patience, though, and dismissed his friends' earnest requests to take better care of his health.

It is not certain when George first became acquainted with Mrs Howard. Their earliest surviving correspondence dates from 1734, but they already seemed to be close friends by then. The fact that it was at Henrietta's request that he had agreed to be a pall-bearer at Gay's funeral suggests that he had been part of her literary circle for some time. Furthermore, they both featured in a painting of an intimate social gathering commissioned in 1730. *A Tea Party at Lord Harrington's House*, by the celebrated artist Charles Philips, shows Henrietta sitting in the centre of three groups playing cards. Standing by the fireplace to her right is Mr Berkeley, and she is inclining her head towards him, as if to suggest some intimacy between them. At the left-hand table is his sister, Lady Betty Germain, who seems to have been the hostess for the occasion.

Lady Betty had been responsible for their introduction. As she herself became acquainted with Mrs Howard around 1730, this corresponds with the evidence from the portrait. She subsequently conveyed messages about him to Henrietta through her niece, Mary Chambers, who little understood the implications of what she was instructed to write. On one occasion, she sent Henrietta two pieces of china decorated with pictures of Adam and Eve in the Garden of Eden, a clear reference to temptation. The bemused Miss Chambers, who had been asked to write a covering note to draw attention to the subject, added: 'I am not to answer, nor to make any remarks upon what Lady Betty pleases to say, so you may easily imagine that what I have writ, is like what a Parrot says without understanding the meaning.'[42]

Henrietta and Berkeley's mutual friends and interests brought them ever closer together as time went on, and it was observed that they spent many long hours in conversation together during the former's supper parties at court and at Marble Hill. Then, in 1733, an unexpected event changed the tenor of their relationship and hastened its progress towards intimacy.

Chapter 13

'Pleasing one not worth the pleasing'

————◦————

JOHN GAY HAD ONCE predicted that Henrietta would never truly be happy while her husband was alive. Charles Howard had devoted his life to plaguing her, from the moment they exchanged vows at the church of St Benet Paul's Wharf on 2 March 1706. Although they had been legally separated for the past five years, he had continued to remind her of his presence by periodic demands for money and, more recently, by the legal wranglings over his brother's will. Nobody – not even Queen Caroline – had the ability to torment her as much as he did, and the fear that he had instilled in her during the miserable years of their violent marriage had never left her.

When a messenger arrived at Lady Suffolk's apartments in Hampton Court at the end of September 1733 with the news that her husband had died at Bath on the 28th of that month, her relief must have been overwhelming. The cause of his death is not certain. Years of heavy drinking may have finally taken their toll, or it may simply have been the deteriorating health associated with advancing years, for the Earl was then approaching sixty. His passing sparked little comment at court. It was afforded a mention in the obituaries of *The Gentleman's Magazine*, as would that of any titled gentleman, but otherwise nobody seemed to notice. Neither Henrietta nor her friends referred to it in their correspondence, although it was no doubt the cause of discreet celebration in her apartments.

Henrietta's son now succeeded as 10th Earl of Suffolk. The estate that he inherited was riddled with the debts that his father had worsened by high living and protracted legal battles. Henry was a much shrewder man of business, however, and restored it to solvency two years later by marrying Sarah Inwen, the daughter of a wealthy brewer. He thus became the first Earl of Suffolk to live at Audley End without debt since the house had been built, well over a century before. Although Henrietta had by now given up all hope of a reconciliation with her son, she may have felt a little pride in hearing of his newfound wealth and prestige.

Charles Howard's death had finally rid his widow of her long-held fears and released her from any lingering notion of marital fidelity. She now openly encouraged George Berkeley's advances. The informality of their correspondence betrays a growing intimacy. The earliest known letter is dated 19 June 1734, and was written almost immediately after George had left London for an excursion to Stowe. Lord Cobham's exquisite gardens were a magnet for Georgian England's most fashionable society, and Mr Berkeley was accompanied by a party of friends that included Alexander Pope. Together they followed a somewhat rambling route through Oxfordshire, calling at Rowsham, the seat of General Dormer, a close friend of the poet. Their first stop, however, was at Shotover, home of Augustus Schutz, a former member of the King's household staff. It seems that this place carried some unpleasant associations for Henrietta from her life with Charles Howard, which she had confided to Berkeley. 'I am not afraid of calling to your remembrance the distress you suffered when you corresponded most with this place,' he wrote, 'since that very suffering was the strongest proof imaginable how little you deserved it.'[1]

Henrietta had clearly been just as eager to write as George was after his departure from London, for their letters crossed. When she received his letter, she wrote another straight away, assuring him that although his reference to Shotover had evoked some bad memories, 'I don't remember that I ever lik'd any of the letters from that Place, better than that I reciev'd last.'[2]

The playful, teasing tone of their correspondence indicates how intimate they had become. Lady Suffolk chided Berkeley for his 'ill breeding and forgetfulness', and told him that if she had little news from Kensington which would amuse him, that was because 'you are dull and want a tast [lack taste] and not that the place do's not abondantly supply both the instructive and entertaining'. In another, she mocked the 'Pride and Arrogancy' which makes men reason that the 'Actions of women are too inconsiderable, to draw any consequences from them'.[3]

Berkeley met such jibes with good grace, and the more Henrietta teased him, the more devoted he professed himself to be. Acceding to her request for detailed descriptions of his travels, he told her that he preferred Rowsham to all the gardens he had visited because 'there is at the bottom of a Sloping hill in the garden a most delightfull stream which runs from thence directly to Marble Hill, and is no small addition to the beautys of the place'. When he visited Stowe, Henrietta bade him pay his respects to the bust of her distinguished ancestor, John Hampden, which was in the Round Temple. He assured her: 'I could not fail paying a due regard to Mr Hampdens memory, for I am sure no body can be more sensible of what England owes to him, than I am.' He added that Lord Cobham was planning to erect a bust of Henrietta nearby, and that if this scheme fell through, he would 'make the Venus of Medicis serve instead of it'.[4]

George obviously missed his friend at court a great deal, for he confessed that he could find little joy in the magnificence of Stowe or the beauty of Rowsham as both were so far from London. 'I can truly pity people who live in the Country,' he declared, 'I who can scarcely bear it a fortnight.' He added that the only source of real pleasure there was the arrival of the post when it brought letters from Lady Suffolk. 'If you wish to be enchanted and leave Stow, you are very unworthy of being there,' she scolded him, but her mock disapproval hid a genuine delight in his attentions.[5]

Henrietta's close friendship with Mr Berkeley set her even further apart from the established order at court. By now, he was in open opposition to Walpole, having been returned as MP for Hedon, Yorkshire, in the general election of May 1734, on the side of his old friend William Pulteney. The latter's influence in government was rapidly increasing. As well as the members of his Tory contingent, he had also gathered a host of disaffected Whigs about him, along with a sizeable number of Jacobites. Such was his power that he was beginning to threaten the predominance that Walpole had so long enjoyed.

Berkeley was one of Pulteney's staunchest supporters, and he became increasingly vocal in his attacks on Walpole's regime. He even published a 'Political Memorandum', in which he accused the ministry of acting against the King's best interests. He claimed that the Jacobites were not responsible for the 'present uncertainty of our affairs', as Walpole had so often asserted, and that this was due to 'those who are in the management of them rather than to those who are not'.[6] This was a bold statement to make at a time of such unease and paranoia within the ministry, with Walpole and his supporters eager to make scapegoats of Jacobite sympathisers. Berkeley had no doubt been egged on by Lord Bolingbroke, who was now in political exile following his defeat by Walpole over the Septennial Act. The two had been friends for some time, and in late summer 1734, he went to join Bolingbroke at Bath. It was on this town that his lover at court now also set her sights.

Lady Suffolk's relationship with George Berkeley had intensified her desire to leave court. Her position there was, in any case, rapidly becoming untenable. Her barely disguised allegiance with political dissidents had added to her isolation and had also invoked the King's displeasure. The latter had been all too easy to achieve in recent years. 'That the King went no more in an evening to Lady Suffolk was whispered about the court by all that belonged to it,' noted Lord Hervey in his memoirs, 'and was one of those secrets that everybody knows, and everybody avoids publicly to seem to know.'[7]

Henrietta had had enough. She had been prepared to tolerate the King's 'contempt, neglect, snubs and ill-humour' as long as her husband had been alive, but now that he was gone and she had the prospect of happiness away from court, she was determined to shake off her onerous duties there. She was, as Horace Walpole shrewdly observed, 'tired of acting the mistress, while she had in reality all the slights of a wife'.[8] On the pretext of ill health, she applied to the Queen for six weeks' leave in Bath. In truth, she wished to test the water rather than take it, and to find out if the King could do without her for such a long period of time.

Perhaps sensing that a refusal would spark her servant's resignation, Caroline acceded to the request, and Lady Suffolk made hasty preparations for her departure. She had long desired to go to Bath, having so often heard its many attractions described in letters and conversations. Her friends had urged her to go there when she had fallen ill in the summer of 1728. 'I can't but think the Bath might give her blood a new turn,' declared Pope, and his opinion was echoed by Henrietta's companion and physician, Dr Arbuthnot.[9] Although she now cited poor health as the reason for her visit, the restorative qualities of the waters were clearly not the main attraction.

Bath was the most fashionable of all the early Georgian spa towns. It had risen to prominence at the beginning of the eighteenth century, when Queen Anne had honoured it with a visit. Huge crowds had soon followed, among them Richard 'Beau' Nash, a professional gamester and adventurer. Through the sheer force of his personality, he had transformed the city into a pinnacle of taste and elegance, and had established strict codes of etiquette. Under his direction, Bath had been rebuilt, with sweeping terraces, elegant promenades, theatres, Assembly Rooms and, of course, the famous Pump Room, into which members of high society crowded to take the waters or exchange gossip. All the new buildings had been crafted from the distinctive local honey-coloured stone, which presented an arresting sight as it glowed in the warm summer sunshine. For all its elegance and diversions, however, the greatest attraction Bath held for Lady Suffolk that summer was the fact that her close friend George Berkeley was among its occupants.

Impatient to reach the city, Henrietta first had to endure a long journey of some two or three days. She set off from Kensington in mid-September, accompanied by Martha ('Patty') Blount – it being inappropriate for a single lady to travel alone. Her departure caused a stir at court, for she had not had a holiday throughout her twenty years' service, and many suspected that she did so now for reasons other than failing health. It was reported in all the newspapers and gossiped about by courtiers and politicians. Berkeley noted to a friend that it had 'occasion'd as much speculation in the family at Kensington as the removal of two or three Minor Ministers would have done'. He defended the excuse that Henrietta had given by claiming that her 'damp and unwholesome' apartments at the palace were aggravating her already fragile constitution – although he could not resist adding that her departure was also intended as a demonstration that she would 'not be such a slave to the court as she has been'.[10]

Several of Lady Suffolk's other friends were at Bath when she arrived, including Lord Chesterfield, who had a house on Pierrepont Street. Bolingbroke and Pope were also on their way there, eager to see their friend 'in Liberty & Health'. 'I am following her chariot wheels 3 days through Rocks & Waters, & shall be at her feet on Sunday night,' the latter wrote on 17 September.[11] The Tory contingent was further strengthened by the arrival of Lord Bathurst, the alleged former lover of Lady Suffolk, who Berkeley jokingly referred to as 'a much younger man than myself and consequently much fitter for her purpose'.[12]

Upon reaching Bath, Henrietta and her companion Miss Blount

were instantly caught up in a glittering whirl of social diversions. New arrivals were traditionally greeted by the pealing of the Abbey bells, followed by a personal welcome from 'Beau' Nash, before hastening to meet their acquaintances at the Pump Room, Assembly Rooms or theatre, depending on the time of day.

A typical day in Bath would begin any time between six and nine o'clock in the morning with a trip to one of the city's five public baths. These were public indeed, for people of the 'lower sort' would crowd into the balconies up above to watch the elegant, fashionable, and occasionally ridiculous figures below. On one occasion, the genteel Mrs Buckley had been enjoying a peaceful hour's bathing when an unfortunate accident had befallen her. The portly Duchess of Norfolk had suddenly plunged into the water and 'like a great Leviathan, rais'd the waters so high, that Mrs Buckley's guide was oblig'd to hold her up in her arms to save her from drowning; and carry her out like a child'.[13]

Bathing was followed immediately by a general assembly at the Pump Room. From there, ladies would either withdraw to their private lodgings for breakfast, or take this repast in company at the assembly rooms. Private concerts or lectures on arts and sciences would sometimes form part of the morning's entertainment, or services at the Abbey if it was a Sunday. The ladies and gentlemen would then repair to separate coffee houses to read the newspapers or trade scandal until noon.

The afternoon would be taken up with promenading along the city's various public walks, during which parties would be formed for cards, dancing or other entertainment in the evening. Dinner was usually taken at four o'clock. For members of high society this would comprise a remarkable abundance of rich food, such as game pies, oyster loaves, potted venison, and sweet puddings and tarts. After these excesses, the more godly would retreat to the Abbey for evening prayers, while those left behind would snooze until the evening. Their consciences thus relieved, they would repair to the assembly rooms, theatres or private functions. A lavish ball would be held twice a week on a Tuesday and Friday to complete the social round.

All this was dictated by Nash's 'Code of Behaviour', which provided strict guidelines on every conceivable scenario, from banning the wearing of gowns and caps by gentlemen in the morning when there were ladies present, to shunning anyone found to be whispering 'lies and scandal' in public. This latter rule was often flouted, but otherwise polite society bowed to Nash's superior judgement and behaved impeccably. Even royalty could not escape his watchful gaze. At the end of a ball one evening, Princess Amelia, the King's second eldest daughter, begged for one more dance, but was curtly informed by the Master of Ceremonies that the music must stop at eleven o'clock, and that nothing would induce him to grant her request, no matter how exalted her status might be.

Although harsh, such strictures transformed Bath into a centre of social excellence and made it a magnet for nobles, aristocrats, men of letters and wit, and every other member of polite society. All the most celebrated figures of Georgian England could be found there at one time or another, from Gay and Pope to foreign dignitaries and members of the royal family. It was a glittering contrast to the dull routines of court life back in London, and Henrietta was at first rather overwhelmed by it. She wrote to her friend Anne Pitt, a Maid of Honour, that she found the celebrated diversions of the place exhausting, and preferred instead to live 'a much more retired life than is fashionable here'. In this she was joined by George Berkeley, who favoured her company above all the public entertainments on offer. Henrietta proudly confided to her friend that he had told her that 'the most agreeable hour he passes in the 24 is at my breakfast table'.[14]

But amidst this tranquil domestic scene, more sinister manoeuvrings were afoot. Bath was a magnet for opponents of the political regime, who used the cover of fashionable assemblies to debate parliamentary affairs and plan insurrections at a safe distance from court. Lady Suffolk was well aware of this. 'The town is full of incindiarys,' she wrote to Miss Pitt, 'but as I am famous for my penetration and observation, I have discovered that, after the waters have past, there issues a sharp humour that can be discharged only at the toung, and into the ear of their next neighbour.'[15]

Amidst this hotbed of rumour and intrigue lay the means to Lady Suffolk's escape from court. Whether she deliberately planned it, or whether she made a virtue of an unexpected turn of events is uncertain, but she soon found herself at the centre of a political scandal. It started with Princess Amelia, who was staying in Bath at the same time as Henrietta. The Princess had the dangerous combination of an insatiable appetite for gossip and a strong aversion to her father's mistress. Suspicious that the latter should be keeping such a low profile in the city, she resolved to discover what company she was mixing with. Much to her delight, she soon found out that Lady Suffolk's private circle included Walpole's greatest enemy, Lord Bolingbroke. Together with her friend Lady Burlington, she put it about that the pair were conspiring to turn the King against his chief minister, and that their acquaintance was of an intimate nature. The latter conjecture was entirely false, and the former had barely more credence, given that Henrietta was by now determined to leave court and therefore cared little about enhancing either her own or her friends' position there.

But the merest hint of insurrection on the part of the King's mistress was enough to create a scandal, and before long the whole of Bath was agog with it. By the time Lady Suffolk made preparations for her departure, news had already spread to the court, and upon her arrival she was caught up in a political storm. She had either failed to predict this, or was secretly glad about it, for she had given no indication to her circle of friends that she might return to St James's to find her position in jeopardy. Lord Chesterfield wrote a light-hearted letter shortly after her departure, assuring her that he would visit her at court in a fortnight's time, where he would regale her with the latest gossip from Bath 'over a hot roll'.[16] The rest of his letter was given over to 'A Generall History of the Bath, since you left it', and described the lamentations at the loss of Lady Suffolk and Miss Blount. The lively account of their daily amusements that followed, including flirtations at the Pump Room, tittle-tattle on the promenades, and drunkenness at the card tables, could not have formed a starker contrast to the scene that confronted Henrietta at St James's.

Henrietta had made sure to arrive in time for the King's birthday on 30 October, as duty and tradition dictated, but her efforts were rewarded with open hostility. When news had reached George II, via his wife and daughter, that she had been conspiring with Bolingbroke and other political malcontents at Bath, he had flown into a rage. He had always hated the thought that he was being manipulated, and that his mistress – whom he had in any case tired of long ago – should attempt to do so was more than he could bear. He therefore vowed never to speak to her or see her in private again.

He made good his threat. Although greatly indisposed with a bad cold, he made a point of being out at the theatre in Haymarket with the Queen and their children when his mistress arrived back at St James's. Upon returning to the palace, he did not pay his accustomed visit to her apartments, but instead snubbed her altogether. He continued to do so throughout his birthday celebrations the following day, and this time it was much more obvious because there were crowds of spectators at the receptions held to mark the occasion.

Henrietta was genuinely shocked by the fierceness of the King's hostility towards her. While she appreciated that it presented the best opportunity she had ever had to escape court, she was anxious not to do so in disgrace. As a member of fashionable society, and a countess to boot, she had her future reputation to consider. She also depended upon the pension that she stood to receive upon her retirement from court. She therefore urgently requested an audience with the Queen so that she might find out – and defend herself against – the allegations that were being whispered about her. Her request was granted, and she hastened to her mistress, 'with whom she was above an hour and a half alone'.[17]

The detail of what passed during this extraordinary meeting was later recorded by Lady Suffolk and can still be found among the Hobart family papers. The Queen also gave her side of it to Lord Hervey, who seized upon it as fodder for his memoirs, and there is a high degree of correlation between the two accounts. Henrietta's objectives were on the one hand to clear her name, and on the other to offer her resignation. But knowing that Caroline had so often refused to release her from service in the past, she had to prepare a very persuasive case. She also had to choose her words extremely carefully. The King's mistress could hardly complain to his wife that he was treating her less kindly than usual, especially as the affair remained something that could never be referred to directly. Henrietta therefore couched everything in terms of his public, rather than private, hostility.

She began by saying that she could no longer stay in Her Majesty's family, considering the 'publick marks the King has given me of his displeasure'. Sensing her rival's discomfort, and trying to bait her into making a direct reference to the affair, Caroline pretended not to understand Henrietta's meaning. 'Child, you dream,' she replied. 'Why, I saw the King speak to you.' Henrietta protested that his words had been nothing but a sharp rebuke, and that he had otherwise ignored her. Enjoying the game, Caroline insisted that he had treated her no differently from any other lady at court, mischievously adding: 'For God's sake, consider your character. You leave me because the King will not be more particular to you than to others.' Pushing home her advantage, she made Henrietta admit that George II had not visited her apartments since her return from Bath, and that this was the real issue.

Nevertheless, Henrietta continued to refer to the King in platonic terms, saying that he had 'been dearer to me than my own brother', and expressing sorrow at the loss of his 'friendship'. But the Queen was having none of it and dismissed the whole matter as little more than a lovers' tiff, caused by the romantic notions that Lady Suffolk had conceived from reading too many novels. In the face of such provocation, Henrietta grew increasingly agitated and demanded to know exactly what she stood accused of, adding that it must be some 'horrid crime' for the King to treat her so severely. The more heated she became, the more calmly the Queen dismissed her foolish notions. 'Oh fie, you commit a crime! Don't talk so,' she chided.

Realising that it was hopeless to push the point any further, even though she could tell by Caroline's looks 'that your Majesty knows of what I am accus'd', Henrietta returned to her main objective and repeated her request to retire from court. The Queen quickly changed tack and argued that if she left court, nobody would want to know her. 'Child, you do not know how differently, when you are out, people will behave,' she warned. Henrietta's response was the cleverest and most perceptive of the entire interview. 'Some people may show me it was the Courtier and not me that was liked,' she reasoned. 'I cannot say that keeping of such acquaintance will be an inducement to keep me at court.'

This particular skirmish clearly lost, the Queen told Henrietta that if she left that day, she would do so without the royal consent. Eventually, however, she suggested a compromise: if, after a week's reflection, she still wished to leave court, then she could do so. Lady Suffolk agreed to this on condition that, given the King's obvious aversion to her, she should be excused from her usual duties at court during this time. Caroline was determined to have the last word, however, and insisted that she should attend her as usual, no doubt confident that she could wear down her resistance during that time. She brought the interview to an abrupt close by dismissing Henrietta from her apartments, adding spitefully: 'Give me your word not to read any romances in that time.'[18]

Henrietta had, of course, no intention of changing her mind, and instead used this week to try and restore her reputation with the King and, by association, with the rest of polite society. Even though George was still refusing to see her in private, she went to seek him out and found him walking in the gardens at Kensington. Immediately irked by her presence, he would hear none of her pleas and she was forced to retreat.

Having failed to win over her old lover in person, Henrietta resorted to her written skills to defend her conduct and beg him to judge her more fairly. The drafts of two impassioned letters that she sent him are still among her correspondence, although they were suppressed in the published version because they leave little doubt about the intimate nature of her relations with the King. 'I Ask Sir but what your meanest, your Guiltiest subject can claim,' she began. 'A Malefactor cannot suffer till his Accusers prove their charge.' Referring to the longevity of their 'attachment', which she claimed had 'made the happiness of my life', she insisted: 'To prove to you with Duty the most sincere the most tender friendship (pardon this expression) attended with the highest sense of Gratitude for the honour of your Esteem has been my business for 20 years past.' She ended the letter with an eloquent (if perhaps not altogether sincere) appeal to the King's affection, assuring him: 'The years to come must be employ'd in the painfull task to forget you as my friend; but no years can ever make me forget you as my King.'[19]

This letter, however impassioned, did little to melt George II's heart, and when his mistress left court a few days later, on 22 November 1734, he showed neither sorrow nor regret. Indeed, if Lord Hervey is to be believed, he was heartily glad to be rid of her. When the Queen told him that she had tried to persuade Henrietta to reconsider, he cried: 'What the devil did you mean by trying to make an old, dull, deaf, peevish beast stay and plague me when I had so good an opportunity of getting rid of her.'[20] Caroline, meanwhile, was careful to show no disappointment at her failure to keep Lady Suffolk at court, and declared herself to be 'both sorry and glad'. She could not, however, resist one final swipe at her rival. 'I have always heard a great deal of her good sense from other people,' she told Lord Hervey, 'but I never saw her, in any material great occurrence of her life, take a sensible step since I knew her; her going from Court was the silliest thing she could do.'[21]

Lady Suffolk's resignation caused a scandal throughout the court, and was soon the talk not just of the city but of fashionable resorts across the country. The Countess of Pembroke observed that it had caused 'a great deal of discourse'. It was also reported in all the newspapers, from *The London Journal* and *The Gentleman's Magazine* to *The Craftsman* and *The Grub Street Journal*. Some railed against the King's cruelty towards a lady who had 'undergone twenty years' slavery to his disagreeable temper and capricious will, after she had sacrificed her time, her quiet, her reputation and her health, to his service and pleasure'. Others said that he had every right to spurn a mistress who had been nothing but trouble, and dedicate himself instead to a wife whom he truly loved.[22]

Whichever view was favoured, speculation as to what had prompted the split was rife. 'The number of story's & contradictory reasons given for Lady Suffolks removing from court wou'd fill more than an ordi nary length of one of my Letters,' wrote Elizabeth Compton to her sister, the Countess of Northampton. Some said that Walpole had 'worked her out of favour'; others that her conspiracy with Lord Bolingbroke at Bath had caused her downfall; and others still that it was due to 'the acquaintance she was known to have with many of the opposing party, and the correspondence she was suspected to have with many more of them'. Only a few people outside her immediate circle guessed the truth. 'My own opinion is that . . . since her Lords death that she was out of danger of falling into his hands I believe she has been desirous to have Liberty & a little more time at her own command,' Miss Compton shrewdly observed.[23]

Henrietta's prediction that her true friends would stand by her was fulfilled. 'Her integrity and goodness had secured the continuation of respect, and no fallen favourite had ever experienced less neglect,' observed one.[24] They had long been aware of her misery at court, and therefore rejoiced at her escape. 'I congratulate her removall from a palace to a house of her own,' wrote the Earl of Peterborough, 'where I hope she will enjoy ease, quiett, & perfect Liberty.' The Duchess of Queensberry, meanwhile, declared that her heart was full on hearing the news, and urged her friend to come and stay with her at the earliest opportunity.

Those friends who knew her less well, although proving equally sincere, expressed some anxiety at what they feared must be her very great distress at leaving court. Mary Herbert, one of Henrietta's former companions in the Queen's household, told her: 'I heartily wish you may make your self easie, tho I know it must be a hard strugle.' Lord Bathurst sent her a letter of condolence, 'for it is a sad thing, without doubt, to be remov'd from the sunshine of the court to the melancholy

Shades of privacy and retirement'. Echoing Henrietta's own words in her interview with the Queen, he predicted that 'all ye beau-monde, that used to crowd about your Toiletts, will avoid you, as if you had got ye plague', but added that it must be a great source of satisfaction to have discovered 'who were friends to ones person and who to ones fortune, which you could never have found out without this Change'.[25]

Back at St James's, there was both celebration and disappointment among the courtiers and politicians. Those who had allied themselves to Lady Suffolk for as long as she was the King's mistress clung to the faint hope that his cruel treatment of her would prompt an outcry and lead to a change of ministry. Members of the opposing party, meanwhile, rejoiced to see 'this back door to the King's ear ... at last shut up'. Although Walpole was counted among the latter, his satisfaction was tempered by a fear that she would be replaced by a mistress who might hate him as much as Lady Suffolk had done, 'but hate him more dangerously'.

A common thought united them all, both friend and foe, and that was the necessity of deterring any other would-be mistress from 'sailing near those rocks on which Lady Suffolk had split'.[26]

Chapter 14

Mrs Berkeley

———◆———

FOR ALL THE GOSSIP and speculation that Henrietta's departure from court occasioned, it proved to be merely the 'novel of a fortnight', and people soon turned to other subjects. Life at court also began to return to normal. Camilla, Countess of Tankerville, was expected to take over both Henrietta's official and unofficial duties, and the other ladies in the Queen's household resumed their daily chores and petty quarrels.

Only Caroline noticed any real difference, and it was an irksome one, for she was now obliged to entertain her husband during the many long hours he had formerly passed with Lady Suffolk. She soon became heartily sick of his company, and her daughter, Anne, the Princess Royal, shared her desire that he might soon find a suitable replacement. 'I wish, with all my heart, he would take someone else,' she told Lord Hervey, 'then Mamma might be a little relieved from the ennui of seeing him for ever in her room.' Deprived of her customary periods of peace and rest, Caroline's health began to suffer, and it was whispered about the court that she was sick with fear that Lady Tankerville was 'not a proper person to preserve the good correspondence between the King and herself that is necessary for her influencing his Majesty in the manner she has been used to do'.[1]

Nevertheless, the Queen resolved to make the best of the materials available to her. If Lady Tankerville was not so ideal a pawn as Lady Suffolk had been, she was at least good-natured and simple – 'a very safe fool' – and was a known quantity insofar as the King had flirted with her in the past. Together with Walpole, she therefore set about engineering a liaison between them, making sure the lady was placed at the King's table for cards. George, though, had already found a far more alluring companion with whom he could while away his hours of leisure.

Lady Deloraine, his daughters' governess, was a vivacious and attractive woman, with 'a pretty face, a lying tongue, and a false heart'.[2] Walpole and the Queen were alarmed at his choice, knowing that, far from being the malleable mistress they required, she was cunning and dangerous. But George was apparently besotted, and before long he was boasting that he had bedded her in his daughters' apartments. Feeling that her hold over the King was slipping away, and all too conscious of her own fading charms, Caroline must have rued the day she allowed Lady Suffolk to quit the court.

Henrietta, meanwhile, had no such regrets. Upon leaving the palace, she had sought refuge in her brother John's house on nearby Pall Mall, opposite St James's Square. The two had remained close throughout her time at court, and he no doubt shared in her joy at being free from it at last. She left his house after a few weeks, eager to take up residence in the Thames-side villa that had been hers for a decade.

Her arrival at Marble Hill inaugurated what was to be the happiest period of her life. She at once set about arranging the interiors to her satisfaction, ensuring that every detail of the decoration, furnishings and art complemented Campbell's elegant structural designs. The crowning glory was the magnificent Great Room, which was lavishly decorated with gilded sculptures, moulded plasterwork and finely carved furniture. Paintings by the Italian artist Panini served as a further reminder to Lady Suffolk's guests that they were living in the new Augustan Age, one which had produced this perfect Palladian villa. The decor also had some darker allusions, for there were a number of prominent portraits of the Stuarts, which hinted at Jacobite sympathies on the part of the hostess.

As soon as it was completed (which was the work of no more than a few weeks), Henrietta put the house to one of the main purposes for which she had intended it: a place of entertainment for her friends. Upon her retirement from court, Lord Bathurst had jokingly warned her that 'to be reduc'd to live within the Circle of one's friends, would be to most people a most dismal retreat'.[3] But in truth, this was the very thing for which she had yearned throughout the long and dreary years at St James's. Alexander Pope was one of the first to visit Marble Hill, delighted by his friend's proximity to his own villa, and he soon became a regular fixture there.

Henrietta must have revelled in the novelty of being able to enjoy her friends and her house without the grim prospect of having to leave either and return to her duties at court. The transformation of her life had an instant effect upon her health, as well as her happiness. 'She has now much more ease and liberty and accordingly her health better,' observed Lady Betty Germain, another frequent visitor to Marble Hill.[4]

So much did the Dowager Countess of Suffolk delight in being mistress of her own house that just a few months after moving there, she decided to buy another. She was eager to have a base in town to complement her country residence, and she set her sights on a new development in a fashionable area just north of Piccadilly. Savile Street (now Savile Row) was at the heart of the Burlington Estate, owned by Richard Boyle, 3rd Earl of Burlington. An acquaintance of Lady Suffolk, he was one of the greatest advocates of the Palladian style in England, and had recently remodelled his mansion at Chiswick so that it formed a perfect homage to it. The Earl also owned Burlington House on Piccadilly (now the Royal Academy of Arts), which Colen Campbell had rebuilt for him in the Palladian style.

In the early 1730s, building work was begun in the area north of Burlington House. Savile Street, named after the Earl's wife, Lady Dorothy Savile, comprised a series of elegant three-storey houses designed for members of London's most fashionable society. William Kent, one of the greatest architects of the age, leased a house at No. 2, and Lord Robert Montagu, Vice-Chamberlain to the Queen, moved into No.17. The lease for No.15 was put up for sale by the builders, Gray and Fortnum, at the beginning of 1735. The house had only just been built, and it was offered in an unfinished state. Relishing the prospect of being able to put her architectural skills to work yet again, Henrietta snapped it up for £2,500 on 12 February 1735, along with an adjoining coach house large enough to accommodate three horses.[5] Some 'allowances' were made by Gray in his bill for finishing the house, and Lady Suffolk again commissioned the Earl of Pembroke and Roger Morris to carry this out – an indication of how satisfied she had been with their work at Marble Hill.

Compared with her first house, the completion of No.15 Savile

Street was a much simpler project, but Henrietta nevertheless threw herself into it with alacrity. Every last detail was described in the instructions she gave her builders, from applying stucco work to the great stairs and hall, to skirting both the public rooms and the servants' quarters, glazing the windows with 'the best Crown Glass', lining them with lead, and installing a 'pump cistern and seat' to the water closet. Everything was finished to the highest possible specification. Even the paintwork, which had been applied only a few days before the sale, was deemed of insufficient quality, and Lady Suffolk sent instructions for 'All the work new painted to be painted over again.'[6]

She could certainly afford such luxuries, for the King had generously agreed to continue her annual allowance of £2,000 by way of a pension after she had retired from court. There was even a suggestion that she might have received an additional lump sum of around £40,000, although her accustomed discretion extended to money matters, and even her closest friends could only guess at the scale of her fortune.[7] Henrietta also continued to receive interest from the money she had been left by her late brother-in-law, albeit a rather more modest sum than her royal pension.

Once completed, Lady Suffolk's new town house presented an impressive prospect to her visitors. All the public rooms were elegant and spacious, their features shown off to best effect by the light that came flooding through the large sash windows. Like Marble Hill, it was a homage to the designs of Palladio. The steps up to the house were flanked by ornate iron railings, and the large front door opened into a thirty-foot-long parlour, flanked by four Ionic columns. Every room beyond was ornamented with richly carved stucco work. There were panelled ceilings with plaster mouldings, dado rails and wainscoting around the walls, and polished wooden floorboards. The overall effect was completed by lavish furnishings throughout, from the highly fashionable 'India paper' in the back parlour to the cherry-coloured silk damask in the twenty-eight-foot high saloon.

The Savile Street house was large enough to entertain a sizeable party of guests, for as well as an impressive dining room, it had a front and back saloon for ladies and gentlemen respectively, a study and four spacious bedrooms. The extensive service quarters were indicative of a house built for entertaining. There was a large kitchen, detached from the main house, containing four stoves, an enormous lead-based sink and many yards of shelving. Adjoining this was a pantry, store rooms and a wash house, together with accommodation for a housekeeper and a butler.[8]

Having such a lavish town house to entertain in, as well as a country villa by the Thames, might seem a little excessive for a lady on her own, no matter how high her status. A countess she might have been, but Henrietta was also a widow, and her only son had long been estranged from her. Custom tended to dictate that a woman in her situation should live in just one house, and that would normally be in town rather than the country, so that she was closer to the social life it offered. Others might choose to live in a dower house on their children's estate. Lady Betty Germain, one of Henrietta's closest friends, had moved out of her country estate at Drayton after her husband's death, and spent the rest of her life with the Duke and Duchess of Dorset at Knole in Kent, where she had her own apartments.

It was therefore rather unusual for Lady Suffolk to have bought a second residence so soon after moving into her first. Of course, it might simply have been that, free at last from the shackles of court, she was determined to make up for all those wasted years. Besides, as a woman who had separated from her husband and had a long-standing affair with the King, she was hardly one to bow to convention. But it is at least equally likely that Henrietta did not plan to entertain alone for long.

As well as Pope, Chesterfield and the other members of Lady Suffolk's circle who came to see her at Marble Hill, there was another friend whose visits she most particularly anticipated. George Berkeley's admiration for the King's former mistress had in no way diminished after she had resigned her prestigious position at court. In fact, he had become an ever more frequent visitor to Marble Hill, and was also among the Duchess of Queensberry's guests at Highclere when Henrietta went there in early summer 1735.

Lady Suffolk had been widowed for almost two years (a respectable period, even for one who had not been estranged from her late husband), she had no further duties to her royal master, and she also enjoyed the luxury of financial independence. It was therefore entirely reasonable – and, in the eyes of polite society, respectable – for her to enter into a courtship with another man. That she had, to all intents and purposes, been doing so with George Berkeley for several years was known only to their closest friends.

The couple were discreet in their courtship, apparently anxious not to reveal it beyond their immediate circle. So successful were they that even those acquaintances who saw them often were astonished when, in July 1735, they joyfully announced to the world that they were married. The wedding had taken place at St Dunstan's Church on the Berkeley family's estate of Cranford, Middlesex, on 26 June. Only a handful of close family members, including Lady Betty, had witnessed the event, and they had kept it secret for almost two weeks. When the couple at last announced it, the whole of the fashionable world was agog at the news. 'The town's surpris'd, & the town talks, as the town loves to do on these ordinary Extraordinary occasions,' observed Lady Betty Germain in a letter to Swift.[9] It was reported in all the newspapers (most of which inaccurately claimed that the wedding had taken place in early July), and was gossiped about throughout the court and polite society.

Henrietta once more found herself the subject of intense speculation. 'Mr Berkeley was neither young, nor handsome, healthy, nor rich,' observed Lord Hervey in typically cutting fashion, 'which made people wonder what induced Lady Suffolk's prudence to deviate into this unaccountable piece of folly.' The cruellest among those who commented on the matter claimed that she had been so long with a companion that she 'could not live without something in that style', but that as she was getting on in years, she could not afford to be too selective so had grabbed the first offer that had come her way. Some asserted that it was a deliberate ploy to salvage her reputation and convince the world that nothing improper had ever passed between her and the King. Others believed the opposite, and that it was designed to pique her former royal lover.

If that had been Lady Suffolk's intention, then she had failed miserably. George II was in Hanover when he received the news in a letter from the Queen, and was reported to have expressed great surprise that his old mistress should have married the 'gouty' Mr Berkeley, who was himself somewhat advanced in years. He added: 'I would not wish to confer such presents upon my friends, and when my enemies rob me, pray God they may always do it thus!' Caroline, meanwhile, was similarly taken aback by the news, and dismissed the match as 'the silliest thing she could do'.[10]

That Henrietta's marriage to George Berkeley should have caused such a stir was perhaps understandable. Her struggle for freedom from the burdens of court service, a violent husband, a protracted and tedious affair with the King, and the persistent solicitations of ambitious place-seekers was well known, and most people had expected her to now sit back and enjoy her newly won independence. But those who knew her best realised that one simple and unforeseen factor had overcome all these considerations: she had fallen in love.

George was an ideal match for Henrietta. He was cultured, witty and sincere, and was as good-natured and mild-mannered as her first husband had been unstable and hot-headed. Here, at last, was her chance to find the happiness in her personal life that had so long eluded her, and she was not about to let it slip away. It was, as one commentator rather aptly put it, her 'Indian summer of love'.[11]

The couple's friends were overjoyed for them, and none more so than the woman who had brought them together, Lady Betty Germain. She declared herself to be 'extreamly delight'd' at the match, and told Swift: 'The Countess of Suffolk . . . has been so good and gracious as to take my Brother George Berkeley for better, for worse, tho I hope in God the last wont happen, because I think he is an honest good natured man.' Referring to the longevity of their acquaintance, she said that her brother 'has appeard to all the world as well as to me, to have long had . . . a most violent passion for her as well as esteem & value for her Numberless good qualities', quickly adding that his 'violent passion' had only dated from the time that Lady Suffolk had become a widow, 'so pray don't mistake me'.[12]

Lady Hervey, meanwhile, who was still a close friend of Henrietta and had also become acquainted with Mr Berkeley, wished them 'all the joy imaginable', and said that if they did not find it, ''twould be very difficult for one to decide on which to lay the blame; tho one of ye wou'd be most excessively in the wrong'. George's friends were similarly delighted, and letters of congratulation came pouring in from all parts of the country. They too could see that he and his new bride were well matched. 'In the choice you have made, where the most agreable beautys of the mind are join'd to those of the body, wishing joy (where it already is & must last) is at any time a meer ceremony,' wrote Lord Lovell from his estate in Norfolk. Thomas Wentworth, Earl of Strafford, joined him in congratulating their friend on having married 'the most agreable lady in Europe', and insisted that these were not mere words said for form's sake, but 'the real dictates of a sincere heart of one who has long known you'. The couple's mutual friend, Lord

Bolingbroke, was also overjoyed when he heard the news in France, and wrote at once to wish them 'a long and uninterrupted scene of felicety'.[13]

The only sour note was sounded by Theresa Blount, who had been put out by Lady Suffolk's neglect of her and her sister Patty during her courtship with Mr Berkeley. Eager to make amends, Henrietta had invited Patty to stay with them at Marble Hill shortly after the wedding, and Theresa had visited them there. 'To behold ye happy Pair; & at night, to see her deaf-Ear, & his Lame-leg: put into Bed on Purpose baught, for ye unexpectid Nuptialls,' she scoffed in a letter to Pope, although she grudgingly admitted that they both seemed to be very happy in their marriage.[14]

Theresa's bitter comments aside, all Henrietta and George's other friends wished them well and confidently predicted a long and blissful marriage. 'I dont think they have above 10 to 1 against their being very happy,' wrote Lady Betty Germain to Swift after the wedding, '& if they should not I shall heartily wish him hang'd because I'm sure twill be wholly his fault.' She was just as assured a few months later, and told her friend: 'I hope whenever you ask me about the Countess & George I shall be able to answer you as I can safely do now, that as yet theres no sort of appearance that they like one another the worse for wearing.'[15]

The couple fulfilled – and even exceeded – their friends' confident expectations. They were clearly very deeply in love. This was not the passing fancy typical of so many marriages – indeed, typical of Henrietta's first marriage. It was founded upon mutual affection, esteem and respect. Once the secret of their marriage was out, Henrietta and George took every opportunity to share their happiness with the world. They commissioned a pair of portraits to mark the occasion, and proudly displayed them in the long gallery at Marble Hill, alongside those of King George and Queen Caroline. The portraits show a couple who are at once at ease and joyful in their union. Mr Berkeley stands in front of a picturesque landscape, as if interrupted from a pleasant walk, a gentle smile playing about his lips. His wife, meanwhile, is dressed in an informal soft pink gown, worn loose around her breasts, and looks considerably younger than her forty-six years. In her left hand is a shell, perhaps a reference to the Goddess of Love, and her enigmatic smile matches that of her new husband.[16]

The couple were quick to open up their house to the wide circle of friends they had cultivated over the years, and before long it was one of the most vibrant centres of society away from London. 'There is a greater court now at Marble hill than at Kensington,' wrote Pope to a friend in August 1735, 'and God knows when it will end.'[17] Mrs Berkeley delighted in playing host with her new husband, and had the added satisfaction of knowing that, in contrast to her days at court, the people who now crowded into her rooms were all there for reasons of friendship rather than ambition. But nothing rivalled her joy at being able to complete this happy domestic scene by once again playing the role of mother.

Soon after her marriage, her brother John's only surviving children, John and Dorothy, came to live with the newlyweds. Henrietta's love for Dorothy has already been documented. She was also very fond of the boy, John, who was twelve years old when they came to live at Marble Hill. George shared his wife's affection for them, and together they raised their young charges in a home filled with love and laughter. Henrietta always favoured Dorothy in arguments, which prompted George to scold her for overindulgence, claiming that it was high time she assumed the 'office of Rebuker' with the girl. He, meanwhile, took John's side, and a light-hearted battle developed between the sexes. 'You have a high opinion of my understanding, which is sufficient proof to me yt you have a good one,' John wrote to his ally, adding: 'I once thought yt silly woman, who has ye honour to call you Husband had been free, at least, from ye glaring foibles of her sex.'[18]

It was agreed that the children would stay at Marble Hill until John was of an age to be sent away to school, and Dorothy reached adulthood. In the meantime, they would be visited often by John Hobart senior when business brought him to London, and would also make regular trips to see him at their childhood home of Blickling.

Henrietta was overjoyed at being given this unexpected chance to experience the contented family life for which she had so long yearned, but which she had resigned herself never to have. She immediately set about transforming Marble Hill into a family home, furnishing the guest bedrooms with all the comforts necessary for a young gentleman and his sister, as well as purchasing a new bed for herself and her husband. She also engaged an extra servant to help run what was suddenly a busy household. These frenzied activities were all related in a letter she wrote, somewhat hurriedly, to her friend Anne Pitt. So often in the past, Henrietta had read wistfully of her friends' ordinary family lives away from court, but now the roles had been reversed, and it was she who was apologising for giving a 'tedious account of my domestic affairs'. For all her panic in trying to arrange everything to the satisfaction of her husband and young charges, she was clearly deeply contented with her new life, and it was with barely disguised pride that she spoke of 'my family'.[19]

The happy domestic scene at Marble Hill was temporarily broken up when Henrietta accepted an invitation to visit her friend Lord Cobham's celebrated gardens at Stowe, towards the end of August 1735. She was reluctant to leave her new family, but her recent poor health proved an incentive. The headaches that had plagued her so often at court had returned, perhaps brought on by the exertion of disrupting her formerly tranquil life in Twickenham, no matter how pleasant the cause had been. George urged her to go, assuring her that he would manage the house and its young occupants in her absence. She duly set off, taking her old friend Patty Blount along for company.

Although the trip only lasted a few days, the Berkeleys obviously found the separation unbearable and wrote to each other every day. The affectionate sentiments expressed in their letters might have been expected from a pair of lovesick newlyweds, but they were no less sincere for that. Indeed, even many years into their marriage, there was no discernible decline in their mutual adoration. 'The moment your Ladyship was gone I went to bed lay half an hour, disliked it extremely, gott up again,' wrote George to his wife the day after her departure, adding that he had 'never found Marble Hill so disagreeable'. Evidently hoping that Lord Cobham's gardens would soon have the desired effect upon her health so that she might return, he ended: 'I begg of you for my sake take more than usual care of your self.'

Henrietta wrote back by return of post and said that she was 'not sorry' he disliked being at home without her, but assured him that she would soon return because her health was greatly improved. Indeed, all the party at Stowe had commented upon how well marriage suited her, for although she was now in her mid-forties, she appeared more radiant than in the bloom of her youth. 'Baron Sparr affirms I look better than I did seventeen years ago, and Lord Cobham says the best looking woman of thirty that he ever saw,' she told him, claiming that all these compliments had quite cured her headaches. She could not resist adding, as a playful afterthought: 'I will follow your advice strictly and expect as I have now told you the method that is proper to keep me in health, that you will repeat the doses as often as is necessary.' The letter ends with a final mark of her affection. 'God bless you,' she wrote, 'I do with all my heart and soul nor do I yet repent that I am H. Berkeley.'

Perhaps this expression of tenderness provoked a sudden impatience to be back with her husband, for she added a hurried postscript urging him to order horses to be ready at Winslow, Buckinghamshire, some fifty miles north-west of London. She proposed setting out very early from Lord Cobham's on the day appointed for her departure so that she might make it back to Marble Hill before nightfall – a journey that would usually take two days.

'My Life! My Soul! My joy!' George replied excitedly. He hastily arranged for the horses to be at Winslow a night earlier than she had instructed, to be on the safe side, and hoped 'to be blessed with your company' the following day. His wife wrote to thank him immediately, and also expressed mock anxiety about his fidelity during her absence. 'I have not heard one word how Madam Pitt and you meet . . . I don't like the silence', she wrote, adding the warning: 'But at your Peril, she has a Brother; I say no more.'

This irrepressibly high-spirited, youthful-looking woman was barely recognisable from the downtrodden royal mistress whose heavy cares had threatened to crush her altogether. Her marriage to George Berkeley, coupled with her freedom from court, had given Henrietta a new lust for life, and she seemed to take joy in everything she experienced. She even learned the theory of cricket during her visit to Stowe, telling her husband that she had 'some thoughts of Practicing this afternoon'.

Mrs Berkeley was up at dawn on the day of her departure and set off before the rest of the household was awake. But for all her efforts, the horses that George had ordered proved frustratingly slow and she was forced to break her journey with an overnight stay. When he heard of this, her husband sent her a hurried note, offering to hire some fresh horses to bring her back from any place that she might wish. 'I miss you even more than I thought I should,' he added as a postscript, 'I cant express it stronger. Heaven preserve you.'[20]

When Henrietta and George were at last reunited, such was their joy that they vowed never to be apart again if it was at all in their power to prevent it. They were true to their word, and during the years that followed, they were almost always in each other's company. Their time was divided between their two homes, as well as visits to friends or fashionable retreats, and even the occasional foreign venture.

The couple spent most of the year at Marble Hill. Henrietta obviously relished her new role as a loving – and much-loved – wife, and George, who had been a city dweller for most of his life, adapted smoothly and delightedly to the slower pace of country living. All this was a far cry from the scandal, intrigue and backbiting of the court, and Henrietta could not have been happier at the transformation. 'We live very innocently, and very regular, both new scenes of life to me,' she told Miss Pitt, going on to describe 'the joys of solitude, and our happiness in it'. She could not suppress the pride she felt in her new husband, who was as different from her first as it was possible to be. 'He rides, walks, and reads; for smoking drinking and hunting I take to be the life of a country brute.'[21]

But for all their simple domestic pleasures, Mr and Mrs Berkeley's new life together was hardly one of complete isolation. The vibrant social scene that they had established at Marble Hill during the first few weeks of their marriage continued to flourish. Many of their visitors were connected in some way to the court. Anne Pitt often called when the royal household was at nearby Richmond, as did Anne Knight, the daughter of James Craggs, former Secretary of State. William Pulteney, who was still at the heart of the opposition to Walpole, was frequently of the party, his long friendship with Henrietta and George deepening as the years went by. He and his wife were grateful to the couple when they offered to take care of their son during a bout of illness. By now adept at looking after young children, they performed the task so well that the boy was soon back to full health. 'If I would take the liberty of carrying a sick Child to any bodys house,' Pulteney vowed afterwards, 'it should be to you & Lady Suffolk.'[22]

Other guests included the Duchess of Queensberry, along with Henrietta's old companion at court, Lady Hervey, and Henry Herbert, Earl of Pembroke. Alexander Pope continued to be one of the most frequent visitors, and despite living only a short distance upstream, he often stayed over rather than risk his fragile health by setting out late at night. Although he had had Henrietta to himself before her marriage, he seemed to grow accustomed to her husband and was always solicitous in enquiring after his health. Pope's only complaint was the lateness of the hour at which the Berkeleys chose to dine. During the early part of the eighteenth century, most of society, including the court,

had tended to take dinner at around midday, but this became gradually later as the century progressed. Ever at the forefront of fashionable taste, within a year or so of their marriage, Henrietta and her
husband were serving dinner at four o'clock in the afternoon. This was
far too late for the stubbornly traditional Pope, who was a slave to a
constitution that would brook no interruption to its accustomed diges-
tive habits. 'I find I must never attempt to dine so late as a fashionable hour,' he complained to an acquaintance, adding: 'I really dread
the consequence of doing it at Marble-Hill.'[23]

Everyone who called on Mr and Mrs Berkeley at Marble Hill found
a warm welcome and generous hospitality. Henrietta had ordered an
ice-house to be built in the grounds, where ice and snow would be
packed in the winter for preserving food and cooling drinks. Guests
were also treated to home-grown fruit and vegetables, as well as fresh
milk, butter and cream from the Marble Hill dairy. A team of household staff and gardeners was employed to keep everything ticking over,
and to ensure that their masters' table was always one of the finest to
be had for miles around.

The constant stream of visitors took its toll on the house and the
guest rooms were frequently redecorated or repaired. This was not
enough to satisfy Henrietta, who decided that more space was needed
to cope with the unremitting round of social calls and receptions. She
therefore commissioned her faithful architect, Roger Morris, to build
a cottage in the grounds. Once completed, this not only created more
space within the main house, but also served as a perfect repository
for Mrs Berkeley's ever-expanding collection of china. She ordered elaborate shelves to be constructed along every wall in order to show this
off to best effect, and also chose a rather garish colour scheme which
included a 'gaily painted ceiling'. 'My Cheney room will make you stare
if not swear,' she told Lord Pembroke, who for once she had not
consulted. 'I must tell you 'tis the admiration of the Vulgar, but my
vanity would be intirely gratified if it shou'd meet your approbation.'[24]
It is doubtful whether the Earl, whose tastes were more inclined towards
classical simplicity, would have given the stamp of approval that she
hoped for.

While Marble Hill remained Mr and Mrs Berkeley's main home,
they made regular visits to their town house in Savile Street and spent
most winters there. They also chose to celebrate their first Christmas
together there in 1735, although it was evidently quite a wrench to leave

Marble Hill. A week before their departure, Henrietta had written to let Anne Pitt know that they would be in town, and to invite her to supper at Savile Street. She confided that she and her husband were both sorry to be leaving their life of solitude in order to 'try again how we like noise, scandal and all the other pleasures your great world abounds in'.[25] She may have said this half in jest, but it is remarkable how quickly she had moved from being at the very centre of fashionable London life to being a passive observer of it. It was a transformation that suited her well.

Nevertheless, when they were up in town, the Berkeleys entertained in style. No.15 Savile Street soon became as lively a social centre as their villa in Twickenham, and also provided a base from which to sample the capital's playhouses, assemblies and other fashionable diversions. But Marble Hill was never far from their thoughts, and they even ordered fresh fruit, vegetables and dairy produce to be sent from there to sustain them and their guests in London.

Consummate hosts though they were, Henrietta and George also made regular visits to the country estates of friends. Their most frequent destination was Lady Betty Germain's. Henrietta's marriage to the lady's brother had deepened their friendship still further, and the three made a very relaxed and convivial party together. Although Lady Betty lived with the Duke and Duchess of Dorset most of the time, she returned to her house at Drayton in Northamptonshire to receive the Berkeleys. This was a considerable journey from Marble Hill, and as the roads were among the most treacherous in the country, it could take several days.

On one trip, Henrietta complained that 'the roads were worse than I had ever gone, and the miles longer'. At the slowest part of the journey, it took two hours to cover just five miles. Things got even worse on this particular trip, for their coach overturned and although nobody was seriously injured, Henrietta sustained a small wound 'in a place where I hope it will be no eye sore'. They found little relief at the coach houses where they stayed en route, which grew less salubrious the further they travelled from London. Mrs Berkeley described one of these to her friend Anne Pitt. 'I, like a good wife, went to see our chamber was clean, aired, and in order,' she wrote. Unfortunately, it fell short on all three counts, and when she and George retired to bed that night, they quarrelled over which side of it smelt the least, eventually concluding that both sides were just as bad.[26]

Such inconveniences were to be expected for an age in which transport was still quite primitive, particularly outside London. 'I find the farther one goes from the capital, the more tedious the miles grow, and the more rough and disagreeable the way,' complained Lord Hervey.[27] Some rural roads dated back to Roman times or even prehistoric trackways, but many more meandered haphazardly up hill and down dale, or wound their way through uneven open fields. This meant a slow, uncomfortable and often hazardous journey for the passengers within. 'If one could fly in ye Aire twould be a charming Countrey,' wrote Henrietta's cousin Margaret Bradshaw during a trip to Cheshire, 'but since there is no such machine I would not live here . . . for ye Kings ransum.'[28]

During the early to mid-eighteenth century, most people travelled in heavy, lumbering coaches, which covered an average of just four miles per hour. Passengers would be in for an uncomfortable ride in summer, as the coaches jolted and bumped their way over the dusty ground; whereas in winter the roads were often so caked in mud that travellers became stuck en route. Added to this was the perennial danger of highwaymen, which was a very real one judging by the number of attacks reported in the papers. Only later in the century did things start to improve, but for Henrietta and her contemporaries, travel was a necessary evil in the pursuit of social pleasures.

The couple did not restrict their excursions to Britain alone. As the century progressed, it became increasingly fashionable for well-to-do ladies and gentlemen to go travelling on the Continent. The 'Grand Tour', which included France, Italy and the Netherlands, became an essential part of an aristocratic son's cultural education. There he would be expected to acquire a knowledge of languages (in particular French, which was spoken by polite society across Europe) and sophisticated Continental etiquette, and above all to develop a taste for the arts and architecture. Many young men returned with crates of art and antiques with which to adorn their country houses. By the 1760s, the Grand Tour had become so popular that much of the paraphernalia associated with modern-day travel had started to be introduced, including published guides to historical monuments and art galleries, and even a few tour guides, who were usually expatriates from Britain.

The Grand Tour aside, other, less formal overseas excursions were made by increasing numbers of England's nobility and gentry during the Georgian period. The vast majority of these headed to France and

Belgium, where certain fashionable stopping-off points became an essential part of any visit. Travellers might take the waters at Spaa or Aix-la-Chapelle (now Aachen) in Belgium, admire the splendid land-scaped gardens surrounding Brussels, or visit the art galleries of Paris. The summer months were the most popular time to travel, and those members of high society who did so could expect to encounter a great many people they knew. 'I found the place swarming with English,' wrote the Duchess of Queensberry from Spaa in August 1738. 'Lord Lonsdale and his brother, Mr and Mrs Poultney, the Duke of Buckingham, Mr Herbert, Mr Newgent, Lord Cornbury ... Lord Scarborough ... Mr and Mrs Pryce, and 10,000 more.'[29]

A number of Henrietta and George's other close acquaintances were also devotees of Continental travel, including Lady Hervey and Lady Betty Germain. Their letters were full of praise for the sights they saw and the lively company they kept, and were no doubt an impor-tant factor in prompting the newlyweds to make a trip of their own during their first full summer together. George Berkeley was, appar-ently, rather against the scheme at first, for he had a well-known aver-sion to the French. Lady Hervey, a fervent Francophile, had chided him for this shortcoming on several occasions. 'Pray tell Mr Berkley that if I did not think of the French as I do, I shou'd think of them as he does,' she wrote to Henrietta upon hearing of their marriage. 'One must love or hate them there is no mean.'[30] But he was a sensible man, and the pleasant prospect of a summer spent with his new wife and their circle of friends soon overcame any initial resistance. Moreover, he was eager to see his elder brother, James, 3rd Earl of Berkeley, who was on a recuperative visit to the Duke of Richmond's house at Aubigny.

They duly set sail in early May 1736, accompanied by their beloved young charge, Dorothy Hobart. Their departure attracted some atten-tion in the press, and was reported in several London newspapers. The contrast with Henrietta's only other overseas excursion, some twenty-two years earlier, when she had wagered everything on an uncertain voyage to Hanover with her first husband, could not have been greater. This time, she was taking her first holiday with a loving new husband, and the objective was to seek pleasure rather than to secure her future.

The party rested at Calais before continuing their journey to Aubigny. The Duke of Richmond and his wife Sarah were old friends of Mrs Berkeley, having served in the households of George II and his consort respectively. The Duke had inherited the title and estate of Aubigny

Lady Suffolks Hair

These locks of 'Lady Suffolk's hair' are mounted on the inside cover of a volume of 18th - century letters. Walpole referred to Henrietta's hair as being chestnut in colour and 'remarkably fine', but she dyed it regularly, no doubt to please her royal lover, who preferred fair hair.

Marble Hill House (the north front), Henrietta's beloved Thames-side retreat in Twickenham.

Henrietta's beloved nephew, John Hobart, 2nd Earl of Buckinghamshire.

Henrietta Hotham, who lived with her great-aunt and namesake at Marble Hill from 1763 until the latter's death four years later.

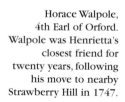

Horace Walpole, 4th Earl of Orford. Walpole was Henrietta's closest friend for twenty years, following his move to nearby Strawberry Hill in 1747.

This portrait, and the one of George Berkeley, was commissioned to celebrate their marriage in 1735. Henrietta looks a very youthful forty-six, and is cast as Venus, holding a shell to gather water from a fountain in the Garden of Love.

George Berkeley at the time of his marriage to Henrietta in 1735. Some four or five years her junior, George was said to have 'long had …a most violent passion for her'.

The Countess of Suffolk's bedchamber, Marble Hill House. This is the room
in which she died, on 26 July 1767.

Marble Hill House from the river (after 1749).

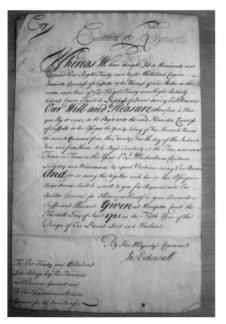

The official order appointing Henrietta Howard, Countess of Suffolk, as Mistress of the Robes – the most senior post in Queen Caroline's household.

The deed of separation that brought to an end Henrietta's marriage to Charles Howard, 29 February 1728.

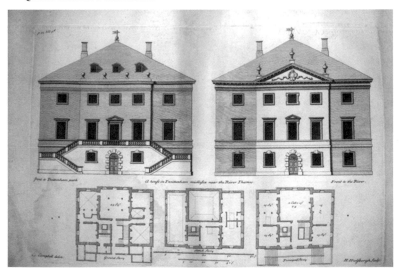

The original plans for Marble Hill House. Drawn up by the celebrated architect, Colen Campbell, these were kept hidden by Henrietta in her apartments, lest her royal mistress should discover them and put an end to the scheme.

(*Left*) John Gay, poet and dramatist, in his mid-thirties. He remained one of Henrietta's closest friends until his untimely death in 1732. (*Right*) Jonathan Swift, Dean of St Patrick's Cathedral, Dublin, and author of *Gulliver's Travels*. Swift was among Henrietta's close circle of literary friends until a bitter row ended their association for good.

Jonathan Swift sits at the table, quill in hand, with Alexander Pope in thoughtful pose on the left and Jonathan Gay in between them. The portrait hanging above them on the left is of Henrietta, who was for many years a member of this intimate literary circle.

A tea party at Lord Harrington's house, 1730. Henrietta sits in the centre of three groups, inclining her head towards her future husband, George Berkeley, who stands just to the left of the fireplace. His sister, Lady Betty Germaine, who introduced the pair, is in the left-hand group, wearing a patterned dress.

Alexander Pope with his dog, Bounce. Pope shared Henrietta's love of dogs, and wrote a poem in honour of their respective pets: 'From Bounce to Fop'.

Queen Caroline (c.1735).
By the time this portrait was painted, Caroline's
famously voluptuous figure had expanded into
portliness and she was suffering so much with
gout that she could barely walk.

(*Left*) Henrietta Howard with one of her lapdogs (she had two at court, named Fop
and Marquise). Henrietta's hair is shown as its natural chestnut colour, which is unusual
because in most other portraits it is blonde. (*Right*) King George II, aged seventy.

upon the death of his grandmother in 1734, and had thereafter spent a great deal of time in that pleasant retreat with his family. He was a genial host and his house soon became an unmissable part of the Continental tour for genteel travellers.

Mr and Mrs Berkeley knew several of the guests who were there upon their arrival, and received a warm welcome. The person whom they were most anxious to see was George's brother James, whose health was showing little sign of improvement. Having lost his other brother, Henry, just a few weeks before, these were anxious times for George. He was greatly comforted by the arrival of his old friend Lord Bolingbroke and his second wife Marie-Claire de Marcilly, who had been living in France since his defeat by Walpole in 1734 and the brief sojourn in Bath that followed. His departure had prompted various disaffected politicians and other opponents to the regime to follow him there, and before long he had gathered quite a body of supporters about him. These included a growing contingent of Jacobites, who used the safety of the Continent to develop fresh plots to restore James 'III' to the British throne.

Lady Suffolk no longer needed to conceal her political allegiance, and therefore openly courted her old acquaintance. Both she and Mr Berkeley were delighted with Bolingbroke's wife, who was renowned for her amiable disposition and good sense, and they maintained a correspondence with her long after their departure from France.

The party at Aubigny also included William Chetwynd, a mutual acquaintance of the Bolingbrokes and Berkeleys, who was known as 'Brother Will' in the close-knit society of disaffected politicians who gathered on the Continent. His attachment to Bolingbroke did not prevent his attaining considerable offices under George II, and he proved a very useful ally at the heart of government. Chetwynd's friendship with the Berkeleys was to develop once they were back in England, and he became a regular guest at Marble Hill and Savile Street.

After spending a pleasant few weeks with this company, Henrietta and George took their leave, sufficiently well assured of James Berkeley's health. Lady Bolingbroke promised to keep them informed of his progress. Together with his wife and her niece, George continued on to Paris, following what had now become the accustomed route for fashionable travellers. The absence of any correspondence to their friends back in England suggests that their time was entirely taken up with the vibrant social scene that greeted them upon their arrival.

Having enjoyed the galleries, theatres and assemblies for a few days, the Berkeleys spent the remainder of their trip recovering at Aix-la-Chapelle and Spaa, where they joined various other members of their acquaintance in taking the waters for their health. They had genuine cause to do so, for Henrietta was still troubled by headaches and poor hearing, and her husband had had a renewed attack of gout. Whilst in Spaa, they received the sad news that James Berkeley's health had taken a turn for the worse after their departure from Aubigny, and he had died on 17 August. This cast a shadow over their carefree adventure, and they prepared to leave for home soon afterwards.

Chapter 15

'The Melancholy Shades of Privacy'

◄○►

NOW WELL INTO THEIR forties, Henrietta and George were aware that death would be an ever more frequent blight on their lives. Up until the mid-eighteenth century, medical practices were largely ineffectual and tended to worsen conditions rather than alleviate them. Purgatives and blood-letting were common, as it was widely believed that ridding the body of phlegm, vomit and toxins in the blood was beneficial. These practices, coupled with a fatty, sugary diet lacking in fresh fruit and vegetables, excessive drinking and a lack of exercise, rendered the population vulnerable to disease. Smallpox was the scourge of the eighteenth century, claiming around 15,000 victims every year in London alone, and influenza often reached epidemic proportions. Gout, with which George Berkeley suffered, was also common, particularly among the wealthier classes, with their rich diet and sedentary lifestyle, and comprised a painful inflammation of the joints which sometimes led to arthritis. All of this considered, it is perhaps not surprising that the average life expectancy was just thirty-eight.

The first year of Mr and Mrs Berkeley's marriage saw the death of two of their closest friends. The first was John Arbuthnot, who had been a physician, friend and confidant to Henrietta throughout her time at court, and whose political leanings had also won him the respect of her husband George. Pope and Chesterfield were with him at his house in Cork Street, Piccadilly, the night before he died, aged sixty-eight. 'He suffered racking pains from an inflammation in his bowels, but his head was clear to the last,' wrote Chesterfield. He had taken leave of them 'without tenderness, without weakness', deriving comfort from his devout Christian faith.[1]

Five months later, in October 1735, Henrietta's old admirer, the Earl of Peterborough, also died. His health had been failing for some years, and he had lost much of his energetic lust for life. He was fond of saying that the world had become so indifferent to him that he amused himself with thoughts of going out of it. When his health began to deteriorate rapidly, several of his closest friends visited him at his home at Bevis Mount, near Southampton. They were amazed by the humour and optimism with which he approached his impending death. 'This man was never born to die like other men any more than to live like them,' wrote Pope, who had been among the friends to visit. Peterborough retained his affection for Henrietta to the end, and urged her to come and see him, saying that it was one of his 'strongest motives' for keeping alive a little longer. 'I want to make an appointment with you, Mr Pope, and a few friends more, to meet upon the summit of my Bevis hill and thence, after a speech and a tender farewell, I shall take my leap towards the clouds . . . to mix among the stars,' he wrote.[2] Sadly, she never made it, and at the end of the summer, Peterborough set sail with his young wife for Lisbon, where he died on 25 October.

Death was also stalking the corridors of St James's Palace. The Queen, who had been suffering with her 'secret rupture' for some time, was becoming noticeably slower and in need of frequent rests. Her condition was not helped by the fact that she was now somewhat obese, years of indulging in hot chocolate and rich food having swelled her portly figure to considerable proportions. Although the King still loved her deeply, he no longer desired her, and he was now finding sexual pleasure elsewhere.

Caroline's long-held fear that once Henrietta had left court, her husband would find a more alluring mistress who would threaten her own hold over him was now being realised. Lady Deloraine had proved a passing fancy, but she had soon been replaced by a more dangerous rival. The year after Lady Suffolk's retirement, George II had paid one of his triennial summer visits to Hanover. Whilst there, he had fallen head over heels in love with a young German noblewoman, Amelia Sophia de Walmoden. Vivacious and high-spirited, she was also cunning and quick-witted, and used all her feminine wiles to seduce the King. Although she was married and already enjoying a series of illicit liaisons with various men at Herrenhausen, Madame Walmoden flattered the King into believing that he was the only man she had ever loved. He was soon so besotted that he showered her with gifts and trailed after her like a lovesick puppy, all the while sending detailed accounts of each stage of the conquest back to his wife in England. 'I know you will love the Walmoden, because she loves me,' he assured her in one.[3]

The whole of London was buzzing with the news, and speculation was rife that the Queen's notoriously tight hold on her husband was now, finally, slipping. Caroline dismissed such notions as ridiculous. She firmly believed that by the time George returned at the end of the summer, the affair would have fizzled out. When he delayed his return because he could not bear to be parted from his new love, however, she began to panic. Her anxiety rose even further as the King's birthday approached and there was still no sign of him: it was inconceivable that he could miss such an important state occasion. In fact, he arrived just in time for the event, but some six weeks later than originally scheduled. What was worse, he had only managed to tear himself away by promising his mistress that he would return the following spring – an unprecedented move that was likely to be as unpopular with his English subjects as it was alarming for his wife.

When at last he arrived back in England, George was in the foulest of tempers, full of bitterness at being forced to leave the 'magnificent delightful dwelling' of Hanover and return to the 'mean dull island' over which he was King. He railed against his ministers, courtiers and the English in general. No Englishman could cook, no English player could act, no English coachman could drive, no Englishman knew how to come into a room, nor any English woman how to dress herself. But it was the Queen who bore the brunt of his ill humour. Everyone at court noticed that his behaviour towards her had completely changed. Everything she did was now a fresh cause for irritation – from hanging some pictures in the wrong place at Kensington to constantly 'stuffing' herself with chocolate.[4] 'The King . . . was now abominably and perpetually so harsh and rough, that she could never speak one word uncontradicted, nor do any one act unreproved,' observed Lord Hervey.[5]

Caroline was greatly troubled by his treatment of her. She had experienced humiliation at his hands in the past, but never anything to compare with this. She confided her fears to Walpole, who told her frankly that after thirty years of marriage, she could not expect to enjoy the same influence over her husband that she had done before, and that 'three-and-fifty and three-and-twenty could no more resemble one another in their effects than in their looks'. This was cold comfort indeed, and she could find no better from her husband. All he could talk about were the charms of his new mistress – a subject that gave him so much delight that he could not understand why his wife apparently failed to share it. When he was not talking about her, he was writing to her, or reading out the letters that she faithfully sent him every post. Blundering on in his insensitivity towards the Queen's feelings, he even had a full-length portrait of the lady installed at the foot of his bed, 'a compliment that shows indeed the violence of his love', one courtier observed.[6]

George II's impatience to return to Hanover was heightened still further by the fact that the object of his passion was with child. While in reality the father could have been one of several men (not least her husband), she swore that the baby was his, and he did not doubt it for a second. He assured her that he would do everything possible to be with her for the birth, but by the time he arrived in early summer 1736, she was already holding their son in her arms. The child proved 'a cement that binds them faster', and George was now more besotted with his mistress than ever.

It was fortunate for her that he was, for it made him blind to her obvious infidelities. One night during the King's sojourn in Hanover, a gardener discovered a ladder beneath Madame Walmoden's window. Fearing that an intruder was at that very moment making away with her jewels, he scoured the gardens and found a man lurking behind a nearby trellis. With the assistance of his fellow servants, he carried him to the captain of the guard then on duty. Rather than a thief, however, the man turned out to be a relation of George I's old mistress, Madame Schulenburg, and an officer in the Imperial Service.

The affair at once created a scandal at Herrenhausen, and Madame Walmoden flew to present her version of events to her royal lover before he heard the gossip from a less favourable (and more accurate) source. Giving the performance of her life, she threw herself at his feet, weeping bitterly and pleading with him to protect her from insult and falsehood. Speaking very quickly, in between sobs, she regaled the bewildered George with an elaborate tale of how the Schulenburg family had plotted to ruin her reputation. Incensed by such an outrage committed against his lady-love, the King ordered that the captain of the guard at Hanover be put under immediate arrest for having released the culprit, and that the latter should again be apprehended. However, the incident had planted a small seed of doubt in his mind, and he wrote to ask the Queen and Walpole's advice on the matter.

The King's shenanigans in Hanover were soon the talk of the English court, and Caroline was determined not to show any sign of humiliation at her husband's foolish infatuation with such a conniving young harlot. Her Gentleman Usher reported that when she overheard some indiscreet whispers about her husband's affair one day at court, she declared that she was 'sorry for the scandal it gave others, but for herself she minded it no more than his going to the close stool'.[7] In truth, however, she was growing increasingly weary of her husband's infidelities. Ill health added to her troubled state, and she was now in almost constant pain and discomfort.

Despite her ailments, Caroline still had all her wits about her, and devised a clever plan to bring her husband to heel. She wrote to suggest that he bring his mistress over to England so that she might be employed in the Queen's service, adding thoughtfully that the lady should be given apartments at St James's so that she would be within convenient reach of the King. To the untrained eye, it seemed as if Caroline had admitted defeat, but her real motive was in fact to have her new rival where she could keep an eye on her. Showing such apparently selfless devotion to her husband's wishes would also sweeten his temper towards her and make him more likely to do her will.

It was a bold move, and one that even the master tactician Walpole had counselled against on the basis that the King's German mistress enjoyed more influence with him than Lady Suffolk had done, and that she would therefore be much harder to manipulate. But the Queen was determined to bring the situation under some sort of control, and saw this as the only way. At first it seemed that her gamble had paid off. Upon receiving her letter, George wrote back at once, praising his wife's understanding and goodness, and instructing her to prepare Henrietta's old apartments so that Madame Walmoden might take up residence there as soon as possible. He also promised to make his own way back to London without delay.

His stay had already been a protracted one, however, and the people of England were growing increasingly hostile towards their absentee monarch. The pamphleteers and satirists had a field day. 'It is reported that his Hanoverian Majesty designs to visit his British dominions for three months in spring,' ran one acerbic comment. For a time, public sympathy was firmly with the Queen, who was viewed as a long-suffering and loyal wife to a man who, at almost sixty years of age, ought to know better than to be chasing after young girls. A particularly daring soul caused great hilarity by posting a bill making fun of the King on the very gates of St James's Palace. 'Lost or strayed out of this house a man who has left a wife and six children on the parish,' it declared. 'Whoever will give any tidings of him to the church-wardens of St James's parish, so that he may be got again, shall receive four shillings and sixpence reward. This will not be increased, nobody judging him to deserve a crown.' As George II's absence grew longer, the jests became ever more inventive. One day, an old horse was set loose in the city with a ragged saddle on its back and a woman's pillion tied behind it. A note was fastened to its forehead which read: 'Let nobody stop me, I am the King's Hanoverian equipage going to fetch his Majesty and his whore back to England.'[8]

George II's protracted stay in Hanover, coupled with his foolish antics whilst there, were bringing shame on the entire royal family. Although she was arguably the greatest victim of his betrayal, Caroline was soon tarred with the same brush as her husband. One evening in mid-November 1736, long after the King should have returned to England, she paid a visit to the opera, determined to maintain the pretence that all was well. The assembled crowds were not to be fooled, however, and to her horror, as she took her seat in the royal box, they started to hiss at her. Worse was to come. She was jeered by a mob of people on her way to Kensington Palace, who cried out that they did not wish to see her there again. Then in December, when she set off to spend the winter at St James's Palace, it was noticed that 'the people did not rejoice as they used to do, but stood sullen as she passed the streets without pulling off their hats'.[9]

This was the greatest crisis the Hanoverian family had ever faced. The tide of public opinion had turned so firmly against them that it seemed unlikely the damage could ever be repaired. It was a dangerous time to lose their subjects' loyalty, for the Jacobites were steadily gathering support for a new offensive. The Queen wrote again and again to her husband, urging him to return. But week after week passed, and there was still no sign of him. His birthday came and went, and the disapproval at his absence was all too evident among the crowds who had gathered for the official reception. It was serious indeed for the

King to miss his own birthday celebrations, and it was the first time that any of the Hanoverian monarchs had done so.

It was now December, and people began to suspect that His Majesty would also miss the Christmas receptions at court. At last, news reached the court that George had left Herrenhausen, after a long and tender farewell to his mistress, and was expected in London within a few days. No sooner had this dispatch been read, however, than another arrived bearing the terrible news that there had been a violent storm at sea on the day that he was due to embark, and it was not known whether or not he had sailed. If he had, then he was surely drowned, for no ship could have survived such angry seas.

Eight agonising days passed with no further news, and the suspense at court was great. Caroline was in extreme distress the whole time, fearing the worst. By contrast, her subjects seemed to care little about the King's fate and casually laid bets on whether he was alive or dead. At last a messenger arrived with news that he had not sailed, and was therefore still safely on the other side of the Channel awaiting a favourable wind. In her relief, the Queen cried out in front of the assembled courtiers: 'The King is safe! the King is safe!' They did not share her enthusiasm. When an official enquired how the wind fared now for His Majesty, one wry soul replied: 'Like the nation – against him.'[10]

George II finally arrived back in London on 15 December, after more than seven months' absence. Courtiers were astonished to find him as cheerful and convivial as he had been foul-tempered and irritable upon his last return. He showered the Queen with praise and affection, prompted no doubt by her generous offer of welcoming his mistress to St James's. But Madame Walmoden demurred, keen to avoid being trapped in a similar situation to Lady Suffolk. She therefore remained in Hanover with only the vaguest promise to join her royal lover in England as soon as she was able.

Caroline could take little satisfaction from this favourable turn of events, for she was by now preoccupied with her own rapidly fading health. George's absence had at least given her the luxury of a rest, and she had been able to forego the exhausting daily route-marches around the gardens of Kensington and St James's. But now he was back, the strain of keeping up the appearance of good health for his sake served only to make her condition worse. Her son, Frederick, was also creating fresh trouble, and in an extraordinary repetition of the scene played out exactly twenty years before, the simmering resentment between him and his parents suddenly broke out into open rupture. He was promptly expelled from St James's Palace and forced to take up residence at Leicester House, which assumed the well-deserved nickname of 'the pouting place of princes'.

All of this served to hasten the Queen's decline, and by the autumn of 1737, her suffering was so obvious that even the King noticed it. One day in early November, she was busying herself with the fitting out of her new library at St James's when she suddenly collapsed with violent stomach pains. Insisting that it was just a passing complaint, she dragged herself to the drawing room that evening, forcing smiles and chatter as if nothing was amiss. By the end of the evening, however, she was in so much pain that she had no choice but to take to her bed and remain there all the following day. The physicians were summoned to bleed and purge her, and when this worked no effect, they made an incision into the part of her bowel that seemed to be causing her most distress. Those who gathered around her bedside were aghast when this 'cast forth so great a quantity of corruption' that the stench was intolerable. The physicians declared that there was a larger abscess inside which would continue to grow 'untill it gains a vital part'.[11]

The King, who had enjoyed the delusion that his wife was merely suffering from a temporary indisposition, was acquainted with the grave news and fell into paroxysms of grief. Day and night he kept a vigil by her bedside, telling anyone who would listen what an incomparable woman his wife was, and how deeply he loved her. Even in the midst of his turmoil, though, he could not help displaying a little of his accustomed short temper. As Caroline shifted restlessly on the bed, trying desperately to escape the pain, he burst out that she should keep still, for he found her constant moving about most irritating. 'How the devil should you sleep, when you will never lie still a moment?' he expostulated. 'You want to rest, and the doctors tell you nothing can do you so much good, and yet you are always moving about.'

Eventually, after two long weeks of suffering, the Queen entered the final stages of her demise and began her farewells to the distraught family members surrounding her bed. To Princess Caroline she recommended the care of her two younger sisters. Her son William, Duke of Cumberland, she begged to support his father and show 'superior merit' to his elder brother, Frederick, whom she still refused to see. And finally, her husband, the King, she urged to marry again after she was dead. This threw him into a renewed fit of weeping, and in between sobs he spluttered: 'Non-j'aurai-des-maîtresses' [No, I will have mistresses], to which his wife sardonically replied: 'Ah! mon Dieu! cela n'empêche pas.' [My God! That won't prevent your marrying.][12]

At about ten o'clock in the evening of 20 November 1737, Caroline's breath started to rasp in her throat. 'I have got an asthma,' she gasped. 'Open the window.' This being hurriedly done, she uttered, 'Pray,' and as her daughter Amelia began to read some verses, the Queen breathed her last. George kissed the face and hands of her lifeless body several times, and then left the bedchamber to weep in private. The sincerity of his grief betrayed a tenderness 'of which the world thought him before utterly incapable', and for a time this made him more popular with his English subjects than he had ever been. He remained inconsolable for many months afterwards. When he opened Parliament in January 1738, the assembled MPs watched in sympathy as he struggled to compose himself enough to read his speech, and then during it 'he often put his hand to his forehead, and as they thought had tears in his eyes'. At a reception later that day, one courtier noted that he talked only of the Queen, and 'cried the whole time'.

The King never tired of saying that there was no other woman on earth who was 'worthy to buckle her shoe'. There was one, however, who might dry his tears just a little. Realising this, Walpole sent for Madame Walmoden to comfort the nation's grieving monarch. The lady duly arrived in June 1738 and took up residence at St James's in the apartments formerly belonging to Henrietta, Countess of Suffolk.

Mr and Mrs Berkeley, along with the rest of polite society, observed the necessary protocols to mark the death of the Queen, such as wearing mourning clothes in public. Whether Henrietta felt any real grief at her former mistress's passing is uncertain, however. The momentous event was afforded no mention in her correspondence, and she and her husband continued to enjoy the pleasant diversions of their life together. Visits to country estates, pleasure gardens and spa towns – both at home and abroad – occupied most of their time, and they were now often away from Marble Hill.

So absorbed was Mrs Berkeley in her joyful new life that she neglected some of her old friends. Most were glad that she had at last found happiness, and were content to see her as and when time allowed.

But Pope was rather less forgiving. 'What vexes me most is, that my female friends who can bear me very well a dozen years ago, have now forsaken me,' he complained to Swift a few months after Henrietta and George's wedding, adding: 'I have nobody now left but you.' His sourness towards his old friend had increased so much by the following autumn that he claimed he had only found out by accident that she and her husband had returned from their holiday in France and were staying at Savile Street. Nor did he expect to see them for many weeks, for he only made the journey up to London 'when Particular Friends are there, and I now think there are but few Particular Friends'.[13]

Pope had, admittedly, always been rather quick to take offence if his friends paid him less attention than usual. When Henrietta had failed to wait for him before setting off on her escape to Bath in September 1734, he had complained to Martha Blount: 'Lady Suffolk has a strange power over me: She would not stir a days Journey either East or West for me, tho she had dying or languishing Friends on each Quarter who wanted & wishd to see her.' He said that he could expect no thanks for his trouble in going to see her there, adding rather pensively, 'I suppose she'll be at cards and receive me as coldly as if I were Archdeacon of the place'.[14]

Of course, he said such things half in jest, always keen to add colour and amusement to his letters. But there was nevertheless a very discernible edge to the criticism that he levelled at Henrietta after her marriage to Mr Berkeley. Jealousy no doubt played a substantial part in it. For many years, Pope had been Henrietta's closest male friend, and the two had met and corresponded often during her time at court. Now she shared all her hopes and fears (and by far the greatest part of her time) with her husband, and Pope – dear friend though he was – no longer occupied centre stage in her personal life.

It is also possible that the poet's feelings towards his 'Lady at Court' extended beyond pure friendship. Pope had a tendency to confuse tender and platonic love in his relationships with women, and had once famously mistaken Lady Mary Wortley Montagu's feelings for the former. When he had duly declared his love for her, she had laughed in his face, scorning the very notion that she should have any romantic inclination towards this deformed little man. In his pain and humiliation, Pope had mounted a campaign to discredit her with his pen, and the two had embarked upon a very public war of words.

His letters to Henrietta certainly suggest an affection that bordered on the romantic. Scarred by his experience with Lady Mary, however, he never openly declared his love – perhaps hoping that once she had finally escaped court and moved to Marble Hill, their relationship would develop naturally. When she subsequently married George Berkeley, any romantic hopes that he might have entertained were dashed. But the secrets of his heart went with him to the grave, so any theories about the nature of his feelings towards the new Mrs Berkeley must remain speculative. What is certain, though, is that he was genuinely put out by the fact that she now had a good deal less time for him than she had in the past.

His hostility towards her boiled over in 1738, when he started making plans to publish his correspondence – a tradition followed by many of his distinguished contemporaries. In the eighteenth century, letters tended to be written for show as much as for the amusement or interest of the recipient, and there was an increasing trend amongst high-profile courtiers, politicians and men of letters to publish their correspondence or memoirs as a way of leaving their mark on history. The more controversial the collection, the more likely it was to be published posthumously – Lord Hervey's memoirs being a notorious case in point. The Earl of Peterborough's letters were apparently so shocking that his widow burnt them after his death, rather than fulfil his last wish to share them with the world.

Alexander Pope's correspondence was not particularly shocking, but it was no less diverting for that. All the wit and eloquence that had made him famous as a poet also shone through in his letters, and the fact that he conversed with some of the most important figures of the age made them even more compelling. Pope was keen to enhance the interest of his collection by including the letters that he had exchanged with George II's most famous mistress. But Henrietta was reluctant to return a correspondence that she had cherished for so many years. She may also have been keen to avoid any further scandal now that she was living so pleasant and retired a life away from public scrutiny. She there-fore demurred, reminding Pope that years ago he had told her that he kept copies of all the letters he sent anyway. When he persisted, she put an end to the matter by telling him (falsely) that she had burned them. Pope was furious. All the resentment that had been building up since her marriage now spilled over, and he exacted revenge through the most effective means at his disposal.

Later that year, he published 'Cloe', a poem about a woman as fickle in her affections as she is shallow in her tastes: a woman who, in short, 'wants a Heart'. While she 'speaks, behaves, and acts just as she ought', he wrote, she 'never, never, reach'd one gen'rous Thought'. Warming to the theme, he continued:

> She, while her Lover pants upon her breast,
> Can mark the figures on an Indian chest;
> And when she sees her Friend in deep despair,
> Observes how much a Chintz exceeds Mohair.

Although some commentators have claimed that Cloe was not based upon Henrietta, the evidence is quite compelling. The traits described resonate with elements of her character, such as her interest in design and furnishings, and 'Cloe' was the name given to her in Peterborough's 'Song'. Furthermore, when the verse was later included as part of Pope's *Characters of Women* anthology, the introduction presented Cloe as someone who was personally known to Patty Blount, which was true of none of the other characters. Horace Walpole also made a note in the margin of his copy that the character was 'meant for Lady Suffolk'.[15] The contrast with the 'handsome and witty' friend of 'A Certain Lady At Court' could not have been greater. Pope's esteem had, it seemed, turned to disdain.

Henrietta was as sanguine in her reaction to the vitriol poured forth in 'Cloe' as she had been to Swift's 'Character' some years earlier. She may have felt an element of guilt at having neglected her old friend in her happiness with Berkeley, or she may have believed that, as a man given to petulant outbursts, his rage would soon pass. She therefore expressed her affection for him by making frequent enquiries after his health and, at the onset of winter, sending him a feather-filled quilt to guard against the cold that she knew he always felt so keenly. 'Pray tell my Lady Suffolk in the first place that I think of her every night constantly as the greatest Comforter I have, under the Edder-down Quilt,' Pope wrote to Patty Blount that December. The concern that he went on to express for her husband suggests that he was a little more reconciled to their marriage. 'I wich Mr Berkley lay as easy, who I hear (& am sorry for it) has had the Gout,' he wrote.[16]

But in truth, he never forgave her, either for the incident with his letters, or for her neglect of their friendship, and thenceforth they were polite acquaintances rather than close companions. They hardly ever corresponded, and only saw each other on the rare occasions that their social circles converged. Henrietta was no doubt saddened by the loss of Pope's good opinion, but the experience with Swift had taught her that no matter how sincere such friendships seemed, their longevity could never be relied upon.

Besides, her own affection for him had suffered something of a decline. The cause was most probably his growing attachment to Patty Blount. He was keen for the two women to become friends, and for a while it had seemed that they would be. But Patty's awkward and, at times, insensitive nature grated on Henrietta, who was perhaps a little jealous of the hold that she had over their mutual friend. As early as 1731, she had complained to Gay: 'I never see Mr Pope, nor Mrs Blount tho I never go to Marble Hill without sending to them: She has been ill, but was well the last time I sent; but you know she has a peculiar pleasure in refusing her friends.' Further criticism of Pope and Patty began to creep into her correspondence, such as Lady Hervey's rather caustic reference to Miss Blount as 'some proud flesh that is grown to his side', which would, she predicted 'prove a mortification'.[17]

The demise of Henrietta and Pope's friendship may not therefore have been solely due to his sense of betrayal and neglect after her marriage to George Berkeley. Whatever the cause, it now seemed irreversible. In the years that followed, Mrs Berkeley turned increasingly to her female friends, in particular Lady Betty Germain. She had need of these when, in the spring of 1741, parliamentary business took her husband up to Yorkshire for a longer period of absence than the couple had yet endured in their marriage. The closeness and love between them had continued to deepen during those six happy years, and the prospect of being apart was even more distressing to them now than it had been when they were newlyweds. Added to this was the fact that Henrietta was again suffering from poor health.

She had come to rely upon her husband's kind and patient efforts to ensure her comfort whenever she had a renewed attack of the headaches that had plagued her for so much of her adult life. 'I am company for nobody but my own husband whose vow obliges him to take care of me in sickness & in health,' she told their friend Lord Pembroke on one such occasion. 'I try his patience sufficiently but he expects his reward in the next world.' In 1741, George took her on a visit to Bath in the hope that it would ease the rheumatism that had now added to her former complaint. Shrugging off concerned enquiries from friends who had heard that he was far from well himself, he assured them: 'I have as much health as any one needs to have as leads so insipid a life. I dare not drink, making love would be ridiculous at my age and I have too much and too little money to game.'[18]

George set out for his constituency at Hedon in Yorkshire in March 1741, accompanied by William Chetwynd. With the prospect of an election looming, their intention was to canvass votes on behalf of Walpole's great adversary, William Pulteney. Anxious for Henrietta's health during his absence, he had asked his sister to come and stay with her in Savile Street. Lady Betty had been happy to oblige, and was assiduous in the task, sending him regular updates on her charge's health.

The first of these caused him great alarm, for it reported that his wife had suffered a relapse soon after his departure and was now taking significant quantities of laudanum to ease the pain. Upon receiving this letter, George was on the point of turning around and coming back, but Henrietta sent him another to reassure him that she was much better and was being well looked after. She was clearly still in a great deal of discomfort, however, and only found release in sleeping for much of the day. Her reliance on laudanum now bordered on addiction, and she later admitted to her husband that although she had resisted it for some days, 'how long my Resolution will hold God knows for the Temptation is at this moment very strong'.[19]

The couple exchanged many letters during George's sojourn in the north of England, and the sincere love and affection they shared was obvious in every page. Henrietta addressed her husband as 'My Dear Dear little George', while he called her his 'Best Beast'. The bond they had developed with Dorothy and John Hobart was also as strong as ever. Mr Berkeley spoke proudly of 'our little girl Miss Hobart' and 'my school fellow Jack', and his wife noted with satisfaction that he showed the 'greatest tenderness' towards them.[20]

With the advent of spring, Henrietta moved back to Marble Hill. Although she loved the place, she found it very lonely without her husband and longed for his return. 'My Duty, affection, inclination and interest makes me my Dear Dear little George yours,' she wrote from 'Mr Berkeleys Dressing Room' the day after her arrival.[21] She did not have long to wait, for he arrived back a week or so later.

During the years that followed, the Berkeleys settled back contentedly into the routine of their life at Marble Hill and Savile Street. Although poor health continued to plague them both, this did not prevent frequent excursions to their accustomed places of retreat and diversion. Their social circle was changing, however, as a number of their long-standing friends died in the 1740s. The first was John, Duke of Argyll, who had been a highly valued friend and adviser to Henrietta throughout her time at court. His protection had saved her from her violent first husband on numerous occasions, and his generous help with her legal affairs had helped her to secure a legal separation from Charles, as well as the purchase of her beloved Marble Hill. Their friendship had continued long after Henrietta had left court, and she was greatly saddened when she learned of his death in 1743.

The following year claimed the life of Alexander Pope. He had long been a slave to his delicate constitution, once referring to 'this long Disease, my life', but in 1743, his friends noticed a marked deterioration in his health. His customary headaches increased, and he began to suffer from asthma and dropsy on the chest. He lingered until 30 May 1744, when he died at his villa in Twickenham.

Pope had evidently not been reconciled with Henrietta before his death. Just a few days earlier, her nephew John had written casually to her that 'Pope & Swift for you lay'd by Satyr, & join'd for once in Panegyrick', as if to suggest that both friendships were now in the past.[22] This is supported by the fact that despite her proximity to his house, she had not been among the friends who had gathered around his bedside to say their farewells. Furthermore, while Pope left gifts for various friends in his will, he left nothing for Henrietta. However estranged they had become, though, it is unlikely that she felt no emotion at his passing. Someone who had been such a close and loving friend could not be easily forgotten.

Less than a year later, she lost another person whom she had once held dear, but who had long been a stranger. This time, her grief was real indeed, for it was her son, Henry, who died at Audley End in April 1745. She had not seen him since he had been a young boy, and had received only the occasional scrap of news about him in the years that followed. The last known reference to him in her correspondence was in 1734, when Lord Bathurst had assured her that she could visit his castle without fear of being 'molested' by him. But she had never got over their estrangement, and the subsequent adoption of Dorothy and John Hobart suggests a desperation to fill the void it had created. Even though she had long since given up any real hope of a reconciliation, the news that death had finally robbed her of him for good must have been devastating. Neither was there the prospect of laying to rest the ghost of their estrangement through the next generation. Henry died without an heir, so his title and estates now passed to Henry Bowes Howard, 4th Earl of Berkshire, a descendant of the 1st Earl of Suffolk.

Lord Bathurst's prediction upon Henrietta's retirement from court, that she would be forced to live in 'the melancholy shades of privacy' was, sadly, now realised.[23] A little more than a year after the death of her son, she lost the person whom she loved most in the world, her 'Dear Dear little George'. His gout had been getting steadily worse during 1746, and by the autumn he was in so much pain that Henrietta took him to Bath in the hope that the waters would offer him some relief. Lady Bolingbroke met them there and was distressed to see her friend so ill. 'Le pauvre Mr de Berkeley, qui en effet a esté fort mal,' she wrote to the Countess of Denbigh, adding that she feared his condition was now very dangerous.[24] She was right, for he died there a few weeks later, on 29 October.

Henrietta was inconsolable in her grief. George Berkeley was, without question, the love of her life, and the eleven years of their marriage were the happiest she had ever known. She had lost not just her husband, but her closest friend and confidant. Evidence (if it was needed) that her love had been reciprocated came at the reading of Mr Berkeley's will some months later. He had left everything he owned – property, goods and funds – 'unto my dear wife Henrietta'.[25] This had been written in his own hand and dated two years after their marriage. It served not only as a testament to his complete trust in and love for his new wife, but as a poignant contrast to the bitter, lengthy and impenetrable legal agreements that had underpinned his widow's first marriage.

George Berkeley's death was afforded a rather curt notice in the papers, which, after listing his various appointments, reported simply: 'he marry'd the countess dowager of Suffolk, but left no issue'. Meanwhile, the men hoping to succeed him as Master Keeper and Governor of St Katharine's Hospital waited impatiently until a respectable period of time had elapsed before laying claim to 'that smug preferment'.[26]

His passing may not have excited any great public interest, but for his widow, Henrietta, life would never be the same again.

Chapter 16

'Where Suffolk sought the peaceful scene'

◦

A S HENRIETTA CONTEMPLATED THE prospect of a solitary life after the death of her beloved husband, so George II was reflecting upon a political scene that had changed dramatically over the past few years. Sir Robert Walpole, who had dominated government for over twenty years, had finally been defeated by his political opponents in 1742. His regime, while it lasted, had been extraordinarily powerful. The King, and more particularly his late wife, Caroline, had given their chief minister a virtually free rein in government, and had put all the household resources at his disposal so that he could further his political ends. Walpole had, in many respects, proved equal to the trust that they had placed in him. He had achieved comparative stability and peace for the Hanoverians after almost half a century of revolution, war and political upheaval. He had managed the public finances with shrewdness and skill, furthering Britain's prosperity by promoting trade, industry and agriculture. Above all, he had been a leader of exceptional strength: his eloquence as a speaker in Parliament and his keen sense of what mattered to the public keeping many faithful to his cause.

But all this had come at a price. The greatest charge levelled against Walpole was that he had governed through corruption, using the Crown's extensive patronage to buy support across government. He had also neglected the affairs of Scotland, which, given the strength of the Jacobite cause there, was a dangerous and short-sighted strategy. His policies had bred widespread distrust and resentment against the government, and the Opposition's ranks grew steadily throughout the 1730s. An alliance of Jacobites, Tories and disaffected Whigs had begun to form under William Pulteney, and the general election of 1734 had been a clear indication that the tide of popular support was turning against the Prime Minister. The death of Queen Caroline in 1737 had further undermined his power, for she had been his most loyal ally for many years and had provided the surest route to the King's favour. Many had expected his fall would come then, but Walpole had won enough of George II's trust and esteem to continue in office for another five years. After the disastrous general election of 1741, however, which reduced his majority from 42 to 19, the Opposition had moved in for the kill. Walpole had known he was beaten, and had tendered his resignation on 2 February 1742. Never again would George II's government be so dominated by one man.

Walpole's collapse was followed by years of political instability as the government lurched from one crisis to another, both at home and abroad. In 1743, war broke out between Britain and France, and a series of costly (and ultimately futile) military campaigns followed. This played straight into the hands of the Jacobites, who exploited the weakness of the government and the growing resentment among the British people to seize the initiative. With support from France, they launched a major uprising in 1745, spearheaded by the charismatic Young Pretender, Charles Edward Stuart – 'Bonnie Prince Charlie'. The Jacobite forces outmanoeuvred the British in Scotland, whose ranks had been depleted by the war on the Continent, and succeeded in capturing Perth and Edinburgh before routing the government army at nearby Prestopans on 21 September. From there, Bonnie Prince Charlie's army advanced southwards and invaded England via Carlisle, which fell after a short siege. They progressed, unopposed, through Penrith, Lancaster, Preston and Manchester, reaching as far south as Derby, which they took on 4 December.

The Hanoverian regime now faced the greatest threat it had ever known. Everything depended upon the loyalty of a people who were already resentful towards a foreign King who had wasted their country's resources for years in pursuit of Hanoverian interests. Their resentment was not matched by action, however, and the general feeling of apathy towards the regime was just enough to sustain it. Furthermore, the Jacobite forces had been fatally weakened by internal divisions and the failure to coordinate with French troops, which had still not arrived as promised in the south of England. Just two days after taking Derby, they were forced to retreat northwards.

Although the Jacobites succeeded in taking Falkirk in January 1746, the British forces, led by George II's younger son, William, Duke of Cumberland, were steadily gaining the initiative, and won a crushing victory at Culloden on 16 April 1746. The Hanoverian dynasty was now finally accepted by the people of Great Britain, and the foundations were laid for the kingdom's emergence as a European and world power.[1]

The events that were unfolding at the centre of Britain's political life carried no greater importance for the Dowager Countess of Suffolk than as an occasional topic for conversation with her acquaintances. Court politics had long since ceased to be of any real relevance for her, and although she had taken an interest in her late husband's parliamentary career, and shared his satisfaction at their friend Pulteney's triumph, after his death they mattered less and less.

The pattern of Henrietta's social life had also changed dramatically. Visits to the country, spa towns or other gentrified retreats had lost much of their appeal now that she could not share them with George. She spent most of her time at Marble Hill and lived vicariously through those friends who continued to enjoy the traditional social round. The Duchess of Queensberry, Lady Betty Germain and Lord Chesterfield regaled her with the latest news and gossip from Bath or Tunbridge Wells, and while many of the names had changed, the scandal remained much the same. Stories of flirtations, betrayals, elopements and 'ravishings' filled the pump rooms and coffee houses as much as they had in Lady Suffolk's heyday.

A new generation of heiresses and beaux were now playing out the familiar scenes in the assembly rooms and on the promenades, while their ageing parents, aunts and guardians looked on. Only very occasionally did the two sides mix. Lady Vere, her late husband's niece, wrote to Henrietta in 1751 with news that Lord Chesterfield's son, a lively young man of nineteen, had been playing court to Lady Betty Germain, who had just turned seventy. 'He invited her to his Ball yesterday, and gave her his Place at the Play the day before,' she related, adding that all eyes were now on the pair and that an engagement was expected daily. Another letter told of how the Earl of Bath, who was the same age as Lady Betty, had started up a flirtation with a young Maid of Honour.[2] There was something faintly ridiculous about these encounters, however, and Lady Suffolk was content to reflect on former glories and leave the rest to her successors. Failing health added to her desire for a quieter, more retired life at Marble Hill, punctuated by occasional visits to her town house in Savile Street.

Her social circle was also quite different to what it had been during the early years of her life away from court. It still included a number of old friends, such as Lady Vere and Miss Pitt. William Chetwynd, a great friend of her late husband, transferred his affection to her and proved 'unalterably kind and zealous'.[3] He was a frequent guest at Marble Hill, and she also visited him from time to time at his estate in Staffordshire. But many more of her former companions had passed away, and Lady Suffolk therefore relied upon new arrivals in Twickenham to bolster her acquaintances. Among them was Richard Owen Cambridge, who settled at an estate nearby in 1751. A witty and amiable man, he was the author of a political journal, *The Scribleriad*. Lady Dalkeith, daughter of the late Duke of Argyll, and Lady Denbigh, wife of the 5th Earl, also moved to Twickenham in the 1750s.

But by far the most significant new arrival was Horace Walpole, son of the former Prime Minister. In May 1747, he acquired a small estate with a cottage attached, in nearby Strawberry Hill. 'It is a little plaything house . . . and is the prettiest bauble you ever saw,' he wrote to a friend a few weeks after the purchase.[4] It was to become his private dream world; the place where he could observe the contemporary social and political scene at a cautious distance.

Horace was a young man of thirty when he moved to Strawberry Hill. The third son of Robert Walpole by his first wife, Catherine Shorter, he was devoted to his mother and resented the indifference that his father had shown towards her in the later years of their marriage. He had had a privileged upbringing, having been educated at Eton and Cambridge before embarking upon a Grand Tour of Europe. Enjoying the advantages of being the son of Britain's most powerful minister, he had been elected an MP during his travels.

But Horace never shared his father's dedication to politics, and upon moving to Twickenham, he declared that he had 'lost all taste for courts & Princes & power, as was natural for one who never felt an ambitious thought for himself'. He preferred instead to pursue his interests in architecture and the literary arts. He was a keen writer and poet, although not a great one. His published works included *Anecdotes of Painting, The Mysterious Mother*, and the romantic novel, *Castle of Otranto*, which was set in Strawberry Hill. Shortly after moving there, he started to keep a detailed journal of political events, which was later published as *Memoirs of the Last Ten Years of the Reign of George II* and ran to twenty-one volumes.

Walpole was of a slight and feeble stature, having been born prematurely, and in both his appearance and mannerisms he was rather effeminate. One of his female acquaintances described him as 'long and slender to excess; his complexion, and particularly his hands, of a most unhealthy paleness'. His style of dress was similarly dandified, and he was often to be seen in a lavender-coloured suit embroidered with silver, together with silk stockings, gold-buckled shoes, and ruffled collars and cuffs made of lace. He preferred delicate food such as chicken or fruit to the roasted meats, pies and other robust dishes favoured by most of his contemporaries. He would share his breakfast with his pampered little pet dog and a squirrel that he had tamed in the gardens at Strawberry Hill.

The epitome of Horace Walpole's effeminate, rather eccentric, nature was the way in which he would always enter a room on tiptoe with his knees bent, 'in that style of affected delicacy which fashion has made almost natural', but which to sniggering onlookers made him seem as if he was 'afraid of a wet floor'. He did not cut an entirely ridiculous figure, however. His eyes were described as 'remarkably bright and penetrating, very dark and lively', and although his voice was 'not strong', it was 'extraordinarily pleasant'.[5] Furthermore, those mannerisms that appeared to some as effeminate, to others seemed rather elegant, and he was undeniably cultured and well bred. His weakness was a love of melodrama and gossip, and he would regularly sit up until one or two o'clock in the morning exchanging tittle-tattle with his acquaintances.

Walpole never married and is not known to have had any mistresses, preferring instead the company of older women. He had a particular liking for wise and spirited dowagers who could satisfy his love of scandal with tales from their younger days. 'The preceding age always appears respectable to us (I mean as one advances in years), one's own age interesting, the coming age neither one nor t'other,' he once observed. Twickenham, with its many ageing widows and distinguished literary associations, was therefore perfect for him. 'Dowagers as plenty as flounders inhabit all around, and Pope's ghost is just now skimming under my window by a most poetical moonlight,' he wrote to a friend soon after moving there.[6]

The woman who, above all others, excited his interest was the

Dowager Countess of Suffolk. The two were introduced by mutual acquaintances, of whom they had several, including Lady Hervey and Lady Betty Germain, and Horace soon became a regular fixture at Marble Hill. The irony of their friendship, given Horace's parentage, was not lost on either. 'I was become known to her, though she and my father had been at the head of two such hostile factions at court,' he later wrote.[7] He usually pursued his father's old adversaries with venomous scorn, but any hostility that he might have harboured towards Lady Suffolk dissolved as soon as he met her. His esteem for her was obvious to everyone, for he was unstinting in his praise, describing her as 'a sincere and unalterable friend, very calm, judicious, and zealous'.[8]

For Walpole, Henrietta had about her that 'peculiar glamour' associated with one who has been the mistress of a king. Like Pope and Gay before him, he was soon inspired to write verses in her honour. His poem, 'The Parish Register of Twickenham', referred to the spot

> Where Suffolk sought the peaceful scene,
> Resigning Richmond to the queen,
> And all the glory, all the teasing
> Of pleasing one not worth the pleasing.

Henrietta was flattered and delighted by the earnest attentions of this cultured and witty young man, while he was astounded at her remarkable memory and sharp intellect, and showed an unstinting enthusiasm for her tales of life at the Georgian court. The pair would spend many a long evening sitting by the fire in Lady Suffolk's elegant Great Room as she regaled her new friend with everything from accounts of major events to the minutest of details about everyday life in the Queen's service, such as the petticoats that Caroline had worn at her coronation, or the mushrooms that had grown in her own damp apartments at Kensington. By now almost completely deaf, she would use a tortoiseshell ear trumpet to help capture Walpole's questions, while he listened intently to her quiet, almost whispered replies.

For his part, Walpole provided a patient and enthusiastic audience. 'She had seen, known, and remembered so much,' he later told a friend, 'that I was seldom not eager to hear.'[9] He was fascinated by the way that she could bring to life a vanished world. Some of the anecdotes he heard from Lady Suffolk were enhanced by the knowledge of court life that he had gained from his father. His description of their conversations proves what a perfect combination they made as orator and listener. 'She was extremely deaf and consequently had more satisfaction in narrating than in listening; her memory both of remote and of the more recent facts was correct beyond belief. I was indulgent to, and fond of, old anecdotes. Each of us knew different parts of many court stories, and each was eager to learn what either could relate more; and thus, by comparing notes, we sometimes could make out discoveries of a third circumstance, before unknown to both.'[10]

Eager to capture his friend's memories for posterity and pursue his own ambition to be a chronicler of the age, Horace began to record their conversations in a series of notebooks, dating from 1759 to 1766. He subsequently compiled these, along with his own observations, and bequeathed them to his favourite nieces, Mary and Agnes Bell, 'for their amusement'. They were later published under the title of *Reminiscences*, and have become one of the richest sources of political history, gossip and scandal for the early Georgian era. Such was their content, particularly about the nature of Lady Suffolk's affair with the King, that Walpole tactfully waited until after her death to bring them to the attention of the world.

Lady Suffolk's friendship with Horace Walpole was strengthened by a number of other common interests, besides her recollections of court life. The most notable of these was architecture. As soon as he had purchased Strawberry Hill, Walpole set about transforming it into an extraordinary Gothic-style villa, complete with lofty towers and pinnacles, pointed arches, cloisters and richly decorated fireplaces. He stuffed the house full of a myriad of curiosities, paintings, china, statues, books and relics. He also loved to be surrounded by portraits of his close friends. The likeness of Henrietta that Pope had commissioned twenty-five years earlier hung in the Round Bedroom, which was in the main tower of the house.

Once he had completed work on the main house (or 'castle', as he called it), he turned his attention to the grounds and erected several weird and wonderful structures, including a Gothic bridge and a chapel in the woods that bordered the property. He also established his own printing press, which churned out a wide variety of books – both his own and other people's – during his time at Strawberry Hill.

Although Lady Suffolk's tastes leaned towards the more understated elegance of the Palladian style, Walpole managed to persuade her to indulge in a little Gothic fantasy of her own. One of her farm buildings was converted into 'The Priory of St Hubert', complete with octagonal spire, buttresses, nave and cloisters. 'My Lady Suffolk,' wrote Walpole in triumph to an architect friend, 'has at last entirely submitted her barn to our ordination.'[11] The Priory must have appeared somewhat at odds with the simple, classical lines of her Palladian villa, and it was pulled down a decade or so later.

As well as providing Henrietta with much-needed companionship, Horace Walpole also helped to widen her circle of friends by introducing her to members of his own. Among them was Isabella Le Neve, with whom he spent a great deal of time, both at Strawberry Hill and at his town house on Arlington Street. That Isabella should also become friendly with Lady Suffolk was remarkable, for she was the eldest daughter of Oliver Le Neve, the man who had killed Henrietta's father in a duel. It is ironic to think of the peaceful meetings, at the tea table or the card table, between these two elderly ladies, whose fathers had fought to the death on Cawston Heath more than half a century before.

Horace's fondness for Lady Suffolk grew ever deeper as the years went by, and his lively company did much to alleviate the sadness that she felt at the loss of Mr Berkeley. He also became close friends with Lady Betty Germain, who often visited Henrietta at Marble Hill and Savile Street. His acerbic wit and overindulgence in gossip won him many enemies, however, and they sneered at his fondness for women who were old enough to be his grandmother. 'Is it not surprising how he moves from old Suffolk on the Thames to another old goody on the Tyne, and does not see the ridicule which he would so strongly paint in any other character?' asked one.[12] But neither Walpole nor Lady Suffolk was overly troubled by such comments. They had both seen enough of courts and society to know that what was ridiculed one week would be lauded the next.

That was not always the case, however. One evening, shortly after her husband's death, Henrietta and Lady Betty attended an assembly hosted by Selina Shirley, Countess of Huntingdon. The Countess was renowned for her devout religious beliefs, and was constantly trying to induce her friends and acquaintances to accept what she held to be the Divine Truth. Her evening assemblies had gained quite a reputation, drawing men and women from both fashionable and intellectual circles.

On the occasion that Henrietta and Lady Betty attended, the hostess had invited her evangelical Methodist preacher, Mr Whitefield, to address the party. The subject of his sermon was the wickedness of marital infidelity, and although he did not know that Lady Suffolk was in the audience, she was convinced that his every word was directed against her. Furious at such an insult, she barely managed to contain herself as his self-righteous sermon rambled on. When at last it was over, the assembled guests looked on in astonishment as she 'flew into a violent passion, abused Lady Huntingdon to her face, and denounced the service as a deliberate attack upon herself'.

In vain her sister-in-law tried to appease her, saying that it had been an unfortunate misunderstanding. Nor would she be silenced by the Duchess of Ancaster or Lady Ellinor Bertie, both of whom commanded her to stop this shameful display. In the end, she calmed down suffi- ciently to apologise (albeit with very bad grace), but then promptly flounced out of the house, never to return again.[13]

The affair was not soon forgotten. Lady Suffolk was clearly still very sensitive to matters concerning her reputation, having spent so many years covering up the shame of her first marriage and the nature of her affair with the King. Her resentment continued long after the incident at the assembly. Some years later, during her last illness, she refused Lady Huntingdon's request to visit her at Marble Hill, and went to the grave hating her.

Henrietta's anxiety to protect her reputation was demonstrated again a few years later. This time it did not involve her own virtue directly, but that of one very close to her. Dorothy Hobart had lived with her for many years, and had grown into a vivacious and attractive young woman. Her presence at Marble Hill had drawn various sons and daugh- ters of local gentry families to the house. The number of male suitors increased after her father, John Hobart, was created 1st Earl of Buckinghamshire, in 1746. Some of these were clearly more interested in her dowry than her physical or intellectual charms. 'I have lately seen the person who enquired for another what Lady Dorothy's fortune was to be,' wrote Lady Betty Germain to Henrietta two years later, 'and on expressing my wonder, that I had never heard of them since I was told point blank that nothing less than twenty thousand pounds would do for the gentleman. I could not help thinking if so, the gentleman either had a small cumbered estate, or was not much in love with one I thought very desirable.'[14] In fact, her father's new title had added little to the Hobart family's fortune, and the maintenance of their crumbling Jacobean mansion at Blickling was still eating up most of their resources.

The discovery of this fact put paid to Dorothy's more mercenary suitors, but there was one who seemed genuine in his admiration for her. Colonel Charles Hotham was the eldest son and heir of Sir Beaumont Hotham, and had been raised in a village near Edinburgh, where his father had been appointed Commissioner of the Customs shortly after his marriage. Charles had been sent to London for his education and had afterwards lived with his widowed aunt, Lady Gertrude Hotham (née Stanhope), sister of Lord Chesterfield, whom he had become close to. He had enjoyed a distinguished military career, rising to the rank of captain in his early twenties.

His father was an old friend of Lady Suffolk, and many years earlier had brought his five young sons to play with Dorothy and her brother John at Marble Hill. Charles and Dorothy became reacquainted in 1752, when he was twenty-three and she some four or five years his senior, and he soon became a regular visitor to Marble Hill. The pair conducted their courtship with as much secrecy as possible, both at Marble Hill and in London, when Miss Hobart accompanied her aunt to her town house in Savile Street. Perhaps recalling her own disastrous courtship with a soldier of the same Christian name many years before, Henrietta strongly disapproved of Hotham and did everything she could to persuade her niece to find a more suitable match. But Dorothy was a spirited young woman, and was so besotted with Charles that she set aside the love and respect she felt towards the aunt who had been more like a mother for most of her life, and instead stubbornly continued on what Henrietta feared was a path to ruin.

Knowing that she would never agree to let them marry, Dorothy took a step that was to shock polite society, and eloped with her lover. Lady Suffolk was aghast when she found out, and at once set about tracking down the couple before the marriage could take place – and before the news sparked a public scandal. She succeeded in the first of these. Dorothy and Charles were discovered at Tunbridge Wells a few days later, still unwed, but their indiscretion had ensured that by now the whole town was abuzz with the news.

Henrietta was mortified. As Miss Hobart's principal guardian, she held herself entirely responsible for the disgrace, and was wretched at the thought of what the news would do to her brother. She was also acutely embarrassed at having been unable to prevent such a scandal unfolding before her very eyes. But above all, she was distraught that her beloved girl looked set to destroy her life through an unsuitable match in the same way that she herself had done almost half a century before.

Lady Suffolk's friends rallied around to support her. 'What can I say or think of, to give You any relief in this your great Distress,' asked Lady Mary Vere upon hearing the news. 'Tis impossible to reflect upon your care, your Affection, and your Indulgence, to this unthinking (and too surely hereafter miserable) Creature, without finding that there is nothing to Plead in her Favour . . . whether you forgive, or forget you certainly have nothing to Answer to your Conscience.' Another acquaintance, Lady Mary Coke, assured Henrietta that she was not at all to blame, and that her niece's shocking behaviour could only be due to 'her being under the influence of an ungovernable passion which has hardly left her reason enough to know what she says, or does'.

But their words could offer little comfort to Henrietta as the days dragged on and she waited anxiously for her niece's return. Meanwhile, every lurid detail that could be gleaned about the affair was pored over in coffee houses, tea rooms and assemblies across London. It soon became clear that the couple's courtship had been rather less discreet than Lady Suffolk believed. 'Tis Certainly no secret to most People,' admitted Lady Mary Vere, 'as many has seen Her often Walk with him alone in the Bird-Cage Walk.' It was equally well known that they had also conducted their liaison at Marble Hill, under Lady Suffolk's very roof, and many sniggered at the disgrace that had thus befallen a lady so renowned for her discretion. Before long, the gossip had spread as far as Norfolk, where people seized upon scraps of information relating to one of the county's most notable families. 'The affair its self is I find generally known,' conceded Lady Mary Coke, though she assured her friend that nobody would hear it from her own lips.

At length, Miss Hobart arrived back at Marble Hill with her lover in tow. But if her aunt had hoped to find her chastened by the whole unfortunate affair, she was to be bitterly disappointed. Dorothy was as steadfast as ever in her determination to marry Colonel Hotham, and not even her aunt's famed powers of reason could work any effect upon her. After a series of bitter rows, Henrietta wrote miserably to her brother, pleading with him to advise her what to do next. He replied at once that she should send Dorothy to Blickling, where he and his son John would force her to her senses. She was to go alone, for the Earl was confident that, once separated, the young lovers' passion would soon fade away.

Dorothy knew her father's intentions all too well, however, and told a friend that she had complied with his request 'to give them a tryal whether time or absence cou'd operate any change in an attachment they so much disapproved'. The Hobarts' friends were confident of success. 'I had some reason to think this unhappy affair wou'd intirely blow over,' Lady Mary Coke assured Henrietta. 'A few Months reflection must I think convince her that the step she was going to take wou'd as infallibly have brought ruin on herself as distress on her Family.'

Like his sister, John Hobart underestimated Dorothy's strength of feeling. She arrived at Blickling as unrepentant as ever, her passion for Hotham 'too deeply rooted to be erased'. But there was another, more compelling, factor that bound her to him: she was with child. Provoked by her father's continued insistence that she must abandon the match, she retorted that it was now far too late, even if she wished to. Horrified by this shocking new twist to her shameful behaviour, Lord Hobart demanded to know how long she had been in this miserable condition. The conception had probably happened during the couple's elopement at Tunbridge Wells almost three months earlier, so if the family was to salvage any respectability from the affair, the need for a wedding was now of the utmost urgency. This was arranged with all due haste, and the couple were married at Duke Street Chapel in Westminster on 21 October 1752.

Henrietta was shocked and distressed when she heard the news of Dorothy's pregnancy and hasty marriage. In vain her friends tried to comfort her with the fact that, apart from his reprehensible behaviour with Lady Dorothy, Charles Hotham's character was otherwise sound. 'Mr Hotham is well spoke of by all his Men acquaintance,' wrote Lady Mary Coke, adding (rather unconvincingly) that she believed Dorothy 'may I think be happy'. Lord Chesterfield, by contrast, was genuinely delighted when he heard of the match, for he had gained a good opinion of Charles when he had met him as a youth. 'I do not wish you and Lady Dorothy Joy, for I am sure that you both have it,' he wrote to 'My Dear Captain'. He had evidently not heard about the pregnancy, for he added that he hoped they might one day be blessed with children.[15] His friend Lady Suffolk was, however, convinced that she would now have to stand by and watch as a very painful history repeated itself before her very eyes.

Happily, her fears were never realised. Dorothy and Charles Hotham's love proved to be more than a passing fancy, and their marriage stood the test of time. Their child – a daughter – was born in the spring of 1753 and, as a conciliatory gesture, was christened Henrietta. Her great-aunt and namesake could not remain angry with the young couple for long, particularly when she saw how happy they were, and they were reunited soon after the birth. So far was Dorothy restored to Henrietta's affection, indeed, that her daughter became as regular a visitor at Marble Hill as she herself had been as a young girl. Lord Hobart, in contrast, could not bring himself to forgive the wayward young lady, and any hope of a reconciliation was extinguished by his death three years later.[16]

The scandal of Dorothy Hobart's elopement has remained hidden in the family archives until now. The editor of Lady Suffolk's published correspondence removed all references to it, and even Louis Melville, who otherwise relished the more colourful details of her life, omitted it from his study on *Lady Suffolk and her Circle*. As almost every historian since has relied upon their accounts, this episode – and several others like it – has hitherto been forgotten. In exploring Henrietta's original letters and papers, a new portrait of her emerges which is at once more human and more compelling than the idealised Woman of Reason.

The more fickle of Lady Suffolk's acquaintances had been quick to disassociate themselves from her during the scandal of Dorothy's elopement. Her true friends, however, had proved the loyalty and sincerity of their attachment, and none more so than Lady Mary Coke, niece of her old friend John, Duke of Argyll. Lady Mary's fierce loyalty towards Henrietta was born out of gratitude, for the latter had come to her aid during a crisis in her own personal life a few years before. The source of this crisis had been all too familiar to Lady Suffolk.

Lady Mary was married to a dissolute and disreputable man whose violent temper was fuelled by excessive drinking. Edward, Viscount Coke, was the son of the Earl of Leicester. It seems that Mary had married him somewhat against her will, his reputation being widely known in Norfolk, and her apprehension proved fully justified. She led a miserable life at Holkham, often falling foul of his violent rages. On one occasion, fuelled by drink, Coke burst into his wife's room and began searching it for proof that she was plotting to have him murdered. Lady Mary pleaded with him to see sense, but he turned on her, and she later described the terrifying scene that followed: 'Lord Coke abused me in the most cruel manner but not content with that, he struck me on my Arm! tore my ruffle all to pieces & told me I deserved to be assassinated.' She was only saved from a further beating by the arrival of a local clergyman, who had come to pay his respects to the couple. Upon hearing the disturbance, he set aside propriety and rushed to Lady Mary's aid, restraining her half-crazed husband until the worst of his temper had subsided.

Although she was humiliated by her husband's treatment, Lady Mary could not suffer in silence and pleaded with her family to help. Her uncle, the Duke of Argyll, at once told Lady Suffolk of her plight, knowing that she would provide a sympathetic ear and, he hoped, some guidance for the young lady. She did not disappoint him, and promised to do all she could to help his wretched niece. Lady Mary was overjoyed to have such a wise confidante, knowing how well Lady Suffolk was qualified to help her, and she soon came to rely heavily upon her guidance. 'Lady Mary wishes extremely to see you & that soon,' her sister Elizabeth wrote to Henrietta. 'She wants your advice about several things.'

Lady Mary used the opportunity of a visit with her husband to London to meet with her new acquaintance. Henrietta braved foul weather to travel up to town so that she might console the girl and devise a plan of escape. Their meeting was conducted in the greatest secrecy. Rumours were already circulating about Lady Mary's marital troubles, and if she had been seen conversing with a woman who had used the law to escape from her own violent husband, then speculation would have been rife. Henrietta counselled her to begin collecting all the evidence she could of Lord Coke's ill treatment, and to keep a detailed diary – well hidden, of course, from his already paranoid gaze. She also urged her to keep her spirits up and her mind alert, no matter what abuses he might inflict upon her body.

Lady Mary was overwhelmed by Henrietta's kindness and assiduity, especially given the shortness of their acquaintance. 'I now find fresh reason to wonder at your goodness,' she wrote upon her arrival back at Holkham. 'The great attention you seem to have for me, and the anxiety you express for my happiness are greatly beyond my expectations.' She added that she had followed her friend's advice to the letter, keeping a record of everything that occurred and sending a copy to her brother-in-law, James McKenzie, the member of the family whom she trusted most.

She had, alas, much to record. Her husband was more violent than ever, and Lady Mary began to fear for her life. 'If my friends shou'd think of acting any thing in my favour for God's sake let it be done soon,' she implored her sister, 'for I am now so ill delays wou'd be dangerous.' But Elizabeth offered her little comfort. Anxious to avoid a scandal in the family, she urged her to show greater fortitude and remember her wifely duties to Lord Coke. Mary received no more sympathy from the friends she consulted, most of whom echoed her sister's sentiments. Only Lady Suffolk proved to be a true and constant supporter. 'The unkindness of friends is infinitely more terrible, then all the injurious usage that can be inflicted on one by Enemies,' Mary lamented in a letter to her. 'I assure your Ladyship that tis you alone that shall ever learn from me this instance of their cruelty.' In reply, Henrietta urged her young protégée not to become paranoid in the face of her distress: 'I must insist that you suspend all hard thoughts and reflections and not add imaginary to real distresses,' she counselled. 'Take comfort my Dear Child be assured you have friends.'

For all Lady Suffolk's calm reflections, she was working earnestly behind the scenes to secure Mary's release from her violent marriage. She begged James McKenzie to visit her in secret at Marble Hill so that they might discuss the matter. Together they agreed that the only course of action left to them was to enlist the services of a lawyer and begin proceedings for a separation. James subsequently instructed his wife, Elizabeth, to go to her sister and tell her of the plan. But Lady Mary was terrified by such an extreme course of action, and one that she thought was bound to fail. Her nerves in tatters, she 'fell into a rage' and was so loud in her objections to the plan that her sister was afraid they would be overheard. James was exasperated when he learned of this, and told Henrietta: 'I shall wash my hands of the affair; for I can be of no farther service to her.'

Meanwhile, Lady Mary's intemperate reaction to her sister's message had indeed been overheard and was soon relayed back to Lord Coke. Furious at his wife's betrayal, he placed her under virtual house arrest at Holkham, taking away her keys and forbidding her to write to family or friends. Only months later did he relent sufficiently to allow her to exchange letters with her sisters, but even then under 'severe restrictions'. She had some time to regret her indiscretion. Cut off from any hope of assistance, she was forced to resign herself to a marriage that would bring her nothing but misery and humiliation. Only death – either her own or her husband's – could now release her.[17]

In the event, Lady Mary only had to suffer her husband's behaviour for a few more years, because he died in 1753. She made the most of her freedom by embarking upon a vibrant social life, travelling regularly in Europe and frequenting the most fashionable gatherings back in England. She never remarried. As with Dorothy Hobart's elopement, Henrietta's involvement in Lady Mary Coke's marital difficulties was omitted by both J.W. Croker and Louis Melville. They were clearly anxious to disassociate their heroine from any more scandal than had already been visited upon her by her liaison with George II. The result was a rather more sanitised version of Henrietta's character than emerges from studying her original letters and papers.

Controversies such as Lady Mary Coke's marital difficulties and Lady Dorothy Hobart's elopement preoccupied much of Lady Suffolk's time during the 1750s, along with the more routine course of her relationships with friends and family. Her attention was also absorbed by some improvements that she was planning to make at Marble Hill. She had managed to secure more land surrounding the property in the late 1740s, and at the turn of the decade she commissioned a number of alterations to the house itself. With Lord Pembroke and Roger Morris both dead, she had to find a new architect to carry out these works. Her brother John recommended Matthew Brettingham, who had recently completed a commission at Blickling, and he began work at Marble Hill in 1750. This included both repairs to the original fabric and some new touches to bring the house up to date. The dining room was fitted with a new floor and ceiling, and was decorated with Chinese wallpaper, which was then high in fashion.[18] Mahogany shelves were installed in the library to house Lady Suffolk's ever-expanding collection of books, and improvements were also carried out to the servants' quarters.

Henrietta was glad of the diversion that these works created. Unfortunately, however, her attention was soon absorbed by a rather less agreeable domestic matter. Marble Hill had been a source of great comfort since her husband's death, and she was fiercely protective of the privacy and tranquillity that it offered. In 1748, Mrs Elizabeth Gray, who lived on Montpellier Row, a smart line of houses adjoining Lady

Suffolk's estate, had written to ask her agreement to the removal of some walnut trees which shielded Marble Hill from the avenue. She had claimed that they were 'not only a very great obstruction, to ye Prospect, but a continual annoyence' because passers-by would throw stones at the walnuts to dislodge them, 'by which some of ye neighbours have had their Windows broke, as indeed wee are all liable to, by yt constant Pernicious Practice'. Henrietta, though, had been more concerned by the prospect of losing the privacy that the offending trees afforded than by the likely damage to her neighbours' windows, and had therefore refused the request.[19]

The loss of some walnut trees seemed a minor inconvenience compared with the intrusion on her privacy that was caused by the arrival of a new, troublesome neighbour a few years later. John Fridenberg, a wealthy merchant, had rented two cottages close to the Thames on the east side of Marble Hill. The only means of access to these cottages was an old right of way that cut across Henrietta's estate. Fridenberg did not just traverse this on foot, but drove carriages and loaded carts across it – an action that contravened the law and infuriated Lady Suffolk. When he showed no repentance for such acts 'Committed with an unparalleled Insolence', she decided to retaliate. With her brother's assistance, she brought a suit of law against Fridenberg, and a protracted legal battle followed.

This caused Henrietta a good deal more stress and anxiety than her new neighbour's original transgression had done, and it was only the constant support of John Hobart, 'the best of Brothers', that kept her spirits up. 'Nothing can give me more uneasiness than to be sensible of what you must feel upon account of the dilatory proceedings against that rascal Fredenberg,' he wrote to her in May 1755, 'and of the uncertainty of what may, after all this plague and expence, be the consequence.' The dispute was to drag on for seven long years, after which time Fridenberg was finally defeated, but the victory had cost Lady Suffolk dear.[20]

Lord Hobart did not live to see the conclusion of the affair. He died in September 1756, aged sixty-two, leaving his sister as the only surviving sibling. His son John inherited the title and estate at Blickling. John had remained close to his aunt. From an early age, it was apparent that he had inherited her keen intellect and wit – although the latter was rather more irreverent than hers. Henrietta had scolded him for being a 'Saucy whelp' as a teenager, to which he had promptly replied:

'I am sorry to say yt your behaviour has convinc'd me yt when people have once got ye Character of being wellbred (by eating with their fingers, never drinking to any body, never taking leave when they go out of an Assembly . . .) they think they have a patent for being impertinent with impunity, & yt every thing they doe is polite because they are esteem'd so, by yt insignificant sect of people who stile themselves fashionable.' For all his jesting, though, it was clear that he adored his ageing aunt. 'You are the only person to whom I fully open my heart & the only one who loves me in the manner I most wish to be lov'd,' he once told her.[21]

John was anxious to ensure Lady Suffolk's wellbeing after the death of his father, and a short time later invited her to stay with him at Blickling. She enjoyed the visit to her childhood home, and was delighted by her nephew's continuing attentions when she returned to Marble Hill. Shortly afterwards, he sent a partridge pie made by the cook at Blickling as a reminder of her stay, and enclosed a note chiding her that although she had told him of her safe arrival, she had made no mention of her health. He comforted himself with the fact that 'there is a cheerfulness in the stile of it which induces me to flatter myself that you are very well'.[22]

Henrietta's nephew provided one of the few links that now remained between her and the court. His rank and status gained him admittance to the formal receptions there, and his ready wit and charming manners provided a further recommendation. He attended his first levée at Kensington Palace in 1756, before which he had sought his aunt's guidance on the proper codes of etiquette and behaviour. The occasion proved a success. He wrote to tell Lady Suffolk that he had done exactly as she had advised, and that as a result the King had been pleased to notice him. Upon hearing that the 2nd Earl of Buckinghamshire was due to attend his levée, George II had enquired into his affairs, aware that he was related to his former mistress. This connection evidently did nothing to prejudice him, though, for both he and Madame Walmoden (now Countess of Yarmouth) treated the Earl with 'the greatest politeness'.[23]

Lady Suffolk also counselled Miss Power, a more distant relative, on the behaviours and duties expected at court. She had helped to secure her the place of lady-in-waiting to Princess Augusta, widow of Frederick, Prince of Wales.[24] 'May the Fair Flower that you have Carefully and Prudently planted at Leicester House Live & Bloom,' wrote Lady

Vere to her friend, 'ever Remembring that 'tis to you she owes the every thing she enjoys in this Life of Happyness, and it will be her own Fault if she does not take care to secure Happyness in the next.' Miss Power's accounts of life at Leicester House must have brought back memories for Henrietta. The daily round of duties, receptions and scandal that she described (and that allowed her barely a moment's peace) was reminiscent of the life that George II's former mistress had led there more than thirty years before.[25]

A few members of Lady Suffolk's old acquaintance, such as Lord Chesterfield and Anne Pitt, continued to attend court, but she herself chose to experience it through the accounts she received from others. It was not incapacity that prevented her. Although she was now approaching sixty and still suffered from bouts of ill health, she was remarkably alert in both mind and body, and continued to make the trip up to Savile Street every winter. Her vitality was such, indeed, that Horace Walpole declared: 'Tis very wholesome to be a sovereign's mistress!'[26] In fact, it was a lack of inclination that kept her from court. She had been overjoyed to quit the onerous life that she had led there, and even the curiosity she may have felt about her old lover and the woman who had succeeded her as mistress was not sufficient to make her undergo what would surely have been an awkward and embarrassing experience.

Lady Yarmouth had now exceeded Henrietta's own length of service to the King, as she had been his official mistress for some twenty-four years. George had had the occasional dalliance with Lady Deloraine during that time, but an incident that had occurred at Kensington in 1742 had put paid to that source of gratification for good. At a drawing room one evening, a mischievous lady of the court had pulled away Lady Deloraine's chair as she had been sitting down. Greatly flustered and annoyed to see that the King had found this prank amusing, she had decided to visit the same upon him. Unfortunately, he had not found it as funny the second time. 'Alas, the monarch, like Louis XIV is mortal in that part that touched the ground and was so hurt and so angry that the Countess is disgraced and her German rival [Lady Yarmouth] remains in sole and quite possession,' recounted Horace Walpole with barely concealed amusement.[27]

Madame Walmoden had proved a rather less faithful and discreet mistress than her predecessor. The transgressions she had committed during the early days of her courtship with George II had been repeated on numerous occasions. A particularly notorious one involved a billet-doux that she had written to her lover in France, who was married to a lady at court. The note had, unfortunately, been misdirected and returned to his wife by mistake. Although Lady Yarmouth had had the good sense not to sign it, she had added a postscript that her lover should direct his reply to her apartments at Kensington, thus placing her very firmly in the frame. When the scandal broke, the King's mistress brazened it out as she had so many times in the past, insisting that she had been entirely innocent in the matter, and that this 'disagreeable mistake' had made people jump to the most 'absurd' conclusions. George was entirely satisfied with her explanation, but those who heard of the tale were more sceptical. The poor lady whose husband had been at the centre of the allegations, meanwhile, was obliged to keep silent in order to retain her position at court.[28]

Although Lady Suffolk stayed away from court, fate ensured that she would once more encounter her former royal lover. In October 1760, during her customary winter sojourn in London, she paid a visit to the gardens at Kensington. This was a popular spot for members of society to promenade and meet their acquaintance, but Henrietta was not aware that on this particular day there was to be a review of the royal guard by the King. As soon as she realised her mistake, she attempted to flee the gardens before George's arrival, but found herself hemmed in by coaches. As she looked about her for a means of escape, she found that the King and Lady Yarmouth were almost upon her, and she therefore had no choice but to steel herself for what looked set to be a very awkward encounter. But George failed to recognise her, and he and his mistress walked straight past without so much as a nod. This proved even more humiliating for Henrietta than a forced greeting would have been. Her friend Horace Walpole noted that she was greatly 'struck' by the incident and remained despondent for some days afterwards.[29]

In fact, this encounter would be the last time that Henrietta would ever see her royal lover. Two days later, George II, King of Great Britain and Elector of Hanover, was dead.

Chapter 17

'An essential loss'

———————<o>———————

O N THE MORNING OF 25 October 1760, George II rose, as usual, at six o'clock. He called for his hot chocolate, as he had done on every other morning since his accession, and drank it down. He then walked over to the window overlooking the gardens at Kensington, opened it, and declared that as it was a fine day, he would walk in the gardens. A little after seven o'clock, he retreated into the water closet, methodical as ever in his habits. His *valet de chambre*, waiting patiently outside while His Majesty completed his evacuations, just as he did every morning, was surprised by 'a noise louder than the royal wind', followed by a thud 'like the falling of a billet of wood from the fire'. He rushed in and found the King lying on the floor. There was a gash on his right temple caused by a heavy fall against the corner of a bureau, and his hand was stretched towards the bell that he had tried to ring for assistance. He whispered, 'Call Amelia,' then spoke no more.

The valet tore off to find help, and arrived back with several doctors in tow, as well as Princess Amelia, the King's second eldest daughter. Together they laid him on the bed and the doctors attempted to bleed him, but 'not a drop followed'. Princess Amelia, who was rather deaf, put her face close to her father's to catch any whispered commands, but finding his cheek cold, she leapt back in horror, realising he was dead. A post-mortem later revealed that he had died from a ruptured ventricle of the heart, the origin of which was probably syphilitic.[1]

As with so much of his life, death had come to George II accompanied by an element of farce. As he lay dying on the floor of his water closet, it was most probably his mistress, not his daughter, whom he had called for. They shared the same Christian name, but the Princess was more commonly known as Emily. It made little difference, however, for by the time his daughter arrived at his side, George was already dead. If he could have chosen the moment of his passing, he might well have preferred something more suited to his royal stature. As it was, this proud warrior king, who had led his troops to glory at Oudenarde and Dettingen, had breathed his last on the toilet.

George II was seventy-seven years of age when he died. He had enjoyed rude health for most of his life, and only in recent years had he been troubled by fading eyesight and poor hearing. He had reigned for thirty-three years, during which time the Jacobite threat had been extinguished for good, the Hanoverian succession had been securely established, and the political regime had been stabilised by the long ministries of Walpole, Pelham, Pitt and Newcastle. At the same time, Britain had been transformed into a great world power. The foundations of the Industrial Revolution had been laid, with new levels of production in industries such as coal and shipbuilding as well as in agriculture, and there had been a rapid rise in population. Overseas trade had been boosted by successes in India, which placed Madras and Bengal under British control, and by the capture of French-held Québec. George had played a personal role in some of his country's military successes, notably at Dettingen in 1743 when he had become the last British sovereign to lead his troops into battle.

The tributes paid to the King upon his death were perhaps more flattering than might have been expected for such a cantankerous monarch. *The London Chronicle* proclaimed that he was 'beloved honoured and regretted by his subjects, for his eminent and royal virtues'. His former minister, Lord Carteret, told his daughter that he had 'lost in common with the public an excellent King but also I can say with great truth a most gracious and good friend in particular'. The Duke of Newcastle, meanwhile, lamented that he had 'lost the best King, the best master, and the best friend that ever subject had. God knows what consequences it may have.' Even Lord Chesterfield, who had long since fallen foul of the King, admitted that he had departed this life unloved 'but not unpraised since he was dead'.

Such accolades were short-lived, however. A little over a month after George II's death, one contemporary observed: 'I can't help still regretting our late Sovereign, if he had some defects, he had certainly many virtues, and he had experience, which nothing but time can give; yet he seems already to be almost forgotten.'[2] Most of his subjects were now looking to his successor with the renewed hope and optimism that so often characterises the beginning of a new reign.

George III was the grandson of the late King, and had become the heir to the throne after the death of his father Frederick, Prince of Wales, in 1751. He was the first of the Hanoverian kings to be born in England, and although he could speak German, he showed little interest in his Hanoverian dominions, and in fact was never to visit them. His popularity was further enhanced by his youth (he was twenty-two on his accession) and enthusiasm, coupled with the fact that he was the first unmarried monarch to ascend the throne since Charles II in 1660. Before long, he had swept away the vestiges of his grandfather's court, including its tedious customs, dreary entertainments, and most of its officials. George II's mistress, Lady Yarmouth, was expelled from her apartments clutching the strongbox he had left her, which was said to contain £10,000. She remained in Britain for a few months before returning to Hanover, where she died of 'a cancer in her breast' in October 1765.[3]

The German mistress's predecessor, Lady Suffolk, profited rather less from the King's death. All that it brought her was the cessation of the pension that she had enjoyed since leaving court twenty-six years earlier. She now faced the prospect of living in straitened circumstances. This in itself was sufficient cause for anxiety, but she also seemed to be genuinely saddened by the King's passing. Horace Walpole observed that she was 'very sensible to his death' and remained rather melancholy for some time afterwards.

The passing of her old royal lover no doubt heightened Lady Suffolk's growing sense of nostalgia and reflection as she looked back over the events of her life. 'We do extremely rejoyce to hear that you are at least left so to yourself, as to be able to think of what is past, so as to be able to judge what is to come,' wrote her friend Lady Mary Vere. At seventy-one years of age, Henrietta was now an old woman. Although she was still plagued by deafness, her health was tolerable and her mind was still sharp. 'She has all her senses as perfect as ever,' marvelled her constant companion, Horace Walpole, 'is clean, gentle upright; and has her eyes, teeth, and memory, in wonderful conversation, especially the last, which unlike the aged, is as minutely retentive of what happened two years ago, as of the events of her youth.'[4]

Henrietta continued to keep abreast of the lives of her friends, and as these now included the statesmen William Pitt and George Grenville, her interest in politics was reignited. 'Don't Mr Walpole think Lady Suffolk gave great proofs of her knowledge and wisdom last Saturday night?' she wrote to her friend in 1761, after accurately predicting that Grenville would be offered the post of Secretary of State in succession to Pitt. The same year, she played an active role in the election to the influential post of Master of the Charterhouse in London, canvassing votes on behalf of Dr Morton, Librarian of the British Museum. She called in some of her connections to help her, including the Earl of Mansfield, Lord Chief Justice of England, and her old court acquaintance, the Duke of Newcastle.[5]

Henrietta also retained some contact with the court. Her advice was sought about the proper ceremonies to be observed at the coronation of George III's new wife, Charlotte of Mecklenburg Strelitz, in September 1761. Even though it had been almost thirty-four years since she had attended the late Queen's coronation, she recalled all the ceremonies, precedents and codes of etiquette in remarkable detail – from the guarding of the robes and jewels at Westminster to the handkerchief used to wipe the Queen's face after she had been anointed.[6]

Lady Suffolk herself attended the coronation. Although an expert on the protocols involved and the clothes that were appropriate, she called upon the assistance of her friend Walpole in dressing her hair. She was later able to return the favour by helping him out of an awkward and embarrassing situation when Queen Charlotte paid an unexpected visit to Strawberry Hill. Unaware who the caller was, Walpole's servant had announced that his master was in bed and could not be disturbed. Greatly flustered upon learning the truth, Horace ran at once to seek his friend's advice, and she helped him write a letter of apology to the palace.

Henrietta was also consulted by William Chetwynd about the extent of his daughter's privileges as Sempstress to the Queen. Miss Chetwynd was eager to attend a drawing room, but her comparatively humble position in the household would not allow her to do so, no matter how well born she might be. Henrietta cautioned that if she ignored the rules, it would be 'a very mortifying circumstance and distress to her', and that she should therefore 'obey them without a murmer'.[7]

Although she dabbled in matters of court and politics from time to time, Lady Suffolk's main preoccupations were closer to home. She did take a trip to Cheltenham in 1762, but otherwise preferred to stay at Marble Hill. She continued to entertain friends both here and at Savile Street, and would also visit Horace Walpole at his Strawberry Hill villa. The latter was with her when a fire broke out near her town house in April 1761. After making sure that she had suffered no ill effects, he persuaded her to remove her most valuable possessions in case the fire should spread. Although Lady Suffolk behaved 'with great composure', she was clearly shaken by the experience and afterwards admitted 'how much worse her deafness grew with the alarm'.[8]

Henrietta came to rely on Walpole more and more as the years passed. When business in town detained him, he would write to her often from his house on Arlington Street. 'I could not help scrawling out a few lines to ask how your Ladyship does, to tell you how I am, and to lament the roses, strawberries, & banks of the River,' he wrote on one such occasion, adding: 'pray keep a little summer for me. I will give you a bushel of politics, when I come to Marblehill, for a teacup of strawberries & cream.'[9] She was therefore distraught when, in the autumn of 1765, he announced that he was taking a trip to France and would probably not return until the following year.

This was the longest period that Henrietta had been deprived of her friend's company, and she felt his absence keenly. She complained that her 'head, eyes, stomach, feet and spirits' had all been adversely affected by his departure, and begged him to comfort her with frequent letters. This Walpole promised to do, and he proved as good as his word. He sent a series of entertaining descriptions of his life in Paris, the company he kept and the sights he encountered. 'All my hours are turned topsy-turvy,' he complained soon after his arrival. 'Indeed Breakfast and Dinner now and then jostle one another.' Very little in France seemed to meet with his approval. 'Their gardens are like Desserts, with no more verdure or shade,' he wrote. 'What trees they have, are stripped up, & cut strait at top; it is quite the massacre of the Innocents.'

Lady Suffolk delighted in his irreverent letters and urged him to write more often. Walpole accused her of being a 'tyrant, who does not allow me many holiday-minutes', but he was clearly glad to obey her request. For all his criticism of France, the longer he stayed there, the more he seemed to like it. By the beginning of December, he was reporting that he had 'seen several people I like', and had become 'established in two or three societies, where I sup every night'. Among his acquaintance there was a family very dear to Henrietta's heart: the Berkeleys. Lady Elizabeth Berkeley, widow of the 4th Earl (George Berkeley's nephew), was a star of the gaming tables, and her son, Frederick, the 5th Earl, was also noted as being among the party. The mention of such a tender connection to her past must have evoked fond memories for Henrietta, who had enjoyed the society of Paris with her late husband George almost thirty years earlier.

Another overseas correspondent to enliven Lady Suffolk's retirement at Marble Hill was her nephew, John, 2nd Earl of Buckinghamshire. John had been rising steadily through the political ranks during the previous few years. In common with many of his contemporaries, he had cut his teeth on elections in his native county, and had been returned as a Whig MP for the city of Norwich in 1747. At the end of 1755, he had secured his first office in government as Comptroller of the Household to George II, and a little over a year later, he had been elected to the Privy Council. To this honour had been added the sinecure of Lord of the Bedchamber to the King, who had apparently taken a shine to his former mistress's lively young nephew.

The Earl had devoted so much of his younger life to politics and the court that it was not until 1761, shortly before his thirty-eighth birthday, that he turned his attentions to more domestic matters and took a wife – Mary Anne Drury, daughter of a Northamptonshire baronet. Perhaps married life was not to his taste, for barely a year into it, he accepted the apparently prestigious commission of concluding a new treaty with Russia. This was something of a poisoned chalice, however, for while the British government's motivation was commerce, the Russians were seeking a political alliance. Such an impasse would have challenged the most seasoned of diplomats, but Buckinghamshire had precious little experience of such matters, and was therefore ill equipped for the situation that greeted him upon his arrival in St Petersburg in the autumn of 1762.

Nevertheless, the Earl's engaging manner made him an instant hit at the Russian court, and he also succeeded in charming its formidable matriarch, Catherine the Great. Before long, she was so fond of him that she habitually requested his attendance, both at court and on more private occasions, such as when she indulged her passion for riding. 'I had the honour of seeing her ride,' he told his aunt a few months after his arrival. 'She was dresst in man's cloaths and it really is not flattery to say that few men ride better.' Riding was a passion that the Earl shared with the Empress, and so highly did she favour him that the year after his arrival, she ordered two horses to be sent over from England so that they might ride them together. During the course of his ambassadorship, she showered him with more gifts, including a magnificent tapestry of Peter the Great, which now hangs at Blickling.

Their mutual affection was obvious to everyone who saw them together, and it was not long before rumours began to circulate that relations between Her Imperial Majesty and the English envoy had deepened into intimacy. They were in each other's company almost all the time, both at the court in St Petersburg and in Catherine's beautiful Summer Palace nearby. When matters of state took her away from there in the summer of 1764, the Earl greatly missed her company and confessed to his aunt: 'The Empress is expected this evening at Peterhoff, about twenty miles from hence, which I equally rejoice at both in my publick and private capacity, as I have sensibly felt in both the difference of her absence.'[10]

Buckinghamshire was both enchanted by his new country and amused by its eccentricities. He described it all to his aunt back in England, who derived real pleasure from his witty and colourful accounts. The weather was a constant theme. 'As yet everything is covered with snow,' he wrote during his first spring there. 'The river has the appearance of a Broad Street and on Sunday is covered with thousands of people who resort there to see Sledge races and Boxing Matches.'

The following year, he had grown more used to the harshness of the climate. 'The Russian spring is begun, that is to say, it freezes all night and thaws all day. Early in the morning you travel upon ice, but all the rest of the day the streets are canals,' he wrote. He still marvelled at the brevity of the warmer months, describing the summers as 'very concise', and observing that 'What we call three seasons are in great measure united here – Spring, Summer and Autumn when the weather is particularly favourable will together make nearly four months.' As well as being 'concise', summer brought other irritations. Writing to his aunt one hot August day, he complained about the flies that had descended upon the city, 'three of those animals (the purpose of whose existence I can as little account for as of my own) taking their evenings walk upon my forehead'.[11]

The food, traditions and etiquette of the Russians were of even greater fascination to John than his typically English obsession with the weather. When his aunt informed him of a likely betrothal that she had heard about between an English lady and a Russian count, he offered the following advice to the bride: 'She must learn Russ, eat mushrooms, fryd in rape oil and pickled cucumbers in Lent; she must forget to courtesy and learn to bow, she must wear red without measure, dance Polish dances, and drink Chisterskij, Quash and Burton Ale, the nature of the first two her dear man will inform her of, the last she will know is the produce of England.'[12]

On another occasion, he described a Russian wedding that he had attended. He had witnessed every part of it: from the bride's dressing party to the wedding ceremony itself and the evening entertainments that followed. While he spoke respectfully of the overall 'dignity and solemnity' of the occasion, he could not resist expressing his amusement at one of the more extraordinary events of the day. Just before the company had set out for the church, the mother of the bride had ordered all those present to be seated and the doors of the room to be closed 'as a prognostick of the future tranquillity of the new marry'd couple'. Unfortunately, however, a young child of the family had 'burst out into a most violent fit of roaring', which, the Earl observed, 'seem'd to me a much apter emblem of what might hereafter insue'.

For all his bemusement at the unusual customs and climate of St Petersburg, Buckinghamshire was clearly enjoying his time there to the full. 'I find myself so much fatigued this morning with dancing last night with the Maids of Honour, that it is with difficulty I can undergo the fatigue of writing,' he observed in one letter to his aunt. In another, he described a lavish reception that he had hosted at his apartments, which had been 'one of the prettiest Balls & cheerfullest evenings I ever was a Party to', and had included twenty 'interesting' young women.[13]

So energetically did the Earl enter into all the social diversions the city had to offer that he scarcely had any time for his official duties. Indeed, these seemed to present an irksome distraction, and on the rare occasions that he did turn his attention to them, he showed neither enthusiasm nor initiative. He had clearly hoped that his secretary would undertake most of this work for him, in the same way as his servant in the English court carried out the duties required by a Lord of the Bedchamber. He was therefore extremely frustrated to find that the man who had been appointed to him was rather incompetent. 'My secretary, is the most disagreeable, illiterate, underbred, wretch in the Universe,' he complained. 'I am forced to do almost everything myself, tho' I pay him two hundred pounds per an. which is full double the usual stipend.'[14] The Earl begged his aunt to use her influence with the politicians back in England to find him a more diligent replacement.

Henrietta did what she could to help him, but her efforts were in vain and he was obliged to endure the less appealing aspects of his posting, as well as enjoying its many pleasures. She performed what was arguably a greater service, however, by looking after his young wife, who was feeling a little neglected by her new husband. A few months before his departure, she had given birth to a daughter, whom they had christened Harriet. Lady Suffolk sent her nephew regular reports of his young family's health, and was clearly delighted to have another child to care for. 'Lady HH is a very fine Child,' she told him, 'very Healthy, forward on her feet and takes great pains to be so with her Tongue.' The little girl had apparently inherited some of her father's capacity to entertain, for one of Lady Suffolk's acquaintances described her as 'the most amusing little Creature I ever saw', when she encountered her at Marble Hill.[15]

Lady Suffolk also kept her nephew informed of political events back in England, although she always pretended that these were far beyond the comprehension of his 'affectionate old aunt'. 'What passes in St Stephens Chaple [the Houses of Parliament] and other matters [are] much to heigh and intricate for my capacity either to judge of, or even to Comprehend,' she insisted in one letter. The insincerity of such protestations was proved by the well-informed insights she provided him with, all of which were based on the conversations she had had with the various high-standing politicians among her acquaintance. The Earl trusted his aunt implicitly and relied upon her advice as he tried to maintain his influence in England. 'There is no person but yourself whom I can talk with confidence upon my situation,' he assured her.[16]

But for all Henrietta's efforts, she was not able to conceal from the English ministers that her nephew was failing to make any progress with the Russian alliance, despite having been there for almost two years. In August 1764, they issued him with an ultimatum: either get the stalled negotiations moving or return to Britain. The Earl knew that such a difficult mission was beyond his capability, and reluctantly agreed to relinquish his position. As he prepared to take his leave from the country that had provided him with so much entertainment over the previous two years, he wrote sorrowfully to his aunt: 'Whatever pleasure a man may promise himself in breathing the air of his native soil and renewing his antient connections, yet the approach of a moment when you are to take eternal leave of those with whom you have lived in an agreeable familiarity and a state of mutual benevolence, cannot but be painful to a feeling mind.' The prospect of seeing his wife and infant daughter again apparently offered little compensation, and he was full of foreboding about the situation that would face him when he returned home. 'What welcome I shall meet with in England except from my own family seems to me rather uncertain, as from the extreme negligence with which my friends have corresponded with me, I almost suspect I shall find myself a little upon the footing of a stranger.'[17]

He was right to be apprehensive. Upon arriving back at court in spring 1765, he was greeted by a rather cool reception from several of his former acquaintances. What was worse, the King seemed to show a growing disapproval of him. His sharp wit and irreverent manner jarred with the more formal behaviour expected in George III's court (not to mention in government) and he often caused offence. Lady Mary Coke once heard him give an address in front of the King in the House of Lords, and noted in her journal that evening: 'His manner is not pleasing.'[18]

Despite the failure of his mission to Russia, Buckinghamshire was offered the ambassadorship of Spain the year after his return. He felt that his position at court was too fragile to leave it, however, so declined. Nevertheless, he remained eager for advancement, but his lack of influence, coupled with his increasing alienation from the King, made this an unlikely prospect. Finally, in November 1767, he was dismissed as Lord of the Bedchamber following his support of a failed plot concerning George III's American dominions. He would have to wait almost a decade before another appointment in government would come his way.

The Earl of Buckinghamshire's correspondence with his ageing aunt continued with the same frequency after his return to England. He was clearly grateful for the care she had taken of his wife and child, and sent regular accounts of their life at Blickling. His return there had brought him little joy at first, for political events in Norfolk seemed to be conspiring against him as much as they had in London. 'I am sorry to find that I have made myself so many enemy's in Norfolk,' he lamented to Lady Suffolk. 'Would I had never seen Blickling!' But he soon succeeded in patching up local relationships, aided in no small part by the plentiful victuals that the county had to offer. He recounted to his aunt how he had dined with the new local sheriff 'upon Venison Swan & Turkey', washed down with 'copious draughts of . . . a coarse homely liquor'. He had managed to remain sober enough to find his way home, and had arrived in time to see 'the Chit' (his young daughter Harriet) before she had been put to bed.[19]

John soon settled down into a life of tranquil domesticity with his family. His wife bore him three more daughters in successive years, between 1767 and 1769, and he doted on them. Having all but given up on his political ambitions for now, he turned his attentions to a programme of repair and modernisation at Blickling. Sharing his aunt's passion for architecture, he threw himself into the task with alacrity and kept her fully informed of progress. 'There is no person in the universe to whom I more willingly communicate my Idea's and no Ideas than to your Ladyship,' he assured her. 'The alterations in the Eating Room go on, Gothick it was, & Gothick it will be, in spite of all the remonstrances of Modern Improvers upon Grecian Architecture. The Ceiling is to be painted with the Lives of Cupid & Psiche, cupid is to hover exactly over the centre of the table to indicate to the Maitre d'Hotel the exact position of the Venison Pasty.' He went on to describe the loss of the 'Nine Worthies' – a set of classical statues that had previously adorned the Great Hall – but assured his aunt that they would be replaced by figures from Blickling's distinguished past. His knowledge of architecture was evidently greater than his knowledge of history, however, for he observed: 'as Anna Boleyn was born at Blickling it will not be improper to purchase her Father Henry the eighth's Figure (which by order is no longer to be exhibited at the Tower) who will fill with credit the space occupy'd by the falling Hector'.[20]

Buckinghamshire's natural energy and exuberance ensured that the works at Blickling soon became more ambitious than he had originally planned. Within a few months, he was supervising a whole host of workmen, and was clearly in his element – although he admitted that paying their bills was a good deal less diverting. His aunt followed the progress at her childhood home with great interest. In spite of failing health and fading eyesight, she faithfully answered each of his letters, and the duel of wits between the elderly lady and her spirited nephew was reminiscent of her correspondence with the likes of Chesterfield and Peterborough many years before. 'Another letter from the Old Woman!' she began one, mimicking her nephew's irreverent terms of address, before scolding him for writing such dull accounts of domestic life at Blickling, which she claimed were an unworthy successor to the lively descriptions he had sent her from Russia. John, meanwhile, scoffed at her 'extensive notions of liberty and the high prerogatives of the female world', and argued that if women were left to follow their own inclinations with regard to such important matters as choosing a husband, 'nineteen times in twenty they will choose wrong'.²¹

Henrietta's nephew provided a much-needed diversion in a life that was increasingly beset by ill health and financial hardship. Although she was hardly destitute, the loss of her royal pension upon George II's death had left her with considerably less money than she had had before, and the cost of maintaining her house and servants was becoming ever more burdensome. John provided for her as best he could, sending her regular parcels of bread, coal and other staples from Blickling. But these were not enough to sustain her, and frequent bouts of illness put a further strain on her meagre funds, requiring as they did the services of doctors and apothecaries. To her old complaints of deafness and headaches were added painful attacks of gout in her joints and even in her eyes, which often laid her low for several days at a time. Her correspondence is littered with concerned enquiries from her friends and family, and hardly a month seemed to go by without some fresh cause for discomfort. Lady Suffolk made light of her illnesses, telling her nephew John: 'I would flatter myself I shall soon be so [healthy]; but head and eyes love contradiction and will not agree with me.'²² Her growing frailty was clear to all, however.

Nothing was a greater source of comfort to Lady Suffolk during these difficult years than the presence of Henrietta, daughter of Dorothy and Charles Hotham. The girl had come to live with her at Marble Hill in 1763, when she was eight years old. This was some considerable distance from her parents' estate in East Yorkshire, fifteen miles north of Hull, but Lady Suffolk was still revered by Dorothy and her brother John after the happy childhood she had given them at Marble Hill, and both had absolute trust in her abilities as a guardian. 'You will tell Miss Harriet [Henrietta] I have but one piece of advice to give her,' wrote John soon after the girl's arrival there, 'that is, to act as you would have her, tell her to try it only for three days, & if at the end of them she do's not confess she never pass'd three days so agreeably, Let blame light upon your most truly affectionate Nephew.'[23]

Henrietta Hotham was a precocious child, and lively to the point of waywardness. Like John, she had inherited her great-aunt's intelligence and humour. Lady Suffolk was instantly charmed by her and did everything she could to ensure her comfort and amusement. She transformed the bedroom next to her own into Miss Hotham's private chamber, furnishing it with a fine walnut dresser and a 'cloaths chest' in the latest 'India' fashion. From this room, the young girl could look out across the gardens or watch the coaches and promenaders who passed by on the road beyond. Lady Suffolk also employed a maid to attend to her every need, and ensured that she was given all the elements of a young lady's education – including dancing, music, reading and embroidery.

But young Henrietta had little patience for such refined pursuits, preferring instead to swim in the river with the local boys or run around doing animal impressions. 'I can grunt like a Hog, Quack like a Duck, sing like a Cuckoo,' she proudly told her parents, although she admitted that her great-aunt had cautioned her that such behaviour was only acceptable for spinsters.[24] The model of propriety that Lady Suffolk presented was not at all emulated by the young girl. In vain, the former had tried to instil some sense of decorum into her wayward namesake by placing a seat in the garden where she could 'retire and meditate'. Miss Hotham would have none of it, however, and instead scrambled up the nearest tree when she needed some solitude.

Lady Suffolk pretended to be exasperated by such conduct, but she was secretly delighted with her young charge and was soon a slave to her every whim. Her friends were equally indulgent towards this charming new addition to the household at Marble Hill – and none more so than Horace Walpole. He paid as assiduous a court to her as he did to his old friend, and delighted in composing poems and rhymes for her amusement. He even went to the trouble of printing one of these, 'The Magpie and Her Brood', at his publishing house at Strawberry Hill. When the coronation of George III took place, he invited Miss Hotham as his special guest to witness the procession from a friend's house in Palace Yard. She adored him in return, and her great-aunt ensured that he was often among the company that gathered at her riverside home.

Another frequent guest was Lady Suffolk's old friend William Chetwynd, who soon became equally besotted with her young charge. A good-natured rivalry developed between him and Walpole as they fought to outdo each other in devising games and pranks to keep the girl entertained. 'Mr Chetwynd I suppose is making the utmost advantage of my absence,' surmised Walpole during his visit to Paris in 1765, 'frisking & cutting capers before Miss Hotham, & advising her not to throw herself away on a decrepit old man. Well, well, fifty years hence he may be an old man too, and then I shall not pity him, tho I own he is the best-humoured lad in the World now.'[25] This 'lad' was in fact an old man of eighty, while Walpole was approaching fifty, and it is amusing to think of the two men prancing around for the sake of the young girl's gratification.

Henrietta Hotham's presence breathed new life into Marble Hill. She was always the centre of attention at her great-aunt's parties and gatherings. Horace Walpole described one such occasion, New Year's Day 1764. The girl had been thoroughly spoilt with gifts from Lady Suffolk and her friends, including a smart new coat which she insisted on wearing for most of the day. Lady Temple, who was among the company, planted a little box on her dressing table. Upon seeing this, the girl seized it 'with all the eagerness and curiosity of eleven years', and was overjoyed to find 'A new-year's gift from Mab our queen'. When she came downstairs, she found another sealed note lying on the floor, and squealed with delight when she discovered that it was from the 'fairies' who had left her the ring. The jest continued into the following day, for when Lady Temple again called upon her friend, she was accosted by Miss Hotham bearing a note from 'Oberon the grand, Emperor of fairy land, King of moonshine, prince of dreams . . . Baron of the dimpled isles That lie in pretty maidens' smiles.' This had been composed with the help of Lady Suffolk and Will Chetwynd, who looked on in amusement at Lady Temple's being thus outwitted.

Adored though she was, Miss Hotham did have a rival for her great-aunt's affections. Lady Elizabeth Berkeley was Lady Suffolk's god-daughter, and spent much of her childhood at Marble Hill. The youngest daughter of the 4th Earl of Berkeley, she would have been the great-niece of Henrietta's second husband George. She was a pretty but somewhat neglected child whose mother had cultivated 'a dislike both unjust and premature' towards her. Lady Suffolk, who was always greatly disposed towards any relative of her late husband, immediately took

pity on the girl and made sure that she came to visit whenever her
family was in London. Lady Betty Germain, Elizabeth's great-aunt, was
often among the party, and the two elderly ladies showered her with
affection. This may have been partly why the girl grew up to be rather
spoilt and self-centred, although she later proudly claimed in her
published memoirs that she had 'made Lady Suffolk a pattern for my
manners'.[26]

The effort of looking after two such wayward charges took its toll
on Henrietta's health. Walpole noted with some concern that his friend
had greatly exerted herself in throwing a party in Miss Hotham's honour,
despite suffering from acute pains in her eyes and going without sleep
for several weeks. 'What spirits, cleverness, and imagination, at that age,
and under those afflicting circumstances!' he marvelled in a letter to a
friend. Indeed, she was so ill at this time that Walpole feared for her
life. 'Alas! I had like to have lost her this morning!' he wrote. 'They had
poulticed her feet to draw the gout downwards, and began to succeed
yesterday, but to-day it flew up into the head, and she was almost in
convulsions with the agony, and screamed dreadfully; proof enough
how ill she was. This evening the gout has been driven back to her
foot, and I trust she is out of danger. Her loss would be irreparable
to me at Twickenham, where she is by far the most rational and agreeable company I have.'[27] She fell ill again later that year, and although
she did her best to conceal her discomfort, it did not escape the sharp
eye of her great-niece. 'I wish it was in my power to give you a better
account of Lady Suffolk,' Miss Hotham wrote to her father in October,
'but she has got a bad cough which keeps her from sleeping.'[28]

As Lady Suffolk's health deteriorated, she became less and less able
to keep up the correspondence with her many friends and acquaintances. She therefore relied increasingly upon Henrietta Hotham and
Horace Walpole to act as her scribes, and it is evident from the resulting
letters that although her body was weak, her mind was as sharp as ever.
She certainly had need of her wit, for one of her correspondents was
her old friend Lord Chesterfield, whose humour had abated little with
the onset of old age. In a letter written towards the end of 1766, he
assumed the character of his footman. 'I cannot well understand why
my lord would rather employ my hand than his own in writing to your
Ladyship,' it began, 'because I have heared him say that there was no
body in the world that he honoured and respected more than your
Ladyship, and that you was the oldest acquaintance, friend and Fellow

servant that he had.' He concluded that his 'maser', who, like Henrietta, was now in his seventies, 'often complains that he feells a sensible decay both of body and mind'.

Lady Suffolk enlisted Walpole's help in replying, and the ensuing letter was written as if from her maid, 'Elizabeth Wagstaff', who apparently spoke with a marked Irish accent. 'Lack a day, Mister Thomas,' she exclaimed, 'here have I been turmoilin and puzelin my poor brains to write to a Jackadandy . . . They says as how your Lord is the greatest Wit in all England, & so I suppose you fansis yourself the second, & will make a mock of a poor Girl.' 'Mrs Wagstaff' went on to report that her mistress was 'pure well', although she 'coffs a litel now & tan all day long', and that she had scoffed at the notion that Lord Chesterfield was growing old, 'for he never was spritlier in his born days, & to be sure between you & I, My Lady is hugely fond of him, & I wishes with all my heart so I do, that it proove a match, for she is as good a Lady as ever trod in shoolether'.

The flirtation between these two old courtiers continued in Chesterfield's reply, although he admitted that he had a 'shattered Carcase' as a result of living 'a little too freely formerly', and was therefore a less energetic lover than he had been previously. Like Henrietta, for all his frailty, he had lost none of his wit, and as a parting shot he made fun of the new fashion among women to wear inordinately high wigs. 'A Gentleman having said at Table that women dres'd their heads three or four storys high, yes said my Lord, and I believe every story is inhabited like the lodging houses here, for I observe a great deal of scratching.'[29]

This amusing exchange between Lady Suffolk and her faithful old friend is among the last of the surviving letters in her collection. Shortly afterwards, her health took a turn for the worse, and throughout much of the long and bitterly cold winter of 1766, she was confined to her bed. Against the advice of all her friends, she managed to venture out for Lady Betty Germain's New Year celebrations in January 1767. The snow had fallen so heavily that she was obliged to wear several layers of clothing in an effort to keep warm in the coach, but by the time she reached the house she was chilled through. She was immediately ushered to a place by the fire, but sat so close to it that her ruffle set alight. The other guests looked on in horror as the flames leapt up her arm. Lord Vere rushed to her aid, getting badly burnt in the process, and it took the intervention of another gentleman to finally extinguish the flames with his hat. The doctor was called to attend Lady Suffolk, who had sustained serious burns to her arm, and it was several weeks before the pain began to subside.

Meanwhile, the attacks of gout continued with increasing severity, and in February Henrietta was so ill with a fever that it was reported she was dead. Frantic with worry, her nephew dispatched his wife and eldest daughter to stay with her at Marble Hill. Although her spirits were lifted by the visit, her health continued to deteriorate, and by May she was no longer able to receive visitors. This was a worrying sign indeed for the members of her social circle, who knew that ill health had never stopped this most committed of hostesses before.

The onset of warmer weather improved her condition sufficiently for her to be able to leave her bed and welcome a small number of guests. Among them was Lady Mary Coke, who noted that Henrietta spent a good deal of time talking about her beloved husband George and his surviving relations, many of whom she had kept in touch with during the years following his demise.[30] Lady Suffolk had apparently rallied so much that her death, when it came, proved a shock to her friends and family.

One evening in late July 1767, Walpole paid one of his regular visits to Marble Hill and was concerned to find his old friend 'much changed', although he did not believe her to be in any great danger. She told him that she was suffering from the effects of gout and rheumatism all over her body, and particularly in her face, but insisted upon sitting and talking 'below stairs' when she should have been in bed. Walpole sent for word of her the following morning, 26 July, and was told that she had had a bad night. By the evening, however, she seemed much better and was able to receive the two visitors who called on her: Lady Dalkeith, daughter of her late friend the Duke of Argyll; and the faithful Will Chetwynd. She was obliged to sit close to the fire, however, for it was an unseasonably cold evening. After Lady Dalkeith had left, Henrietta told Will that she would take her supper in her bedchamber. He escorted her up there and thought she appeared well enough to enjoy a good night's sleep. But upon sitting in her chair to prepare her toilet, she suddenly gripped her side and collapsed. She died half an hour later.

News of Lady Suffolk's death spread quickly throughout polite society. It was published in the newspapers, which refrained from making any reference to her affair with the King and instead described her simply as 'for many years Keeper of the Wardrobe to her late Majesty Queen Caroline'.[31] Her friends and family were devastated by her death, and none more so than Horace Walpole. 'I am very sorry that I must speak of a loss that will give you and Lady Strafford concern,' he wrote to his friend Lord Strafford three days later, 'an essential loss to me, who am deprived of a most agreeable friend, with whom I passed here many hours ... as it was not permitted me to do her justice when alive, I own I cannot help wishing those who had a regard for her may now, at least, know how much she deserved it than even they suspected. In truth, I never knew a woman more respectable for her honour and principles, and have lost few persons in my life whom I shall miss so much.' He continued in another letter: 'She was discreet without being reserved: & having no bad qualities, & being constant to her connections she preserved uncommon respect to the end of her life.'[32] Miss Hotham was just as inconsolable at her great-aunt's death, and Will Chetwynd had to stay with her at Marble Hill until her family could come from East Yorkshire to take her away.

Lady Suffolk's will was read a few months later. She had made it in September 1758, two years before her pension from George II had ceased, and had evidently expected to have a rather greater fortune to bequeath than actually proved to be the case. It included generous gifts of money, such as £8,000 for her niece, Dorothy, which, although not considerable when compared to the vast sums bequeathed by wealthy noblemen and women, was generous within the context of Henrietta's more modest resources. She also left half a year's wages to her servants, and various other monetary bequests to friends and family.

In fact Henrietta had lived in increasing hardship after the King's death, and had had to apply such strict economy that she had gained an ill-deserved reputation for covetousness. She had also been unable to make the necessary repairs to her Thames-side house, which had begun to show signs of considerable neglect during the last years of her life. By the time of her death, it was estimated that it would cost between £2,000 and £3,000 to put it right. In spite of such frugality, Walpole claimed, she had exceeded her income considerably, and the 'anguish of the last years of her life, tho' concealed, flowed from the apprehensions of not satisfying her few wishes, which were, not to be in debt, and to make a provision for Miss Hotham'. Unaware that his friend had made her will at a time when her prospects had been rather better, he predicted that its reading would 'surprise those who thought her rich'.[33]

While Lady Suffolk's ability to fulfil her financial bequests may have been in doubt, there was one possession that she could dispose of as she chose: her beloved house, Marble Hill. She had clearly been anxious to ensure that the house, contents and estate that she had so lovingly created over the past forty years should stay together, for she had made detailed provisions to this effect. The will specified that 'all the Household Goods and Furniture . . . shall go along with my said house as Heir Looms'. The recipient of this most treasured bequest was her nephew, John, and on his death without male heirs, it was to pass to Henrietta Hotham and her heirs. Lady Suffolk's affection for her great-niece was further demonstrated by the provision of a dowry of £3,000 for her, as well as 'all my State Jewells China and Japan in whatever shall be contained in cabinets chests or Boxes under Lock and Key'.

Lady Suffolk's decision to bequeath Marble Hill to a female relative in the event of there being no male heirs to inherit after her nephew was extraordinary for the time. In a male-oriented society, women were all but barred from inheriting titles, property or estates. If there was no direct male heir, these almost always passed to distant male relatives rather than to the wives or daughters of the deceased. Indeed, this had been the case when Lady Suffolk's own son had died. But the inheritance of Marble Hill by a female relative was far from being intended as a last resort: Henrietta had stipulated that after Miss Hotham's death it should pass to her daughters, or if she had none then to those of her uncle, John Hobart. Although this provision was highly unusual, it was typical of a woman who had fought so long for independence in a world dominated by men.

Lady Suffolk's will also proved her enduring love for her late husband, George. She bequeathed a number of legacies to his family, including £2,500 in trust for Lady Betty Germain and £1,500 to be divided amongst the sisters of the present Earl of Berkeley, 'as a mark of my respect to Mr Berkeleys Memory'. The most touching indication of this love, however, was the request that came before all others in the will: that she should be 'buried as Mr Berkeleys widow very Privately as he was and with the Earl of Berkeley's leave near him'.[34] This wish was honoured, and the mortal remains of Henrietta, Dowager Countess of Suffolk, were interred next to those of her second husband in the family mausoleum at Berkeley Castle.

Epilogue

A MONG LADY SUFFOLK'S BEQUESTS to her nephew John was the voluminous collection of letters and memoirs that she had preserved with great care from the time of her entry into the Georgian court to her death at Marble Hill. In terms of their historical worth, they were perhaps the single most valuable item of her entire inheritance. Many years later, they would breathe new life into the characters, events and places of one of the most fascinating periods in Britain's history.

But in the years immediately following Henrietta's death, it was her estate that most preoccupied her nephew. As executor and chief beneficiary of her will, the disposal of her property fell to him. He sold the Savile Street town house in February 1768,[1] and also attempted to sell Marble Hill. This might seem a betrayal of his aunt's last wishes, but the estate comprised a complicated series of leases and agreements, for Lady Suffolk had gradually extended it over the years by investing in plots of adjacent land as they became available. She had, however, protected the house and estate too carefully in her will for it to be sold off by her heirs, and John therefore resigned himself to its care and upkeep. A detailed inventory of the contents was drawn up, which survives intact today and conjures up an image of an elegant country villa, tastefully decorated with fine ornaments and furnishings – from the large marble tables and 'looking glasses' in the Great Room, to the mahogany card table and 'India fire screen' in the Paper Room.

The Earl let Marble Hill, fully furnished, to various tenants during the first few years of his ownership, before moving there himself in 1772 and subsequently using it as an occasional retreat. Horace Walpole once visited him there, but was saddened by the memories of his old friend that it invoked and described it as 'a melancholy day to me, who have passed so many agreeable hours in that house and garden with poor Lady Suffolk'.[2] On Buckinghamshire's death in 1793, the house finally passed to Lady Suffolk's great-niece, Henrietta Hotham. Perhaps, like Walpole, she found it too poignant, for she only lived there a short time before deciding to let it out to others.

The first of Miss Hotham's tenants was Maria Fitzherbert, the mistress (and almost certainly secret wife) of George II's great-grandson, the future George IV. Anxious to escape London before the day appointed for her lover's 'official' marriage to Caroline of Brunswick, Mrs Fitzherbert chose this most fitting of rural villas as her refuge. In order that the gossips at court would not hear of her absence, she left instructions that her town house was to be illuminated on the wedding night. However, Prince George heard of her flight and rode furiously to Twickenham to see her. Maria refused to grant him an audience, and he rode backwards and forwards outside Marble Hill for some considerable time, before reluctantly turning back to face his future bride. As she waited for news that the marriage had been concluded, Mrs Fitzherbert may have reflected wryly on the appropriateness of her surroundings. Sixty years earlier, another mistress of a Hanoverian prince had fled there to escape her royal lover – albeit for rather different reasons.

It was an irony that would not have been lost on Henrietta.

Notes

◅◦▻

Abbreviations

BM Add. MS	British Museum Additional Manuscripts collection
HMC	Historical Manuscripts Commission
NRS	Norfolk Record Society
PRO	Public Record Office manuscripts, The National Archive
RA	The Royal Archives
UHA	University of Hull Archives
Wilton MSS	Wilton Manuscript Collection
WRO	Wiltshire Record Office

CHAPTER I 'A BACKWATER IN TIME'

1. Narcissus Luttrell, *Diaries*, 6 vols. (London, 1867).
2. The best account of the duel, and the circumstances surrounding it, is given in R. W. Ketton-Cremer, 'Oliver Le Neve and his duel with Sir Henry Hobart', in *Norfolk Portraits*, 58–68.
3. According to the National Trust staff who now manage the property, the screams can still be heard from time to time, reverberating around the house and grounds.
4. Luttrell, op. cit.; NRS MC 1601/78 862 X8.
5. HMC, *Lothian*, 81.
6. The Characters of Lord Coke and Lord Hobart by Judge Jenkins', BM Add. MS 22629 f.225.
7. J. Maddison, *Blickling Hall* (National Trust, 1989), 5.
8. Pocock, x.

9. According to Horace Walpole, Maynard had given his granddaughter to Sir Henry out of gratitude because he owed his distinguished legal career to Hobart's grandfather, who had first advised him to 'pursue that branch of the law which he afterwards practised'. Walpole, *Reminiscences*, 129–30.

10. NRS 21089 71 X5.

11. Baird, 18.

12. Francois de Salignac de la Mothe-Fenelon, 'Treatise on the Education of Daughters' (1687), quoted in Jones, 102. In a similar vein, Richard Allestree, a Royalist clergyman, proclaimed that women were naturally 'below men' in their intellects: 'The Ladies' Calling' (1673), quoted in Hill, *The First English Feminist*, 22.

13. Mary Astell, 'A Serious Proposal to the Ladies, for the Advancement of their True and Greatest Interest' (1694), quoted in Jones, 197.

14. Reynolds, 175; Halsband, III, 28.

15. Halsband, *Letters*, III, 24; Baird, 18; Jonathan Swift, *Gulliver's Travels* (1726). See also Jones, 46.

16. Ketton-Cremer, 60.

17. NRS 11129 25 E5.

18. This was later moved a short distance to the garden of the Woodrow Inn on the Norwich to Holt road. The inn has since been replaced by a petrol station.

19. Ketton-Cremer, 61.

20. NRS 14020 28 F5.

21. NRS 11129 25 E5 23.

22. No likenesses of Lady Hobart are known to have survived.

23. P. Hounswell, *Ealing and Hanwell Past* (London, 2003).

24. When the estate was sold in 1739, the tapestries in the 'Great Room' were valued at £1,000. HMC, *Lothian*, 147.

25. 22 August had proved a singularly unfortunate date for the Hobarts. Lady Elizabeth Hobart, Sir Henry Hobart and his father Sir John Hobart had all died on this date.

26. The Hobart family accounts for November 1702 record items sent from Blickling to Gunnersbury, including 'stockens, and pin-money for ye children'. NRS 16334 32 C2.

27. See, for example, NRS 10385 25 A6, 20 December 1703.

28. Mary died in April 1704, aged 18; Philippa died in September 1704, aged 10; and Elizabeth died in April 1705, aged 18.

CHAPTER 2 'MAN'S TYRANNICK POWER'

1. Addison, 52.
2. Sedgwick *Some Materials*, I, 40.
3. Mahon, *Letters*, II, 440, 459.
4. NRS 22953 Z76.
5. The church still survives today, sandwiched between the modern buildings of London's financial district, and close to the Monument to the Great Fire of 1666.
6. It was not until late into the reign of Queen Victoria that white became the traditional colour for bridal gowns. The fashion for evening dresses at this time was for low square necks, three-quarter-length sleeves and full skirts, and most were made from silk.
7. BM Add. MS 22627 ff.40–1; Walpole, *Reminiscences*, 58.
8. Mahon, *Letters*, II, 459; 'The Present State of Matrimony, or The Real Causes of Conjugal Infidelity in Marriages', in Jones, 80.
9. The records do not reveal any details about these lodgings, beyond the fact that the rent was just £25 per year. BM Add. MS 22627 f.41.
10. Summerson, 21.
11. BM Add. MS 22627 f.41.
12. Ibid. ff.41, 45.
13. Ibid. f.44.
14. Ibid. f.41.
15. Ibid. ff.43, 46.
16. Ibid. f.41.
17. Ibid. f.43.
18. Ibid. f.45.
19. BM Add. MS 22727 ff.40–2.
20. Again, there is no record of where these lodgings were, and because the couple were going by a false name (probably still Smith), it is almost impossible to find out for certain.
21. BM Add. MS 22727 f.41. Some secondary accounts have, erroneously, claimed that Henrietta considered selling her hair in order to fund a dinner for some courtiers once she and her husband had arrived in Hanover. There is no evidence to substantiate this within the original sources, and Henrietta's own written testament states that it was to fund the voyage.

CHAPTER 3 HANOVER

1. Wharncliffe, I, 135, 138.
2. Ibid., 138.
3. Mahon, *Letters*, II, 452; Halsband, *Letters*, I, 6.
4. Kroll, *Letters*.
5. Wharncliffe, I, 6.
6. Walpole, *Reminiscences*, 29–30.
7. Mahon, *Letters*, II, 458.
8. Wharncliffe, I, 13.
9. Mahon, *Letters*, II, 453.
10. Sedgwick, *Some Materials*, II, 321.
11. Mahon, *Letters*, II, 454; Sedgwick, *Some Materials*, II, 320.
12. People with this condition tend to talk continuously, unaware of the listener's interest, and may also appear insensitive to their feelings. They commonly excel at learning facts and figures, and often develop an almost obsessive interest in a hobby or pastime. Any change to their routine will cause them great distress and they prefer to order their day according to a set pattern.
13. Ibid., I, 261.
14. Wharncliffe, I, 13.
15. RA Geo. Add. MS 28/52.
16. Arkell, 19.
17. Wharncliffe, I, 13.
18. Kroll, *Sophie*, 216.
19. Wharncliffe, I, 13–14.
20. Walpole, *Reminiscences*, 142.
21. BM Add. MS 22627 ff.41–2.
22. Ibid., f.42.
23. BM Add. MS 22628 ff.29–30.
24. Walpole, *Reminiscences*, 121.
25. HMC, *Portland*, V, 200.
26. Burgess, 12–15.
27. Walpole, *Reminiscences*, 28.
28. Wilkins, 81.
29. Wharncliffe, I, 13.
30. Wilkins, 80.
31. Kroll, *Sophie*, 243.
32. HMC, *Portland*, V, 480.

CHAPTER 4 ST JAMES'S

1. Clarke and Ridley, 12; *The London Gazette*, 3 August 1713.
2. Mahon, *Letters*, II, 452.
3. Kroll, *Letters*, 167.
4. *The London Gazette*, 4–7 September 1714.
5. *The Weekly Journal*, 22 September 1714.
6. Beattie, 9; Saussure, 41; Defoe, I, 357.
7. Picard, 37.
8. Chenevix Trench, 21.
9. Cowper, 102.
10. *The Daily Courant*, 12 October 1714.
11. Cowper, 5.
12. Ibid., 7–8.
13. Lady Cowper incorrectly cited Henrietta's appointment as 2 December 1714, stating that 'In the afternoon came Mrs Darcy, to desire me to speak to the Princess to make Mrs Howard a Bedchamber Woman. She urged that Mrs Howard had had a promise of it from Hanover in Princess Sophia's time.' Lady Cowper's tendency to overstate her own influence at court led her to make such inaccurate claims on many other occasions, and more reliable sources state that all of the Women of the Bedchamber were appointed on 26 October. See for example the Institute of Historical Research's lists of office-holders in modern British households, which can be accessed online at www.history.ac.uk/office. Henrietta's own account implies that her appointment happened very shortly after the coronation. BM Add. MS 22627 f.42.
14. Graham, 302.
15. Beattie, 162.
16. Wharncliffe, I, 214–15.
17. Van der Kiste, 79.
18. The equivalent of £61,000 and £37,000 today.

CHAPTER 5 IN WAITING

1. The best account of the royal household in early Georgian England is provided by Beattie.
2. This post later became known as Mistress of the Robes.
3. Cowper, 10.
4. Walpole, *Reminiscences*, 91.
5. Sedgwick, *Some Materials*, I, 67–8.
6. Carelessness.

7. Walpole, *Reminiscences*, 60.

8. Mahon, *Letters*, II, 42.

9. Wilkins, 137.

10. Ibid., 138.

11. HMC, *Portland*, VII, 423.

12. Longford, 292–3.

13. Cowper, 99; Wilkins, 133.

14. Cowper, 43.

15. Ibid., 98.

16. Ibid., 46.

17. Stead, 73.

18. Saussure, 162–4.

19. Griffith Davies, 42; Matthews, 310.

20. Cowper, 120.

CHAPTER 6 THE SWISS CANTONS

1. Matthews, 298–9, 310.

2. Sedgwick, *Some Materials*, I, 72.

3. Mahon, *Letters*, II, 463; Walford, 99.

4. Law, III, 208.

5. BM Add. MS 22628 f.19. Hartshorn was a leavening agent commonly used in making bread, but was also occasionally taken as a tonic in the eighteenth century.

6. Thurley, 248.

7. Cowper, 123.

8. Wilkins, 208–9.

9. Thurley, 254.

10. Wharncliffe, I, 311.

11. Walpole, *Reminiscences*, 40–1; HMC, *Portland*, V, 541–4.

12. BM Add. MS 22627 f.42.

13. Hill, *Eighteenth-Century Women*, 93.

14. BM Add. MS 22627 f.13.

15. Ibid. f.16.

16. Ibid. f.17.

17. Ibid. f.18.

CHAPTER 7 'THESE FOOLS MAY NE'ER AGREE'

1. HMC, *Portland*, V, 544.

2. Wilkins, 229; Plumb, *Sir Robert Walpole*, I, 260.

3. HMC, *Portland*, V, 547.

4. Walpole, *Reminiscences*, 132; HMC, *Portland*, V, 548.

5. Walpole, *Reminiscences*, 59.

6. Mahon, *Letters*, III, 12.

7. Impey, 72.

8. Wright and Tinling, 215; Sherburn, I, 412–13.

9. Groom and Prosser, 30.

10. BM Add. MS 22626 f.43.

11. Walpole, *Reminiscences*, 59.

12. Sherburn, II, 201–2.

13. Ibid., 141.

14. Melville, *Lady Suffolk*, 86; Russell, II, 165; Chenevix Trench, 83.

15. Russell, II, 315; BM Add. MS 22625 ff.50, 66, 125.

16. Ibid. ff.54–5, 82, 92.

17. Ibid. f.98.

18. BM Add. MS 22626 f.22.

19. BM Add. MS 22625 f.68; 22626 ff.27, 31.

20. BM Add. MS 22626 ff.29–32, 64.

21. Ibid. f.32.

22. Ibid. ff.105–6.

23. Ibid. f.61.

24. Sherburn, II, 201–2.

25. NRC MC 3/284 f.70; HMC, *Polwarth*, I, 176; Mahon, *Letters*, I, 301.

26. Mahon, *Letters*, I, 300; BM Add. MS 22625 f.46.

27. BM Add. MS 22625 ff.21, 114; Williams, *Correspondence*, IV, 111–12; Sherburn, II, 141, 182, 322.

28. BM Add. MS 22627 f.87; Sherburn, II, 446; Lewis, XXXI, 266; Sedgwick, *Some Materials*, II, 380.

29. BM Add. MS 4805 f.158; 22629 f.10.

30. BM Add. MS 22628 f.20; *The Gentleman's Magazine*, January 1731; Walpole, *Reminiscences*, 66, 67n.

CHAPTER 8 'J'AURAI DES MAÎTRESSES'

1. Sedgwick, *Some Materials*, I, 41.

2. Gay, 'Welcome to Pope from Greece'.

3. BM Add. MS 22627 ff.90–1.

4. Ibid. f.89.

5. Walpole, *Reminiscences*, 61.

6. Ibid., 61–2.

7. Sedgwick, *Some Materials*, I, 41.

8. Walpole, *Reminiscences*, 62.

9. Hardy, 64.

10. Walpole, *Reminiscences*, 62; Sedgwick, *Some Materials*, I, 42.

11. She later miscarried.

12. Sedgwick, *Some Materials*, I, 41; HMC, *Egmont*, II, 134; Walpole, *Reminiscences*, 68. In his *Reminiscences*, Horace Walpole cites the time of their meetings as nine o'clock, but in the original draft of this work he says it was seven o'clock. The latter is most likely, given the timing of the formal routines of court.

13. Sedgwick, *Some Materials*, I, 41.

14. Wharncliffe, I, 12.

15. Mahon, *Letters*, II, 453; Walpole, *Reminiscences*, 66; Walpole, *Memoirs*, I, 154.

16. BM Add. MS 22629 ff.4–5.

17. BM Add. MS 22627 ff.97, 107.

18. Walpole, *Reminiscences*, 66.

19. BM Add. MS 22627 f.107.

20. BM Add. MS 22628 f.9; 22629 f.122.

21. W. A. Shaw (ed.), *Calendar of Treasury Books*, XXXII, part ii (London, 1957).

22. Sedgwick, *Some Materials*, I, 43.

23. Ibid., I, 253–5.

24. Wharncliffe, I, 13. See also Mahon, *Letters*, II, 457.

25. Plumb, *The First Four Georges*, 70; Walpole, *Reminiscences*, 50–1.

26. Sedgwick, *Some Materials*, II, 498.

27. Wharncliffe, I, 13; Coxe, I, 278–9.

28. HMC, *Egmont*, II, 134.

29. Sedgwick, *Some Materials*, II, 474; Walpole, *Reminiscences*, 68.

30. BM Add. MS 22625 f.27.

31. Sedgwick, *Some Materials*, II, 474.

32. Hardy, 15.

33. Sedgwick, *Some Materials*, II, 474.

34. Ibid., I, 43.

35. HMC, *Egmont*, II, 134.

36. Llanover, I, 137; Walpole, *Reminiscences*, 65.

37. Russell, II, 278; Mahon, *Letters*, II, 459.

38. Wright and Tinling, 262.
39. Arkell, 132.
40. Hardy, 33.
41. Sedgwick, *Some Materials*, II, 385.
42. Mahon, *Letters*, I, 315.
43. Sedgwick, *Some Materials*, I, 44.
44. Ibid.
45. Mahon, *Letters*, I, 441.
46. Coxe, I, 281.
47. BM Add. MS 22627 f.114.
48. Ibid. f.121.
49. Ibid. f.96.
50. HMC, *Portland*, V, 553.
51. Walpole, *Reminiscences*, 38.
52. Cowper, 142.
53. Ibid.
54. Ibid., 143.
55. BM Add. MS 22629 f.8.
56. Walpole, *Reminiscences*, 37.
57. Cowper, 152.
58. HMC, *Portland*, V, 96.

CHAPTER 9 'A HOUSE IN TWITTENHAM'

1. HMC, *Portland*, V, 599; BM Add. MS 22629 f.8.
2. HMC, *Portland*, V, 606; Sherburn, II, 52–3.
3. 'Character of Sir Robert Walpole by Dean Swift', BM Add. MS 22625; Mahon, *Letters*, II, 473.
4. D. W. Hayton, 'Ascending the Greasy Walpole', *History Today*, January 2006, 67.
5. Wilkins, 301.
6. Mahon, *Letters*, II, 468.
7. BM Add. MS 22627 f.96.
8. BM Add. MS 22626 f.87; 22627 f.70.
9. BM Add. MS 22627 f.94.
10. Ibid. f.21.
11. Ibid. ff.22, 24, 39, 95.
12. £1.5 million today.
13. NRS 22955 Z76.
14. BM Add. MS 22627 f.96.

15. BM Add. MS 22626 ff.29, 30.
16. BM Add. MS 22627 ff.55–7.
17. Wharncliffe, I, 348. This was something of an exaggeration, for the population at that time was less than 1,500.
18. Sherburn, II, 116, 307.
19. Ibid., 236–40, 257; Draper, 15.
20. Sherburn, II, 197.
21. BM Add. MS 22625 f.107.
22. BM Add. MS 22626 f.17.
23. Wharncliffe, I, 367, 369.
24. Sherburn, II, 262–3, 298–9.
25. Ibid., II, 261.
26. Girouard, 204.
27. BM Add. MS 22626 f.92; 22629 ff.115–16.
28. BM Add. MS 22628 f.15.
29. R. White, *Chiswick House and Gardens* (English Heritage, 2001), 37.
30. BM Add. MS 4805 f.120.
31. See also J. H. Pye, William Gilpin, Illustrated Notebooks, 1781, GB 0161 MSS. Eng. e. 3326-9, p.25. *A Short Account of the Principal Seats and Gardens, In and About Twickenham* (1760).
32. Sherburn, II, 436.
33. BM Add. MS 22627 f.93.
34. Sherburn, II, 257.
35. Ibid., II, 322.
36. BM Add. MS 22625 ff.7–8; 22626 ff.9–10.
37. BM Add. MS 22625 ff.6, 7–8; Sherburn, II, 412.
38. BM Add. MS 22625 f.13.
39. Sherburn, II, 387.
40. BM Add. MS 4805 f.126; Sherburn, II, 407.
41. BM Add. MS 22625 f.6.
42. Ibid. ff.111, 160.
43. Sedgwick, *Some Materials*, I, 93.
44. BM Add. MS 22627 f.25.
45. Ibid. ff.26, 27.
46. Ibid. ff.28–9.
47. Ibid. ff.30, 31, 37.
48. Ibid. ff.37–9.
49. Sedgwick, *Some Materials*, I, 93; Walpole, *Reminiscences*, 63.
50. BM Add. MS 22627 f.35.

51. Sherburn, II, 436.
52. Ibid., 435–6.

CHAPTER 10 'DUNCE THE SECOND REIGNS LIKE DUNCE THE FIRST'

1 Wilkins, 315–16.
2. HMC, *Polwarth*, V, 5.
3. Saussure, 226–7.
4. Sedgwick, *Some Materials*, I, 25.
5. Ibid., I, 28; Sherburn, II, 437.
6. Sedgwick, *Some Materials*, I, 28.
7. Ibid., I, 39.
8. Mahon, *Letters*, II, 460; Coxe, I, 276.
9. BM Add. MS 22626 f.117; 22627 f.79; 22629 f.20.
10. BM Add. MS 22626 f.6.
11. Ibid.
12. BM Add. MS 22625 f.14.
13. Sherburn, II, 455, 460.
14. Williams, *Correspondence*, III, 471.
15. Ibid., III, 352; IV, 100.
16. Ibid., IV, 135; Sherburn, III, 251.
17. Williams, *Correspondence*, IV, 98–100, 110–12.
18. 'Character of the Honourable Mrs Howard, Written and given to her by Dr Swift, Dean of St Patrick's', BM Add. MS 22625 ff.4–5.
19. BM Add. MS 4805 ff.44–5. The 'Crown and Plad' were a trinket and some Irish cloth that Swift had given her during the early days of their friendship.
20. BM Add. MS 22627 f.10; Saussure, 258.
21. Llanover, I, 137.
22. Ibid., 138.
23. Saussure, 256.
24. Llanover, I, 139.
25. This impressive feat was achieved by suspending fine cords of cotton wool, almost invisible to the eye, along the rows of candles, each soaked with flammable liquids such as spirits and wine, which carried the flame rapidly from one candle to another. 'This arrangement had been so skilfully prepared that hardly a single candle failed to take fire,' observed one of the guests. Saussure, 262.
26. Ibid., 264–5.

CHAPTER 11 'THE INDISSOLVABLE KNOT'

1. Sedgwick, *Some Materials*, I, 45.
2. Black, *The Hanoverians*, 96.
3. Walpole, *Reminiscences*, 70–1.
4. Sedgwick, *Some Materials*, I, 68–9.
5. Walpole, *Reminiscences*, 72.
6. Mahon, *Letters*, II, 461.
7. BM Add. MS 22628 f.21.
8. BM Add. MS 22627 ff.4–5.
9. Sedgwick, *Some Materials*, II, 473.
10. Ibid., I, 93.
11. Sherburn, II, 445–6.
12. BM Add. MS 22626 ff.94, 96; 22625 ff.28–9.
13. BM Add. MS 22626 ff.34–5.
14. BM Add. MS 22627 f.36.
15. Jones, 80.
16. Ibid., 143, 217.
17. Ibid., 112.
18. BM Add. MS 22627 f.35.
19. Ibid. ff.40–2.
20. Ibid. ff.43–6.
21. Sedgwick, *Some Materials*, II, 473–4.
22. Ibid., I, 94.
23. NRS 22956 Z76.
24. Sherburn, II, 478, 491.
25. NRS 8862 21 F4; BM Add. MS 22626 f.96.
26. BM Add. MS 22626 f.26; 4805 f.160.

CHAPTER 12 'COMFORTING THE KING'S ENEMIES'

1. Ilchester, 169.
2. Ibid.
3. BM Add. MS 22626 ff.26, 99.
4. BM Add. MS 22628 ff.19–20.
5. Ashdown, 144.
6. BM Add. MS 22626 ff.28–9.
7. BM Add. MS 22628 f.29.
8. Ibid. f.21.
9. Ibid. f.27.

10. Sherburn, II, 446; BM Add. MS 22626 f.13.
11. Walpole, *Reminiscences*, 68.
12. Sedgwick, *Some Materials*, II, 379–80.
13. Walpole, *Reminiscences*, 73–4.
14. Hone, 378.
15. Wilkins, 427–8.
16. BM Add. MS 22626 f.43.
17. Sherburn, II, 141.
18. BM Add. MS 22626 f.51.
19. Ibid. f.53; NRS 21089 71 X3.
20. BM Add. MS 22626 f.53.
21. Ibid. ff.30, 55; 22625 f.30.
22. BM Add. MS 22625 f.22.
23. BM Add. MS 22626 ff.53, 55.
24. Thomson, I, 242–3. See also ibid., 232–3, 237, 240.
25. BM Add. MS 27732 ff.57, 216.
26. W. A. Shaw, *Calendar of Treasury Books and Papers 1731–34* (London, 1898), 550; BM Add. MS 22626 f.20.
27. BM Add. MS 22626 f.55.
28. Sedgwick, *Some Materials*, I, 98–100; Llanover, I, 193.
29. Williams, *Correspondence*, III, 324, 326.
30. Ibid., 326.
31. BM Add. MS 22626 f.74.
32. Sedgwick, *Some Materials*, I, 172–3.
33. i.e. the statute of treason.
34. BM Add. MS 22626 ff.103–4.
35. Sedgwick, *Some Materials*, II, 371.
36. Ibid., II, 384.
37. BM Add. MS 22627 f.99.
38. Williams, *Correspondence*, IV, 85.
39. BM Add. MS 22626 f.80.
40. BM Add. MS 22628 f.69.
41. BM Add. MS 22629 ff.191–2.
42. BM Add. MS 22627 f.101.

CHAPTER 13 'PLEASING ONE NOT WORTH THE PLEASING'

1. BM Add. MS 22629 f.33.
2. Ibid. f.35.

3. Ibid.
4. Ibid. ff.35, 38.
5. Ibid. f.37.
6. Ibid. f.228.
7. Sedgwick, *Some Materials*, II, 381.
8. Walpole, *Memoirs*, I, 514.
9. Sherburn, II, 514; BM Add. MS 22626 f.26.
10. BM Add. MS 22628 f.100.
11. Sherburn, II, 409.
12. BM Add. MS 22628 f.98.
13. BM Add. MS 22626 f.112.
14. HMC, *Fortescue*, 92–3.
15. Ibid., 92.
16. BM Add. MS 22626 f.111.
17. Sedgwick, *Some Materials*, II, 383.
18. NRS MC3/285 f.50; Sedgwick, *Some Materials*, II, 472.
19. BM Add. MS 22627 f.6. Another draft of the letter can be found at f.7.
20. Sedgwick, *Some Materials*, II, 601.
21. Ibid., 471–2.
22. Thomson, 248; Sedgwick, *Some Materials*, II, 383.
23. NRS BL/T/5/2; Sedgwick, *Some Materials*, II, 382.
24. Lewis, V, 59–60.
25. BM Add. MS 22625 f.122; 22626 ff.19, 78; 22627 f.77.
26. Sedgwick, *Some Materials*, II, 382, 385.

CHAPTER 14 MRS BERKELEY

1. Sedgwick, *Some Materials*, II, 382, 385; HMC, *Egmont*, II, 134. In fact, Caroline eventually decided not to appoint another Mistress of the Robes, and the post remained vacant for the rest of her reign.
2. Sedgwick, *Some Materials*, II, 491.
3. BM Add. MS 22626 f.19.
4. Williams, *Correspondence*, IV, 314.
5. NRS 21140 X3. The houses along Savile Street were later renumbered, and the one occupied by Henrietta is now at No.17. It is not in the form that it would have been in her day, however, for the original house was demolished and rebuilt in the nineteenth century. In common with most other houses along the street, it is now occupied by a prestigious tailor's.
6. Ibid.

7. Williams, *Correspondence*, IV, 362.

8. PRO C104/262 bundle no.11.

9. Williams, *Correspondence*, IV, 362.

10. Sedgwick, *Some Materials*, II, 471–2.

11. Melville, *Maids of Honour*, 114.

12. Williams, *Correspondence*, IV, 362.

13. BM Add. MS 22628 ff.37–8, 89–91.

14. Sherburn, III, 474.

15. Williams, *Correspondence*, IV, 422.

16. It is rather ironic that both portraits are now hung at Audley End House, the seat of Henrietta's estranged late husband. How they came to be there is not known.

17. Sherburn, III, 478.

18. BM Add. MS 22629 ff.51, 60.

19. HMC, *Fortescue*, I, 93.

20. BM Add. MS 22629 ff.39–44.

21. HMC, *Fortescue*, I, 94.

22. BM Add. MS 22628. While the boy overcame this childhood illness, he did not survive into adulthood and died at the age of seventeen.

23. Sherburn, IV, 38–9.

24. WRO Wilton MS 2057/F4/25.

25. HMC, *Fortescue*, I, 94.

26. Ibid., I, 106–7.

27. Melville, *Bath*, 79.

28. BM Add. MS 22627 f.110.

29. HMC, *Fortescue*, I, 105–6.

30. BM Add. MS 22628 f.37.

CHAPTER 15 'THE MELANCHOLY SHADES OF PRIVACY'

1. Mahon, *Letters*, I, 467.

2. Russell, 326, 334; Croker, *Letters*, II, 127–30.

3. Walpole, *Memoirs*, I, 513.

4. Sedgwick, *Some Materials*, II, 486–90.

5. Ibid., II, 497.

6. Ibid., II, 490; HMC, *Egmont*, II, 370.

7. HMC, *Egmont*, II, 299.

8. Wilkins, 583.

9. HMC, *Egmont*, II, 311.

10. Sedgwick, *Some Materials*, II, 638–9.

11. HMC, *Egmont*, II, 44.

12. Sedgwick, *Some Materials*, III, 877–915.

13. Sherburn, IV, 4, 33.

14. Ibid., III, 434.

15. Ault, 266–75. Valerie Rumbold provides an excellent account of Henrietta's
    relationship with the poet: Rumbold, 225–31.

16. Sherburn, IV 212.

17. BM Add. MS 22626 f.58; 22628 ff.34–5.

18. BM Add. MS 22628 f.94; WRO Wilton MS 2057/F4/25.

19. BM Add. MS 22629 ff.45–6, 52.

20. Ibid. ff.47–55.

21. Ibid. f.54.

22. Ibid. f.58. Swift himself died a year later, in 1745.

23. BM Add. MS 22627 f.77.

24. HMC, *Denbigh*, V, 152–3.

25. NRS 8549 21 B6. The will does not specify what property George Berkeley
    owned, and there is no evidence of this in the other contemporary papers
    that I have studied. He spent his early years at his family seat, Berkeley Castle,
    and lived in London from at least the mid-1720s, when he was appointed
    Master Keeper and Governor of St Katharine's Hospital, although there is
    no indication of exactly where.

26. *The Gentleman's Magazine*, November 1746; HMC, *Buckinghamshire* et al., 154.

CHAPTER 16 'WHERE SUFFOLK SOUGHT THE PEACEFUL SCENE'

1. The following sources provide excellent accounts of the Jacobite defeat and
    the fall of Walpole: Plumb, *England in the Eighteenth Century*; O'Gorman;
    Black, *The Hanoverians*.

2. BM Add. MS 22627 f.105; 22629 ff.81–2.

3. Lewis, VII, 120–2.

4. Cobbett, 296.

5. Ibid., 308–10.

6. Ibid., 296; Fothergill, 106.

7. Walpole, *Reminiscences*, 64.

8. Fothergill, 121.

9. Ibid., 120–1.

10. Walpole, *Reminiscences*, 65.

11. Fothergill, 117.

12. Lewis, XXXI, ix.

13. Tytler, 49–50.

14. BM Add. MS 22627 f.81.

15 UHA DDHO/4/4/23.

16. BM Add. MS 22629 ff.126–7, 138, 166–8.

17. Ibid. ff.139–63, 172, 178, 180.

18. English Heritage has recently restored the room to its 1750s appearance and has hung an exquisite replica of Lady Suffolk's Chinese wallpaper.

19. NRS 8899 21 F6.

20. Ibid.

21. BM Add. MS 22629 ff.58–9; NRS MC 3/285 467 X.

22. BM Add. MS 22629 f.71.

23. HMC, *Lothian*, 170.

24. The Prince had died in March 1751 from an injury sustained some time before when he had been hit on the head by a cricket ball.

25. BM Add. MS 22627 f.105; 22629 ff.62–4.

26. Walpole, *Reminiscences*, 65.

27. Impey, 79.

28. BM Add. MS 22629 f.82.

29. Melville, *Lady Suffolk*, 244.

CHAPTER 17 'AN ESSENTIAL LOSS'

1. Walpole, *Memoirs*, 454; *The London Chronicle*, 25–29 October 1760; *The Gentleman's Magazine*, 25 October 1760; Impey, 81.

2. Black, *The Hanoverians*, 110.

3. BM Add. MS 33069 f.295.

4. BM Add. MS 22629 f.127; Fothergill, 118.

5. Lewis, XXXI, 24.

6. BM Add. MS 22627 ff.10–11.

7. BM Add. MS 22629 f.83.

8. Fothergill, 119.

9. BM Add. MS 22626 f.121.

10. NRS MC 3/285 f.9.

11. Ibid. ff.1, 73, 467x.

12. NRS MC 3/284 f.62.

13. NRS MC 3/285 ff.15, 62.

14. NRS MC 3/284 f.66.
15. BM Add. MS 22629 f.93; Coke, I, 211.
16. BM Add. MS 22629 f.98; NRS MC 3/285 f.7.
17. NRS MC 3/285 f.16. For the entire collection of the Earl's correspondence with Lady Suffolk during his stay in St Petersburg, see: NRS MC 3/284, 285; BM Add. MS 22629 ff.90–103.
18. Coke, I, 96.
19. NRS MC 3/284 f.75; BM Add. MS 22629 f.108.
20. BM Add. MS 22629 ff.110–11.
21. Ibid. f.114; NRS MC 3/285 f.19.
22. BM Add. MS 22629 f.94.
23. NRS MC 3/284 f.65.
24. UHA DDHO/4/20/114.
25. Lewis, XXXI, 40.
26. A. W. M. Stirling, *The Hothams* (2 volumes, London, 1918), II, 96–7.
27. Lewis, V, 59–60.
28. UHA DDHO/40/26/41.
29. BM Add. MS 22626 ff.114–16.
30. Coke, I, 138–9, 233, 238–9.
31. See for example *Lloyd's Evening Post*, 27–29 July; *The Gentleman's Magazine*, 26 July. These reports inaccurately cited her age as 86, rather than 78.
32. Croker, *Letters*, II, 341–3.
33. Ibid., II, 342–3.
34. NRS 8549 21 B6.

EPILOGUE

1. The London property market was clearly less buoyant than it is now, for the house was sold for £2,110 – some £390 less than the original purchase price had been more than thirty years earlier.
2. Fothergill, 121.

Select Bibliography

———————— ‹◦› ————————

Manuscript Sources

Bodleian Library	GB 0161 MSS. Eng. e. 3326-9
British Museum	Add. MSS 4805, 4806, 22358, 22625–22629, 27732, 29732
Lambeth Palace Library	Talbot MS 3129
The National Archives	PRO C104/262
Norfolk Record Office	NRS 8549, 8862, 8899, 21089, 21140, 23508, 22785, 22953, 22955, 22956, 22976, 22977, 22979, 24492, 27094, MC 3/284, MC 3/285, MC 3/578, MC 3/608, BL/T/5/2
The Royal Archives	RA Geo. Add. MSS 1/49, 28/52, 15743-4
Suffolk Record Office	941/78/7/1
University of Hull Archives	DDHO/4/5/23, DDHO/40/26/41
Warwickshire Record Office	CR2017/C246/68
Wiltshire Record Office	WSRO 2057/F4/25

PRINTED PRIMARY SOURCES

C. F. Burgess (ed.), *The Letters of John Gay* (Oxford, 1966)

Lady Mary Coke, *The Letters and Journals of Lady Mary Coke* (2 volumes, Bath, 1970)

Hon. S. Cowper (ed.), *Diary of Mary Countess Cowper, Lady of the Bedchamber to the Princess of Wales, 1714–20* (Murray, 1865)

W. Coxe, *Memoirs of the Life and Administration of Sir Robert Walpole, Earl of Orford* (2 volumes, London, 1898)

J. W. Croker (ed.), *Letters to and from Henrietta, Countess of Suffolk, and her second husband, the Hon. George Berkeley from 1712 to 1767* (2 volumes, London 1824)

J. W. Croker (ed.), *Memoirs of the Reign of George the Second From His Accession to the Death of Queen Caroline* (3 volumes, London, 1884)

D. Defoe, *A Tour Thro' the Whole Island of Great Britain* (2 volumes, London, 1927)

K. Deighton (ed.), *Coverley Papers from The Spectator* (London, 1964)

W. Graham (ed.), *The Letters of Joseph Addison* (Oxford, 1941)

Robert Halsband (ed.), *The Complete Letters of Lady Mary Wortley Montagu* (3 volumes, Oxford, 1965)

Sir Charles Hanbury Williams, *The Works of the Right Honourable Sir Charles Hanbury Williams, KB, Ambassador to the Courts of Russia, Saxony & c. with notes by Horace Walpole, Earl of Orford* (3 volumes, London, 1882)

Historical Manuscripts Commission, *Manuscripts of the Earl of Buckinghamshire, the Earl of Lindsey, the Earl of Onslow, Lord Emly, Theodore J. Hare, Esq., and James Round, Esq., MP*, 14th Report Appendix Part IX (London, 1895)

Historical Manuscripts Commission, *Report on the Manuscripts of the Earl of Denbigh, preserved at Newnham Paddox, Warwickshire*, Part IV (London, 1911)

Historical Manuscripts Commission, *The Manuscripts of the Earl of Egmont. Diary of Viscount Percival Afterwards First Earl of Egmont* (3 volumes, London, 1920–3)

Historical Manuscripts Commission, *The Manuscripts of J. B. Fortescue Esq., preserved at Dropmore*, Volume 1 (London, 1892)

Historical Manuscripts Commission, *Report on the Manuscripts of the Marquess of Lothian preserved at Blickling Hall, Norfolk* (London, 1905)

Historical Manuscripts Commission, *Report on the Manuscripts of Lord Polwarth, preserved at Mertoun House, Berwickshire* (5 volumes, London, 1911–61)

Historical Manuscripts Commission, *Report on the Manuscripts of his Grace the Duke of Portland, preserved at Welbeck Abbey*, Volumes 4 and 5 (London, 1905)

Historical Manuscripts Commission, *The Manuscripts of the Marquess of Townshend* (London, 1887)

W. Hogarth, *Anecdotes of William Hogarth ... Written by himself: with essays on his life and genius, and criticisms of his works, selected by Walpole, Gilpin, J. Ireland, Lamb, Phillips and others* (London, 1833)

Earl of Ilchester (ed.), *Lord Hervey and His Friends 1726–38. Based on letters from Holland House, Melbury and Ickworth* (London, 1950)

M. Kroll (ed.), *Letters from Liselotte. Elisabeth Charlotte, Princess Palatine and Duchess of Orléans, 'Madam', 1652–1722* (London, 1970)

W. S. Lewis (ed.), *The Yale Edition of Horace Walpole's Correspondence* (48 volumes, London, 1937–83)

Lady Llanover (ed.), *The Autobiography and Correspondence of Mary Granville, Mrs Delany* (3 volumes, London, 1861)

Lord Mahon (ed.), *The Letters of Philip Dormer Stanhope, Earl of Chesterfield* (5 volumes, London, 1845–53)

W. Matthews (ed.), *The Diary of Dudley Ryder 1715–1716* (London, 1939)

E. Morris (ed.), *Letters of Molly Lepel, Lady Hervey* (London, 1821)

F. Rye and A. Rye (eds.), *Calendar of Correspondence and Documents relating to the family of Oliver Le Neve, of Witchingham, Norfolk, 1675–1743* (Norwich, 1895)

C. de Saussure, *A Foreign View of England in the reigns of George I and II* edited by B. van Muyden (London, 1902)

R. Sedgwick (ed.), *Some Materials Towards Memoirs of the Reign of King George II, By John, Lord Hervey* (3 volumes, London, 1931)

G. Sherburn (ed.), *The Correspondence of Alexander Pope* (5 volumes, Oxford, 1956)

K. Thomson (ed.), *Memoirs of Viscountess Sundon, Mistress of the Robes to Queen Caroline* (2 volumes, London, 1847)

H. Walpole, *Memoirs of the Last Ten Years of the Reign of George II* (2 volumes, London, 1822)

H. Walpole, *Reminiscences: written in 1788 for the amusement of Miss Mary and Miss Agnes* edited by Paget Jackson Toynbee, (Oxford, 1924)

Lord Wharncliffe (ed.), *The Letters and Works of Lady Mary Wortley Montagu* (2 volumes, London, 1887)

H. Williams (ed.), *The Correspondence of Jonathan Swift* (5 volumes, Oxford, 1963–5)

L. B. Wright and M. Tinling (eds.), *William Byrd of Virginia, The London Diary 1717–1721 and Other Writings* (New York, 1958)

CONTEMPORARY NEWSPAPERS

The Craftsman
The Daily Courant
The Daily Journal
The Gentleman's Magazine
The Grub Street Journal
Lloyd's Evening Post
The London Chronicle
The London Gazette
The Weekly Journal
The Weekly Miscellany

SECONDARY SOURCES

W. Addison, *Audley End* (London, 1953)

R. L. Arkell, *Caroline of Ansbach* (Oxford, 1939)

D. Arnold, *The Georgian Villa* (Gloucestershire, 1996)

D. Arnold, *The Georgian Country House: Architecture, Landscape and Society* (Gloucestershire, 1998)

D. M. Ashdown, *Ladies in Waiting* (London, 1976)

N. Ault, *New Light on Pope* (USA, 1967)

F. E. Baily, *Sophia of Hanover and Her Times* (London, 1939)

R. Baird, *Mistress of the House: Great Ladies and Grand Houses* (London, 2003)

R. Bayne-Powell, *Eighteenth Century London Life* (Murray, 1937)

J. M. Beattie, *The English Court in the Reign of George I* (Cambridge, 1967)

A. Beckles Wilson, *Strawberry Hill: A History of the Neighbourhood* (Twickenham, 1995)

A. Beckles Wilson, *Alexander Pope's Grotto in Twickenham* (London, 1998)

J. Black, *Robert Walpole and the Nature of Politics in Early Eighteenth Century Britain* (London, 1990)

J. Black, *The Hanoverians: The History of a Dynasty* (London, 2004)

Blickling Hall (National Trust, 2003)

F. Boucher, *A History of Costume in the West* (London, 2004)

C. Brewer, *The Death of Kings. A Medical History of the Kings and Queens of England* (London, 2004)

J. S. Bromley, P. G. M. Dickinson and A. Whiteman (eds.), *Statesmen, Scholars and Merchants. Essays in Eighteenth Century History presented to Dame Lucy Sutherland* (Oxford, 1973)

J. Bryant, *Finest Prospects: Three Historic Houses* (English Heritage, 1986)

J. Bryant, *Mrs Howard: A Woman of Reason* (exhibition catalogue, English Heritage, 1988)

Burke's Peerage

E. Burton, *The Georgians at Home* (London, 1973)

A. Campbell, *The Countess of Suffolk and her Friends* (exhibition catalogue, London, 1966)

T. H. R. Cashmore, D. H. Simpson and A. C. B. Urwin, *Alexander Pope's Twickenham: Eighteenth Century Views of his 'Classic Village'* (Twickenham, 1988)

C. Chenevix Trench, *George II* (London, 1973)

C. Christie, *The British Country House in the Eighteenth Century* (Manchester, 2000)

I. Christie, 'The Personality of George II', *History Today*, V (1955)

J. Clarke and J. Ridley, *The Houses of Hanover and Saxe-Coburg-Gotha* edited by Antonia Fraser (London, 2000)

R. S. Cobbett, *Memorials of Twickenham: parochial and typographical* (London, 1872)

G. E. Cockayne, *Complete Peerage of England, Scotland, Ireland, Great Britain and the United Kingdom* (London, 1887)

W. Connely, *Beau Nash, Monarch of Bath and Tunbridge Wells* (London, 1955)

R. Crisp, *Richmond and its Inhabitants from the Olden Time* (London, 1866)

H. Davis (ed.), *Pope: Poetical Works* (Oxford, 1978)

H. T. Dickinson, *Bolingbroke* (London, 1970)

D. Doran, *Lives of the Queens of England of the House of Hanover* (2 volumes, London, 1855)

M. Dorothy George, *London Life in the Eighteenth Century* (London, 1976)

M. P. G. Draper, *Marble Hill House and its owners* (London, 1970)

A. Drayton Greenwood, *Lives of the Hanoverian Queens of England* (London, 1909)

I. Ehrenpreis and R. Halsband (eds.), *The Lady of Letters in the Eighteenth Century* (Los Angeles, 1969)

E. Eriberg and J. Jacob, *Marble Hill House: A Catalogue of Recent Purchases and Loans* (London, 1969)

B. Fothergill, *The Strawberry Hill Set. Horace Walpole and his circle* (London, 1983)

L. Garfield, *The House of Hanover: England in the Eighteenth Century* (London, 1976)

J. Gay, *Selected Poems* (London, 2003).

M. Girouard, *Life in the English Country House: A Social and Architectural History* (London, 1978)

Sir Charles Grant Robertson, *England Under the Hanoverians* (London, 1934)

J. D. Griffith Davies, *A King in Toils* (London, 1938)

S. Groom and L. Prosser, *Kew Palace. The Official Illustrated History* (London and New York, 2006)

S. Gwynn, *The Life and Friendships of Dean Swift* (Thornton Butterworth, 1933)

R. Halsband, *Lord Hervey: Eighteenth Century Courtier* (Oxford, 1973)

A. Hardy, *The King's Mistresses* (London, 1980)

A. D. Harvey, *Sex in Georgian England: Attitudes and Prejudices from the 1720s to the 1820s* (London, 2001)

R. Hatton, *George I Elector and King* (London, 1978)

E. Herman, *Sex With Kings* (London, 2004)

B. Hill, *Eighteenth Century Women: An Anthology* (London, 1984)

B. Hill (ed.), *The First English Feminist. Reflections on the marriage state and other writings by Mary Astell* (Aldershot, 1986)

W. Hone, *The Table Book*, Volume I (London, 1827)

E. Impey, *Kensington Palace. The Official Illustrated History* (London and New York, 2003)

W. H. Irving, *John Gay's London* (Cambridge, 1928)

W. H. Irving, *John Gay: Favourite of the Wits* (North Carolina, 1940)

K. Jeffrey (ed.), *Audley End* (English Heritage, 2002)

V. Jones (ed.), *Women in the Eighteenth Century: constructions of femininity* (London and New York, 1990)

R. W. Ketton-Cremer, *Norfolk Portraits* (London, 1944)

J. van der Kiste, *George II and Queen Caroline* (Stroud, 1997)

M. Kroll, *Sophie Electress of Hanover* (London, 1973)

E. Law, *The History of Hampton Court Palace* (3 volumes, London, 1885–91)

W. E. H. Lecky, *A History of England in the Eighteenth Century*, Volumes 1 and 2 (London, 1907, 1909)

London Borough of Hounslow, *Gunnersbury Park and Museum* (London, 1984)

E. Longford, *The Oxford Book of Royal Anecdotes* (Oxford, 1989)

J. Maddison, *Blickling Hall* (National Trust, 1989)

Lord Mahon, *History of England – from the Peace of Utrecht to the Peace of Aix-la-Chapelle* (3 volumes, London, 1836–7)

Marble Hill, Twickenham (English Heritage, 2002)

Marble Hill House, Twickenham: A Short Account of its History and Architecture (London, 1966)

L. Melville, *Bath under Beau Nash* (London, 1907)

L. Melville, *The First George in Hanover and England* (2 volumes, London, 1908)

L. Melville, *Lady Suffolk and her Circle* (London, 1924)

L. Melville, *Maids of Honour* (London, 1927)

W. Michael, *England Under George I* (Macmillan, 1939)

J. Munson, *Maria Fitzherbert. The Secret Wife of George IV* (London, 2001)

F. O'Gorman, *The Long Eighteenth Century. British Political and Social History 1688–1832* (London, 1997)

K. O'Morgan (ed.), *The Oxford Illustrated History of Britain* (Oxford, 1997)

W. M. Omrod (ed.), *The Kings and Queens of England* (Stroud, 2001)

L. Picard, *Dr Johnson's London. Life in London 1740–1770* (London, 2003)

J. H. Plumb, *The First Four Georges* (London, 1956)

J. H. Plumb, *England in the Eighteenth Century* (London, 1966)

J. H. Plumb, *Sir Robert Walpole: The Making of a Statesman* (3 volumes, London, 1972)

J. H. Plumb, *Georgian Delights* (London, 1980)

T. Pocock, *Norfolk* (London, 1995)

M. Reynolds, *The Learned Lady in England 1650–1760* (Boston and New York, 1920)

V. Rumbold, *Women's Place in Pope's World* (Cambridge, 1989)

Colonel F. S. Russell, *The Earl of Peterborough and Monmouth* (2 volumes, London, 1887)

R. Sedgwick (ed.), *The History of Parliament. The House of Commons, 1715–54*, Volume I (London, 1970)

E. Sitwell, *Alexander Pope* (London, 1930)

R. A. L. Smith, *Bath* (London, 1948)

J. Stead, *Georgian Cookery. Recipes and History* (English Heritage, 2003)

D. M. Stuart, *Molly Lepel: Lady Hervey* (London, 1936)

J. Summerson, *Georgian London* (London, 1969)

J. Swift, *Gulliver's Travels* (London, 1994)

S. Taylor, R. Connors and C. Jones (eds.), *Hanoverian Britain and Empire: Essays in Memory of Philip Lawson* (New York, 1998)

W. M. Thackeray, *The Four Georges* (London, 1866)

S. Thurley, *Hampton Court: A Social and Architectural History* (New Haven and London, 2003)

J. Treasure, *Who's Who in History. England 1714–1789*, Volume IV (Oxford, 1969)

A. S. Turberville, *English Men and Manners in the Eighteenth Century* (Oxford, 1926)

E. S. Turner, *The Court of St James's* (London, 1959)

Twickenham Local History Society, *Twickenham 1600–1900: People and Places* (Twickenham, 1995)

S. Tytler, *The Countess of Huntingdon and her Circle* (London, 1907)

A. Vickery, *The Gentleman's Daughter: Women's Lives in Georgian England* (New Haven and London, 1998)

E. Walford, *Greater London: A Narrative of Its History, Its People and Its Places* (London, Paris and New York, 1898)

A. W. Ward, *Great Britain and Hanover* (Oxford, 1899)

A. Weir, *Britain's Royal Families: The Complete Genealogy* (London, 1996)

W. H. Wilkins, *Caroline the Illustrious, Queen-Consort of George II and sometime Queen-Regent* (London, 1904)

B. Williams, *The Whig Supremacy 1714–1760* (Oxford, 1962)

Wren Society, *The Royal Palaces of Winchester, Whitehall, Kensington and St James's*, Volume VII (Oxford, 1930)

T. Wright, *England Under the House of Hanover* (2 volumes, London, 1848)

Index